Contents

List of Illustrations	vii
List of Music Examples	ix
Contributors	xi
Acknowledgements	xiii
Introduction	1
1 Scotch Drink & Irish Harps: Mediations of the National Air *Celeste Langan*	25
2 "Suspended" Sense in *Alastor*: Shelley's Musical Trope and Eighteenth-Century Medical Discourse *Kimiyo Ogawa*	50
3 On Music Framed: The Eolian Harp in Romantic Writing *Susan Bernstein*	70
4 Music and Inspiration in Blake's Poetry *John Hughes*	85
5 "Music their larger soul": George Eliot's "The Legend of Jubal" and Victorian Musicality *Ruth A. Solie*	107
6 Musical Reactions to Tennyson: Reformulating Musical Imagery in "The Lotos-Eaters" *Michael Allis*	132
7 "Monna Innominata" and Christina Rossetti's Audible Unhappiness *Yeo Wei Wei*	174

8	The "silent song" of D.G. Rossetti's *The House of Life* *Phyllis Weliver*	194
9	"The Music Spoke for Us": Music and Sexuality in *fin-de-siècle* Poetry *Emma Sutton*	213
10	Sappho Recomposed: A Song Cycle by Granville and Helen Bantock *Yopie Prins*	230
Index		259

List of Illustrations

8.1   Rossetti's illustration for the introductory sonnet of *The House of Life*. Dante Gabriel Rossetti, *The Poems of Dante Gabriel Rossetti: with illustrations from his own pictures and designs*, ed. William Michael Rossetti, vol. 2 (London: Ellis & Elvey, 1904) faces page 164. BL shelf mark TAB.537.a.9. By permission of the British Library, London.   197

10.1   Frontispiece and title page, Henry Thornton Wharton's *Sappho: Memoir, Text, Selected Renderings, and a Literal Translation*. Owned by the author, Yopie Prins. Published in London by Lane, 1895.   238

10.2   Cover illustration, piano-vocal score, *Sappho, Nine Fragments for Contralto*. Words selected by Helen F. Bantock, set to music by Granville Bantock, Deutsche Übersetzung von Joh. Bernhoff. Northwestern University Music Library owns the piano-vocal score, which was published by Breitkopf and Hartel in 1906. The University of Michigan Photo Services reproduced the front cover.   239

List of Music Examples

6.1	Hubert Parry, *The Lotos-Eaters* (1892), opening of stanza 1	146
6.2	Parry, *The Lotos-Eaters*, stanza 2	147
6.3	Parry, *The Lotos-Eaters*, orchestral introduction	148
6.4	Richard Wagner, *Parsifal* (1882), Act II	150
6.5	Parry, *The Lotos-Eaters*, opening of stanza 8	154
6.6a	Parry, *The Lotos-Eaters*, opening of stanza 3	156
6.6b	Parry, *The Lotos-Eaters*, opening of stanza 7	156
6.6c	Parry, *The Lotos-Eaters*, stanza 7, figure BB	157
6.7	Parry, *The Lotos-Eaters*, ending	158
6.8	Edward Elgar, "There is sweet music" (1907), opening	164
6.9	Elgar, "There is sweet music," bars 8–11	165
6.10	Elgar, "There is sweet music," bars 26–28	167
6.11	Elgar, "There is sweet music," bar 17	168
6.12	Elgar, "There is sweet music," ending	169
6.13	Elgar, "There is sweet music," bars 36–41	170
10.1	Granville and Helen Bantock, *Prelude*, bars 1–4. From *Sappho: Prelude and Nine Fragments* (1898-1906).	244
10.2	Bantock, "Hymn to Aphrodite," Song I, bars 1–12. In *Sappho: Prelude and Nine Fragments*.	247

10.3 Bantock, "Hymn to Aphrodite," Song I, bars 113–121. 252
      In *Sappho: Prelude and Nine Fragments*.

10.4 Bantock, "I loved thee once, Atthis," Song II, bars 64–68. 254
      In *Sappho: Prelude and Nine Fragments*.

10.5 Bantock, "Muse of the golden throne," Song IX, bars 41–57. 256
      In *Sappho: Prelude and Nine Fragments*.

Contributors

Michael Allis is Senior Tutor in Postgraduate Studies at the Royal Academy of Music, London. His publications include editions of Parry's chamber and piano music, along with articles on Stanford, Samuel Butler, Elgar and narrative, and Liszt reception in Britain. His book, *Parry's Creative Process*, was published by Ashgate in 2003.

Susan Bernstein is Associate Professor of Comparative Literature at Brown University. She is the author of *Virtuosity of the Nineteenth Century: Performing Music and Language in Heine, Liszt and Baudelaire* (Stanford, 1998) and has published widely in European Romanticism, literature and the arts, architecture, poetics and philosophy.

John Hughes is Senior Lecturer in English at the University of Gloucestershire. He has published widely on nineteenth-century literature and twentieth-century philosophy, particularly Wittgenstein and Deleuze. He has written two books, *Lines of Flight* (Sheffield Academic Press, 1997) and *"Ecstatic Sound": Music and Individuality in the Work of Thomas Hardy* (Ashgate, 2001).

Celeste Langan is Associate Professor of English at the University of California, Berkeley. Author of *Romantic Vagrancy: Wordsworth and the Simulation of Freedom* (Cambridge, 1995), she has also published essays on Scott, Byron and Coleridge. She is currently working on a book-length project called *Post-Napoleonism*.

Kimiyo Ogawa is a Lecturer at Sophia University in Japan and expects her PhD from Glasgow University in 2004. She has published articles on Mary Shelley, Radcliffe and Percy Bysshe Shelley in *Osaka Literary Review* and a chapter on Toni Morrison in *Dramatic America* (Eiho-sha, 2002), edited by Hisashi Ishida.

Yopie Prins is Associate Professor of English and Comparative Literature at the University of Michigan. She is the author of *Victorian Sappho* (Princeton, 1999) and has published various articles on Victorian poetry and prosody, nineteenth-century Hellenism, and the reception of Greek tragedy.

CONTRIBUTORS

Ruth A. Solie is Sophia Smith Professor of Music at Smith College and a former president of the American Musicological Society. She is editor of *Musicology and Difference* (California, 1992) and the nineteenth century volume of Strunk's *Source Readings in Music History* (Norton, 1998), and author of *Music in Other Words: Victorian Conversations* (California, 2004).

Emma Sutton is Lecturer in English at the University of St Andrews. Her research interests include the role of music in late Victorian British literature and cultural history. She is the author of *Aubrey Beardsley and British Wagnerism in the 1890s* (Oxford, 2002) and is currently working on a study of music, Modernism and British writing.

Phyllis Weliver is Assistant Professor of English at Wilkes University. She is the author of *Women Musicians in Victorian Fiction, 1860–1900: Representations of music, science and gender in the leisured home* (Ashgate, 2000). Currently, she is working on a book on music and imagined community in Victorian fiction.

Yeo Wei Wei is Assistant Professor of English at the National University of Singapore. She has co-edited and contributed chapters on Singaporean narratives and national identity to *Postcolonial Urbanism* (Routledge, 2003) and *Beyond Description: Space, Historicity, Singapore* (Routledge, forthcoming). She is currently working on a book about Dante's presence in the nineteenth and twentieth centuries.

Acknowledgements

My thanks to Bennett Zon's unfailing support, both in his immediate enthusiasm for the idea of this volume of essays and for his subsequent assistance in all steps of the production process. Thank you also to the contributors to the volume for their hard work, Rachel Lynch for her expertise, Heidi May and all the Ashgate staff. My conversations with Sophie Fuller about this collection were invaluable and inspiring, and I appreciate the opportunity to link it with *The Idea of Music in Victorian Fiction*, edited by Sophie Fuller and Nicky Losseff. Wilkes University reduced my course load for one semester and funded work-study students for me, Greg Specter and Andrew Amoroso, whom I also thank for their assistance in preparing the volume. Mary Watkins's speedy processing of interlibrary loan requests went beyond the call of duty, the staff of the New York University Elmer Holmes Bobst Library were very helpful, Robert Adlington provided information at an essential stage, and the hospitality Naomi Gurt Lind and Bill Lind made it possible for me to use the NYU library while writing the introduction and editing the essays.

Introduction

Included in Amy Levy's second collection of poetry, *A Minor Poet and Other Verse* (1884), are poems that express erotic love alongside and through a palpable, physically-charged experience of music. For example, "Sinfonia Eroica (*to Sylvia*)," describes a crowded June concert where

> Far off, across the hush'd, expectant throng,
> I saw your face that fac'd mine.
>   Clear and strong
> Rush'd forth the sound,[1]

Because of the indentation and lineation, "Clear and strong" references both Sylvia's face and the music, suggesting physically-present music as well as making it uncertain whether the concert begins simultaneously with the sighting of Sylvia or whether the music is only experienced by the speaker in response to Sylvia (or to passionate feelings in general). Indeed, the speaker expresses uncertainty as to "which was sound, and which, O Love, was you" (35), perhaps because running through the poem is a corporal description and experience of music, which "smote the air" (30). Similarly, in "June-Tide Echo (*After a Richter Concert*)," the speaker imagines a June lover (or June, the lover) whose presence is linked to music:

---

[1] Amy Levy, "Sinfonia Eroica (*to Sylvia*)," *A Minor Poet and Other Verse* (London: Unwin, 1884) 11–13. The title of this poem plays on the similarities of sound between "erotic" and Beethoven's Symphony No. 3, Op. 55, commonly known as the *Eroica Symphony* (heroic). The poem in its entirety can be read beyond the literal meaning of a concert; it is also an extended metaphor for love-making (the *Eroica*). Other poems within *A Minor Poet and Other Verse* that treat the theme of music are "In a Minor Key (*An Echo from a Larger Lyre*)," "A Dirge," and "To Sylvia," which has a few bars of musical staff notation after the title. For another poem that takes place at a concert and was written within the same time period, see Levy, "A Ballad of Last Seeing," *Cambridge Review* (1 May 1883) 337. Levy returned to the theme of music throughout her poetic career as seen, for instance, in *A London Plane-Tree and Other Verse* (London: Unwin, 1889). Sylvia was often used as a name for the beloved in poetry. See Virginia Blain, ed., *Victorian Women Poets: A New Annotated Anthology* (Harlow: Longman, 2001) fn 336; Linda Hunt Beckman, *Amy Levy: Her Life and Letters* (Athens, OH: Ohio University Press, 2000) 88. My thanks to Robert Adlington, Yopie Prins and Jenny Bourne Taylor for reading and commenting on drafts of the introduction, and to Thomas Hamill for some reading suggestions.

> Sweet sounds to-night rose up, wave upon wave;
> Sweet dreams were afloat in the balmy air.
> This is the boon of the gods that I crave –
> To be glad, as the music and night were fair.
>
> For once, for one fleeting hour, to hold
> The fair shape the music that rose and fell
> Revealed and concealed like a veiling fold;
> To catch for an instant the sweet June spell. (13–20)

Dreams may float on the "balmy air" but, far from figuring dreams and air as insubstantial, the speaker brings in the physics of sound (sound waves). Just as her longing for a lover has physical urgency, so it is given bodily presence through this configuration of air, making it so thick with sound waves that music reveals, conceals and veils a "fair shape" that can be held, even if only momentarily. Levy's poems therefore play with conceptions of music as transcendent and also as so materially present that it can be seen and felt. "Sweet sounds" are the stuff of "Sweet dreams" and are appropriate for describing a lover who is simultaneously there and not there; June is present through the speaker's own erotic longing, and so is physically felt and yet literally absent.

Besides expressing the experience of imagination and music in physical terms – a formulation that Levy was not alone in using[2] – the poems contribute to our understanding of Victorian concert-going and constructions of the sexual self. Levy's verse does not simply express the physics of *sound*; it refers specifically to *musical* experience. It relies on knowing what certain repertoire signified while also increasing our understanding of what the public experience of music meant to the private individual. For instance, Hungarian conductor Hans Richter (1843–1916), referred to in the subtitle of "June-Tide Echo," was a close friend of Richard Wagner's and frequently conducted his music – a fact so well known that it figures in Sigmund Freud's case studies in *The Interpretation of Dreams* (1900).[3] As Emma Sutton's essay in this volume documents, Wagner's music

---

[2] See my *Women Musicians in Victorian Fiction, 1860–1900: Representations of Music, Science and Gender in the Leisured Home* (Aldershot: Ashgate, 2000) and Emma Sutton's essay in this volume.

[3] Richter was an influential figure in nineteenth-century England, arriving for the first time as Wagner's assistant and conducting most of the Albert Hall Wagner Festival in 1877, with the composer sitting in an armchair beside him. One eye-witness writes of "the all-controlling power of Hans Richter, hidden behind Wagner's conducting desk, but really conducting everything; for Wagner, in the enjoyment of his own splendid creations, frequently forgot the baton altogether." See Myles B. Foster, *History of the Philharmonic* Society, 358; cited in Percy A. Scholes, *The Mirror of Music, 1844–1944*, 2 vols (London: Novello and Oxford University Press, 1947) 1: 254. Richter returned a couple of years later to Britain, conducting the "Richter Concerts" or the "Orchestral Festival Concerts" in London from 1879 to 1897, and subsequently serving as conductor for the Hallé orchestra in Manchester until 1911. Between 1885 and 1911, Richter also conducted the Birmingham Festivals. Besides conducting Wagner's music, Richter's performances of Beethoven, and later of Elgar, were noteworthy to British concertgoers. See Scholes, 1: 384–385. See also George Bernard Shaw, "The Wagner Festival," *The Hornet* (6 June 1877), rpt. *Shaw's Music (The Bodley Head*

was frequently invoked by aesthetic writers and *fin-de-siècle* sexologists as "excessively" sensual and erotic. With the physicality of musical experience that is expressed in poems like "June-Tide Echo" and "Sinfonia Eroica," Levy's poetry was an early example of this discourse.[4]

What seems especially interesting in Levy's poems, however, is that this intensely private experience is awakened in public, among a "hush'd, expectant throng", which contributes to findings about audiences and concert attendance in Victorian Britain. In another essay, I investigate how *fin-de-siècle* novels like George Du Maurier's *Trilby* (1894) integrate crowd psychology with audience scenes; whether audience members have musical ability or not, they respond alike to the all-encompassing sway of an almost mesmeric diva's performance.[5] The result is an audience grouped together by an *en masse* response to musical sensation, to the point where their imaginative response is expressed as unified, as if a single social body were experiencing the same images rather than being disparate individuals. But in Levy's verse, it seems that the public, aesthetic sphere of the concert hall is a necessary aid to personal imagination, erotic experience and the intimate connection between people seen from afar. A bridge is formed between public and private, where private dreams and sexual identity are dependent upon public experiences. This state is even eagerly anticipated by the speaker in "Sinfonia Eroica" before the concert begins:

> And all the eager people thronging came
> To that great hall, drawn by the magic name
> Of one, a high magician, who can raise
> The spirits of the past and future days,
> And draw the dreams from out the secret breast,
> Giving them life and shape.
>   I, with the rest,
> Sat there athirst, atremble for the sound; (3–9)

"Magic name" and "magician" suggest that the dream state created within this group experience will be led by one person, similar to the dynamics of

---

Bernard Shaw), ed. Dan H. Laurence (London: Reinhardt, The Bodley Head, 1981) 1: 126-127; Shaw, *Music in London, 1890–94*, 3 vols (London: Constable, 1932); Christopher Fifield, *True Artist and True Friend: A Biography of Hans Richter* (Oxford: Clarendon, 1993); Sigmund Freud, Chapter 6, *The Interpretation of Dreams* (1900) in *The Standard Edition of the Complete Psychological Works of Sigmund Freud*, trans. James Strachey (London: Hogarth, 1953) 5: 342–343.

[4] See Sutton's essay in this volume, "'The Music Spoke for Us': Music and Sexuality in *fin-de-siècle* Poetry" for a further discussion of these issues. While Oscar Wilde's *Poems* (1881) predates Levy's *A Minor Poet and Other Verse* (1884), and sexology was indeed developing as early as the 1880s, most of Sutton's examples are from the 1890s, both in terms of verse and the writings of sexologists like Magnus Hirschfeld, Marc-André Raffalovich and Havelock Ellis.

[5] See my "Music, crowd control and the female performer in *Trilby*," *The Idea of Music in Victorian Fiction*, eds Nicky Losseff and Sophie Fuller (Aldershot: Ashgate, 2004).

Victorian crowd theory where a charismatic individual was thought to lead the people through tapping into their unconscious minds and playing upon their suggestibility.[6] But instead of creating a situation whereby these thoughts are then shared between the collective through a process of "infection" or "contagion" – popular notions at the time – the result is to give "life and shape" to secret, individual dreams of erotic fulfillment. Sensation is invoked, but for the purpose of giving physical life to imaginative processes that remain private. These passionate imaginings literally exist, and co-exist, with the bourgeois society thronging the concert hall, but are not subsumed into it nor subsume it; a parallel world occurs for same-sex lovers, which is interesting not only for existing within the bourgeois public sphere, but also for being in some degree dependent upon it. This formulation occurs even in "June-Tide Echo" which takes place "After a ... Concert" rather than during it; "June-Tide Echo" depicts the speaker as alone, but still incorporates the musical experience, sensuality and suggestiveness of the Richter concert into solitary dreams. While it is usual to examine Levy as a poet expressing alienation and while these poems do express dreams rather than real love affairs, it seems to me that in attending the symphony the speaker finds at least some sense of community and connection; it is here that her dreams seem real, even if her inner life runs parallel to, rather than merging with, the rest of the audience.[7]

Music, poetry and culture

As this brief example shows, poems were part of larger cultural movements in the nineteenth century that helped to construct the idea of music, and were in many cases reciprocally constructed by an on-going debate about the meaning of music. This volume investigates how music was depicted in and mediated through British poetry of the long nineteenth century (c.1789–1914) in order to elucidate music's significance, both within the culture and within poetic practices. The essays range from the verse of William Blake and Robert Burns at the end of the eighteenth century through to that of Michael Field and Arthur Symons at the turn of the twentieth century, and demonstrate that music in poetry partook of and commented on a wide range of scientific and cultural discourses. In this, the book contributes to exciting, recent scholarship that not only explores music's relationship to religion, aesthetics and the other arts in nineteenth-century Britain, but also to evolutionary theory, medicine, mental science, and constructions of

---

[6] Unusually, it seems to be the composer who elicits this entranced response (Beethoven, as implied by the title), instead of the star performers, who are the ones usually depicted in these terms (e.g., Liszt, Paganini and the fictional Trilby).
[7] Sutton's chapter further explores the notion of this type of *poetry* as comparable to bourgeois *musical* experience. Our findings complement each other, although they differ in how we come to the conclusions of parallel worlds. My argument is based on music, Victorian crowd theory, the group and the individual, while Sutton's discussion of music as "used to delineate a sense of public, social sexual identity" depends on how it interacts with the conception of the public, performative role of the poet in verse of the 1890s.

class, nation, gender and sexual identity.[8] Featured in this volume are essays by literary scholars and musicologists that propose in various but complementary ways how music in nineteenth-century poetry is socially and even physically rooted. The book, therefore, extends beyond notions of music as evocative, which has been a critical commonplace in literary scholarship of nineteenth-century poetry, and also unveils new information and methodologies for musicologists interested in the contextualized study of music.

The aim of this book is to provide a meeting ground between the two disciplines, yielding information and methodological approaches that are of musicological import as well as literary, and also to define the field by discussing a number of poets and by ranging through various topics of cultural and aesthetic significance. These disparate topics and methodologies work together to investigate nineteenth-century British music and music-making as significant for what it tells us, not just about music and its place within culture, but also for ideas about what music itself might be. Indeed, there is no doubt now that music was deeply entrenched in and a dominant part of British life during the nineteenth century, and musicologists generally agree the period from 1840 to 1940 to be a Musical Renaissance in England.[9] This essay collection builds from this fact in order to ask more specifically how literature constructs the meaning of music.[10] The answer to this query is complex. In his study of current

---

[8] See Alison Winter, *Mesmerized: Powers of Mind in Victorian Britain* (Chicago: University of Chicago Press, 1998); Bennett Zon, *Music and Metaphor in Nineteenth-Century British Musicology* (Aldershot: Ashgate, 2000); Emma Sutton, *Aubrey Beardsley and British Wagnerism in the 1890s* (Oxford: Oxford University Press, 2002); Paula Gillett, *Musical Women in England, 1870–1914* (New York: St Martin's Press, 2000); and my *Women Musicians in Victorian Fiction*.

[9] See Meirion Hughes and Robert Stradling, *The English Musical Renaissance, 1840-1940: Constructing a National Music*, 2nd ed. (Manchester: Manchester University Press, 2001). For a fascinating consideration of the phenomenon from the point of view of women, see Sophie Fuller, "Women Composers During the British Musical Renaissance, 1880–1918," diss., King's College, University of London 1998, 9–20. The starting date of the Musical Renaissance is open to debate, with many musicologists suggesting 1880. However, Hughes and Stradling make a convincing argument for 1840 because in this decade there begins to be greater value placed on music in British society.

Also of note are the biennial conference on Music in Nineteenth-Century Britain, held at the University of Hull (1997), University of Durham (1999), Royal College of Music (2001), and University of Leeds (2003); one day conferences at the University of Reading (2000) on The Idea of Music in Fiction, and at the Open University on nineteenth- and twentieth-century literature and music (London, 2001; Oxford, 2002); and Ashgate's series on Music in Nineteenth-Century Britain.

[10] The interdisciplinary study of music and literature is a recent growth field. For books on music in nineteenth-century British fiction, see Nicky Losseff and Sophie Fuller, eds, *The Idea of Music in Victorian Fiction* (Aldershot: Ashgate, 2003); Beryl Gray, *George Eliot and Music* (London: Macmillan, 1989); Delia da Sousa Correa, *George Eliot, Music and Victorian Culture* (Basingstoke: Palgrave, 2002); John Hughes, *"Ecstatic Sound": Music and Individuality in the Work of Thomas Hardy* (Aldershot: Ashgate, 2001); Alisa Clapp-Itnyre, *Angelic Airs, Subversive Songs: Music as Social Discourse in the Victorian Novel* (Athens, OH: Ohio University Press, 2002); Phyllis Weliver, *Women Musicians in Victorian Fiction,*

musicology, Alastair Williams discusses the "idea of music" by summarizing how Claude Lévi-Strauss and Paul De Man deal "more with what we might call the idea of music than actual musical practices" and also how Lawrence Kramer distinguishes between "the idea of music (music as cultural trope) and the way music is studied (music as disciplinary object)."[11] My point is that examining literature potentially allows us to resolve some of this bifurcation: in literature we can investigate the idea of music *and* musical practices (as contributing to reception history). Moreover, even focusing on music as cultural trope does not preclude applying the information gleaned to the study of music as object, as Michael Allis's and Yopie Prins's chapters in this volume demonstrate. Of course, this means that the page of music will be interpreted in part through cultural information, rather than being strictly formalist and so without referentiality. The break with traditional musicology is also made because this collection of essays, despite its emphasis on history, does not align itself with the practices of positivist musicology.[12]

1860–1900: Representations of music, science and gender in the leisured home (Aldershot: Ashgate, 2000).
    While fiction has been the focus of this work in recent years, especially within Victorian studies, an equal, on-going consideration is needed of how music was imagined in poetry. No collection of essays on music in British poetry of the long nineteenth century exists, although there are essays on individual poets scattered through various scholarly publications (see the footnotes provided in each of the chapters). Other books about music in nineteenth-century British poetry address Romantic poets, not Victorian, and focus on literary studies, rather than being a true dialogue between the fields of music and literature, where each field is of at least fairly equal importance. This is not to say that the information contained would not interest musicologists, especially because in some cases the books deal with the aesthetics of music or music as iconography, but rather that the books are mostly geared toward a literary audience. For books on music and Romantic poets, see John A. Minahan, *Word Like a Bell: John Keats, Music and the Romantic Poet* (Kent, OH: Kent State University Press, 1992); B.H. Fairchild, *Such Holy Song: Music as idea, form, and image in the poetry of William Blake* (Kent, OH: Kent State University Press, 1980). Although he mostly addresses eighteenth-century poets, Kevin Barry also dips into the Romantics in *Language, Music and the Sign: A study in aesthetics, poetics and poetic practice from Collins to Coleridge* (Cambridge: Cambridge University Press, 1987).

[11] See Alastair Williams, *Constructing Musicology* (Aldershot: Ashgate, 2001) 3, 24, 32, 56; Lawrence Kramer, *Classical Music and Postmodern Knowledge* (Berkeley: University of California Press, 1995) 61; Paul De Man, "The Rhetoric of Blindness: Jacques Derrida's Reading of Rousseau," *Blindness and Insight: Essays in the Rhetoric of Contemporary Criticism* (London: Methuen, 1986) 102–141; Claude Lévi-Strauss, *The Raw and the Cooked*, trans. John and Doreen Weightman (London: Cape, 1969) 15–16, 18.

[12] Traditional musicology could be further broken down into the history of Western art music, music theory and analysis, and ethnomusicology – divisions that are more prominently made in American academe than they are in British. Old-style musicological approaches within these categories are: (1) sonic relationships as determining meaning – a formalist approach used in music theory and analysis, and (2) a positivist methodology, used in music history. Alastair Williams calls these "quasi-scientific methodologies" which themselves replace previous ways of formulating music's meaning (nineteenth-century aesthetics; associations made between a composer's biography and compositional meaning). See Williams, *Constructing Musicology*, vii–ix, 1–3; Joseph Kerman, *Contemplating Music: Challenges to Musicology* [published as *Musicology* in the UK] (Cambridge, MA: Harvard University Press, 1985).

Of course, pairing music and poetry is not a new undertaking. Explorations of text setting obviously focus on the two arts,[13] while Lawrence Kramer's influential *Music and Poetry* (1984) addresses "when and how a poem and a composition can be rewardingly discussed in tandem" suggesting a manner of analysis that supports a consideration of the two through "a shared pattern of [structural] unfolding".[14] Slightly pre-dating Kramer, James Anderson Winn provides in *Unsuspected Eloquence* (1981) a history of music and literature that complements Kramer's; although covering ancient Greece to Schönberg and Stravinsky, and although ranging through topics as varied as emotional expression, text setting and comparing the autonomy of twelve-tone music to I.A. Richards's practical criticism, Winn also posits that the kind of formal analysis practiced by the fields of linguistics and music theory can be mutually informative.[15] This work on the structural similarities between music and literature has been followed by musicologists and literary scholars alike, with Kramer's writing, especially, forming a model for much work in this interdisciplinary field.[16]

---

[13] See, for example, Edward T. Cone, *The Composer's Voice* (Berkeley: University of California Press, 1974); Richard Kramer, *Distant Cycles: Schubert and the Conceiving of Song* (Chicago: University of Chicago Press, 1994); Lawrence Kramer, ed., *Walt Whitman and Modern Music: War, Desire, and the Trials of Nationhood* (New York: Garland, 2000); Ruth A. Solie, "Whose life? The gendered self in Schumann's *Frauenliebe* songs," *Music and Text: Critical Inquiries*, ed. Steven Paul Scher (Cambridge: Cambridge University Press, 1992) 219–240; Susan Youens, *Schubert's Poets and the Making of Lieder* (Cambridge: Cambridge University Press, 1996); Youens, *Schubert, Müller and* Die Schöne Müllerin (Cambridge: Cambridge University Press, 1997).

[14] Lawrence Kramer, *Music and Poetry: The Nineteenth Century and After* (Berkeley: University of California Press, 1984) 4, 10. Although Kramer writes that no interdisciplinary method exists between "twentieth-century advances in literary interpretation and musical analysis" (4), and his analysis certainly draws on later twentieth-century methods of analysis, the idea of comparing music's formal structures with poems (and fiction) had been anticipated by Calvin S. Brown in *Music and Literature: A Comparison of the Arts* (Athens: University of Georgia Press, 1948). As Robert Samuels comments, Adorno's familiar statement might also predate Kramer's way of reading music: "It is not that music wants to narrate, but that the composer wants to make music in the way others make narratives." See Theodor W. Adorno, *Mahler: A Musical Physiognomy* (1960), trans. E. Jephcott (Chicago: University of Chicago Press, 1992) 62. Cited in Robert Samuels, *Mahler's Sixth Symphony: A Study in Musical Semiotics* (Cambridge: Cambridge University Press, 1995) 133. For a discussion of musicology and narrativity, see Samuels, 133–140.

[15] For James Anderson Winn's writing on the nineteenth century, see *Unsuspected Eloquence: A History of the Relations between Poetry and Music* (New Haven: Yale University Press, 1981) 259–331.

[16] Winn is known among literary scholars, but is virtually unheard of among musicologists, while Kramer is an acknowledged leader in the recent paradigm shift in musicological practices. For scholarship following Kramer's model, see Samuels, 133–165; Anthony Newcomb, "Once More 'Between Absolute and Programme Music': Schumann's Second Symphony," *19th Century Music* 7 (1984): 233–250; "Part II: Literary models for musical understanding: music, lyric, narrative, and metaphor," *Music and Text: Critical Inquiries*, ed. Steven Paul Scher (Cambridge: Cambridge University Press, 1992) 59–136. Essays in Part II include Paul Alpers, "Lyrical modes"; Marshall Brown, "Origins of modernism: musical structures and narrative forms"; Thomas Grey, "Metaphorical modes in nineteenth-century

While I am emphasizing Kramer's model as oriented toward structure, it is crucial to note that Kramer breaks with previous, formalist traditions. Since at least the mid 1980s in musicology (and the late 1970s in literary studies) there has been increasing interest in cultural context, and Kramer is at the cutting edge of this changing paradigm. Indeed, in *Music and Poetry* he carefully defines his approach as including referential qualities, not least because he places a poetic text and a musical composition side by side. In this, music is not being interpreted by sonic relationships only, nor is a poem read as autonomous, outside of cultural context; Kramer differentiates his approach from "the formalist equation of pure music with pure form" and "the extreme poststructuralist view that poetic language (indeed all language) is non-referential" (5). These are important and valid distinctions, making Kramer a pioneer in the so-called new musicology, which emphasizes an increased awareness of music within cultural context.

That being said, Kramer's approach moves from this careful cultural awareness to a type of analysis that still aligns with "traditional" approaches because it focuses on the inner structure of literary works and of musical compositions. This was the pivotal point of a by now famous debate between Kramer and Gary Tomlinson, conducted in the pages of *Current Musicology* in 1993.[17] Tomlinson suggests that even though Kramer argues for a postmodern musicology which is aware of context, webs of meaning and multiple voices, he still ends up focused on the score:

> Indeed Kramer unreservedly identifies the "work" as the locus of the new musicology, even though it is one of the modernist categories contested most rewardingly in postmodern thought. In the very moment that he holds out hope for an extramusical broadening of the notes' signifying potential, he draws our attention back to the work, making it the primary (almost exclusive) matrix of its own meanings. (Tomlinson, 20)

Tomlinson considers himself postmodern, just as Kramer does. He argues that focusing on the work positions Kramer's method within what are usually considered more traditional (modernist) approaches in musicology, but Alastair Williams is correct that the Kramer/Tomlinson debate ultimately springs from the fact that the scholars do not agree on what postmodernism means.[18] In other

---

music criticism: image, narrative, and idea"; Anthony Newcomb, "Narrative archetypes and Mahler's Ninth Symphony."

[17] Kramer's article originally appeared as "The Musicology of the Future" in *Repercussions* 1 (1992): 5–18 and was reworked and republished as Chapter 1, "Prospects: Postmodernism and Musicology," *Classical Music and Postmodern Knowledge*, 1–32. The debate following the *Repercussions* article was published as Gary Tomlinson, "Musical Pasts and Postmodern Musicologies: A Response to Lawrence Kramer"; Lawrence Kramer, "Music Criticism and the Postmodernist Turn: In Contrary Motion with Gary Tomlinson"; and Tomlinson, "Gary Tomlinson Responds" in *Current Musicology* 53 (1993): 18–24, 25–35, 36–40. For a pro-Kramer discussion of the debate, see Williams, 121–123.

[18] Williams, 122. Far from being a personal quarrel, the Kramer/Tomlinson debate is ultimately a productive discussion of key points regarding the nature of postmodernism and the new

words, just as new historicism is slippery because of its methodological diversity, so is postmodern musicology thick in varied definitions and self-questioning.

It is not my intention to debate the nuances of what it is to take history and cultural context seriously within musicology, but rather to point out that while Kramer's approach has cultural relevance because it lays a poem next to a musical composition, this volume of essays engages in a different type of cultural contextualization – a process whereby Kramer's approach seems, in contrast, more traditional because of its ultimate focus on the internal structure of text and composition. This is not to invalidate Kramer's model – indeed, it is important, theoretically rigorous and highly influential – but instead to flag the differences between our undertaking and Kramer's. Simply put, this essay collection differs from Kramer's model by developing a wider range of approaches to cultural contextualization; it considers how the topic of music is conceptualized within poems according to different historical contexts and musical practices. This is a localized study of one culture (even if it is national instead of regional), one long century, and contains myriad voices – the essays are not only varied in topic and methodology, but also frequently address plurality. Further, I am proposing an intertextuality not through juxtaposing a musical composition with a poem and considering similarities in structure, but rather through an awareness that the meaning of music is partially constructed by texts, just as poems that mention music reference and interpret ideas of music already present within the culture. The concept of networks or webs of meaning is not new, nor is the notion that contextualization will open up how we interpret music as, in part, beyond the notes on the page.[19] However, in this it is crucial to emphasize that our project is not necessarily a dispersing "into context of what we usually grasp as the immediacy of music", to use Kramer's words of rebuttal to Tomlinson (27); some of the essays in this volume do indeed examine ideas of music as re-represented in musical composition, suggesting permeability between types of texts – music and poetic. Analysis of music can sometimes be influenced by deeper understandings of "the idea of music," then, but the primary task here is to examine the conceptualization and representation of music in poetry, which helps to decode music's very solid presence in nineteenth-century British thought and culture.

Situating art firmly within society is an important point not just for understanding general movements within musicological and literary studies, but also for the idea that poetry specifically has a statement to make about culture. After all, Romantic and Victorian verse has traditionally been seen as a private

---

musicology. It is worth noting that the issues debated by Kramer and Tomlinson are much more complex than I address; they also include issues of ethnomusicology and otherness, Foucaultian power dynamics in the relation of critic to subject (music), and the nature of music as speech-act.

[19] For "webs of connections" see Donna Haraway, *Simians, Cyborgs, and Women: The Reinvention of Nature* (New York: Routledge, 1991) 191. See also Susan Bernstein's essay in this volume, "On Music Framed: The Eolian Harp in Romantic Writing"; Gary Tomlinson, "The Web of Culture: A Context for Musicology," *19th-Century Music* 7.3 (1984): 350–362.

discourse, although more recently poetry has been investigated in terms of the public and political.[20] While the field of Romantic poetry has been ahead in this project, scholars of Victorian poetry have also begun to investigate the political aspects of poetry, resulting in a complex, on-going conversation about the subject. On the one hand, even the most private poems can be politicized now, as Isobel Armstrong articulates in *Victorian Poetry: Poetry, Poetics, and Politics*. "Art occupied its own area, a self-sufficing aesthetic realm over and against practical experience" she writes. "And yet it was at once apart and central, for it had a mediating function, representing and interpreting life."[21] Armstrong explores the power relationships between self and world, suggesting that the private, often dreamy realm of Victorian verse is also inherently political – a position in line with much current critical thinking that politicizes sexual relations, language and epistemology.[22] On the other hand, Matthew Reynolds demonstrates in *The Realms of Verse* that there were specific connections between poems and British and European political activities – or what the nineteenth century would consider to be political (activities having to do with government [7–9]). This carries forward ideas about Romantic poets who were frequently social radicals, a point made by Anne Janowitz in *Lyric and Labour* where she discusses lyric identity as coming from the external (especially community, but also "customary and rationalist philosophical, economic, and political rhetorics", and landscape) as well as from the internal.[23] The process of linking the public to poetry is not limited to poetic *response* to the larger world, however. Janowitz investigates Chartist poets who help to construct Chartism itself, building it through collective poetry and song writing (135–136), and Reynolds indicates an exchange between politicians and poets, whereby each regarded the other with greater respect than occurs today: "[poets'] claims to be, in some more or less figurative way, legislators, were taken seriously by those men ... who were involved in the day-to-day business of actual legislation." (7) Not only were poems and poets constructed by their society, but they were also significant in constructing English culture, as Antony H. Harrison proves in his exploration of how "poets operated as a mode of cultural intervention", in part "under the guise of eliciting pleasure."[24] In *Victorian Poets and the Politics of*

---

[20] For Romantic poetry see, for example, Carl Woodring, *Politics in English Romantic Poetry* (Cambridge, MA: Harvard University Press, 1970); John Whale, *Imagination Under Pressure, 1789–1832: Aesthetics, Politics and Utility* (Cambridge: Cambridge University Press, 2000); Richard Cronin, *The Politics of Romantic Poetry* (London: Macmillan, 2000).

[21] Isobel Armstrong, *Victorian Poetry: Poetry, Poetics, and Politics* (London: Routledge, 1993) 4.

[22] Armstrong, 7. Reynolds makes the same point in his discussion of Armstrong. See Matthew Reynolds, *The Realms of Verse, 1830–1870: English Poetry in a Time of Nation-Building* (Oxford: Oxford University Press, 2001) 9.

[23] Anne Janowitz, *Lyric and Labour in the Romantic Tradition* (Cambridge: Cambridge University Press, 1998) 5. Despite the title, Janowitz bridges the Romantic and Victorian periods.

[24] Antony H. Harrison, *Victorian Poets and the Politics of Culture: Discourse and Ideology* (Charlottesville: University Press of Virginia, 1998) 1.

Culture, Harrison opposes Utilitarianism to the pleasurable effects of language and its influence on ideology.[25] Taking as a subject political stances that were positioned for or against poetry is quite different from politicizing private topics and thereby suggests that Victorian poetry anticipates deconstructive strategies, which is different again from arguing that the political world and the poet were in dialogue. In all cases, however, the public and the political are now seen to be integral to British poetry of the long nineteenth century, even if each project defines "political" differently and utilizes various methodologies.

Thus poetry mediates, constructs and debates life, from the realistic depiction of current sociopolitical realities and intellectual debates to the imaginative realms of mythical worlds, which might still speak to contemporary issues. Moving beyond the need to prove verse to be culturally constructing and constructed, then, this book focuses on a particular topic: music. Doing so deepens the discussion about poetry as paradoxically "private and public," "apart and central,"[26] individualistic and communal, taking as the focal point the subject of music, which, because of its transcendent qualities, has shared with poetry the notion of being "apart." Not only did nineteenth-century aesthetic debates give music this function, but poets have been seen to play upon this quality of music, making the Aeolian harp a central image for poetic inspiration and thereby helping to construct the notion of the nineteenth-century poet and poem as occupying the realm of imagination. However, when music is focused on as a topic that actually is engaged with cultural realities, particularly interesting points emerge regarding the place of poetry not as extraneous to nineteenth-century culture, but rather as energetically engaged with discourses that cross the public/private divide, from issues of sexual identity to expressions of nationalism, and which continue to challenge the perception of imaginative realms as separate from physical life. Concentrating on music does indeed bring up issues of imagination, evanescence and transience in nineteenth-century poetry, but it equally questions the notions of that insubstantiality, often expressing itself in physiological terms. Besides space, time is at issue, since poets of the period often play with the notion of music as simultaneously indicating an historical present and the eternal. In this, we find music a potent nexus for debates about humanity and the divine, the cultural and the natural, self and other.

Looking at how music is depicted in nineteenth-century poetry as a concrete, sometimes even corporal presence, these essays make a sharp break with the way in which many literary scholars have borrowed musical vocabulary to describe what are actually elements of poetic discourse, often meaning something entirely different from what a musician would mean by the term. For instance, Gerard

---

[25] Harrison, 3–15. Harrison's argument is considerably more nuanced and complex than I have indicated here, going beyond a simple argument against Utilitarianism by bringing discourse theory into his discussion of ideology. For a detailed critique of the book, see Isobel Armstrong's review essay, "When is a Victorian Poet Not a Victorian Poet? Poetry and the Politics of Subjectivity in the Long Nineteenth Century," *Victorian Studies* 43 (2001): 279–292.

[26] Reynolds, 10; Armstrong, 4.

Manley Hopkins's use of "counterpoint" to mean the "systematic reversal of iambic stress patterns" indicates a process quite different from the counterpoint of a musical composition, which has two or more simultaneous melodic lines.[27] John Hollander aptly summarizes this metaphoric use of musical language in poetry: "[b]y the 'music of poetry' we generally mean all of the nonsemantic properties of the language of a poem including not only its rationalized prosody, but its actual sound on being read, and certain characteristics of its syntax and imagery as well."[28] This idea of a "musical poetry" is so prevalent that it informs what we think a "musical poet" might be. As Deborah Vlock-Keyes writes, "[w]hile Tennyson is often considered the musical Victorian poet, Browning's choppy, prosaic verse actually imitates music in a way that Tennyson's more lyrical poetry does not."[29] This is one of many examples, but it has the merit of using music as a means of contrasting two of the most prominent Victorian poets, one of whom was and is frequently described in musical terms.

This metaphoric use of music is not limited to the vocabulary of scholars; poets at both ends of the period worried about the sound conveyed by their poems. As Eric Griffiths documents, William Wordsworth and W.B. Yeats sought help with punctuation in letters written respectively to Humphry Davy and to Robert Bridges, and Yeats revealed years later that "I spoke them [the lines of his poems] slowly as I wrote and only discovered when I read them to somebody else that there was no common music, no prosody."[30] This idea of equating music and prosody (the study of meter) demonstrates that poets themselves use a musical lexicon to discuss the ability of print to convey what they intended in the writing process, a point made clear in Seamus Heaney's 1978 lecture at the University of Liverpool, *The Makings of a Music: Reflections on the Poetry of Wordsworth and Yeats*. Investigating poetic composition and the "music" of the final product, Heaney stated that "I want to explore the way that certain postures and motions within the poet's incubating mind affect the posture of the voice and the motion of rhythms in the language of the poem itself."[31] Voice and rhythm are communicated quite literally

---

[27] John Hollander, *Vision and Resonance: Two Senses of Poetic Form* (1975), 2nd ed. (New Haven: Yale University Press, 1985) 5.

[28] Hollander, *Vision and Resonance*, 9. See also Steven Paul Scher, "How Meaningful is 'Musical' in Literary Criticism?" *Yearbook of Comparative and General Literature* 21 (1972): 52–56.

[29] Deborah Vlock-Keyes, "Music and Dramatic Voice in Robert Browning and Robert Schumann," *Victorian Poetry* 29.3 (Autumn 1991): 227.

[30] Letter of 29 September 1800 in *The Letters of William and Dorothy Wordsworth: The Early Years 1787–1805*, ed. Ernest de Sélincourt (1935), 2nd ed., rev. Chester L. Shaver, 2 vols (Oxford: Clarendon, 1967) 1: 289; letter of July 1915, in *The Letters of W.B. Yeats*, ed. Allan Wade (London: Hart-Davis, 1954) 598; W.B. Yeats, *Reveries over Childhood and Youth* (1915), rpt. in *Autobiographies* (London: Macmillan, 1955) 67. All cited in Eric Griffiths, *The Printed Voice of Victorian Poetry* (Oxford: Clarendon, 1989) 61–62.

[31] Seamus Heaney, *The Makings of a Music: Reflections on the Poetry of Wordsworth and Yeats*, Kenneth Allott Lecture given on 9 February 1978 (Liverpool: University of Liverpool, 1978) 1.

through the "language of the poem"; this includes issues of punctuation, such as those that Wordsworth and Yeats worried about, and also word choice, meter, and so on.

While exploring the metaphoric "music of poetry" is certainly a worthwhile pursuit – indeed, the issues involved are crucial to considerations of voicing – this volume does something quite different. Some of the essays do explore formal issues that might be said to depict a "musical poetry," but the essays all specifically link their discussion to how the figure of music is addressed in verse. Creating angst for poets of the period, the accuracy of communicating and disseminating sound through print was obviously important, and this issue cannot help but be foregrounded when a poem depicts a musical scene or image. It seems to me that music's obviously aural nature is useful for highlighting considerations of how sound works in a poetry created in a newly emergent print culture – where sound is communicated and delivered, even, through the printed word. Recent scholarship is laying the foundation for how these issues might be explored, even when the focus is not directly on music.[32]

The essays in this book further define the field, partly by developing the ideas mentioned above and even more by highlighting a number of issues that increase our understanding of specifically musical practices in nineteenth-century Britain, despite prevalent notions that the poetry of the period does not lend itself to such disclosures. For instance, Hollander makes Robert Browning the one exception in the century who *does* include "musical images" in his poems.[33] Hollander bases his point on the idea that the music of "the concert hall, the drawing-room and the opera house" is largely excluded in British poetry of the period, unlike German Romanticism, and when musical images like the Aeolian harp do occur in British Romantic poetry they tend to emphasize issues about sound rather than music. Browning, however, is not the only poet of nineteenth-century Britain to examine what Hollander calls "cultural music" (71). To give just two examples: George Eliot's *Armgart* provides an account of an opera singer and Aubrey Beardsley's "The Three Musicians" clearly references Wagner and Gluck, as Emma Sutton discusses in her chapter. Indeed, Hollander even contradicts himself by citing Leigh Hunt as making concert music of imaginative concern in poetry like "The Lover of Music to His Pianoforte" and the verse fragments "Paganini"

---

[32] For instance, Griffiths's influential ideas about prosody in *The Printed Voice of Victorian Poetry* (1989) seem to be moving into the relation of poetry and music, as do recent essays such as Celeste Langan, "Understanding Media in 1805: Audiovisual Hallucination in *The Lay of the Last Minstrel*," *Studies in Romanticism* 40.1 (2001): 49–70; Yopie Prins, "Victorian Meters," *The Cambridge Companion to Victorian Poetry*, ed. Joseph Bristow (Cambridge: Cambridge University Press, 1999) 89–113. Susan Bernstein's book, *Virtuosity of the Nineteenth Century*, while not being a study of British poetry, does address ideas about music and poetry as situated within a new print culture. See Susan Bernstein, *Virtuosity of the Nineteenth Century: Performing Music and Language in Heine, Liszt, and Baudelaire* (Stanford: Stanford University Press, 1998).
[33] John Hollander, "Browning: The Music of Music," *Robert Browning*, ed. Harold Bloom, Modern Critical Views Series (New York: Chelsea House, 1985) 69.

and "A Thought on Music: suggested by a Private Concert, May 13, 1815."[34] The essays in this collection therefore offer a conclusion different from Hollander's thesis, where the poems are seen to emphasize music (not just sound) and to reveal important findings for musicologists studying nineteenth-century Britain. What this suggests is that we need to continue widening our repertoire of nineteenth-century poetry and also that musical images do not necessarily need to reference "cultural music" to have cultural significance.

Indeed, the centrality of music to poetry runs through the verse of the century, continuing past the Romantic period where it was a commonplace that music in poetry suddenly became more important than the eighteenth-century emphasis on the pictorial. As studies in Victorian poetry continue to widen beyond the triumvirate of Tennyson, Browning and Arnold, first discovering and now engaging in critical analysis of other poets, the study of music as a theme or topic in nineteenth-century British poetry bears further investigation by musicologists and literary scholars alike.

Interdisciplinarity: A web of connections

This volume, in bringing together considerations of music historically and within text, aims to examine how nineteenth-century British poetry constructed the idea of music, both through historic image and imagination. Taken together, the result of the essays is a rich exploration of nineteenth-century poetry, music and culture that will appeal to both musicologists and literary scholars, not least by suggesting new ways of intersecting the two fields to their mutual benefit. Situating literary texts and music within cultural context is of central importance in part because one of the things shared by the two fields is an increasing interest in recent years in the study of art within social context. However, while this seems to indicate a confluence of approach, it actually means that the time is ripe for bending disciplinary boundaries and that this can occur in various ways. Speaking on the simplest level, the essays in this volume are balanced differently: some are more obviously historical in nature, others concentrate to a greater degree on close reading, and some find the study of language and society to be mutually constituted.

The goal is to open up how we read texts so that they can beneficially cross disciplines; the contributors' methodological differences are an asset to this project and a hallmark of what it means to think in interdisciplinary ways. To some extent this aligns interdisciplinarity with other types of criticism that have developed in the last two or three decades. Certainly, recent discussions have stressed the inherent theoretical and disciplinary diversity of new

---

[34] See "Browning," 74–79, and also Hollander's 1968 Churchill College Overseas Fellowship Lecture at Cambridge, published as *Images of Voice: Music and Sound in Romantic Poetry* (Cambridge: Heffer, 1970) 8.

historicism as well as postmodern musicology.[35] Subsumed within these discussions is a consideration of interdisciplinarity. However, if we were to look for an overarching critical methodology in this volume, it would require pulling interdisciplinarity out from the shadow; the essays in this collection come together to make interdisciplinarity the keyword, not the subcategory. In other words, the chapters cohere first by looking at the interdisciplinary subject of music and poetry, but then further complicate the notion of interdisciplinarity by utilizing a variety of approaches to the topic, including drawing in other disciplines besides music and literature and stepping outside of established critical approaches. In this, we get such innovative methodologies as Celeste Langan's rethinking of Benedict Anderson, environmental science, capitalism and the circulation of music within print culture, and Susan Bernstein's figurative work where music is integrally intertwined with language, making her theoretical orientation itself interdisciplinary. We get investigations of triangulations that exist between science, music and literature in Kimiyo Ogawa's and Emma Sutton's chapters, which then branch out to other considerations (e.g., the spirit, poetry's public role), and Ruth A. Solie's idea of using a poem as an anchor from which to pivot through an impressive range of cultural discourses to explicate moral historiography and music. Yeo Wei Wei engages with feminist concerns that are similar between music and poetry, and applies Harold Bloom's anxiety of influence. The chapters by John Hughes and myself examine concerns familiar to musicologists, but with a twist. Hughes politicizes the aesthetic function of music, bringing philosophic arguments into his discussion of how music dramatizes the escape from rational understanding and social institutions to express an innocent, even transcendent, self. My chapter considers the reflexive function of language in poems that construct the idea of music as historical object and yet as transcendent – seemingly conflicting notions which elucidate Victorian musical practices, but in ways that go beyond reception history to brush against psychology and the materiality of language. Finally, traditional ideas of text-setting are inverted through Michael Allis's and Yopie Prins's awareness that not only were poets discussing music in nineteenth-century Britain, but British composers became eager to reformulate the

---

[35] For new historicism, see Catherine Gallagher and Stephen Greenblatt, *Practicing New Historicism* (Chicago: University of Chicago Press, 2000) 3; Louis Montrose, "New Historicisms," *Redrawing the Boundaries: The Transformation of English and American Literary Studies*, eds Stephen Greenblatt and Guiles Gunn (New York: MLA, 1992) 392. Catherine Gallagher details the issues involved in close reading and new criticism versus new historicism (including interdisciplinary studies) in "The History of Literary Criticism," *Dædalus: Journal of the American Academy of Arts and Sciences* 126.1 (1997): 133–153. Good companion pieces are H. Aram Veeser, introduction, *The New Historicism*, ed. H. Aram Veeser (New York: Routledge, 1989) ix–xvi; Montrose, "New Historicisms," 392–418; Harrison, 5–6; Cronin, 1–16. For new historicism and music, see Williams, 123–124. New historicism can be opposed to the autonomy of the literary text. For the autonomous text, see Jonathan Culler, *Structuralist Poetics* (Ithaca: Cornell University Press, 1975), especially Chapters 3 and 8.

meaning of music and lyric back into heard music, suggesting that in the text setting we find voices other than that of the composer only: in heard music we begin to hear the idea of music and, lifted off the poetic page, these new configurations become comments in their own right on the constructs of poetry.

Thus the orientation of this volume shares with new historicism and postmodern musicology a sense of expansion, diversity and contextualization, but its practices frequently demonstrate types of interdisciplinarity that do not necessarily neatly fit into the boxes of current critical approaches. Indeed, this is a movement seen in other recent books about nineteenth-century poetry. As Isobel Armstrong suggests in a 2001 review article, a dialogue exists between the variety of methodologies that are being applied to nineteenth-century British poetry, and this conversation demonstrates just how complex nineteenth-century culture was: "[t]heoretical work has been a late-comer, on the whole, to the study of 'Victorian' poetry," she writes, "but now that it has arrived, some new and intellectually exacting questions arise, questions that could not have arisen so sharply had they been posed of texts outside of the nineteenth century."[36] In this volume of essays is collected just such a multifaceted dialogue, where it is not merely poetry of the nineteenth century that elicits such diverse approaches, but also the complex debate about the idea of music in nineteenth-century Britain. Perhaps, then, we should avoid speaking of one methodology as subsuming the others and instead envision them as standing together with permeable boundaries; we need to be aware that interdisciplinary criticism is truly postmodernist in that it not only brings together various disciplines and discourses, but it also utilizes myriad critical approaches, whether new or previously existing. Multiple strategies are viable for understanding a single subject (music and poetry), because a subject is now seen as plural; it is understood not only through many texts, but also through many approaches. Indeed, even envisioning the interdisciplinary subject of music and poetry as single is debatable, for it is also double (music *and* poetry). This kaleidoscope method is successful in this essay collection because it digs deep. Through techniques such as demonstrating webs of connections between seemingly disparate discourses, or even the conversation between various methodologies, it illustrates how fields of knowledge rely on and inform each other.

The metaphor of "webs" for this process of interconnectedness is particularly apt in studying the nineteenth century since the web was a favorite

---

[36] Armstrong, "When is a Victorian Poet Not a Victorian Poet?" 280. The books under review are Janowitz, *Lyric and Labour*; Harrison, *Victorian Poets and the Politics of Culture*; Yopie Prins, *Victorian Sappho* (Princeton: Princeton University Press, 1999); Colin Graham, *Ideologies of Epic: Nation, Empire and Victorian Epic Poetry* (Manchester: Manchester University Press, 1998); Kerry McSweeney, *Supreme Attachments: Studies in Victorian Love Poetry* (Aldershot: Ashgate, 1998). Armstrong describes them as having the approaches of poststructuralism, "cultural materialism, ideological and discourse analysis in a new historicist mode, and Bakhtinian critique" (288).

image for poets, novelists, scientists and philosophers of the period, as Gillian Beer documents in *Darwin's Plots*. Moreover, the web was itself a deeply plural notion, approached using a variety of metaphors that brought to "web" a layered understanding. Nineteenth-century thinkers, Beer demonstrates, associated it not only with the spatial configuration of spiders' webs, but also with woven fabric, "chemical affinities," nerve and tissue connections that make up a single body, family relations, and the temporal idea of descent. The process of weaving was even sometimes treated as analogous to how waves function (waves of light and of ether, which were further compared to sound waves in nineteenth-century Britain).[37]

The concept of "web" becomes even more complex when we realize that it takes us beyond "mere analogy", as William Herschel writes, explaining what he means in terms of the "constituents of the planetary system": "they are bound up in one chain – interwoven in one web of mutual relation and harmonious agreement."[38] In this, although related parts are in agreement, the individual threads making up this "web of mutual relation" also maintain their own identities. Using an example from G.H. Lewes's *The Foundations of a Creed* (1873–1875), Beer demonstrates that the nineteenth-century "web" included the notion that threads come from "the general web of Existence" to be rewoven into new webs or fabrics, "but whatever different arrangement the threads may take on, they are always threads of the original web, they are not different threads."[39] As Susan Bernstein's essay demonstrates in terms of Fourier analysis, the same could be said for the construction of a sound wave or "a periodic motion" that "can be decomposed into a series of simple harmonic motions"[40] which retain their original configuration while coming together to form a single pitch. Taken one step further, "vibrations" through air and ether were frequently used in Victorian science and literature to explain communication between like-minded or sympathetic people, where the similarity was registered as literally vibrating through the human body. The wave, the vibration of commonality and mutual identification, did not

---

[37] Gillian Beer, *Darwin's Plots: Evolutionary Narrative in Darwin, George Eliot and Nineteenth-Century Fiction* (1983; London: Ark, 1985) 167–170. For the connections made between waves (water, sound, light, ether), see my *Women Musicians*, 63, 194. In discussing nineteenth-century uses of "web," Beer starts with Darwin's phrase, the "web of affinities" from *On the Origin of Species*, and then continues to explore the use of the word by J.S. Mill, G.H. Lewes, John Tyndall, Alexander Bain, George Eliot, Thomas Hardy, René Descartes, and William Herschel. See Charles Darwin, *On the Origin of Species By Means of Natural Selection, or the Preservation of Favoured Races in the Struggle for Life* (London: Murray, 1859) 415.
[38] William Herschel, cited by Robert Chambers, *Vestiges of the Natural History of Creation* (London: Churchill, 1844) 11–12. Cited by Beer, 169.
[39] Beer, 168. The citations are from G.H. Lewes, *The Foundations of a Creed* (London, 1873–1875) 1: 26.
[40] Robert T. Beyer, *Sounds of our Times: Two Hundred Years of Acoustics* (New York: Springer Verlag, 1999) 44–45. Cited by Susan Bernstein "On Music Framed: The Eolian Harp in Romantic Writing."

transform, but rather was shared between two bodies, which were envisioned as resonant instruments.[41]

What all this suggests is that one thread or one wave was conceived in the nineteenth century as able to be woven into or vibrate through various phenomena, making them physically related if not mutually constructed. This nineteenth-century perception of a world made up of many subjects that are interconnected in their very weave and fabric is extremely useful in the postmodern world, too, which stresses multiplicity rather than an overarching, single stance while also looking at how disciplines can be usefully studied together. Interdisciplinary work, then, is a way of pulling on several threads of a single subject, unraveling how it is constructed by using a variety of discourses and stances. This sense of construction is both spatial and temporal (the radiating web as a visual representation, the web as created through threads weaving together).[42] This is a useful construct because it demonstrates the solid presence of a subject, but also the notion of it being built. Evolution, transformation, and variation occur in subjects through time, while the individual threads making them up retain their own identity. This notion aligns nicely with interdisciplinary work, which may not only pull on several threads of a single subject, but also demonstrate how several subjects are constructed using the same thread or threads. These are webs of connection and interdependence.

Put another way, interdisciplinary work forces us to question our categories, making it an apposite way of studying nineteenth-century Britain, where disciplinary boundaries were not as rigid as they are today. Thinking in this way foregrounds issues of genre. The essays in this volume explore the meaning of music, but they also implicitly investigate the meaning of poetry. Indeed, given that the idea of poetry was itself in flux in nineteenth-century Britain (it was not a self-evident category) it seems odd that literary studies do not have a similar catch phrase to musicology's "the idea of music" for investigating how an ideology of poetry was forming. This is not to say that the subject has not already received critical attention. Certainly, one of the most useful investigations for the study of music and poetry is centered on what it meant for poetry to suddenly find itself within a print culture.[43] As I discussed above in terms of the anxiety of poets over communicating sound through print, a poem in the early nineteenth century was suddenly both an object (a printed page) and a sound, existing beyond the page. The same considerations of lyric as transcending print are part of musicological debates: examining music as an object versus a transcendental idea of music (formalist

---

[41] See my *Women Musicians*, 64–70, 132, 149, 194–201, 210–211, 215, 235–236.

[42] I am indebted to Gillian Beer for this idea of the web as spatial and temporal. See *Darwin's Plots*, 167–170.

[43] For an excellent discussion of the lyric as disseminated within print culture, including a brief consideration of the lyric's changing confrontation of "song culture", see Matthew Rowlinson, "Lyric," *A Companion to Victorian Poetry*, eds Richard Cronin, Alison Chapman and Antony H. Harrison (Malden: Blackwell, 2002) 59–79, especially 59–60.

analysis and/or positivist musicology versus the aesthetic debates of the nineteenth century).[44] Moreover, as seen in Prins's chapter on Sappho, the figure of poetry is found in music in the nineteenth century, as much as the idea of music is found in poetry. Music and poetry, far from being fixed mediums in nineteenth-century Britain, were mutually constructing each other through this kind of dialogue. Not only might we coin a term, "the idea of poetry," then, but we might also find the term to be exchangeable or reversible with "the idea of music," especially because poets themselves frequently conflated the terms singer and poet, song and sonnet. At very least, we can understand that the ideas of poetry and music are historical concepts that are illuminated and better understood through studying them together.

Overview of essays

Although I have been referring to poems as being Romantic or Victorian in order to situate them within acknowledged periods, this volume of essays is organized towards a consideration of British poetry of the long nineteenth century. In terms of music's significance, the essays demonstrate that period boundaries are flexible and that certain themes carry through the century, developing in some cases and remaining relatively static in others.[45] That is, later writers reference earlier texts and ways of imaging music, even if only implicitly. The idea that Victorian poets refer to Romantic poems is not new. Antony H. Harrison usefully likens the idea of intertextuality to a palimpsest and suggests that the uses of alluding to previous poems includes the desire to pay homage to the earlier writer, to draw upon his/her text as an authenticating source, to debate, or to subvert previous ideas and beliefs (1). While the contributors to this book did not always deliberately set out to comment on this process, certain thematic patterns do emerge in discussing music in nineteenth-century British verse. For instance, the Aeolian harp is not only a recurring motif in Romantic poetry, but it is also found in Victorian texts, and so is the idea of musical strings being like human nerves. To highlight progressions such as these, the chapters are roughly organized chronologically and thematically. The Romantics come first, then the Victorians, but within these broad categories the order of the essays juxtaposes those with thematic connections.

The volume begins with Celeste Langan's chapter, which demonstrates the importance of collections of "national songs" and "national airs" published around 1800; these were, significantly, texts printed without music. While

---

[44] See Kramer, *Classical Music and Postmodern Knowledge*, 61. In terms of transcendence and transcending signification, Kramer examines how "both music and language seek the absolute" and how they are defined by this intention and their respective failure or success (14).
[45] For further discussion on the limitations and distortions that result from using the term "Victorian" to denote a period, see Armstrong's review essay, "When is a Victorian Poet Not a Victorian Poet?"

Benedict Anderson's discussion of print-capitalism and the post-Enlightenment concept of "nation"[46] has been crucial to considerations of prose, Langan highlights the limitations of his ideas when the focus is poetry. In studying the publishing of folk song texts by Robert Burns and Thomas Moore, capitalism itself (not only print-capitalism) is shown to play a crucial role in the formation of subaltern national identities, as is the idea of what is perceived as absence. In collections of new verses for traditional folk melodies is the hovering presence of the original air referenced by the texts, even if it is not provided in musical staff notation. This idea of "national air," then, exists outside of print, beyond the printed page, just as the atmospheric air is generally perceived to be an ephemeral presence, while also demonstrably made up of measurable chemical compounds. Implicitly building from Noam Chomsky's theories of language as a formation of matter, Langan's essay emphasizes the materialism of the national air; she elucidates the ideas of "air" with the discourses of Marxism and eighteenth-century chemistry, where the material substance "air" becomes a term indicating formal equivalence in the discourses of music, chemistry and the commodity-form of labor, rather than being inherently regional, national or universal.[47]

Beginning her essay with a statement about the atmospheric vibrations made by musical sound, Kimiyo Ogawa furthers the link between science and music in her discussion of Percy Bysshe Shelley and the Aeolian harp. Her emphasis is on shared metaphors used by medical science and music that are found in Shelley's poetry, most notably in his conception of imagination, processes of association, and the poet's voice as something that triggers motion, similar to the vibration of sound waves. Chapter 2 investigates this idea of the poet's body as musical instrument by reviewing eighteenth-century medical discourse on the nerve, which uses musical instruments as a metaphor for the mind and body. This furthers the notion in Langan's chapter of music as material substance, but develops the topic in terms of human agency rather than the idea of nation. Exploring musicologists' debates about the physical effect of sound on listeners' bodies and scientists' use of music as a conceptual aid for understanding physiology, Ogawa explicates the use of the Aeolian harp in Shelley's poetry as an equivalent for the sensible, corporal poet in *Alastor*, and also as figuring contemporaneous investigations into the relations between sensations, the spirit and the cause of life.

Susan Bernstein, likewise, examines the Aeolian harp, but her chapter concentrates on the harp as a framing device, which seems to figure a unity while also allowing an interplay between voices. The essay complements Ogawa's work since Bernstein discusses acoustics as well as the harp, but in this third chapter the emphasis is on Fourier analysis and how the presence of converging sound waves exemplifies the idea that unity and difference can be

---

[46] Benedict Anderson, *Imagined Communities: Reflections on the Origin and Spread of Nationalism* (1983), rev. ed. (London: Verso, 1991).
[47] For generative grammar and "language as a natural object," see Noam Chomsky, *New Horizons in the Study of Language and Mind* (Cambridge: Cambridge University Press, 2000).

co-present, and how metaphoric exchange between two fields works. Concentrating on poems by Shelley and Coleridge, Bernstein examines the nexus of music, poetry and science, suggesting in her discussion of metaphorical networks that one discourse does not collapse into another in the Romantic image of the harp or in the figure of Fourier analysis. This kind of "co-reading of various fields" is, as Bernstein notes, also Ogawa's approach in Chapter 2, where science is not the "ground" or the base that determines the discourse of music. Rather, the play between nature and culture embodied in the notion of the Aeolian harp (an empirical instrument yet also a poetic creation) appeals to Romantic writers, she argues, because it figures a dual agency; the presence of dual voices counteracts traditional readings where the lyric "I" is emphasized. In this, Bernstein problematizes the notion of the lyric subject as "one," asking us to revise our notions to admit plurality.

Chapter 4 leads on from Bernstein's work since it concentrates on the recurring theme of music in William Blake's poetry as dramatizing individuality and relatedness: individuals respond to the world and others through exuberant song, and music also figures unity between the material and the spiritual worlds, between thought and feeling. In particular, John Hughes explores how innocence, inspiration and music are entwined in *Songs of Innocence and Experience*. The two previous chapters also explored lyric poetry and situated it culturally, but while they found the discourses of science and music to be mutually illuminating, in looking at the *Songs*, Hughes's focus is on the ethical and redemptive properties perceived to be shared by music-making and innocence, and on politicizing the reciprocity and joyful expression of these states precisely because they exist outside political and religious institutions. While Blake's position against Church and State is a commonplace, Hughes's essay demonstrates the poet's enthusiasms as well as his indignations, suggesting that identity based on responsiveness instead of cogent thought is the site of his affirmative ethics. In the second half of the chapter, Hughes turns his attention to how music is similarly made prominent as inaugurating the prophetic imagination or the vision in Blake's epic and prophetic poems. These genres bring together the notions of music as eternal, but also rooted in history, and continue to link music and politics.

With the fifth chapter we move into the Victorian period, and yet in its focus on George Eliot and moral historiography it complements the spiritual properties of music highlighted in Hughes's chapter on Blake. Ruth A. Solie concentrates on "The Legend of Jubal," a poem whose primary concerns surface throughout George Eliot's writing and, indeed, throughout Victorian thought and culture. Music as linking human and divine creativity, as measuring and expressing an individual's sympathy and the importance of community, and as an agent of memory demonstrate a use of music to explore literary and philosophical themes that are similar to other Victorian writers and thinkers. Unlike the first three chapters, Solie's methodology does not oscillate between two or three discourses to demonstrate shared networks of understanding, but instead it uses music as the continuum for showing that an array of popular texts from those published in *Macmillan's Magazine* to those by oft-quoted Victorian sages found music of central importance, making it a well-known and widely-applied metaphor of the day. Using "The Legend of Jubal" as the point of departure and then drawing on an extensive range of cultural areas, Chapter 5 explores the idea of music and its relation to religion, to emotional development, and to the ideal structuring of the social order.

Chapter 6 is founded on the prevalence in Victorian culture of musical ways of conceptualizing human behavior, but instead of focusing on morality as the previous chapter does, it looks at music's connections to the unconscious mind, sensuality and the siren. Michael Allis's essay parallels Solie's in taking a single poem by a Victorian sage as its starting point – this time the verse is that of the Poet Laureate – but instead of then asking how similar themes are raised in Victorian culture at large, Allis probes settings of Tennyson's "The Lotos-Eaters" by Hubert Parry and Edward Elgar to ask how literary representations of musical ideas are refigured in music by prominent British composers. This task is possible because Allis takes well-established notions such as the Victorian fascination with the figure of the siren, and then asks how late nineteenth-century musical compositions responded, reformulated, critiqued and conversed with popular representations of music's seductive effects. What the essay demonstrates is that despite the connections often made between music and morality in Victorian Britain, when given the chance to revise the Laureate's use of music to seductive purpose, the composers chose instead to promote the link made by nineteenth-century mental scientists between music and the unconscious mind.

In contrast, Yeo Wei Wei's chapter on Christina Rossetti as a Christian poet continues the association of music with morality, but adds gender issues and historicity to the discussion: what does it mean for a woman to participate in the lyric tradition? While the "siren" was a favorite, if angst-ridden, musical figure used in her brother's writing and painting, C. Rossetti eschews this figuration, opting instead for a polyphonic voice: in "Monna Innominata," she not only cites Dante, Petrarch, Barrett Browning and Shakespeare, but she makes her own identifiable voice the same as that of the female speaker – one of the troubadours' ladies who had traditionally been the silent subject of poems. In finding her voice, the speaker questions gender assumptions made about song and the lyric tradition, which are very similar to restrictions felt by women composers in Victorian Britain. Yeo argues that C. Rossetti breaks free of these constraints by comparing herself to Dante, in part through continuing in her own sonnet sequence the associations of music with heaven made in *Paradiso*. In music is read the younger poet's anxiety of influence in relation to Dante, but it is also the key to resolving the unhappiness resulting from such a comparison; music as associated with the divine emphasizes humility and self-surrender. The tensions felt between these Christian virtues, woman's place in song traditions, and poetic vocation (where the lyric "I" is continually asserted) result in a conflicted and complex poetic voice and treatment of music.

Chapter 8 examines the sensuality of music as Allis's chapter did, and like Yeo's essay the topic is a sonnet sequence by one of the Rossetti siblings. However, brother and sister differ in that D.G. Rossetti figures music as double: as presence and absence, as powerfully persuasive and yet impotent, as rhythmic but silent. In this, D.G. Rossetti's use of music in *The House of Life* anticipates aesthetic writing, where music helped to create the notion of an autonomous art because distinctions between form and matter ideally collapse. The chapter focuses on how structure and hermeneutics are emphasized over what might seem to be historic or symbolic uses of musical figures. For instance, medieval and Romantic instruments are depicted only to have their traditional meanings subverted, and the eloquent Orpheus is reconfigured into a poet anxious about the meter that he calls "music." Through close reading and reference to various Victorian musical practices, my chapter describes how history and representation are not excluded, but rather hauntingly present. As an ephemeral voice emerges from the structure on the page, so too a parallel emerges regarding how music figures the connection between body and soul. Fusing matter and form, the sequence exemplifies Walter Pater's notion of the "*condition of music*"[48] while also illuminating the angst of contemporaneous discussions about the "condition of music" in British society, where music is similarly perceived as present, but feared absent.

While Chapter 8 looks at how D.G. Rossetti anticipates music's importance to the aesthetic movement, Emma Sutton's chapter explores in earnest *fin-de-siècle* British poetry and aesthetic theory, focusing on the associations made between music and erotic love in the poetry of Oscar Wilde, Arthur Symons, Michael Field, Aubrey Beardsley, John Gray and John Davidson. Methodologically similar to the first three chapters, Chapter 9 examines how the late nineteenth-century discourses of music and sexuality were mutually constituted. The chapter also continues threads found in Allis's examination of the seductive elements of music, founded as it was on the work of associationist psychologists and mental scientists, whereby the associations between music and seduction were understood in concrete, corporeal terms. Sutton provides important new research on how *fin-de-siècle* psychologists, aesthetes, critics and artists explored what musical sensibility might indicate about sexual identity, and whether it was an index of expressive potential or musical and sexual pathology. The chapter then considers the implications of these analogies for poetry of the 1890s, and adds to the mixture a consideration of various preceding poetic traditions, including the homoerotic associations of Greek lyric poetry and the images of music in French decadent poetry. This verse might finally be considered as running parallel or perhaps counter to the role of music within bourgeois cultural life; as existing simultaneously, but articulating a private and controversial realm of aesthetic and sexual experience.

---

[48] Walter Pater, "The School of Giorgione" (1877), *Walter Pater: Three Major Texts*, ed. William E. Buckler (New York: New York University Press, 1986) 156. Original emphasis.

Following Sutton's exploration of *fin-de-siècle* poetry, Yopie Prins's chapter opens with a definition of how voice is perceived in decadent poetics as forever fading.[49] Sappho, whose verse exists mostly in fragments and whose music is unknown, not only embodies this notion of voice as present and absent, but also figures the relationship perceived to exist between poetry and music. This interface can be seen in how the personification of lyric (Sappho) is refigured, or recomposed, in Granville and Helen Bantock's song cycle, *Prelude and Nine Fragments* (1905). Prins's discussion is similar to Allis's examination of how literary constructions of the "idea of music" were recomposed in music itself, but ultimately differs because Prins suggests a reciprocity between music and poetry. She argues for a relationship that furthers Kramer's notion of an "agonic" interruption or transformation of speech as it becomes song (*Music and Poetry*, 130–132). Song transcends speech in Lawrence Kramer's figuration, but Prins proposes that the reverse is also true in the Bantock song cycle; ultimately, the two arts *interrupt* each others' idealizations. This equalizing, equivocating process differs from Bernstein's notion of shared metaphoric networks. Like Bernstein, Prins problematizes the unity of the lyric subject, but instead of exploring plurality, Prins posits an ultimately unheard voice. The song cycle enacts a constant reaching toward, and interrupting of, a unified voice. In the echoing interstices between vocal and instrumental lines, lyric (Sappho) emerges as the paradoxically unvocalized voice. Music and poetry, then, construct while also deconstructing each other.

---

[49] For a definition of "voice," see Chapter 8, footnote 16.

Chapter 1

Scotch Drink & Irish Harps:
Mediations of the National Air

Celeste Langan

> Sometime early in the nineteenth century, or perhaps the late eighteenth, students of the science of music discovered the national idea, adopted it, lived and wrote within it, and often, but not always, made it central to their assessments of what music was excellent and what not, where music had come from and where it was going.[1]

> After Williams & I had sung one of the Irish Melodies, somebody said, "Every thing that's national is delightful" – "Except the national Debt, Ma'am" says Poole ...[2]

It was not primarily "students of the science of music" who discovered the "national idea" in the nineteenth century – unless, that is, we extend our definition of "students" of music to include poets and lyrists of the Romantic period. Musicians who began to cite or thematize folksongs in a variety of musical genres in order to gesture toward the national idea frequently owed their knowledge of those folksongs to the collaborative efforts of poets and publishers who, around

---

[1] Celia Applegate, "How German Is It? Nationalism and the Idea of Serious Music in the Early Nineteenth Century," *Nineteenth Century Music* 21.3 (Spring 1998): 275. The question of whether the "national idea" was central to developments in British music is complicated by the longstanding assumption that there is little "development" of any significance in the nineteenth century. But Celia Applegate's point – that the "national" was first identified *against* metropolitan culture – would seem to hold true of the "British" case as well, in the sense that the idea of the national was modified by the adjectives "Irish," "Scottish" and "Welsh," and rarely by "English," except defensively. For the latter, see Joseph Ritson, *A Select Collection of English Songs, in three volumes; with an Historical Essay on the Origin and Progress of National Song* (London: Johnson, 1783). For the tendency to conflate "British" and "English," see Nicholas Temperley, "Xenophilia in British Musical History," *Nineteenth-Century British Music Studies*, ed. Bennett Zon, vol. 1 (London: Ashgate, 1999).
[2] Thomas Moore, *The Journals of Thomas Moore*, ed. Wilfred S. Dowden (Newark: University of Delaware Press, 1964) 2: 461.

1800, flooded the market with collections of "national melodies," "national songs," "national airs." Indeed, interest in what is now called the folksong tradition began first as an interest in all things "national," despite the fact that, as Carl Dahlhaus puts it, "folk music ... is more regional and social than national in its definition and localization."[3]

That poets should have contributed significantly and substantially to the development and popularity of the "national idea" may seem hardly surprising; we are used to thinking about literature as national expression. While the discipline of literary study is ostensibly organized by reference to "history," in fact the national idea continues to take precedence, even in periods prior to the emergence of the modern idea of the nation, and even now, when the power of nationality to organize identity and expression is recognizably put in question by global capitalism. But my purpose in this essay is to argue that, even in the period where the "national idea" powerfully informed the production and reception of the work of art, that idea is more complex than the version of nationality often associated with the Romantic movement: organic, essentialist, transhistorical. By focusing on how the idea of the "national air" is understood by its two chief popularizers, Robert Burns and Thomas Moore, I seek to demonstrate how the "factitious"[4] idea of the national that they promote offers an antidote both to the undertheorized assumption that literature, music, and other arts are forms of national expression, and to the counterargument that national expression is largely an ideological illusion.[5]

First, a definition: in *The New Grove Dictionary*, there is no separate entry for "national air," but a partial definition can be found in the entry on Scotland – itself a significant fact, since it suggests the way in which the "national" in music is usually identified with a category like "ethnicity" or "culture" in opposition to Culture (the "high" tradition of "Western" music whose name is Beethoven).[6] Describing the contribution to Scottish folk music made by the poets Allan Ramsay and Robert Burns, the entry reads,

---

[3] Carl Dahlhaus, *Nineteenth-Century Music*, trans. J. Bradford Robinson (Berkeley: University of California Press, 1989) 38.

[4] This is the term eighteenth-century chemists applied to component gases of the atmosphere. See discussion of Joseph Priestley below.

[5] For the latter position, see Ernest Gellner, *Thought and Change* (London: Weidenfeld and Nicholson, 1971) 169; see also Dave Harker, *Fakesong: The Manufacture of British "Folksong," 1700 to the Present Day* (Philadelphia: Open University Press, 1985).

[6] Applegate notes that in the *New Oxford History of Music* devoted to Romanticism, "national music" is discussed exclusively in relation to non-Germanic composers. In a recent essay, Andrew Bowie suggests that even Adorno's musical insights are conditioned by this tendency to identify the "universal" with the Germanic: "Too much of Adorno's position with regard to Western music depends ... on a link between Hegel's claim to achieve the final philosophy and Beethoven's establishment of new forms of integration for musical material. The link is the source both of some significant insights and of Adorno's ultimately ethnocentric perspective." See Andrew Bowie, "Adorno, Heidegger, and the Meaning of Music," *Thesis eleven* 56 (1999): 1–16.

> It can be said that the poets mentioned above created a golden age of Scots song ... It was not allied to the true evolutionary process of folksong, but to literary creation expressly intended for the printing press and for enjoyment in the drawing room ... Though these songs may contain some traditional elements, they cannot be termed folksong in the real sense of the word; "national" is the more accurate description.[7]

However distant the national air may be from the supposedly "true" or "real" meaning of folksong, it became a virtual obsession during the Romantic period, inspiring not only Burns's work in collecting "Scotch airs" for publication in a *Scots Musical Museum* (as the volumes published by James Johnson in 1787–1790 were titled), but also creating such a taste for Moore's *Irish Melodies* (1808–1834) that, even after his supposed farewell to Irish airs in "Dear Harp of My Country" (one of the few *Irish Melodies* still included in anthologies of the Romantic poetry), he produced four more volumes of *Irish Melodies* (ten, all told) as well as a collection of European melodies called *A Select Collection of National Airs* (1818).[8]

It is certainly the case that, as *Grove* suggests, the emergence of the "national" air was intimately linked to print; in each case the publishers (James Johnson and George Thomson in the case of Burns; William and James Power in the case of Moore) were instrumental not only in soliciting new lyrics for the traditional airs from poets with a recognizably "national" (that is to say, not English) identity, but also in soliciting new musical settings from those composers whose fame seemed likely to attract buyers.[9] In fact, the publishing ventures themselves may offer the

---

[7] *The New Grove Dictionary of Music and Musicians*, ed. Stanley Sadie, 2nd ed. (New York: Macmillan, 1980) 11: 74–75.

[8] The first edition of Moore's *Irish Melodies* was published in 1808, but their popularity was such that Moore continued to produce nine more "numbers." The last new collection appeared in 1820, but various editions were published by Moore's publisher, John Powers, to 1834. At first, Moore was averse to publishing his lyrics without the music, but finally acquiesced in 1820. For more complete bibliographical information, see the entry on Moore in *The New Grove Dictionary of Music and Musicians* (1980).

[9] James Johnson was the publisher of the *Scots Musical Museum* (Edinburgh: Johnson, 1787–1790), which collected words and music for traditional Scottish songs, both of the Highlands and Lowlands. Burns's (voluntary and unremunerated) relationship with Johnson was much happier than was his subsequent collaboration with Thomson, who sought to capitalize on the success of Johnson's venture. As the title-page of one edition (Edinburgh, 1802) suggests, Thomson's project was designed to *elevate* the airs to the status of art music; he highlights the contributions of well-known cosmopolitan musicians over those of Burns: *A Select Collection of Original Scottish Airs for the Voice. With Introductory and Concluding Symphonies & Accompaniments for the Piano Forte, Violin & Violincello by Pleyel, Kozeluch, and Haydn. With Select and Characteristic Verses both Scottish and English adapted to the Airs including upwards of One Hundred New Songs by Burns*. Moore's relationship with the publishers of *Irish Melodies* was complicated by a financial dispute between the two brothers, William and James Power. Siding with William, stationed in Dublin, was the original composer of the accompaniments, the Irish musician Sir John Stevenson; Moore remained loyal to James Power, the London publisher, who was forced as a consequence of the falling-out to seek a new arranger – the Englishman Henry Bishop. See Thomas Moore, *Notes from the Letters of Thomas Moore to His Music Publisher, James Power* (New York: Redfield,

clearest evidence of how the "national" character of artistic expression began to be articulated. The publishers of *A Select Collection of Original Scottish Airs* and *A Selection of Irish Melodies* were eager to secure a poet with a recognizably "national" identity for the new verses (in English) that were to accompany and so to make popular the traditional airs; but for the musical arrangement, no such national identity seemed required – perhaps because the "air" itself, prior to the addition of harmonies and ornaments, was deemed sufficiently national.

One might say, then, that, insofar as the "national air" is defined as the annexation of new verses and harmonies to traditional melodies in printed collections, it confirms Benedict Anderson's influential argument that nineteenth-century nationalism is largely a product of print culture, print capitalism.[10] Indeed, there are few more interesting cases of an emergent "print capitalism" than the speculations of Burns's second publisher, George Thomson, as he negotiated with Beethoven to make his arrangements for Burns's songs sufficiently simple for the British piano-playing public.[11] Here we discover a certain tension between what Thomson calls "national taste" and high musical "Culture": when Thomson writes to Beethoven that "your great predecessor Haydn [also commissioned by Thomson for settings to Scottish airs] invited me to point out frankly everything which was likely not to please *the national taste*," (original emphasis) it quickly becomes clear that by "national taste" he means the taste of a piano-playing, book-buying public. "There is not in this country one pianoforte player in a hundred who could make both hands go properly together in the first *ritornello*; I mean, play four notes with one hand and three with the other at the same time," he writes of one objectionable setting; "for a work like mine to succeed," he insists, Beethoven must keep in mind that "there is not one young lady in a hundred who will so much as look at an accompaniment if it is ever so little difficult" (Haddon, 323–324).

Anderson's description of the nation as an "imagined" community, "conceived in language, not in blood" (133), has had considerable appeal both because of its anti-essentialist stance and because it has seemed to confirm the value of the nation as an organizing principle for the study of cultural expression. But what is most interesting about the peculiar product of print capitalism known as the

---

1854).

[10] Phyllis Weliver reminded me that Anderson specifically mentions "the vernacularization of another form of the printed page: the score" (Anderson, 75). "Vernacularization" is a complex process, according to Anderson's argument; not a simple shift to a demotic register, it implies standardization or normativization as well. "Harmonization" is the mark of a similar normativization in the musical score. One collection of Scottish airs published in the 1790s describes them as "harmonized and *improved*"; Moore, in his prefatory letter to the third number of *Irish Melodies*, explains that "the irregular scale of the early Irish, (in which, as in the music of Scotland, the interval of the fourth was wanting), must have furnished but wild and refractory subjects to the harmonist" (Thomas Moore [1820], 225). See my discussion of Burns's "sanguinary scores" below.

[11] See J. Cuthbert Haddon, *George Thomson, Friend of Burns: His Life and Correspondence* (London: Nimmo, 1898).

national air, I suggest, is that it disables too easy an identification of print-language as the basis of national identity, and, as I will argue, demands more attention to the understudied role of capitalism, not just print-capitalism, in the formation of subaltern nationalisms. Anderson points out, of course, that there is no isomorphism between language and nation; indeed, he argues that a separate creole nationalism develops despite the fact that a colony might share the language of the metropolis from which it seeks distinction. Moreover, the dominant "print-language" bears chiefly an imaginary relation to the variety of languages and dialects spoken within the space of a putative nation. The national airs produced by Burns and Moore certainly prove this point: even if one were to accept unequivocally the idea that Burns's poetic idiom adequately represented the "lallans" dialect spoken in the Lowlands, he also employed that idiom when providing verses for airs collected from the Highlands, where Scots Gaelic, or Erse, was still spoken. Likewise, Moore famously "Englished" versions of airs that had been traditionally accompanied by Gaelic verses. The projects of both writers, in other words, are best characterized as prototypes of the "cover," that practice most usually associated with the advent of recorded sound.[12] It is the peculiar character of this practice, in which a song popularized by one singer, sometimes of a different era, is reprised by another performer, that the affect of the song depends on the perception of difference. The difference between the "naïve" and "sentimental," famously proffered by Friedrich Schiller in 1798, while it is only one such possible affect, is one that seems peculiarly pertinent to understanding the work of Burns and Moore.[13] While readers of the *Scots Musical Museum* and the *Irish Melodies* could not be expected to *know* the originals thus "covered," the print matter itself pointed to that material as a significant absence, or rather a haunting presence. Whether the verses were published with music or not, in both cases the printed text would usually identify by title (often Gaelic) the original "air" for which the new verses and harmonies had been created.[14] This

---

[12] I find the anachronistic term "cover" here useful because it highlights the extent to which the projects of Burns and Moore were quite distinct from attempts at some sort of "authentic" ethnography. In the case of Burns, for example, the idea of "covering" a naked melody with respectable clothing is almost literal: he sometimes supplies more suitable lyrics for the same airs that are referenced in his pornographic collection (circulated in manuscript), *The Merry Muses of Caledonia*. See James Barke and Sidney Goodsir Smith, eds, *The Merry Muses of Caledonia* (New York: Putnam, 1964).

[13] Schiller's essay, *Über naïve und sentimentalische Dichtung*, first published in 1795, is a *locus classicus* of Romantic aesthetic theory (see M.H. Abrams, *The Mirror and the Lamp: Romantic Theory and the Critical Tradition* [NewYork: Oxford University Press, 1953] 238). Schiller characterizes modern, or "sentimental" poetry, as a mode of "reflection," of the artist's self-conscious *mediation* of feeling.

[14] See *A Selection of Irish Melodies, with symphonies and accompaniments by Sir John Stevenson, and characteristic words by Thomas Moore* (London: Power, 1808–1813); James Kinsley, ed., *Burns: Poems and Songs* (New York: Oxford, 1969) 418, 554.

It might be interesting to connect the appearance in print of the lyrics to "airs" that were only referenced by title to the later practice, also associated with the drawing-room and the piano, of improvisation. Lord Byron's collaboration – not altogether a successful one – with Isaac Nathan

naming of the air or "tune" foregrounds the text as an act of *mediation* – the transmission of one (oral-acoustic) medium by another (print-visual) medium.[15] The "national" is identified partly by its *difference* from print, by its identification with the remainder, "air," that print cannot fully capture. The "air" thus referenced seems to haunt, or to hover slightly beyond, the printed page, in the same manner, one might say, that the "national" character of music seems to depend on a certain distance from metropolitan centers of cultural and political power. For in the early nineteenth century, in London and even in Edinburgh, the "national air" was definitely not a local product; it was, crucially, imported from the periphery.

What follows might be described as an extended meditation on what it means to identify the nation with "air." For if at first that identification threatens to reinforce the illusoriness of the nation, its reduction to "airy nothing," I will argue that Burns and Moore both resist this reduction by narrating the transformation of "airy nothing," into *something*. For Moore, this something will frequently be no more substantial than a tear or a sigh. William Hazlitt, in unfavorably contrasting Moore to Wordsworth (that most "English" of poets), nonetheless offers the most telling assessment of what constitutes the "national" character of his verse:

> The fine aroma, that is exhaled from the flowers of poesy, everywhere lends its perfume to the verse of the bard of Erin .... [Moore] enjoys an ethereal existence among troops of sylphs and spirits, and in a perpetual vision of wings, flowers, rainbows, smiles, blisses, tears and kisses .... Mr Moore hardly ever describes entire objects, but abstract qualities of objects .... It might as well be the lights of heaven he describes, or the voice of Echo – we have no human figures before us, no palpable reality, answering to no substantive form in nature.[16]

Too often these *topoi* of the *Irish Melodies* have been read – and criticized – as signs of Moore's sentimentalization of Ireland and Irishness.[17] When read in the

---

on a number of "Hebrew Melodies" suggests such an improvisational practice already at work. Byron, a good friend of Moore and an admirer of the *Irish Melodies*, was offered a chance to try his hand, and he composed several lyrics – *without ever having heard* the Hebrew melodies Nathan would adapt and harmonize. A decade later, L.E.L. (the popular poet Letitia Elizabeth Landon) would compose a series of "Stanzas for Music" that were published in *The Keepsake*, an expensive literary annual published at Christmas and intended for gift-giving. Piano-playing readers invented melodies to accompany the lyrics.

[15] I mean here to invoke the classic formulation of Marshall McLuhan, that "the content of one medium is always another medium." See Marshall McLuhan, *Understanding Media: The Extensions of Man* (Cambridge, MA: MIT Press, 1994), and Friedrich A. Kittler, introduction, *Gramophone, Film, Typewriter*, trans. Geoffrey Winthrop-Young and Michael Wutz (Stanford: Stanford University Press, 1999) 2. For an account of the relevance of media theory to the "musicality" of printed poetry, see my "Understanding Media in 1805: Audiovisual Hallucination in *The Lay of the Last Minstrel*," *Studies in Romanticism* 40.1 (Spring 2001): 49–70.

[16] William Hazlitt, *Works*, ed. P.P. Howe (London: Dent, 1930–1934) 16: 412, 414.

[17] For the best of such accounts, see Leith Davis's important essay, "Irish Bards and English Consumers: Thomas Moore's 'Irish Melodies' and the Colonized Nation," *Ariel* 24.2 (April 1993): 7–25.

context of Burns's prior experiments with the national air, however – experiments which include the *Poems, Chiefly in the Scots Dialect* (1786) – we learn to recognize in Moore's tears and sighs what we might call the lyrical equivalent of Burns's thematic and narrative emphasis on the national value of "Scotch Drink." In both cases, the moment of distillation or liquidation is crucial. Prior to this distillation or liquidation – prior to its nationalization, that is – the air which is its material basis must be regarded as either too universal or too particular.

The same might be said of the general term for which "air" is the national representative in the Romantic period: music. The philosopher of music Peter Kivy has insisted both that "we know better than to think that music is the 'international language'" and that, once we dispense with the dream that music transcends the contingencies of time and place, and functions as a kind of universal grammar, then we must also recognize that music is "not even national."[18] By this double negative, Kivy succeeds in avoiding the essentializing fictions – usually denominated as "Romantic" – of absolute music and of cultural nationalism, but we are left to wonder at the persistence of these apparently contradictory claims within Romanticism. If Herder declared in 1785 that "the music of a nation, in its most imperfect form, and favorite tunes, displays the internal character of the people ... more truly and profoundly, than the most copious description of external contingencies,"[19] the Scotsman James Beattie had already (in 1778) argued that, without a discursive framing, what is "national" in music is unrecognizable:

> It is true, that to a favourite air, even when unaccompanied by words, we do commonly annex certain ideas, which may come to be related to it in consequence of some accidental associations: and sometimes we imagine a resemblance (which however is merely imaginary) between certain melodies and certain thoughts or objects. Thus a Scotchman may fancy, that there is some sort of likeness between that charming air he calls *Tweedside,* and the scenery of a fine pastoral country: and to the same air, even when only played on an instrument, he may annex the ideas of romantic love and rural tranquility; because these form the subject of a pretty little ode which he has heard sung to that air. But this is the effect of habit. *A foreigner who hears that tune for the first time, entertains no such fancy.*[20]

Tellingly, the fantasy of music's "national" meaning is assigned to a Scotsman.[21] For the true distinction of the national air, for both Burns and Moore, lay in its

---

[18] Peter Kivy, *Osmin's Rage: Philosophical Reflections on Opera, Drama, and Text* (Princeton: Princeton University Press, 1988) 178.
[19] Johann Gottfried von Herder, *Reflections of the Philosophy of the History of Mankind*, ed. Frank E. Manuel (Chicago: University of Chicago Press, 1968) 40.
[20] James Beattie, *Essays: On Poetry and Music, As They Affect the Mind* (London: Dilley, 1779) 464.
[21] One imagines a "foreigner" in the character of the Englishman Samuel Johnson, whose travels in

non-English character. Soliciting contributions to the *Scots Musical Museum*, Burns writes, "There is a certain something in the old Scotch songs, a wild happiness of thought and expression, which peculiarly marks them, *not only from English songs,* but also from the modern efforts of song-wrights, in our native manner and language" (emphasis added).[22] The "certain something" that is the "national" element in the Scotch air cannot wholly be identified with "native" melodies or language, but depends on a perceived difference from English identity. This difference or distinction is even more clearly marked by Moore, who in the "Advertisement" to his *Selection of Popular National Airs* describes "the abundance of wild, indigenous airs, which almost every country, *except England,* possesses" (emphasis added).[23] Moore's motives for representing England as a "land without music" (*das Land ohne Musik*) are articulated in the "Advertisement" to the first number of the *Irish Melodies*, which quotes his letter to the composer Sir John Stevenson (1761–1833):

> Our National Music has never been properly collected, and while the composers of the Continent have enriched their Operas and Sonatas with Melodies borrowed from Ireland, very often without even the honesty of acknowledgement, we have left these treasures in a great degree unclaimed and fugitive. Thus our Airs, like too many of our countrymen, for want of protection at home, have passed into the service of foreigners.[24]

Staging a veiled attack on English imperialist policies in Ireland in terms of Continental appropriation, Moore suggests that the "national" can be thought, in part, as a reaction against the hegemony of trade.

Theodor Adorno, among the most influential of modern theorists of music, offers an account of the role of music in the process of economic rationalization that explains Burns's and Moore's eagerness to attach a "national" character to the "native" air particularly well:

> Within the global development in which music shared in the progressive emergence of rationality, music at the same time always remained the voice of all who fell by the wayside or were sacrificed on the altar of the rational. This defines the central social contradiction of music .... The very element that raises music above ideology is also what brings it closest to it. As a carefully cultivated preserve of the irrational in the midst of the rationalized universe, music becomes negativity pure and

---

Scotland were undertaken partly to demystify such nationalist Scottish fantasies as "second sight."
[22] Robert Burns, *The Letters of Robert Burns*, ed. J. DeLancey Ferguson (Oxford: Clarendon, 1931) 1: 134–135.
[23] Thomas Moore, *A Selection of Popular National* Airs (London: Cramer, Addison, & Beale [J. Power], 1818).
[24] Thomas Moore, *Irish Melodies, and a Melologue upon National Music* (Dublin: William Power, 1820) 277. All subsequent references are to this edition.

simple, as this is rationally planned, produced, and administered by the Culture Industry.[25]

Yet if we might anticipate, from such an account, Adorno's disdain for the "regressive" tendencies of the national air, we might balance such a critique against his earlier claim that "all forms of music ... are sedimented contents. In them survives what is otherwise forgotten and can no longer speak in a direct manner" (Bowie, 10). Trying to read the national air as an expression of the "social contradiction" of Romantic conceptualizations of music – and of the "musicality" of poetry – we might understand the musical "air" at once as a material substance and a material substance exposed to conditions that tend to alter or dissolve that substance. The social contradiction takes the form of print-capitalism's celebration of, and attempt to manufacture a profit from, the traditional air. The *national* air is the product of the air's exposure to print-capitalism.

The chemical composition of the national air

If imagining music as universal or as "national" are to be regarded as equally essentialist illusions, it is the apparent immateriality of music – registered so precisely in the vague term "air" – that abets such essentialism. And insofar as the musical air represents on a grand scale what Roland Barthes calls "the myth of respiration" – the Romantic myth that music is the unmediated expression of the soul – it seems worthwhile to try to counteract the effects of such naturalization or spiritualization by reminding ourselves that air is in fact a material substance.[26] For that reason I want – quite seriously – to link the emergence of the national air in the Romantic period to a key materialist text of the Enlightenment: Joseph Priestley's 1774 *Experiments and Observations on Different Kinds of Air*. A foundational moment in the history of chemistry, Priestley's record of experiments he undertook when living in a neighborhood of a brewery is prescient in its speculations about what we now call "greenhouse gases" and the role of

---

[25] Theodor Adorno, "Some Ideas on the Sociology of Music," *Sound Figures*, trans. Rodney Livingstone (Stanford: Stanford University Press, 1999) 5–6.
[26] Roland Barthes, "The Grain of the Voice," *Image/Music/Text*, trans. Stephen Heath (New York: Hill and Wang, 1977) 83. Barthes expresses a dissatisfaction with prevailing norms of music criticism, which he sees as caught between what he calls "the dilemma of either the predicable or the ineffable" (180). The "predicable" is the reduction of music to an adjective – "warlike" or "voluptuous," for example. While the "ineffable" is self-explanatory, Barthes interestingly ties its conceptual emergence to a historically specific musical practice: composers begin to supplement the traditional indication of tempo (allegro, etc.) with more "poetic" descriptions, "which are given in the national language" (180). In the context of the national air, such poetic descriptions (Moore's "Come O'er the Sea" instructs that it be played or sung "with impassioned melancholy") become at once a sign of vernacularization (the "national" coding of a "universal" language) and a sign of hybridization (the sentimental coding of a naïve artifact, perhaps).

rainforests and oceans in restoring the atmosphere. Priestley calls the atmosphere the "common air"; other component gases he manages to extract or produce in the course of his experiments are known by the collective name of "factitious airs." Of course, to Priestley, what comes to be called the "national air" would be not merely factitious but an actual fiction; the modulations of the Irish harp and the Scotch snap do not alter the chemical composition of the air through which they resonate; nor could it be scientifically asserted that the chemical composition of the air produces what is distinctive in the Irish and Scots musical traditions. In fact, Priestley's experiments might be described as having inadvertently exploded the myth of national or local specificity; one of his more important contributions to chemical knowledge was his technique for producing the equivalent of "Pyrmont" or "Seltzer" water, so named to mark its local habitation, its "nationality," merely by adding the "factitious air" he calls "fixed air" (carbon dioxide) to any water at all.[27]

Nonetheless, Priestley's work in isolating and examining several component gases and their effects has the important consequence of exposing the variable character of what might otherwise appear to be a universal medium: air. Through a series of experiments, Priestley demonstrates how different concentrations of various component gases will have different effects on plant and animal life. Two such experiments have an odd pertinence to the well-known lyrics of Burns ("To a Mouse") and Moore ("'Tis the Last Rose of Summer"): in one, Priestley traps a mouse and places him in an inverted beer-glass filled with the "fixed air" that floats on the surface of fermenting barley, measuring how long the mouse can survive in the absence of "common" air; in another, he discovers that "a red rose, fresh gathered, lost its redness, and became of a purple colour, after being held over the fermenting liquor about 24 hours."[28] But equally important, plant and animal life affect the composition of the air; it is, after all, the brewery that produces the carbon dioxide for his experiments, and later, Priestley discovers how living plants can "restore vitiated air":

> One might have imagined that, since common air is necessary to vegetable, as well as to animal life, both plants and animals had affected it in the same manner; and I own I had that expectation, when I first put a spring of mint into a glass-jar, standing inverted in a vessel of water: but when it had continued growing there for some months, I found that the air would neither extinguish a candle, nor was it at all inconvenient to a mouse, which I put into it. (50)

---

[27] Joseph Priestley, *Directions for Impregnating Water with Fixed Air* (London: Johnson, 1772). Of course, Priestley (1733–1804) had no intention of exposing the "national idea" as an ideological illusion; the point is that enlightenment procedures of empirical observation and analysis (not unrelated to alphabetization and standard musical notation) reduce an apparently organic whole into component, technologically reproducible parts.
[28] Joseph Priestley, *Experiments and Observations on Different Kinds of Air* (London: Johnson, 1774) 36.

Despite the fact, therefore, that most of Priestley's experiments involve an initial attempt to isolate and to "fix" each component gas in order to discover its specific properties, they also reinforce an understanding that "common air" by contrast is remarkably *un*fixed, undergoing incessant chemical transformation. Successful in extracting and isolating the gases, Priestley fails in his efforts at recomposition: "I once imagined that, since fixed and flammable air are the reverse of one another, in several remarkable properties, a mixture of them would make common air," he writes, but "whatever methods I took ... they were all ineffective" (*Experiments*, 63).

Priestley identifies each of the isolated gases by specific adjectives – "fixed" (carbon dioxide), "nitrous" (nitrous oxide), and "flammable" (oxygen, or what Priestley calls phlogiston) – but defends retaining the common word "air" because "to the eye, they appear to have no difference at all," and because "it is certainly convenient to have a common term by which to denote things which have so many common properties" (*Experiments*, xxii). Notice how "air" here becomes a "common" medium in a different sense, more akin to money than to "atmosphere"; no longer does it name "common" (unfixed) air, but rather a formal equivalence. Perhaps it was for this reason that Marx seized upon the chemical analysis of air to describe the commodity-form of labor:

> The recent scientific discovery, that the products of labour, so far as they are values, are but material expressions of the human labour spent in their production, marks, indeed, an epoch in the history of the development of the human race, but by no means dissipates the mist through which the social character of labour appears to us to be an objective character of the products themselves. The fact, that in the particular form of production with which we are dealing, viz., the production of commodities, the specific social character of private labour carried on independently, consists in the equality of every kind of that labour, by virtue of its being human labour, which character, therefore, assumes in the product the form of value – this fact appears to the producers, notwithstanding the discovery above referred to, to be just as real and final, as the fact, that, after the discovery by science of the component gases of air, the atmosphere itself remained unaltered.[29]

Earlier in *Capital*, Marx had insisted even more strongly on an analogy to chemistry to expose the fact that "exchange-value" represents a common "something" that is not a "natural" property of the object:

> To borrow an illustration from chemistry, butyric acid is a different substance from propyl formate. Yet both are made up of the same chemical substances, carbon (C), hydrogen (H), and oxygen (O), and that, too, in like proportions – namely, $C_4H_8O_2$. If now we equate

---

[29] Karl Marx, *Capital*, trans. Samuel Moore and Edward Aveling (New York: International Publishers, 1967) 1: 79.

> butyric acid to propyl formate, then, in the first place, propyl formate would be, in this relation, merely a form of existence of $C_4H_8O_2$; and in the second place, we should be stating that butyric acid also consists of $C_4H_8O_2$. Therefore, by thus equating the two substances, expression would be given to their chemical composition, while their different physical forms would be neglected. (57)

Since butyric acid has the smell of rancid butter, whereas propyl formate is a pleasantly aromatic ester often used as an additive in perfumes, Marx's point here is that the different physical composition of "essences" drastically changes the properties of those essences. If we were to imagine the formula $C_4H_8O_2$ for a moment as describing the musical air, we can see how representing Scottish and Irish airs as "merely a form of existence" of that air would therefore inadequately describe their purposes and effects. To make the relevance of this analogy more concrete, consider that the "air" titled "Robin Adair" by Burns is formally the same as the air referred to by Moore as "Aileen Aroon" (and rewritten as "Erin! The Tear and the Smile in Thine Eyes"). Both Burns and Moore supply new lyrics. But since these lyrics are themselves supposedly "nationalized" by their annexation to the air, we cannot really contend that the lyrics make the air recognizably Scottish or Irish. Obviously this (al)chemical alteration can only be understood within a wider context of *social* exchange.

Marx's favorite representation of ideology as a "mist-enveloped region" that is by no means dissipated by chemical analysis or scientific rationality is one of the reasons I have developed at some length an analogy between the national air and the "factitious" airs that Priestley extracted from the common air. Marx encourages us to read the "social hieroglyphic" of exchange-value, and thereby to "dissipate the mist through which the social character of labour appears to us to be an objective character of the products themselves" (79). Too often, analysis of the work of art – perhaps especially the musical work of art – has only exchanged one mist for another, regarding the work as either a product of the properties of the medium (music as formal arrangements of "natural" sounds, a universal language and value), or a product of "independent" labor (of the artist in the case of the poem, of the "folk" or nation in the case of the air). Because they labor to be "national," Burns and Moore valuably remind us that the nation too is a product. It is not "natural," on the order of the "common air" of a given region. But nor is it fictitious, having no real existence. Like the "factitious" air that Priestley artificially isolates, its purpose is partly to expose the differences made invisible by the assertion of a "common" identity.

The national air and the excise officer

As proof of the factitious or illusory character of what, after the Act of Union of 1707 became "Great Britain," one might cite the frequency with which Great Britain was identified as "England." Likewise, the imagining of the United Kingdom as a single island rather than an archipelago persists long after the 1800 union with Ireland made it an obvious solecism. Saree Makdisi argues that this imaginary geography was linked to "the formation of a national economy ... (increasingly the center of) a world-economy."[30] Robert Burns, who already felt the effects of this economic and political centralization, expressed great irritation at the tendency to use the adjective "English" to describe state institutions that were supposed to represent the Scottish as well; a letter registers his on-going annoyance with "the common terms, 'English ambassador, English court,' &c. And ... that most equivocal character, Hastings, impeached by the Commons of England."[31] This letter, we should note, bears little trace of the "lallans" dialect for which Burns had become famous; Burns uses an English language that has become "common" even as he recognizes the extent to which Scotland's assimilation to England – the abstraction of differences into a "common" British identity – has had the effect of impoverishing Scotland. This impoverishment affected far more than forms of cultural expression; Burns attributed his own family's agricultural woes to the tendency to set rents at *national* (i.e., English) rates:

> Farming is also at a low ebb with us. Our lands, generally speaking, are mountainous and barren; & our Landholders, full of ideas of farming gathered from the English, and the Lothians and other rich soils in Scotland; make no allowance for the odds of the quality of land, and consequently stretch us much beyond what, in the event, we will be found able to pay.[32]

Thus, although Burns does not include the "Bank of England" in his list of solecisms that expose the hegemony of English political power, his critique of the "factitious" character of the British state will be played out chiefly by reference to "national Debt." In contrast to the (Scottish) nation, the identity of the British nation becomes entirely negative.

Well in advance of the period where Burns actually took up his commission as an officer of the Excise, he understood how the centralization and rationalization of fiscal power affected Scotland. The Wash Act of 1784 and the 1786 revised code that first elicited Burns's wrath in "Scotch Drink" were designed, as Vivien Dietz points out, to increase revenues by standardizing the "excise" tax on distilleries.[33] However, the tax also demonstrates quite powerfully the effect of economic rationalization on national identity. What Burns identifies as "the odds of the quality of land in Scotland" made the project of standardization difficult; stills in the Highlands were small and geographically dispersed, which made regular visits by an excise officer impractical. The solution of the Wash Act was

---

[30] Saree Makdisi, *Romantic Imperialism: Universal Empire and the Culture of Modernity* (New York: Cambridge University Press, 1998) 61.
[31] Burns to Mrs. Dunlop, 10 April 1790, *Letters*, 2: 18.
[32] Burns to James Burness, 21 June 1783, *Letters*, 1: 15–16.
[33] Vivien Dietz, "The Politics of Whisky: Scotch Distillers, the Excise, and the Pittite State," *Journal of British Studies* 36.1 (January 1997): 35–69.

to draw a formal distinction between Lowlands and Highlands and to tax their distilleries at different rates; as David Daiches points out, "The Highland line, which separated the two forms of duty, was precisely defined in the Act – the first time that a specified area of Scotland was separated from the rest."[34]

In "The Author's Earnest Cry and Prayer," a poem addressed pointedly "To the *Scotch* Representatives in the House of Commons" (my emphasis), Burns first links the peculiar character of his poetic idiom to the economic rationalization represented by the British state.[35] Playing upon the etymological connection of whisky to the Gaelic (Highland Scots) "usque beagh," or "water of life," Burns declares, "Alas! My roupet Muse is hearse!" (7). What might otherwise be identified as his "native" idiom is instead registered as the effect of higher taxes and lower hydration, which leaves the poet "scriechin' out prosaic verse, / An' like to burst" (11–12), in a remarkable series of slant rhymes ("hearse," "pierce," "arse," "verse"). Given that the poem already displays a fine mastery of Burns's favorite stanza form (Standard Habbie, or "Burns stanza"), "prosaic verse" might be read as an allusion to poetry or verse unaccompanied by music, as "scriechan" rather than singing, as well as a more obvious account of the poem's orthographic dialect.

The slant rhymes are carefully designed to indicate the roughened timber of a voice denied its usual (Scots) measure of whisky, and thereby to identify the poem as a distinctively "national" form of expression on a par with Scotch whisky itself. But the analogy does not identify Burns's voice as *essentially* "native"; rather, it is the British imposition, the excise, and its *effect* on his native Muse, which produces the distinctive timber of Burns's Scots verse. Perhaps the most interesting aspect of the poem's representation of Scottishness as a deformation of English eloquence brought about by the excise tax and similar measures of regulation is the parodic epigraph of the poem: "Dearest of distillation! last and best – / – How art thou lost! –". Burns parodies that canonically English poet, Milton, who in *Paradise Lost* had described Eve as "fairest of Creation, last and best" (9:896). In another poem titled and addressed directly to "Scotch Drink," Burns had already figured whisky as his "Muse," and parodied conventional inspiration as an ingestion of "spirits": "Inspire me, till I lisp an' wink" (11). Here, it is by virtue of the parody on Milton that we are asked to recognize in the commodity-form of taxable whisky the debased (fallen) form of the aesthetic.

Since Burns encourages us to take figures of speech literally, to think of what Barthes calls "the grain of the voice" by the name of (fermented and distilled) barley (see his famous poem "John Barleycorn"), it seems worthwhile to recall the process by which whisky is actually produced.[36] David Daiches's useful account

---

[34] David Daiches, *Scotch Whisky* (London: Deutsch, 1969) 33.
[35] Burns, "The Author's Earnest Cry and Prayer," *Poems, Chiefly in the Scots Dialect* (Kilmarnock, 1786).
[36] Barthes, 179–189. See especially his discussion of the German *lied*. Acknowledging that the *lied* is commonly thought to signify the "national" because of its lyrics, Barthes nonetheless insists on the importance of the "popular" origin of the music; what he calls the "grain" of the voice is an

identifies four basic steps. First, harvested barley is malted by being soaked in water and spread on a floor to dry. During this stage the barley "breathes" – taking in oxygen and expiring carbon dioxide. After the malted yeast is mashed (mixed with hot water), yeast is added, which has the effect of converting the carbohydrate mash into alcohol and carbon dioxide. (Daiches remarks, "It is a violent and noisy process".) The last step is distillation, which, as Daiches points out, is actually a double distillation: "distilling is essentially turning a liquid into vapour and then condensing the vapour back into liquid" (6–15).

If distillation is a useful trope for Burns, it is so because the proliferation of distilleries (and alcoholism) in Scotland can be linked to the high rents associated with the rationalization of agriculture. The *Statistical Account of Scotland* (1791–1799) to which Burns was a contributor includes the justification of whisky production by a Presbyterian minister: "It will be asked, Why then so many distilleries? For these reasons: Distilling is almost the only method of converting our victuals into cash for the payment of rent and servants; and whisky may, in fact, be called our staple commodity."[37] Could we imagine a description of Scotch whisky production that offers a clearer account of the commodification of the "gross national product" of Scotland? The historian John Brewer identifies the Excise Office as crucially important to the consolidation of state power; by the end of the eighteenth century, the excise tax (on "domestically produced commodities, especially alcoholic drinks") had "replaced the landtax as the most important source of state income."[38]

Were Burns merely to repeat, in his account of the process by which a "spirit" is extracted in response to exterior fiscal pressures, this picture of "distillation" as a distortion of national essence, his account of the national air could be entirely associated with Ernest Gellner's account of nationalism as a byproduct of modernization, and Adorno's account of music as a "distraction" from rationalization. But Burns consistently represents Scottish song as a product of *double* distillation, as we see in his commentary on one of the songs he collected for *The Scots Musical Museum*, entitled "The Scots Recluse." The lyrics could easily be Burns's:

> When I upon thy bosom lean
> And fondly clasp thee a' my ain
> I glory in the sacred ties
> Than made us ane, wha once were twane. (9–12)

We learn, in Burns's *Notes on Scottish Song*, that

---

insistence on materiality at the interface of music and language.
[37] Quoted in Daiches, 36.
[38] John Brewer, *The Sinews of Power: War, Money, and the English State, 1688–1783* (New York: Knopf, 1989) 92, 95.

> This song was the work of a very worthy, facetious old fellow, John Lapraik, late of Dalfram, near Muirkirk; which little property he was obliged to sell in consequence of some connexion as security for some persons involved in that villainous bubble, the AYR BANK. He has told me that he composed this song when his wife had been fretting o'er their misfortunes.[39]

This narrative offers to explicate the song's "reclusive" domestic feeling – a feeling of union – as a Scottish revaluation of "attachment" that responds to the liquidation of more material assets. In that sense, it might be seen merely as an etherealization of Scottish national identity, parallel to the ingestion of Scotch drink that allows Burns to transcend the Wash Act's formal division of Highlands and Lowlands. But in another sense, the song is less an etherealization than a materialization, a process Burns elsewhere describes as "localization": "As music is the language of nature: and poetry, particularly songs, always more or less localized (if I may be allowed the verb) by some modifications of time and place, this is the reason why so many of our Scots airs have outlived their original, and perhaps many subsequent sets of verses."[40] Localization, we learn from the example of "The Scots Recluse," is a recondensation of what had been rendered "air" by the effects of capitalization.

"Localization" as it is explained and put in practice by Burns (and Moore) can therefore be distinguished from the cultural nationalism that David Lloyd sees at work in the (northern) Irish poet Seamus Heaney's "reterritorialization" of national identity via the place-name.[41] When attached to the air as a subordinate element designed to keep the air in circulation (parallel to the chemical process that "fixes" carbon dioxide in limestone or chalk), the words or lyrics must themselves be understood as the medium, so that neither the language of the lyrics nor the place-names they employ represent the song's "national" content. Over their lifespan, the airs have been "localized" repeatedly, so that no particular place or phrase can be regarded as the air's "true" referent or origin. Precisely because "Scotia" and "Coila" (the factitious cognate of Kyle in Ayrshire that Burns names as his particular Muse), like Moore's "Erin," are evocations rather than place-names, they both emblematize the project of the national air and suggest how the national air represents not an essentialization in the manner of *Geist* (the

---

[39] James C. Dick, ed., *Notes on Scottish Song* (Edinburgh, 1908) 42.
[40] Dick, *Notes to Scottish Song*, 6.
[41] David Lloyd, "Pap for the Dispossessed: Seamus Heaney and the Poetics of Identity," *Anomalous States* (Durham: Duke University Press, 1993) 13–40. For the term "reterritorialization," Lloyd draws on the work of Gilles Deleuze and Felix Guattari, who in *Anti-Oedipus: Capitalism and Schizophrenia* (Minneapolis: University of Minnesota Press, 1983) described the "de-territorializing" effects of capital, whose circulation seems to dematerialize the boundaries that formerly organized existence. Lloyd's argument is that Heaney's elevation of the place-name to preserve a sense of "authentic" Irishness is flawed because it reintroduces an essentialist nationalism ("blood and soil") and therefore ignores the socially produced character of national identity.

"spiritualization" of national identity by German idealism) but rather as a material substance that is distilled and reproduced in order to *resist* etherealization. Burns's interest in localization as materialization is what explains, I suggest, his foregrounding of the *medium of communication* which, as Raymond Williams reminds us, is also a means of production.[42]

In *Poetry as an Occupation and an Art*, Peter Murphy raises the question of why Burns's literary activity, after the early success of the *Poems, Chiefly in the Scots Dialect*, was so absorbed in song-writing. He proposes that song-writing, as a "minor" form, allowed Burns a certain freedom from the dependency that patronage instituted. In fact, Burns refused payment for his contributions to the *Scots Musical Museum*, preferring to regard the enterprise as a patriotic collaboration, having the character of "social labor" prior to its abstraction and commodification. But Burns was by no means unaware of the effects of print-capitalism on such labor. Of his unsatisfactory negotiations for a second edition of his *Poems*, Burns reports,

> By his [Wilson's] account, the paper of a thousand copies would cost about £27, and the printing 15 or 16; he offers to agree to this for the printing, if I will advance for the paper; but this you know is out of my power; so farewell hopes of a second edition till I grow richer, *an epocha which, I think, will arrive with the payment of the British national debt.* (emphasis added)[43]

In fact, as Burns probably knew all too well, the exorbitant price of paper was, like the tax on Scotch whisky, an innovation of the Excise Office. Sir John Sinclair (1754–1835), who wrote a *History of Public Revenue* as well as the *Statistical Account of Scotland*, was almost as outraged as Burns over the price and the quality of paper available in Scotland:

> By the present mode of allowing paper to be stamped only at London, the manufacturers in Scotland are deprived of a considerable market for their paper .... The paper brought from London is considerably dearer than it could be got for in Scotland, and is frequently so bad as to be unfit either for writing or printing.[44]

According to Brewer, the Excise Office led the way in modeling economic efficiency and bureaucratic rationalization in the eighteenth century. "No detail was too small," he reports; when the Post Office began charging the office by weight, the Excise "bought thinner paper for the gauger's [excise officer's] petty accounts" (112).

---

[42] Raymond Williams, "Means of Communication as Means of Production," *Problems in Materialism and Culture: Selected Essays* (London: New Left Books, 1980).
[43] Burns, *Letters*, 1: 287.
[44] Sir John Sinclair, *History of Public Revenue* (London: Cadell, 1785) 345. The *Statistical Account of Scotland* was published between 1791 and 1799.

Explaining to a correspondent his reluctant decision to take a position as an excise officer, Burns writes, "I know how the word, Exciseman, or still more opprobrious, Gauger, will sound in your ears. – I too have seen the day when my auditory nerves would have felt very delicately on this subject, but a wife & children are things which have a wonderful power in blunting these kinds of sensations."[45] Burns's allusion to "auditory nerves" here wonderfully suggests how the Excise and the British national debt are associated with a foreign idiom, like foreign music harsh and grating to the unaccustomed ear;[46] but it is another letter which most fully explains how Burns's song-writing is an attempt to "localize" the costs of political and fiscal rationalization. In 1786 Burns writes a letter to his friend, the bookseller Peter Hill, on Excise stationery. Rather than apologizing for this misuse of state property, Burns presents his letter as a parodic instance of economy:

> I will make no excuses, my dear Bibliopolus, (God forgive me for murdering language) that I have sat down to write you on this vile paper, *stained with the sanguinary scores of 'thae curst horse leeches o' th' Excise."* – It is economy, Sir; it is that cardinal virtue, Prudence; so I beg you will sit down, & either compose or borrow a panegyric (if you are going to borrow, apply to our friend Ramsay, for the assistance of the author of those pretty little buttering paragraphs of eulogiums on your thrice-honoured & never-enough-to-be-praised Magistracy – how they hunt down a housebreaker with the sanguinary perseverance of a bloodhound ...) – I was going to say, but this d-mn'd Parenthesis has put me out of breath, that you should get that manufacturer of tinsell'd crockery ... to compose or rather compound, something very clever on my remarkable frugality; that I write to one of my most esteemed friends on this wretched paper, which was originally intended for the venal fist of some drunken Exciseman, to take dirty notes in a miserable vault of an ale-cellar. (emphasis added)[47]

In this remarkably *un*economical letter, Burns brilliantly demonstrates how even the most apparently "abstract" mechanisms of state power – print-language, taxation, law – still require a material substrate – paper – that also provides a

---

[45] Burns to Robert Ainslee, 1 November 1789, *Letters*, 1: 364.
[46] By suggesting that the English words "Exciseman" and "Gauger" are harsh or grating, Burns reverses the usual eighteenth- and nineteenth-century dismissal of "primitive" music for not understanding the principles of harmony; according to Burns, it is "foreignness" (albeit a foreignness perceived as a relation of power) that is the only distinction between (English) "noise" and (Scots) music. See Jacques Attali, *Noise: The Political Economy of Music* (Minneapolis: University of Minnesota Press, 1992). On the prospect that media (whether the musical score or the phonograph) have the capacity to rationalize acoustic experience and so transform noise into articulate sound, see Kittler, "Introduction": "Following a suggestion made by the musicologist von Hornsbostel, it is possible to fix the chaos of exotic music assailing European ears by first interpolating a phonography, which is able to record this chaos in real time and then replay it in slow motion" (4–5).
[47] Burns to Peter Hill, 2 April 1789, *Letters*, 2: 318–19.

material basis for *resistance*. The Excise stationary is *lined*, a fact which reminds Burns of its institutional origin and function, its association with economic rationalization, with bookkeeping. Describing the lines as "sanguinary scores," Burns suggests that the Excise Office actually works by *incision*, through taxation draining the life-blood of Scotland.[48] Perhaps as well, the word "scores" reminds him of the *musical* score, a technology of writing and of print that is also associated with rationalization, especially in connection with the "wild, indigenous" airs that many felt were *spoiled* by the addition of harmonies and the elimination of what Moore called the "lawlessness" of the original melodies. Yet these oppressive lines are themselves written over – scored – by Burns's grand "Parenthesis," so full of breath and spirit that it puts in doubt the capacity of even the most Latinate English truly to "murder" language. The "compound" of languages that Burns himself produces here – Latinate English, quotations of his own Scots dialect poems, and the speech that not even the sanguinary scores can kill – offers the best evidence of how Burns understood the national air.[49]

The air of the exile

> sung to them in the evening, & saw in Lady Helena's eyes those beads (to use the language of distillers) which show that the spirit is proof – (or rather *not* proof, perhaps)[50]

In her important essay on Thomas Moore, "Irish Bards and English Consumers," Leith Davis reminds us that Moore was required to sing for his supper: "Part of Moore's contract of five hundred pounds per year included his recitation of the *Melodies* in English parlors" (14). An emblem of the situation of "cultural nationalism in a colonized country," Moore's dependence on English ("British") patronage demonstrates for Davis how a "national" project, in such a situation, is

---

[48] The word "score" is derived from Old Norse and Old English words meaning "incision."
[49] In a critical review of Burns's *Poems*, James Montgomery offers a definition of the "peculiar character" of the Scottish language remarkably consonant with what we find in Burns's letter. Insisting that "what is now called Scottish is only a written language," Montgomery comments,
> Its basis was undoubtedly a national dialect now almost obsolete, but its superstructure consists of vulgar idioms, and its embellishments of pure English phrases. Hence the language, as it is written, is an arbitrary one, and its force and eloquence depend principally upon the skill with which the poet combines its constituent parts, to make a *common chord* of its triple tones; and we may venture to pronounce that style the most harmonious and perfect, in which the national dialect is the *key-note*, and the vulgar and the English are subordinate. The muse of Burns disdained to confine her song to any peculiar accordance of these, but ran, as it suited her subject or her caprice, through the whole diapason of her country scale, and tried her skill in every modulation of which her mother-tongue, copious and flexible beyond any now in use, was capable. (my emphases)

See Donald A. Low, ed., *Robert Burns: The Critical Heritage* (Boston: Routledge & Kegan Paul, 1974) 212.
[50] Thomas Moore, *Journals* (3 January 1821) 2: 531.

"always partially created by the desires of the colonizers" (7). I'd like to provide a new angle on that argument, by suggesting that it is *only* in response to colonial power – or, in the postcolonial era, in response to the hegemony of capital – that the "national idea" can develop. Just as, without comparison to the "common air," Priestley would have been unable to distinguish the properties of the factitious airs he extracted from it, so Moore seeks to define "Irishness" in the *Irish Melodies* by identifying it with the indigenous "air" that the English language and its musical traditions cannot quite absorb.

At one of the dinner parties at which he probably performed, Moore reports a conversation about the national character of language:

> Humboldt mentioned at dinner a theory of Volney's (I think) with respect to the influence [of climate] upon language – that in a cold, foggy atmosphere, people are afraid to open their mouths, and hence the indistinctness & want of richness & fullness in the sounds of their language, whereas in soft, balsamic air, which the mouth willingly opens to exhale, the contrary effect takes place. (*Journals*, 2:477)

In most of his commentary on the *Irish Melodies*, however, he rejects such (Herderian) characterizations of language as a reflection or expression of something natural; for instance, he praises the Irish musical tradition for having "avoided that puerile mimicry of natural noises, motions, &c." If the title of *Irish Melodies* obviously gives the airs it contains a "programmatic" quality, the reference is not geographical – or at least not "territorial," since the "Erin" to which many of the lyrics allude is not a place-name. And even though, in the later numbers, Moore provides notes that identify political, historical, and mythic references in the lyrics, the fact that he attaches new words and new references to traditional airs disables any attempt to read the *Melodies* as an authentically Irish form of cultural memory. For example, since his elegy to the executed leader of the United Irishmen, Robert Emmet, entitled "Oh! Breathe Not His Name," is attached to an air that circulated years before Emmet's execution in 1798, Moore does not suggest that the melody is itself a memorial. (We might also notice here Moore's suggestion that the "national" air is not a "natural" act of respiration; national inspiration is here signified instead by a *refusal* to breathe.) Even more radically, however, Moore calls into question even the authentic character of the airs themselves; he insists in "doubting the antiquity of our music," and assigns the power of Irish music to "the acts against minstrels in the reigns of Henry VIII, and Elizabeth" (*Irish Melodies*, 229–230). The national for Moore is an agon, not an essence.

If, on the one hand, Moore rejects the identification of music and language as being authentically national in character, he also challenges the claims of music to universality, though in more subtle ways. His "Melologue upon National Music," which was appended to a collection of *Irish Melodies* published in 1821 (the first to publish the verses without music), is particularly interesting in this regard.

Moore begins with what appears to be a celebration of music precisely on the grounds of its universality:

> There breathes the language, known and felt
>   Far as the pure air spreads its living zone;
> Whenever rage can rouse, or pity melt
>   That language of the soul is felt and known. (1–4)

Not only is music conflated with the earth's atmosphere, defined as a *universally* common air, but it is also identified as a language of feeling, prior or transcendent to words. But if at first the global reach of music – the first scene takes place in Peru – appears to have the usual homogenizing effects associated with globalization, Moore appends a footnote that disrupts such appearances. Glossing the following lines,

> The soft Peruvian pour'd his midnight strains,
> And call'd his distant love with such sweet power
> That, when she heard the lonely lay,
> No worlds could keep her from his arms away (7–10)

Moore writes, "A certain Spaniard, one late night, met an Indian woman in the streets of Cozco, and would have taken her to his home, but she cried, 'For God's sake, Sir, let me go; for that pipe, which you hear in yonder tower, calls me with great passion, and I cannot refuse the summons; for love constrains me to go, that I may be his wife and he my husband'" (*Irish Melodies*, 220–271). The peculiar character of the "national" air – its production as material resistance to hegemony/homogeneity, is nicely registered here by its association with the "Peruvian" pipe, which "hails" or interpellates the "Indian" maid into a new form of (national) identity, antithetical rather than natural.

Leith Davis has also noticed – and criticized – the fact that Moore's *National Airs* sound – at least on the level of the verse – remarkably like the *Irish Melodies*. (No doubt the harmonies – composed, as in the case of the later numbers of the *Irish Melodies*, by Henry Bishop – contributed to their homogenization.) "One problem with Moore's nostalgic depiction of the 'spirit of the nation'," she writes, "was that it could be superimposed on other situations" (21). But the force of this criticism depends on the extent to which we accept the premise that Moore's representation of Ireland as *the* "national idea," a "universal prototype of Romantic nationalism in defeated countries," somehow represents a dilution or attenuation of Irish national identity (Davis, 21). If instead we see in Moore's *Irish Melodies* and *National Airs* a consistent and coherent attempt to expose the factitious claims of English and Continental imperialism to universality, then we are poised to understand *both* his attraction to the national air as a form *and* his refusal to regard the musical air as expressing a national essence.

There are more stories to tell of Moore's ironization of essentialist nationalism – for instance, the episode where, after a melody of his *own* composition meets with the approval of Henry Bishop, he contemplates including it in his collection of *National Airs* under the cover of "a Moorish air." (Moore, *Journal*, 1: 185) More pertinent to the example of Burns, perhaps, is Moore's inclusion of a number of drinking-songs ("Fill the Bumper Fair," "Come Send Round the Wine," "One Bumper at Parting") in the *Irish Melodies*; in "Oh! Blame not the Bard," Moore suggests that such songs of pleasure are deformations of the national air produced by English colonization: "His soul might have burned with a holier flame" (4), he writes, but national feeling is rendered treasonable by the Act of Union: "Tis treason to love her, and death to defend" (12). No doubt it was partly the publishing success of the *Melodies* that encouraged Moore to offer such lyrical arguments for the "national" character of the melodies as he could collect from Irish antiquarians; but it is, after all, the (English) national debt that Moore, like Burns, holds responsible for the defensive production of Irish national identity.

In *Bardic Nationalism,* Katie Trumpener suggests that interest in the Celtic periphery was a necessary counterpart to the centralization of English power:

> British centralization implies not only the spread and enforced imposition *but also the systematic underdevelopment of Englishness.* To the degree that England becomes the center of the empire, its own internal sense of empire accordingly fails to develop. And to the degree that the English language, coercively imposed on the British peripheries, comes to serve as the means of imperial absorption, it becomes an increasingly minimal basis for identifying Englishness. The peripheries, in comparison, struggle with the contradictions of underdevelopment, yet they retain their distinct, national, and non-English character. Their very ways of speaking and using English remain highly distinctive, marked by a particular cultural and political history. In contrast, the language and cultural landscape of England come to seem ever paler, even to the English themselves. (emphasis added)[51]

In Trumpener's suggestion that the "national" character of the English language can only be peripherally inflected, we hear the echo of Moore's claim that England has no "wild and indigenous airs" of its own. One might say that England, *c.* 1800, was perceived as a land not only without music, but also without tone, without a notable inflection. Likewise, what she describes as the growing *pallor* of the English language allows us to conceive of "imperial absorption" in Priestley's chemical terms, terms that also are given figural form in Moore's account of the *Irish Melodies.* Consider Moore's famous defense against the charge that the *Melodies* were "a vehicle of dangerous politics." In the "Prefatory Letter" to the third number of the *Irish Melodies,* addressed to an Irish noblewoman, Moore writes that

---

[51] Katie Trumpener, *Bardic Nationalism: The Romantic Novel and the British Empire* (Princeton: Princeton University Press, 1997) 16.

> It is not through the gross and *inflammable* region of society, a work of this nature could ever have been intended to circulate; it looks much higher for its audience and readers; it is found upon the Piano-fortes of the rich, and the educated; of those, who can afford to have their national zeal a little stimulated. (231)

Most of Moore's readers have read this passage as an admission of defeated political purposes, or at least of political intentions compromised by social ambitions. But it also quite pointedly uses the background of Priestley's chemical experiments to suggest that the consolidation of financial and political power has itself produced the correlative "factitious" air Priestley calls flammable. And if the subordination of the Irish has concentrated and identified as "national" certain properties that threaten combustion, Moore also suggests that their recirculation can help to restore the "vitiated" air breathed in the English parlor. Thus when he reports seeing in Lady Helena's eyes "those beads (to use the language of distillers) which show that the spirit is proof – (or rather *not* proof, perhaps)," we begin to understand how the reduction of Irishness to sentiment works, as in Burns, like a "double distillation."

To clarify, let me offer an example of how "distillation" as a concept works in Moore's lyrics. In "Erin! The Tear and the Smile in Thine Eyes" we rightly note the prevalence of "wings, rainbows, smiles, blisses, tears and kisses" to which Hazlitt objects:

> Erin! The tear and the smile in thine eyes
> Blend like the rainbow that hangs in the skies;
> Shining through sorrow's stream,
> Saddening through pleasure's beam,
> Thy suns with doubtful gleam
> Weep while they rise. (1–6)

Structured as an invocation to the factitious national identity named "Erin," Moore's lyric places "no human figures before us, no palpable reality, no substantive form in nature," to quote Hazlitt's criticism of Moore once again. Instead, it offers a vision of nationality that is always *mediated,* and of national expressions (smiles and tears) as forms of sentimental resistance to a prevailing condition (sorrow's stream, pleasure's beam). And if the poem seems to play upon the theory attributed to Volney that expressive forms depend on *climate,* closer attention to Moore's lyrical skill will demonstrate how completely Erin is identified with a single sound, the long vowel *i,* which reverberates through the poem's two stanzas. Erin, in other words, is entirely the product of a vocalization, of a sigh. No doubt a version of that Romantic nostalgia that Philippe Lacoue-Labarthe and Jean-Luc Nancy in *The Literary Absolute* define as "the evocation of an evocation," Moore's poem also cannily suggests how such an apparently ethereal substance might realize itself materially; when sounded aloud, the air makes possible the *double entendre* of "sons" rising in political resistance.[52]

My aim has not been to defend the politically subversive or enabling qualities of Moore's lyrics, but to highlight the extent to which Moore, like Burns, finds in the figure of "air" a way to understand the "national idea" as a "certain something" that is produced by the alchemical operations of British economic imperialism. It is striking that both Burns and Moore represent those operations in exactly the same way: as the negating, abstracting effect of the "national Debt." Understood in this context, the financial motives of Moore in attempting to "nationalize" those airs which had passed without remuneration into foreign service need not be regarded as more compromised, less authentic, than Burns's largely unremunerated labors of collection. In order truly to understand the sources of delight in "every thing national," both poets suggest, it is necessary to recall the agency of the "national Debt" in producing the national idea.

To have discussed Burns and Moore together is to leave oneself open to criticism for a failure to attend to the specific conditions affecting cultural production; for example, I have not really addressed the difference that Burns's continued residence in Ayrshire and Moore's migration to the metropole might have made to their senses of nationality. I have therefore risked the paradox so often affecting cultural studies, which, as Timothy Bahti has recently suggested, "trades in the majoration of the minority, the universalization of the diverse, the globalization of the local and the subaltern."[53] I have taken that risk because I believe that the Romantic trade in national airs actually offers an historical antecedent for this tendency in cultural studies, as well as a valuable lesson for its critique. For the oddly similar form taken by Burns's and Moore's "private" labors allows us to read the "social hieroglyphic" of the national air. The emergence of national expression thus takes place in the space created by the uneven relation between one place and another; it is this relation which effectively *localizes* the nation.

Burns and Moore demonstrate how traditional airs that circulated orally and were certainly not confined to specific territorial borders can be effectively "nationalized." This nationalization is certainly an ambivalent process; on the one hand, the growing dominion of English as a standard language and print as a standard medium gives the traditional air an exotic quality, and makes the national air "regressive" in Adorno's sense: the "national taste" is a version of primitivism. On the other hand, precisely because Burns and Moore insist on the national as a material byproduct – an unintended residue – of political and economic operations of rationalization and abstraction, they make of the national air something *more* concrete, more recognizably a social product, than the high-cultural musical tradition that minoritizes it. That latter musical tradition, which will subsequently *cite* the national air (folk-melodic motives become increasingly common over the

---

[52] Philippe Lacoue-Labarthe and Jean-Luc Nancy, *The Literary Absolute: The Theory of Literature in German Romanticism*, trans. Philip Barnard and Cheryl Lester (Albany: SUNY Press, 1988) 1.
[53] Timothy Bahti, "Anacoluthon: Cultural Studies," *MLN* 112.3 (April 1997): 371.

course of the nineteenth century, as Dahlhaus and others have noted) achieves its *apparent* universality by making the national air into a mere citation, thereby distinguished from the *un*localized, *non*-national language to which the composition as a whole aspires. But because the national air, as popularized in the work of Burns and Moore, was already a "citation," as it were (the printed scores and verses only *alluding* to the traditional air), its capacity to remind us of the social, economic and political conditions that affect or mediate pure artistic "expression" remains intact.

I'll give Priestley the last word, except in substituting the term "national air" for his own neologism *phlogiston*:

> Some philosophers may not like the term [*national air*]; but, for my part, I see no objection in giving that, or any other name, to a *real something*, the presence or absence of which makes so remarkable a difference in bodies ... and which may be transferred from one substance to another, according to certain known laws, that is, in certain definite circumstances. It is certainly hard to conceive how any thing that answers this description can only be a mere *quality*, or mode of bodies, and not a *substance* itself, though incapable of being exhibited alone. (*Experiments*, 282)

Chapter 2

"Suspended" Sense in *Alastor*: Shelley's Musical Trope and Eighteenth-Century Medical Discourse

Kimiyo Ogawa

A few years before Percy Bysshe Shelley began writing *Alastor*, a columnist in *The Monthly Magazine* made a scientific statement in a short essay titled "Proximate Cause of Light, Heat, and Sound": "[m]ay not SOUND be the effect of rapid *mechanical vibrations*, radiating in and upon the universal medium, (not on our gross atmosphere,) and modified by contact with the atmosphere, and by reflections from all surrounding bodies?"[1] At the turn of the nineteenth century, the linking of music and science raised the critical awareness of those who characterized them as mutually exclusive. Where music is concerned the mechanical approach expressed by *The Monthly Magazine* essay was not wholly accepted. Calling it a kind of "quackery in musical science," another columnist had incisively criticized the view that "strain[s] musical sound to represent mechanical motions in nature."[2] The resistance against containing music within the bound of mechanism resembles Shelley's reproachful tone against the cultivation of "sciences" which have "proportionally circumscribed those of the internal world." Shelley, who aimed at the "production and assurance of pleasure in [the] highest sense" with his poetry, problematizes "sciences" but was himself ambiguous when using a musical instrument as a metaphor for the physiological body.[3] But how is one to define "musical sound" or "voices" apart from mechanical explanations? In other words, to what extent did contemporary discourse in music and medical science, which shared the same metaphysical space of the body, feed into Shelley's imagination?

---

[1] Anon., "Proximate Cause of Light, Heat, and Sound," *The Monthly Magazine* 35 (March 1813): 121. Original emphasis.
[2] Anon., "Superiority of the Ancient Music," *The Monthly Magazine* 35 (February 1813): 33.
[3] Percy Bysshe Shelley, *A Defence of Poetry* in *Shelley's Poetry and Prose*, eds Donald H. Reiman and Sharon B. Powers (New York: Norton, 1977) 501–503. Unless otherwise noted, all the quotations from Shelley's poetry are from *Shelley's Poetry and Prose* and are hereafter cited in the text with line references in parentheses.

Music was meaningful to Shelley not merely because music and poetry are both media of aesthetic experience, but more importantly perhaps because "music" could figuratively embody the vocal quality in a poet, as it is reified by a singing bird: "[a] Poet is a nightingale, who sits in darkness and sings to cheer its own solitude with sweet sounds; his auditors are as men entranced by the melody of an unseen musician, who feel that they are moved and softened, yet know not whence or why" (*Defence of Poetry*, 486). Conversely music is a valuable source of new sensations and associations for a poet. As Captain Kennedy (1795–1870) recollects, "Shelley liked music chiefly as it brought associations."[4] Just as a musician is alert to his own sensations and their associations as well as evoking new sensations in an audience, the creative process of a poet involves the same sensitivity about the reader. Shelley's view on creativity is presented in his preface to *Prometheus Unbound*: "[p]oets, not otherwise than philosophers, painters, sculptors and musicians, are in one sense the creators and in another the creations of their age."[5]

The notion of music and poetry as the media of aesthetic experience reiterates the idea that creativity is both inherent and also comes from one's sense experience in the external world, which is represented by the word "interchange"[6] in Shelley's "Mont Blanc":

> Thy caverns echoing to the Arve's commotion,
> A loud, lone sound no other sound can tame;
> Thou art pervaded with that ceaseless motion,
> Thou art the path of that unresting sound –
> Dizzy Ravine! And when I gaze on thee
> I seem as in a trance sublime and strange
> To muse on my own separate phantasy,
> My own, my human mind, which passively
> Now renders and receives fast influencings,
> Holding an unremitting interchange
> With the clear universe of things around; (30–40)

The streams passing through the channels of the River Arve signify the stream of sensations or impressions that pass through the mind, universal or individual, and it is this universal force that also penetrates the body of an individual in the form of "sensation," which Shelley was deeply fascinated by. He had a perennial interest in this unknown actuating force, referred to as "Power" (16, 96), which could well be termed the "First Cause." This belief in

---

[4] Edmund Blunden, *Shelley: A Life Story* (London: Oxford University Press, 1965) 97. Captain Kennedy heard Shelley play several times on the piano an air which his cousin, Harriet Grove, used to play.
[5] P.B. Shelley, preface, *Prometheus Unbound* (1820), by Percy Bysshe Shelley in *Shelley's Poetry and Prose*, 135.
[6] Wordsworth had used this word in *Prelude*, Book xiii: "A balance, an ennobling interchange / Of action from without and from within". See William Wordsworth, *The Prelude* (1850), ed. Ernest De Selincourt (Oxford: Oxford University Press, 1968) 13: 375–376.

a "Power" that moves everything has a profound bearing upon what I will discuss in this paper: voice (particularly with reference to musical voice) or its sound that triggers "motion."

The contemporaneous discussion about "musical sound" in relation to its mechanism reverberates with the polemical issue over the cause of motion or "life" in the eighteenth century and early nineteenth century. The debate centered round the problem of how to conceptualize musical sound: whether to see it as part of a mechanical system of the body or as an immaterial principle caused by an unknown entity, or "God."[7] The juxtaposing of scientific and musical discourses may seem to distort the interpretation of Shelley's poetics, for past critical approaches to Shelley's poetry have tended to treat these two subjects separately.[8] However, the apparently unrelated discourses of music and science (including physiology), in attempts to define this motion and life already shared a common lexical ground from which Shelley devised his linguistic dispensation. As I will discuss, some musicians were concerned with the scientific effect of music on the bodies of the audience, and some physiologists used music as a metaphor for the functions of bodily organs.

Shelley fuels the reader's imagination by using musical metaphors and making them richer by manipulating the image of the physiological system. This is typically observed in his prose work "On Love," the dating of which I will address below. Using the Aeolian harp as a metaphor for man, Shelley states that "a soul within our soul" resembles or corresponds with another, and an imagination should "enter into and seize upon the subtle and delicate peculiarities ..., with a frame whose nerves, like the chord of two exquisite lyres strung to the accompaniment of one delightful voice, vibrate with the vibrations of our own".[9] In discussing Shelley's poetry, the musical metaphors that I highlight are those suggesting the Aeolian harp. In *The Poetics of Sensibility*, Jerome McGann discusses the harp-as-man metaphor as the philosophical and poetic legacy of Enlightenment culture of sensation and sensibility. He calls it an "emblem" for "an experience of non-conscious orders" and connects it with the idea that "nature is 'animated' with spirit."[10]

---

[7] The turn of the century saw an intensification of debate over the causality theme of motion, life and creativity among medical men, philosophers and literary writers. Some of the most well-read treatises may be Thomas Reid's *Essays on the Intellectual Powers of Man* (1785) and Thomas Brown's *Inquiry into the Relation of Cause and Effect* (1835). See also the reviews of Reid's theory in *The Analytical Reviews* 1 (May–August 1788): 145 and in *The Monthly Magazine* 43 (February 1817): 30–32.

[8] Desmond Kind-Hele's *Shelley: His Thought and Work* (London: Macmillan, 1960) and A.M.D. Hughes's *The Nascent Mind of Shelley* (Oxford: Clarendon Press, 1947) view Shelley's poetry (especially the early works) as his political statement, which is the embodiment of eighteenth-century Enlightenment philosophy of materialism. Those who study the musical aspect of Shelley's poetry focus on the musical metaphors and his musical circle of Leigh Hunt, Thomas Peacock and Vincent Novello. See Erland Anderson's *Harmonious Madness: A Study of Musical Metaphors in the Poetry of Coleridge, Shelley and Keats* (Salzburg: Universitat Salzburg, 1975).

[9] P.B. Shelley, "On Love" in *Shelley's Poetry and Prose*, 474.

[10] See the chapter on Coleridge's "Eolian Harp" in Jerome McGann's *The Poetics of*

Given that an increased sensitivity toward the body occurred in early nineteenth-century poetry, I consider it crucial to investigate what is evoked by the harp-as-man metaphor, such as the physicality and sensibility of a poet.

The Aeolian harp comes from "Aeolus," god of the winds in ancient Greek myth, and is a stringed instrument sensitive enough to produce sounds when exposed to wind.[11] Shelley said in *A Defence of Poetry* that the Aeolian harp as a metaphor does not simply represent man, but "sentient" man. This testifies to what Richard Cronin writes in his revealing book *Colour and Experience in Nineteenth-Century Poetry*, that the central problem explored by nineteenth-century poets is "how the self, the feeling, thinking human consciousness, is related to the world in which it lives."[12] Music was a crucial component of mental science and a central metaphor for explaining and conceptualizing theories of consciousness.[13] I would further argue that mental science was increasingly charged with the idea that it could be studied within the bound of physiological science, and that the movement of "thought" could keep abreast of the vibration of "the chord" or "nerves." At this junction, I would like closely to examine Shelley's *Alastor; or, The Spirit of Solitude*. To study Shelley's musical metaphors without reference to the musical climate of the time may be reductionist. Yet in order to discuss the cross-referentiality of Shelley's figurative language, I will limit my argument to observing how the harp-as-man metaphor was framed by eighteenth-century medical discourse. Specifically, I will discuss the period around 1815 when Shelley was beginning to take an interest in music as well as medicine.

Musical motion and "life"

Before analyzing Shelley's musical background and use of musical metaphors, I want to demonstrate how scientific discourse penetrated discourse on music, taking as my sources publications about contemporary concerts, music aesthetics, and Shelley's own writing. Some late eighteenth-century writers were using certain scientific terms such as "pulsation," "sensation," and "vibration" to evaluate the affective power of music. Foremost among them is Charles Burney (1726–1814) who, in writing about the 1784 Handel

---

Sensibility: A Revolution in Literary Style (Oxford: Clarendon Press, 1996).
[11] Jonathan Mansfield, *Aeolian Harp*, vol. 1 (Cambridge: Bois de Boulogne, 1970) 16–17. It is recorded that the instrument was reproduced following the models of A. Kircher in 1650 or the contemporary, R. Brookfield. In Shelley's time the harp was made into a rectangular shape measuring about three feet to fit the Georgian sash window.
[12] Richard Cronin, *Colour and Experience in Nineteenth-Century Poetry* (London: Macmillan, 1988) 5.
[13] Phyllis Weliver writes extensively on the scientific writings in the latter half of the nineteenth century, but I will focus on the earlier period and show that music in relation to scientific studies was already significant in the late eighteenth century. See Weliver, *Women Musicians in Victorian Fiction, 1860–1900* (Aldershot: Ashgate, 2000) 8.

Commemoration in Westminster Abbey, described the "wonderful powers of his [Handel's] harmony":

> And, as the power of gravity and attraction in bodies is proportioned to their mass and density, so it seems as if the magnitude of this band had commanded and impelled adhesion and obedience, beyond that of any other of inferior force. The pulsations in every limb, and ramifications of veins and arteries in an animal, could not be more reciprocal, isochronous, and under the regulation of the heart, than the members of this body of Musicians under that of the Conductor and Leader.[14]

The totality of sound or "harmony" which seemed to proceed from one voice, and one instrument, according to Burney, produced "new and exquisite sensations" in the audience. Thomas Twining (1735–1804) in his *Two Dissertations in Poetical and Musical Imitation* (1789) also acknowledged the importance of musical effects on senses. The whole power of music, according to him, can be reduced to three distinct effects: those that effect the ear, the passions, and the imagination.[15] A little earlier than Burney, Daniel Webb (1719–1798), in his *Observations on the Correspondence between Poetry and Music* (1769), investigated the relations between sound and its effect on sentiment or feelings. He categorized musical impressions depending on the types of "motion" involved. For instance, "[t]he more gentle and placid vibrations shall be in union with love, friendship, and benevolence" and "[i]f the nerves are relaxed, the spirits subside into the languid movement."[16] Thus scientific or, rather, medical language is effectively used to illustrate the "union" of sound and sense.[17]

There is certainly a parallel between this union and that of poetry and sense, which recalls Shelley's claim that poetry acts upon sense to induce corresponding or sympathetic vibrations. In his *Defence of Poetry* he writes that "by wondrous sympathy" poetry "transmutes all that it touches": "a word … will touch the enchanted chord, and reanimate, in those who have ever experienced [the] emotions [of virtue, love, patriotism, and friendship]" (505). The linguistic referentiality of the "chord" is two-fold (musical and medical), for Shelley often used this word to allude to the chord of the Aeolian harp and

---

[14] Charles Burney, *An Account of the Musical Performances in Westminster-Abbey, and the Pantheon, in Commemoration of Handel* (London: Payne, 1785) 15.

[15] See Thomas Twining, *Aristotle's Treatise on Poetry, and Two Dissertations, on Poetical, and Musical, Imitation*, 2nd ed., 2 vols (London, 1812).

[16] See Daniel Webb's *Observations on the Correspondence between Poetry and Music* (London, 1769) 202–203.

[17] In an essay "On language, as an universal accomplishment," James Dumbar, a philosophy professor at King's College, Aberdeen in the late eighteenth century, touches upon this "union of sound and sense" or "*simultaneous harmony*." He also commented on Burney's scientific ideas, stating that Burney "exhaust[ed] on his favorite science so much ingenuity and learning." James Dumbar, *Essays on the History of Mankind in Rude and Cultivated Ages* (1781; Bristol, 1995).

also to celebrate the vibrating chord of the nerve. The association with the sensory faculty suggests not so much "mechanical" vibration as organic reaction. Shelley was deeply versed in eighteenth-century medical discourse and read medical books such as *Zoonomia* (1794–1796) by Erasmus Darwin,[18] and *A View of the Nervous Temperament* (1807) by Thomas Trotter (1761–1832). Shelley's physiological interest is already observable in his early poem *Queen Mab*:

> How wonderful! that even
> The passions, prejudices, interests,
>   That sway the meanest being, the weak touch
>   That moves the finest nerve,
> And in one human brain
> Causes the faintest thought, becomes a link
>   In the great chain of nature. (II. 102–108)

His notion of "nature's laws" is thus illustrated; they operate according to the principle of "Necessity." What seems to be a mere materialist statement such as this may be regarded as a comprehensive specimen of the way Shelley could refine the reader's imagination to the scale of "the finest nerve." Such a metaphorical device demonstrates Shelley's point that words would touch the chord to reanimate the reader's thought. This passage, however, has a pessimistic tone with regard to the "chain of nature," lamenting the "nerve" which is vulnerable to the existing social institutions sustaining prejudices and custom. In this poem, the chain is thematized as that which is irrevocable, "bound / Ere it has life" (IV. 133–134). It is puzzling that the same loathsome mechanism which "sways" and "moves" the nerve enables a poet to call forth "wondrous sympathy," reanimating the emotions of love and friendship in the reader.

One element that may have shifted Shelley's views on "nature's laws" may be musical motion or what Leigh Hunt calls Shelley's "musical feeling." Hunt, who introduced Shelley to the musical circle of Vincent Novello (1781–1861), said of Shelley's poetry: "[t]he secret of musical, as of all other feeling, lies in the depths of the harmonious adjustments of our nature; and a chord touched in any one of them vibrates with the rest,"[19] clearly echoing Shelley's notion of vibrating chord. The cross-referential word, the "chord," is thus appropriated by many, but most representative of all is Abraham Rees's *Cyclopaedia*, compiled at the beginning of the nineteenth century. *Cyclopaedia*, which

---

[18] For Erasmus Darwin's (1731–1802) influence on Shelley, see Carl Grabo, *A Newton Among Poets: Shelley's Use of Science in Prometheus Unbound* (Chapel Hill: North Carolina University Press, 1930) and Desmond King-Hele, *Erasmus Darwin and the Romantic Poets* (London: Macmillan, 1986).
[19] Leigh Hunt, preface, *Stories in Verse: Containing Remarks on the Father of English Narrative Poetry; on the Ill-understood Nature of Heroic Verse; on the Necessity, Equally Ill-understood, of the Musical Element in Poetry to Poetry in General* ... in *Selected Writings*, ed. David Jesson-Dibley (1855; Manchester: Fyfield Books, 1990) 85.

Shelley is said to have consulted,[20] defines NERVE as "a solid chord" composed of "a soft white or medullary substance" and what is said to be "connected either immediately or remotely with the brain, spinal marrow, or certain small bodies called ganglia," and it forms "the instrument by which eternal objects act on the brain."[21] The nerve in a physiological sense is equated with a passive "chord" which is acted upon. The word "instrument" denies any form of agency, as is also suggested by Hunt. The secret of musical feeling lies deep in "nature's law."

William Lawrence (1783–1867), the author of *Lectures on Physiology, Zoology and the Natural History of Man* (1819), is also committed to the idea of "nature's law." When Shelley became ill in 1815, Lawrence, as his physician, came to examine him. There is no sufficient proof that Shelley read Lawrence's work at any point in his life, but it is highly conceivable that Shelley, an impassioned philosopher, had heated discussions with his physician about physiological theories and the vital properties of life. Certainly, there are some passages in *Lectures* reminiscent of Shelley's theory of necessity.[22] Lawrence subtly differentiates the vital powers from "mechanical" motion and asserts that the operation of "those natural laws, to which living, as well as all other bodies are subject, is constantly modified ... by the vital powers: and this essential element in all mathematico-physiological considerations, is, by its very nature, fluctuating and indeterminate."[23] Thus his search for "the vital powers" terminates at a philosophical impasse, not dissimilar to the *Monthly Magazine* columnist who placed "musical motion" away from mechanical theory. Despite his conviction that "the physical sciences are ... applicable to the science of life," Lawrence is uncertain whether to determine that "the internal movements of the animal machine are explicable by the laws of mechanics and hydraulics; whether the changes of composition, incessantly going on in all parts of the frame, can be assimilated to the operations of our laboratories" (70). In other words, he has no conclusion as to what the cause of life is, though he touches upon its lexicology: that it is related to the Latin *spiritus*, or the original of our spirit.[24]

---

[20] Shelley, for instance, cites the entry on "Man" from Abraham Rees's *The Cyclopaedia; Universal Dictionary of Arts, Sciences, and Literature* (London, 1819). There is no page reference in this dictionary. See Timothy Morton's *Shelley and the Revolution in Taste: The Body and the Natural World* (New York: Cambridge University Press, 1994) 133.

[21] Rees, *Cyclopaedia*. See the entry of "nerve."

[22] Shelley's theory of necessity is based on the non-dogmatic idea of power unconcerned with human values. The first cause of motion that starts the chain of necessity is the natural cycle of destruction and rebirth. This is based on the materialist idea that the mind is dependent on matter or external objects. Like the Aeolian lyre whose strings are moved by the winds, the mind is necessitated to be passive. The passivity of the mind was, however, modified by Berkeley's theory of perception, and further by the contemporary medical discourse which ascribes the cause of motion to the vibration of the nerves and muscles and which, as it were, became the conduit between the matter and the mind.

[23] William Lawrence, *Lectures on Physiology, Zoology, and the Natural History of Man* (London, 1819) 71.

[24] Lawrence, however, does explicate the derivation of the words, "life" and "spirit." He finds

Likewise, Shelley searched for the secret of life and "spirit" by applying the concepts to his verse, the outcome of which is his *Alastor; or The Spirit of Solitude* written in the same year he met Lawrence. From the subtitle, it is generally supposed that the representation of the spirit becomes the central issue in the poem. The title was Thomas Peacock's suggestion, drawing from the Greek meaning, "evil genius," or a spirit of evil. The word "spirit," which Shelley may also have derived from the earlier medical term "animal spirits," became one of the crucial concepts that enabled physiologists to theorize the communication between the bodily organs, or how one part of the body affected another. Shelley's conception of life was, consciously or not, linked with music and with motion. Hunt who avers that "[m]usic affected [Shelley] deeply"[25] remembers that Shelley expressed a sense of "the great Mover of the universe" when an organ was playing in the Pisa cathedral. Although there is very little in Shelley's biography to support the idea that he had a ruling interest in music in his early poetic career, there are hints that he started showing a more active interest in music as early as 1813 when Captain Kennedy heard Shelley play the piano in the Lake District. Shelley became acquainted with musical knowledge through his friend Thomas Peacock, and it is also recorded that he enjoyed his outings with the family of Dr John Frank Newton to Vauxhall Gardens in 1813, where he heard lively music (Anderson, 47). Therefore, even before Shelley began to see Hunt and Novello in 1816 and 1817, he must have been fairly familiar with music as being that which brings "associations." We can tentatively conjecture that the way Shelley felt about the materialist theory of Necessity was in some way altered by his growing attachment to music, for Shelley's musical themes often appear in a positive and productive light.[26] For, as Nora Crook and Derek Guiton have aptly pointed out, Shelley does not so much denounce the body as lament its transitory nature.[27] The idea that the self in its whole and part is "sentient" formed the basis of Shelley's image of vibration, which gave rise to an equivocal power not only to bind self to the "chain of nature" but also to enrapture it with harmony.

---

that the Latin *anima*, or "the breath" (from the Greek word "wind"), which popularly marks and expresses "the vital principle" of life has the same meaning as "the Latin *spiritus*, the original of our spirit." See Lawrence, 60.

[25] Leigh Hunt, *Lord Byron and His Contemporaries* (1828), in *Selected Writings*, ed. David Jesson-Dibley (Manchester: Fyfield, 1990) 101.

[26] For example, when Shelley wrote a poem "With a Guitar; To Jane," depicting Jane Williams in the role of Miranda from Shakespeare's *The Tempest*, he characterizes himself as the spirit, Ariel. It thematizes the theory of association and musical harmony: the guitar is created to "echo all harmonious thought" and "for it had learnt all harmonies / Of the plains and of the skies, / Of the forest and the mountains, / And the many voiced fountains" (44–68).

[27] Nora Crook and Derek Guiton, *Shelley's Venomed Melody* (Cambridge: Cambridge University Press, 1986) 183.

Spirit and musical tropes in eighteenth-century medical discourse

As C.E. Pulos observes, Shelley's materialism is largely drawn from the theory of causation as applied by David Hume (1711–1776) and Sir William Drummond (*d.* 1828), and Godwin's theory of the mind.[28] Shelley's fundamental idea about creativity reflects the Godwinian enigma that "thought may be the source of animal motion, and at the same time be unattended with consciousness."[29] A radical thinker and a novelist, William Godwin, who was also Shelley's father-in-law, compares the "human body" to "the strings of a musical instrument," and, exploring the mechanism of the mind, he asserts that "[t]hese vibrations, having begun upon the surface of the body, are conveyed to the brain; and, in a manner that is equally the result of construction, produce a second set of vibrations beginning in the brain, and conveyed to the different organs or members of the body."[30] Here Godwin, with some reservation, is restating the doctrine of vibration propagated by David Hartley (1705–1757) in his *Observations on Man* (1749).[31] Richard Holmes, Shelley's biographer, regards Hartley as an important eighteenth-century author who made a factual inquiry into the internal constitution or mental phenomena including imagination, dreaming and reveries, and was still generally current in Shelley's time. Hartley's materialism, or what Godwin unfavorably called "the scheme of material automatism," offered the theory of the mind which connects sensation or "motion" with its corporeal or vibratory effect on "the medullary substance of the brain" (Godwin, 362; Hartley, 512).

Shelley first read Hartley's *Observations* in the summer of 1812,[32] and its profound influence is evident from his introspective poems such as *Alastor*, "Mutability," "Mont Blanc" and *Hymn to Intellectual Beauty*.[33] Equally introspective are his essays, "On Love" and "On Life." The latter is concerned with the problem of motion and creativity of the mind:

> Mind, as far as we have any experience of its properties, and beyond that experience how vain is argument, cannot create, it can only perceive. It is said also to be the Cause? ... – It is infinitely improbable that the cause of mind, that is, of existence, is similar to

---

[28] Shelley is said to have been deeply influenced by Sir William Drummond's *Academical Question* (1805), the first work to be acknowledged as the work of a metaphysician. Drummond's date of birth is not ascertained. See C.E. Pulos, *The Deep Truth: A Study of Shelley's Scepticism* (Lincoln: University of Nebraska Press, 1954) 112.

[29] William Godwin, *Enquiry Concerning Political Justice and Its Influence on Modern Morals and Happiness* (1793; Harmondsworth: Penguin, 1985) 364.

[30] See Chapter 9, "Of the Mechanism of the Human Mind," in William Godwin, *Enquiry Concerning Political Justice and its Influence on Modern Morals and Happiness* (1793), ed. Isaac Kramnick (Harmondsworth: Penguin, 1976) 361.

[31] David Hartley, *Observation on Man, His Frame and His Expectations*, 2 vols (1791; Washington, D.C.: Woodstock, 1998).

[32] Richard Holmes, *Shelley: The Pursuit* (London: Weidenfeld, 1974) 295.

[33] These poems were produced in 1815 and the succeeding year.

mind. It is said that mind produces motion and it might as well have been said that motion produces mind.[34]

Hartley's materialism offered Shelley an image of the mind as something simultaneously static and vibrant, or mobile. These essays – "On Love" and "On Life" – are likely to have been produced when *Alastor* was conceived or composed. While D.H. Reiman and S.B. Powers suggest that the essays were written in the summer of 1818 and in 1819 respectively,[35] Richard Holmes argues that the dating goes back to 1815. Holmes's rationale is credible, because, like all his poems from the period of the summer and autumn 1815, "Shelley was clearly advancing towards the notion of an objective psychology" which "has the hallmark of psychological introspection, and attempts to reach a position of philosophic balance" (288). When the poem, *Alastor*, is read within this context, the poem becomes "allegorical of one of the most interesting situations of the human mind" as Shelley states in the preface. In the poem, the traveling Poet sees a vision of a veiled maid, and the narrator observes that "[h]er voice was like the voice of his own [the Poet's] soul" (153). The idea that music is a condition whereby two kindred sounds or voices are interwoven or sympathized is articulated: "[t]he intellectual faculties, the imagination, the functions of sense, have their respective requisitions on the sympathy of corresponding powers in other human beings."[36] In addition, there are passages strongly evocative of the Aeolian harp in these introspective poems: "forgotten lyres" (5) in "Mutability," the "strings of some still instrument" (34) in *Hymn to Intellectual Beauty*, and not least the passage I cited earlier from "On Love." Shelley makes use of musical images when elaborating on motion and sympathy. Like Hartley, Shelley saw the body as the constellation of external forces, just as diet forms "solids" and "fibers" of his body, but he uses the metaphor of music and harmony as a way of re-imagining the physicality of the body and of re-developing the ideas about human agency, materialism and the power of the mind which inspired *Alastor*.

The theory of vibration, according to Hartley, equally applies to musical sounds which "afford, like articulate ones, various instances of the power of association" (321). "Words," which Shelley said "touched the chord," can also be considered corporeal in that, as Hartley has theorized, the sound of the words causes vibration through the air to reach the so-called "membrana tympani" of the auditory nerve (223). For Hartley, it was the medullary particle that enabled the communication between the organs of the body, and, for previous physiologists, it was the "animal spirits" that gave rise to the idea of the "sympathy" of the body. Hartley's theory of vibration is, as he admits, predicated upon eighteenth-century medical theory propagated by "physiologists and physicians" (72).

---

[34] See "On Life" in *Shelley's Poetry and Prose*, 478.
[35] See *Shelley's Poetry and Prose*, 473–474.
[36] See the preface to Shelley's *Alastor* in *Shelley's Poetry and Prose*, 69.

In his famous *English Malady* (1733), George Cheyne (1671–1743) called the animal spirits the "sentient principle," but the idea that the spirits are dispersed among all parts of the body only occurred in the middle of the eighteenth century when Edinburgh physician Robert Whytt (1716–1766) figuratively dissolved human agency to all the sensible organs. What is most interesting about Whytt's rhetoric in his medical treatises is that he remapped the topography of the sensory faculties by comparing them to various musical instruments constituting an orchestra:

> It will be unfair to object here, that we ascribe the intelligent powers of the mind to the bodily organs: for as the best musician cannot make a flute give the sound of a violin, nor a harpsicord that of a French horn, nor without these several instruments produce their sounds and notes at all; in like manner, the soul, in the present state can only exercise its rational powers in the brain; it can only taste in the tongue, smell in the nose, see in the eyes, hear in the ears, and feel hunger in the stomach.[37]

The idea that a sensory faculty, which he calls "the soul," could be in the brain as well as in the tongue, nose, eyes or ears was revolutionary. Cheyne's metaphor is akin to Whytt's musical metaphor except that the former believed that there is a sole cause of motion. It is curious to observe that Cheyne's metaphysical body is turned into an organ, for its performer is usually a single person and the motive force is one. He imagined the nerves to be the keys of the organ which the musician plays and hears in his "Organ chamber." This figures the winding and convoluting nerves from the extremities of the body, whose vibration then reaches the sentient principle in the brain.[38] Cheyne's idea that the keys of the organ require a certain elasticity and tone in maintaining the proper solids was pervasive throughout the eighteenth century, and was used in describing both the musical instrument and the nerves of the body.

The definition of the "Aeolian harp" given by Rees's *Cyclopaedia* retains some of these cross-referential characteristics. It defines the harp as an "instrument so named, from its producing an agreeable harmony, merely by the action of the wind." It follows that the "string, by its elasticity, returns to its former position: so as thus to continue vibrating and exciting pulses in the air, which produced the tone of the ... string."[39] Above all, the lexical field within which the Aeolian harp was so-defined in the early nineteenth century had underscored the images of bodily resilience. Therefore, the Aeolian harp is

---

[37] Robert Whytt, *Physiological Essays containing I. An Inquiry into the Causes which promote the Circulation of the Fluids in the very Small Vessels of Animals, II. Observations on the Sensibility and Irritability of the Parts of Men and other Animals, occasioned by Dr Haller's late Treatises on these Subjects* (Edinburgh, 1745) 171–172.

[38] George Cheyne, *The English Malady*, ed. Roy Porter (1733; London: Routledge, 1991) 88.

[39] See the entry on the Aeolian harp in Rees's *Cyclopaedia*. Given that Shelley's language has a strong resemblance, it is likely that he has read this particular article in Rees's *Cyclopaedia*.

meaningful not merely for what it stands for – the sensible body as Shelley suggests – but also for what it historically implicates, reflecting the vicissitudes of the place or places that "spirit(s)" have occupied in the musical tropes, which eventually paved the way for Shelley's notion of "wondrous sympathy." What makes this correspondence crucially relevant to Shelley's *Alastor* is that the poem, in my reading, follows the footsteps of those who investigated the cause of life.

Maiden's voice in *Alastor*

Alastor; or the Spirit of Solitude was written in the fall and early winter of 1815. I consider this period to be marked by two changes. First, as Erland Anderson has pointed out, Shelley began to move towards more personal experience, or in Holmes's words "introspective" themes, in his poetry, expanding with it his interest in and allusion to music (174). Second, it is plausible that his precarious health made him more conscious of his own body. In her note on *Alastor*, Mary Shelley wrote: "[i]n the spring of 1815 an eminent physician pronounced that he [Shelley] was dying rapidly of a consumption; abscesses were formed on his lungs, and he suffered acute spasms" (Holmes, 286). Thus Shelley had suffered a serious illness just before writing *Alastor*.

Alastor is a story of an uncorrupted Poet who sees, or rather experiences, a vision of a veiled maid, whom he subsequently seeks; he dies without finding the "prototype" of this vision. The Poet's search for the spirit figures Shelley's ontological quest for life. Critics have debated whether this spirit is supernatural or natural, immaterial or material, external or internal,[40] for some believed that a spirit was a supernatural being sent from outside to punish the Poet by presenting the evil dream. The following passage in the poem adds to their conviction: "The spirit of sweet human love has sent / A vision to the sleep of him who spurned / Her choicest gifts" (203–205). However, when we take into account that Shelley was familiar with eighteenth-century medical discourse, we could re-read the poem from a different angle. Contrary to the commentary of these critics, the medical notion of spirit invites us to conceive that the "spirit" in *Alastor* is internal to the Poet. The preface conforms to this idea, for the vision, Shelley says, is created by the Poet's imagination, sense and intellectual faculties.

In Canto IV of *Queen Mab*, he had defined soul as that which "Is active, living spirit" and said that its "Every grain / Is sentient both in unity and part" (143–144). This echoes Cheyne's theory in which life in the "sentient principle," and Whytt's theory which dissolved it to every sensory faculty in the body. It is more than befitting that Shelley in *Queen Mab* reduces "self" down to the size of an atom or what he calls "the universal element" in

---

[40] See Evan K. Gibson's argument for a more elaborate analysis on why the spirit is not supernatural in "*Alastor*: A Reinterpretation," *PMLA* 62 (1947): 1022–1042.

Defence of Poetry. In *Queen Mab* Shelley says that every "atom" is not only materially sentient but morally so, asserting that these atoms "beget / Evil and good" (145, 146–147). In a sense, *Alastor* is a meditation on the nature of sensory experience, and an attempt to explore its relation with life.

The narrator's account that the Poet's "infancy was nurtured" represents not only Rousseauvian innocence, but also a self that is created by the sensory impressions it receives: "Every sight / And sound from the vast earth and ambient air, / Sent to his heart its choicest impulses" (68–70). Also, the epistemology is strictly based on feelings, for the pleasure of sensation is intact with the Poet's learning: "The fountains of divine philosophy / ... and all of great / Or good, or lovely, ... / ... he felt /And knew" (71–75). His attention to the physiological system must have been increasingly focused on the nerve, for the medical approach Shelley absorbed was a holistic one,[41] which implied that the debility of a bodily organ was largely to do with the state of the nerve. As Simon Haines has rightly stated, having dissolved the moral realm into the material one, human life into atoms, Shelley has nothing left to hold on to.[42] The lack of a hypostatic element or what we may call "human agency" is the natural consequence of the endless regression that the theory of association or Necessity posits. The passionate search for the cause may be the Poet's natural urge in *Alastor*, which eventually leads him to the journey in search for the source, eventually finding a tranquil nook in the recesses of Nature. It may be no coincidence that Shelley had been reading Rousseau's *Reveries of the Solitary Walker* in the same year when he was writing this poem. *Reveries* is concerned with solitude, the yoke of Necessity, the laws of motion, moral cause, spontaneity and human agency.[43]

The opening invocation of *Alastor* is ultimately addressed to "Mother of this unfathomable world" (18), or in other words to "the great Mover of the universe." The narrator could not find her "inmost sanctuary" and he only says that he has watched "Enough" (38, 39)

> that serenely now
> And moveless, as a long-forgotten lyre
> Suspended in the solitary dome
> Of some mysterious and deserted fane,
> I wait thy breath, Great Parent, that my strain
> May modulate with murmurs of the air,
> And motions of the forests and the sea,
> And voice of living beings, and woven hymns
> Of night and day, and the deep heart of man. (41–49)

---

[41] Nora Crook and Derek Guiton, *Shelley's Venomed Melody* (Cambridge: Cambridge University Press, 1986) 23.
[42] Simon Haines, *Shelley's Poetry: The Divided Self* (London: Macmillan, 1997).
[43] Jean-Jacques Rousseau, *Reveries of the Solitary Walker* (1782; Harmondsworth: Penguin, 1979) 117, 126–129.

The passage suggests the narrator's vain attempt to seek the cause of motion, physical and mental; now he awaits external motion to vibrate upon his "long-forgotten lyre". The human agency is absent in this passage, for it is not the narrator's will, but "my strain," suggesting the nerve, that modulates with murmurs of the air and motions of the forests and the sea.

When the Poet experiences the vision, it is the voice, the auditory sensation, that he experiences, followed by the visual sensation. The Poet first hears the voice stifled into the tremulous sobs, the beating heart in the pause of the song, the tumultuous breath, and when he turns round he "sees" the bare arms, the floating locks, the beamy, bending eyes, the trembling lips:

> He dreamed a veiled maid
> Sate near him, talking in low solemn tones.
> Her voice was like the voice of his own soul
> Heard in the calm of thought; its music long,
> Like woven sounds of streams and breezes, held
> His inmost sense suspended in its web
> Of many-coloured woof and shifting hues. (151–157)

Throughout the poem, there are references to this "web." Shelley calls it the "web of human things" or "Nature's vast frame" (719), by which "A fragile lute" (667), or the poet, is jostled by "influxes of sense," (641) such as "Hope and despair" (639) and "mortal pain or fear" (640). However fragile the body is, it rests on the premise of physicality and sensibility. This is reiterated in Shelley's prose work. One's feelings, he says, are the "combined result of a multitude of entangled thoughts, of a series of what are called impressions, planted by reiteration."[44] This imagery reappears in Shelley's later poem "Mutability," in which the figurative strings of forgotten lyres "Give various response to each varying blast, / To whose frail frame no second motion brings / One mood or modulation like the last" (6–8), suggesting perpetual change in one's feeling due to its connection with external objects.

To grasp adequately Shelley's materialistic idea of self by the workings of "spirits," it may be pertinent to cite the *OED*'s entry of "sympathy" in medical usage, which gives a more physical than psychological definition. Besides the common understanding of the word, such as "[c]onformity of feelings" or "harmony of disposition," sympathy is defined as "[a] relation between two bodily organs or parts, or between two persons such that disorder or any condition, of the one induces a corresponding condition in the other."[45] This is what Whytt calls the "sentient and sympathetic power of the nerves."[46]

---

[44] See "On Life" in *Shelley's Poetry and Prose*, 477.
[45] The earliest record of the physiological or pathological meaning of sympathy in the *Oxford English Dictionary* is from 1603, though it refers less to sympathetic nerves than to conduits between various parts of the body. The other meaning, "Conformity of feelings," predates this, with the first reference being Spencer's *Hymn Beauty* (1596).
[46] Robert Whytt, *Observations on the Nature, Causes, and Cure of those Disorders which have been commonly called Nervous, Hypochondriac, or Hysteric*, 2nd ed. (Edinburgh, 1765) v.

Whytt's metaphor of the orchestra, in other words, is an illustration of the communicative sympathy, which theoretically makes it possible for the sentient principle to travel between the extremities of the body, consequently revolutionizing the idea that it is the mind/brain that moves the body. Interestingly, the view that the brain is merely one sensible organ was later to be absorbed by William Lawrence and Shelley.

If we take a look at a much earlier poem, "The Retrospect" (1812), we see that Shelley has already ontologically connected matter and spirit, as in the "chain of nature" in his *Queen Mab*. Shelley has learned to "scorn / The chains of clay" which bound his aspiring soul (71–72). For him, the world is a dunghill or a charnel house, and the body, the dungeon or coffin of the soul. On the other hand, Shelley is perpetually struggling against this prison trope by imagining the body as the lyre on which the divine music of love is played.

The musical metaphor of the Aeolian harp potentially transmutes the body from the yoke of necessity to the power of life. "[I]f we feel," Shelley says in "On Love," "we would that another's nerves should vibrate to our own, that the beams of their eyes should kindle at once and mix and melt into our own".[47] Therefore, the bodily sensation encapsulates life and can also reach out to mingle with another, causing harmonious and sympathetic vibration. Shelley's notion of sympathy is contained within the physical or "sentient" realm. The corresponding element on both sides, "lips of motionless ice" he says, "should not reply to lips quivering and burning with the heart's best blood" (473). Similar expressions are observed in Shelley's later poems, especially in "To Constantia," written between mid-1817 and early 1818. The poem celebrates the singing voice of Claire Clairmont for whom he bought a piano from Vincent Novello. Claire's voice is likened to a "Spirit" with "The blood and life" residing in her fingers, and the corresponding blood in Shelley is "listening" in his frame, while his heart is "quivering like a flame" (1, 3, 6, 9).

The device of the harp-as-man metaphor is most effective when it represents an entity which is endued with motion and which hears voices. As Evan K. Gibson has argued, Shelley presents various images of all that we know of our existence, with caves giving forth a thousand confused voices.[48] For Gibson, the cave is perhaps merely a figure of an acoustic instrument, but it strangely fits in with this passage from *Alastor*:

> A fragile lute, on whose harmonious strings
> The breath of heaven did wander – a bright stream
> Once fed with many-voiced waves (667–669)

The mutable nature of life is reified by multiple voices whose motions are each transient. Shelley may be imagining "many-voiced waves" that carry music,

---

[47] See "On Love" in *Shelley's Poetry and Prose*, 473.
[48] Gibson (1947) n.p. Cited in *Shelley's Poetry and Prose*, 564.

with each voice is associated with disparate scenes and life events, similar to Hartley's statement about music:

> When [the pleasures of music] are arrived at tolerable perfection, and the several compounding parts cemented sufficiently by affection, they are transferred back again upon a great variety of objects and ideas, and diffuse joy, good-will, anger, compassion, sorrow, melancholy, &c. upon the various scenes and events of life. (233)

In Shelley's poem, when the spontaneous strings of the musical instrument or the nerves are touched by these "many-voiced waves," the affection ceases to fix itself on one voice. The external stimuli, particularly that of music, will disturb one's engagement in the present and excite one's memory of the past, thereby making associations. According to Hartley, the pleasures of music are composed partly of the original, corporeal pleasures of sound and partly of associated ones. The sounds or ideas that can be associated with certain scenes or events will strike the auditory nerves themselves and, without the intervention of the will, these voices will affect the emotion or the bodily condition of the hearer. The Poet in *Alastor* remembers the maiden's voice corporeally just as if he had heard it in reality: "sweeping from some strange harp / Strange symphony, ... / The eloquent blood told an ineffable tale. / The beating of her heart was heard to fill / The pauses of her music" (166–170). He also remembers it strongly for the voice is associated with his feeling of joy. This is demonstrated when joyful birdsong reminds the Poet of the maiden's voice. The ideal state of being unaffected by change is symbolized as one voice in his own vision, to which he can attach himself in solitude and dreams.

The narrative in *Alastor*, however, is disrupted in the portrayal of what at first glance appears to be a sympathetic tie between the Poet and the maiden. The maiden's voice does not so much cause vibration on the Poet's inmost sense as "suspend" it. The passage could possibly express what Shelley articulates in "On Life," namely man's desire to "disclaim alliance with transience and decay," or the existence of a "spirit" (476) which works against change and extinction. Indeed, the only companion to the Poet is that "one voice" of the veiled maiden which now echoes. This is reminiscent of Rousseau's solitary reflection in *Reveries of the Solitary Walker*:

> Nothing keeps the same unchanging shape, and our affections, being attached to things outside us, necessarily change and pass away as they do .... But if there is a state where the soul can find a resting-place secure enough to establish itself and concentrate its entire being there, ... with no other feeling of deprivation or enjoyment, pleasure or pain, desire or fear than the simple feeling of existence, a feeling that fills our soul entirely, as long as this state lasts, we can call ourselves happy (88)

The suspension of the Poet's sensation significantly reflects the Rousseauvian desire to find the immutable space in the body. What makes the maiden's harp and symphony "Strange" is that the maiden's music does not produce motion which would move the poet's senses. Therefore, it is not the realism of the vision that needs attention, but how the voice alienates the Poet from the sympathy of another and reinforces his spirit of solitude.

The Poet's journey is symbolic not only of this spirit, crucially echoing Rousseau's solitary walks in the woods, but also of his life, both in the physiological sense and the historical sense. Half obsessed with the imaginary maiden, the Poet searches for her voice which is "far sweeter" than the "dying" music of a "Beautiful bird" (286, 280). He then leaps into a boat and travels through the river. Now, the boat is likened to "that frail and wasted human form" (350) just like the harp is compared to man, and words such as "straining boat" (320, 389) draw the two metaphors closer. The "frail joints" of the boat (302) are possibly suggestive of Shelley's own ill health at the time. Despite the frailty and the waters overflowing, the boat catches the wind, and "with gentle motion" (399) sails heading toward the "searchless fountain" (507). In exploring the secret of life, Shelley's imagination extends to the physical universe of the mountain and river which "rolls its rapid waves," as he writes in "Mont Blanc" (2), where the river is like the spirit or the power of life which rolls through all things.

As Carl Grabo has argued, there seems to be an assumption in the poem that thought and Power are one and that they flow like a river through the mind of the perceiver. Through "[t]he windings of the dell" (494), the Poet seeks the source of the stream, where allegorically he finds the source of life. The Poet exclaims, "O stream! / Whose source is inaccessibly profound, / Whither do thy mysterious waters tend?" (502–504). The most significant irony may be that the image of decay and death remains throughout the journey, while the Poet searches for the opposite. He reaches a "silent well" (484) and sees his reflection in the "dark depth / Of that still fountain" (471–472). In the narrative framework, in place of the fountain, the Poet's soul was characterized as "still" (224), suggesting that his soul is not in sympathy with another. This fountain is likened to the grave over which the human heart gazes in dreams. Finding his "Spirit" personified, or his alter-ego, he realizes that they are the only existence; the feeling of solitude is here accentuated: "as if he and it / Were all that was" in the scene (487–488). When the Poet steps into the shade of trees; ghastly "change" (532) was there. It seems that time has elapsed, "as fast years flow away, / The smooth brow gathers, and the hair grows thin / And white" (533–535). From his steps "Bright flowers departed ... / With all their odorous winds / And musical motions" (537–539). The receding of Nature represents the gradual loss of its musical motion. Musical motion hence becomes the synecdoche of life.

What he calls the "passive being" has become a "long forgotten lyre" in solitude, whose strings would otherwise move with "many-voiced waves." The voice of the veiled maiden that the Poet imagined, as I have pointed out, does not so much act upon the Poet's sense as suspend it. The voice that brings about true sympathy, which is observed in poems like "To Constantia," is totally lacking in *Alastor*. The depiction of the veiled maiden is, for example, somewhat morbid. Despite signs of life such as "glowing limbs" and "panting bosom," her "parted lips" are "pale" and "quivering" (176–184). Just as the Rousseauvian solitary walker pursued a figurative "resting-place" that is unaffected by the influxes of sense, the Poet finds the final repose in the "silent nook" (572). In reaching the "tranquil spot" (577), the Poet finds the "stillness of its solitude" (590). "Hope and despair, / The torturers, slept; no mortal pain or fear / Marred his repose, the influxes of sense, / And his own being unalloyed by pain" (639–642). In his journey, he has "Rolled through the labyrinthine dell" (541) or its "curves" (542), and metaphysically reached "some dim latticed chamber" bearing "sweet music" (632, 631), just like Cheyne's perception of convoluted nerves that terminate at the organ chamber. Indeed, Cheyne illustrated the physiological body using the images of "channels" and "pipes" through which fluid flows:

> the Human Body is a Machin [*sic*] of an infinite Number and Variety of different Channels and Pipes, filled with various and different Liquors and Fluid, perpetually running, gliding, or creeping forward, or returning backward, in a constant Circle, and sending out little Branches and outlets, to moisten, nourish, and repair and Expenses of Living. That the Intelligent Principle, or Soul, resides somewhere in the Brain, where all the Nerves, or Instruments of Sensation terminate, like a Musician in a finely fram'd and well-tun'd Organ-Case; that these Nerves are like Keys, which, being struck on or touch'd, convey the Sound and Harmony to this sentient Principle, or Musician. (4–5)

The Poet's search for the source of musical motion had already been carried out metaphysically in eighteenth-century medical writings. Cheyne was keen to define where the end of sensation terminates.

Shelley has the Spirit or the "soul within our soul" explore the workings of life only to find that the prolonging of his "inmost sense" or sensation (in musical terms, the "suspension" of his chord) is not possible, much less sustaining to his life. To suspend, in a standard usage of the term, of course, means to "put a stop," "interdict" or "abrogate," but it may also signify "[o]f a note of a chord: Prolonged into the following chord, usually so as to constitute a temporary discord" (*OED*). In *Alastor*, the word suspension becomes ambivalent in that it represents the Poet's ardent desire to prolong his sensibility or to sustain idealized harmony, but it also leads to its inevitable dissonance: immortality and (mortal) life are mutually exclusive. One has no choice but to shut off the sensation to give forth an ideal harmony. In *Alastor*, the Poet physically surrenders to the final impulses of the spirits or the "sentient principles" that hover in his body, and his being rests "motionless" (636) and "still" (650), and "the Poet's blood, / That every beat in mystic sympathy / With nature's ebb and flow, grew feebler still" (651–653). Shelley does not make the voice immortal, for the sentient being whose nerves vibrate in harmony with that which acts upon them belongs to the earthly realm. Just as the Aeolian harp needs elasticity and tension to produce pleasurable sounds when activated by wind, man's body must hold tension in the muscular and nervous fibers, which are only sustainable by a vital force. Hartley says: "[t]he degree of sensibility both in the membrane [of the nerve] itself and in the whole organ, is probably greater when the tension is greater" (224). The body beats in mystic sympathy so long as it has bodily strength enough to sustain resilience. Therefore, the poet's frailty does not sustain the vibration of the maiden's music: the voice that "endued / ... motions, render[s] up its majesty" and "Scatter[s] its music on the unfeeling storm" (595–596, 597). Thus Shelley sets two subject-positions in the poem: the narrator as a spectator, and the Poet figuratively as the "Spirit" that travels through the body. He explores the metaphorical space drawn up by the medical writers, in the process of which the body, or rather the nerve, metamorphoses into the chord of the harp, the boat floating on a river, and back to the body again.

The Poet's illusion is merely suspended at the impasse where death awaits. Shelley does not permit immortal or immutable space for the Poet to sustain the ecstatic feeling that he experienced in his vision. What is true of Shelley's poetry is true of Romantic poetry in general. It is a poetry of alienation, of *irony*.[49] This is why illusions are the central preoccupations for Romantic poets. The lack of a hypostatic element in "self" – soul within a soul – was expressed in the Poet's search for self, but cannot we see this wavering sense of self as the effect of alienation?[50] The Poet "spurned" the vision, the spirit's "choicest gift," not because he literally did so, but because he misunderstood "human love." Far from spurning the vision, the Poet attached his soul to it. Shelley's theme of human love is "suspended" in the web of immortality, but this is expressed in an ironic way because there is "No sense, no motion, no divinity" (666). The image is "silent, cold, and motionless / As their own voiceless earth and vacant air" (661–662). This is comparable to the energetic voice of "The Cloud." There is a sense of triumph in the poem when the cloud, which is both metaphysically earthly and heavenly, exclaims, "I pass through the pores, of the ocean and shores; / I change, but I cannot die" (75–76). I say "irony" because two opposite philosophical ideas coexist in *Alastor*: the optimistic sense of an "overflowing and exhaustless vital energy" in the world (a sense of possibility in the future, that the Ideal moment is forever there), and the pessimistic "denial of any absolute order in natural or human events" (a

---

[49] Susan Bernstein also discusses the "failed desire for unity" in *Alastor* in her essay in this volume, "On Music Framed: The Eolian Harp in Romantic Writing."

[50] Stephen Bygrave suggests that "alienation" is one of the possible unifying factors of Romanticism. "If we think of Clare's 'I Am' with its wavering sense of self, couldn't we now see this as the effect of alienation?" Stephen Bygrave, *Romantic Writings*, ed. Stephen Bygrave (London: Routledge, 1996) 274.

terrible sense of limitations, that reality is forever changing).[51] The absence of such energetic voice in *Alastor* does not necessarily indicate Shelley's denial of it. Rather, we can read the poem as his didactic narrative which emphasizes the importance of physical voice that vibrates on strong elastic nerve, opening up the way to "wondrous sympathy" and the function of association.

In his *Essay on Percy Bysshe Shelley*, Robert Browning rightly captures Shelley's poetical force, by which the whole being is "moved and suffused with a music at once of the soul and the sense, expressive both of an external might of sincere passion and an internal fitness and consonancy."[52] While reason is contemplative, imagination is active and creative. The impressions are not merely recorded, for the mind or organic "thought" responds to them and composes them to harmony. Figurative expressions, as Hartley argued, illuminate our discourses and writings by transferring the properties, associations, and emotions, belonging to one thing upon another, by augmenting or diminishing (430). Man, according to Shelley, is "an instrument over which a series of external and internal impressions are driven, like the alternations of an ever-changing wind over an Aeolian lyre, which move it by their motion to everchanging melody" (*Defence of Poetry*, 480).

---

[51] Anne Mellor, *English Romantic Irony* (Cambridge, MA: Harvard University Press, 1980) 7.
[52] Robert Browning, *An Essay on Percy Bysshe Shelley* (London: Reeves and Turner, 1888) 18.

Chapter 3

On Music Framed: The Eolian Harp in Romantic Writing

Susan Bernstein

This paper is part of an ongoing project. The interest of this project is to complicate, or at least render more interesting, what is often perceived to be the Romantic obsession with unity. For many, the reduction of the Romantic point of view to a privileging of unity – organic or otherwise – is enough to dismiss it as even potentially interesting to us today. Many Romantic texts of course contribute to the mythological fusion of mind and matter, subject and object, or man and nature. These moments of fusion, however, can emerge only when properly framed. The frame produces a fictional or figurative region in which phantasmatic images of unity can appear temporarily.[1] But if we redirect our attention to the framing device or technique, we see that the dream of unity is always posited elsewhere, carried away by another.

The Eolian harp presents the components of the logic I have just outlined. The play between nature and culture embodied in the figure of the Eolian harp appeals to Romantic writers because it allows a dual agency to persist; it presents a kind of commingling of voices that counteracts a traditional reading of the supremacy of the lyric "I."[2] The figure of the Eolian harp presents a

---

[1] The figure of the "frame" makes possible the distinction between "inside" and "outside." At the same time, it destabilizes this difference because the position or nature of the frame itself is impossible to define with finality. This problem comes up in Kant's discussion of the parergon in the *Critique of Judgement*, especially para. 14. See Immanuel Kant, *Kritik der Urteilskraft* (Frankfurt am Main: Suhrkamp, 1981) 139–142. Jacques Derrida analyzes the problem of the frame in *The Truth in Painting*, trans. Geoff Bennington and Ian McLeod (Chicago: University of Chicago Press, 1987) especially 37–82. In "The Frame of Reference," Barbara Johnson extends the problem of the frame, reading it in terms of narrative frame, but finally arguing that the "frame" is comparable to writing itself: like the "literal" figure of a (picture) frame, language is often understood as a mere marker presenting some "content," or a secondary material support only there to allow an "inside" meaning to appear. See Barbara Johnson, "The Frame of Reference," *The Purloined Poe: Lacan, Derrida, and Psychoanalytic Reading*, eds John P. Muller and William J. Richardson (Baltimore: Johns Hopkins University Press, 1988) 213–267. Johnson also plays with the sense of "framing" as false conviction.

[2] This critical commonplace is virtually omnipresent; but here is a clear statement of it in the present context: "a lyric poem is a highly organized pattern of sound and meaning which produces a cantabile or singing effect. This form represents intense subjective feelings united

syncopated subjectivity in which music and language cooperate to form a bond between self and other.[3] Similarly, the Eolian harp is a *topos* where the discourses of music, poetry and science meet.

The notion of the *figure* or *image* of the Eolian harp raises the question of the relationship between the empirical instrument and the poetic figure. But this is a question about the nature of poetic language itself and the relation it has to the historical world, or of the relation between the literal and the figurative. The Eolian harp hovers between these two regions, being both a creation of science, especially some of its more popular practices, and of poetry.[4] What follows here will provide only some preliminary hints at how we might ask the question about this relationship by considering the figure of the Eolian harp in some poetic texts of Percy Bysshe Shelley and Samuel Taylor Coleridge. In particular, I will look at how the language of Fourier analysis might describe the relationship of oscillating identity and difference brought into play by the Eolian harp. In 1822, Jean-Baptiste-Joseph Fourier demonstrated that a "finite and continuous periodic motion can always be decomposed into a series of simple harmonic motions of suitable amplitudes and phases."[5] The convergence of waves explains the moment of apparent unity while allowing for a continuing process of differentiation.

It is tempting to draw upon scientific discourse to explain musical figures, or likewise to draw upon musical figures to explain scientific discourse. With such a methodology, however, one must assume or posit a stable field of meaning within one discourse in order to transfer it to another. The figure of the Eolian harp, however, engages the very process of this transfer or exchange itself. In *Music and Metaphor in Nineteenth-Century British Musicology*, for example, Bennett Zon investigates the application of "metaphorical templates" from the areas of science, religion and the arts to that of musicology. Such a procedure finds similarities and subsumes them within a unifying structure ("metaphor"), suggesting a general "correspondence" between various fields of discourse. This process of substitution and projection of correspondence is itself an act of metaphor, of transferring one set of terms to another with a view

---

in a single mood and usually attributed to an "I" or first-person persona." E. San Juan, Jr, "Coleridge's 'The Eolian Harp' as Lyric Paradigm," *The Personalist* 48 (1967): 77–88.
[3] I borrow the term "syncopation" in relation to a critique of subjectivity from Jean-Luc Nancy, *Discours de la Syncope* (Paris: Flammarion, 1976).
[4] I follow here Alison Winter's approach in *Mesmerized: Powers of Mind in Victorian Britain* (Chicago: University of Chicago Press, 1998). In this study, Winters argues that science is a field still being constituted, and that what might be called popular or pseudo-science today was equally constitutive and indicative of cultural formations as what later comes to canonized in scientific discourse (5–9).
[5] Robert T. Beyer, *Sounds of our Times: Two Hundred Years of Acoustics* (New York: Springer Verlag, 1999) 44–45. See also Frederick Vinton Hunt, *Origins in Acoustics: The Science of Sound from Antiquity to the Age of Newton* (New Haven: Yale University Press, 1978); Stephen Handel, *Listening: An Introduction to the Perception of Auditory Events* (Cambridge, MA: MIT Press, 1989).

towards replacing them all with a single meaning.[6] The difficulty thus is not due to "vagaries attendant to its [metaphor's] meaning" (Zon, 3), but rather to the fact that this kind of analysis cannot or does not account for its own figurative activity. Jacques Derrida has explored the vertiginous relationship between metaphor and philosophical discourse, as a discourse that both erases and depends upon metaphor, especially in "White Mythology: Metaphor in the Text of Philosophy."[7] Here he focuses particularly on the way in which metaphor has been understood as a process of spiritualization, internalization or idealization that subsumes differences under a single unity and replaces a "material" beginning point with a "spiritual" end as its meaning. Metaphor thus describes the very emergence of thought or meaning out of what is seen to be its literal conveyor, body or linguistic signifier. This metaphysical understanding of metaphor, which in the end must consider it a "form" for a "content," or a mere "exterior" conveying a single "inner meaning," must produce and reproduce both the "literal" and the "figurative" poles between which it moves, transfers, or translates. The difficulty lies in the fact that a metaphysical understanding of metaphor cannot account for itself, for there is no "original" or "first" metaphor by means of which other instances of metaphor can be known; the "field" (itself a metaphor) of metaphor is structured by the absence of its origin or ground. While Derrida writes explicitly about philosophy, his comments extend to any discourse of knowledge based on a metaphysical organization of the binaries inside/outside, literal/figurative, or material/spiritual: "If one wished to conceive and to class all the metaphorical possibilities of philosophy, one metaphor, at least, always would remain excluded, outside the system: the metaphor, at the very least, without which the concept of metaphor could not be constructed, or, to syncopate an entire chain of reasoning, the metaphor of metaphor" (220). "Syncopation" occurs here as a kind of abbreviation, a naming of a linguistic process or an infinite series that cannot be reduced to a name. "Syncopation" has several definitions. According to the *Encyclopedia Britannica*, it indicates "in music, the displacement of regular accents associated with given metrical patterns, resulting in a disruption of the listener's expectations and the arousal of a desire for the reestablishment of metric normality; hence the characteristic 'forward drive' of highly syncopated music."[8] It refers also to the shortening of a syllable by dropping a letter, or a brief loss of consciousness due to anemia. Thus syncope, or syncopation, indicates a process extending through time that connects two moments through an experience of disruption – whether of

---

[6] Bennett Zon writes, for example: "It goes without saying that the word 'metaphor' connotes a spectrum of meanings. My use of the word is, of course, not intended to compound the vagaries attendant to its meaning, but rather to unify under one heading various types of musicological discourse of the period under consideration." See Bennett Zon, *Music and Metaphor in Nineteenth-Century British Musicology* (Aldershot: Ashgate, 2000) 3.
[7] In Jacques Derrida, *Margins of Philosophy*, trans. Alan Bass (Chicago: University of Chicago Press, 1982).
[8] "Syncopation": *Encyclopedia Britannica*, 7 December 2002, <http://search.eb.com/eb/article?eu=72582>.

musical beat, syllabic form or consciousness. The restoration of the wholeness of a recognizable pattern does not sublate or undo the disrupted series through which it emerges, but remains congruent with that series.[9] Derrida's reading of metaphor as syncopation, then, stresses discontinuities and would prevent the collapse of the terms it connects into a single identity. This is what Jeffrey Wallen aims at in a recent article, "Physiology, Mesmerism, and Walter Pater's 'Susceptibilities to Influence.'"[10] Here Wallen looks at the connections between these discourses stressing the way in which "influence" implies an excess of effect that cannot be reduced to its material cause, yet also cannot be separated from it. The resistance to the unifying function of metaphor ends up destabilizing the limits or frames that would separate an "inside" from an "outside," or establish any kind of stable identity.

For this reason, I have chosen to draw on the figure of Fourier analysis here; on the one hand, it suggests a parallel between the science of sound and the poetic figure of the Eolian harp; on the other, it does not allow for a collapse of poetry into science, or an interpretation of one as the ground and the other as the figure. The science of sound is not the "ground" or cause of metaphor. The lure of the explanatory force of "ground" and "figure" is strong indeed; there is a temptation to view the discourse of "science" or perhaps of "economics" as determining those of music, language or literature. Yet to allow such a collapse is to reintroduce a model of correspondence that organizes all discourse as instances of a single structure; it would be to set up the same kind of "harmony of the spheres" initiated by Pythagoras and renewed in the eighteenth and nineteenth centuries by Swedenborg and other champions of synaesthesia and correspondence.[11] This would be the result of non-reflective historical discourses that claim to simply "find" similarities and offer their compilation as a form of explanation. On the other hand, a co-reading of various fields may expand the "field" of metaphor itself and can work against a reductionist discourse that mirrors the idealistic kinds of interpretation it was supposed to critique. Kimiyo Ogawa's essay in this volume, "'Suspended' Sense in *Alastor*: Shelley's Musical Trope and Eighteenth-Century Medical Discourse," for example, shows a common set of terms, comparisons and figures operating in medical, musical and poetic

---

[9] I am also drawing on the elaboration of the term "syncopation" in relation to a critique of subjectivity in Jean-Luc Nancy's *Discours de la Syncope*. Nancy focuses on the way syncopation articulates consciousness: "Ainsi, ce qu'on appelle une conscience ne se laisse sans doute jamais appréhender comme une identité que lorsqu'elle s'évanouit: c'est la syncope" (13). (Thus what is called consciousness can only be apprehended as a unity at the very moment it is vanishing: that is syncope.)

[10] Jeffrey Wallen, "Physiology, Mesmerism, and Walter Pater's 'Susceptibilities to Influence,'" *Walter Pater: Transparencies of Desire*, eds Laurel Blake, Leslie Higgins, and Carolyn Williams (Greensboro, NC: ELT Press, 2002) 73–93.

[11] The difficulty of talking about the relation between different arts is the focus of my book, *Virtuosity of the Nineteenth Century: Performing Music and Language in Heine, Liszt and Baudelaire* (Stanford: Stanford University Press, 1998). The whole project might be understood as an effort to co-articulate the fields of music and language without presupposing and putting into operation a model of correspondence.

discourse, focusing on Shelley's *Alastor*. Likewise Phyllis Weliver's *Women Musicians in Victorian Fiction, 1860–1900* documents shared metaphoric networks in the areas of music, mesmerism and mental science in a way relevant here. As she notes, "The boundaries between analogy and literal truth blur when science relies on metaphors like music and fluid to explain universal laws."[12] The question is how otherwise music or fluid could be understood, if both "figuratively" describe the process of understanding itself. The opposition of literal and figurative itself induces this epistemological vertigo. Paul de Man analyzes the implication of understanding in metaphor in an interpretation of Locke focusing on the figure of "light." Locke, de Man writes,

> takes pains to explain that the work "light" does not refer to the perception of light and that to understand the causal process by which light is produced and perceived is not at all the same as to understand light ... To understand light as idea is to understand light properly. But the word "idea" (*eide*), of course, itself means light, and to say that to understand light is to perceive the idea of light is to say that understanding is to see the light of light and is therefore itself light.[13]

In the end, we cannot understand either light or understanding through the metaphor of light.

Like "light" for Locke, the Eolian harp has been interpreted as a figure of the processes of perception and understanding. The Eolian harp gained popularity during the Romantic period and is generally taken to be an important Romantic image.[14] Often cited is M.H. Abrams essay "The Correspondent Breeze: a Romantic Metaphor" (1984), in which he writes:

> The wind-harp has become a persistent romantic analogue of the poetic mind, the figurative mediator between outer motion and inner emotion. It is possible to speculate that, without this plaything of the eighteenth century, the Romantic poets would have lacked a conceptual model for the way the mind and imagination respond to the wind, so that some of their most characteristic passages might have been, in a literal sense, inconceivable.[15]

Abrams points out that the Eolian harp not only links man and nature, but provides a model for thinking about this relationship as well. Recalling

---

[12] Phyllis Weliver, *Women Musicians in Victorian Fiction, 1860–1900* (Aldershot: Ashgate, 2000) 62.
[13] Paul de Man, *Aesthetic Ideology* (Minneapolis: University of Minnesota, 1996) 38.
[14] "The supernatural, ghostly sound of these chords, changing, increasing and fading away with the wind without any player or any artificial contrivance, was wholly romantic. Between 1780 and 1860, therefore, Aeolian harps were much in favor in parks, on roofs and on ruins of medieval castles, especially in Germany and England." See Curt Sachs, *The History of Musical Instruments* (New York: Norton, 1940) 402.
[15] M.H. Abrams, *The Correspondent Breeze: Essays on English Romanticism* (Norton: New York, 1984) 26.

Derrida, we could say that it is both a metaphor and a metaphor of metaphor. The Eolian harp is a kind of technical supplement which would allow us to hear nature's own music, nature's own voice, directly; it is supposed to bring about precisely one of the moments of unity between man and nature for which Romanticism is famous. If we forget about the labor, the knowledge – the *techné* – implied in the harp, we hear only the resonance of this other. But if we attend to the framing device, we see that the animated resonance projected towards us is a momentary fiction supported by a surrounding narrative. The Eolian harp, as a figure, presents not an immediate unity between self and other, man and nature, but rather a temporary eclipse of separation that can only be articulated poetically – that is, in some manner figuratively, indirectly.

The Eolian harp is itself a duplicitous object: both a historical artifact and a poetic image. We are tempted to look first towards the literal or material definition of the harp as its beginning point. Eolian harps, popular in the Romantic period especially in England and Germany, are constructed by extending strings across some kind of box. The strings are all one length but differ in width. The harp is then typically placed at a window, or more eccentrically, somewhere else where it can be stroked and played by the wind. Windows were the preferred place in England, while on the continent the harps were placed in gardens, grottoes, on medieval ruins, or between trees.[16]

The history of the Eolian harp begins with the legend of David hanging his harp over his bed to catch the divine wind. Athanasius Kircher, "a German polyhistorian, theologian and music theorist," (*Grove*, 619) is credited with creating the first Eolian harp, which he called a "musical autophone" in his *Musurgia Universalis* (1650). The instrument was connected to Eolus, the god of the winds, by J.J. Hoffmann in his *Lexicon Universale* of 1677. James Thompson's poem "The Castle of Indolence," published in 1748, describes the Eolian harp; he also wrote an ode on the same subject in 1750.[17] Following an article on the Eolian harp published in 1781 (in W. Jones's *Physiological Disquisitions*), W. Jones, the author, took up production of the harp in cooperation with various London instrument makers. As Eolian harps came into vogue towards the turn of the century; they were produced mostly in London and imported to the continent, especially to Germany. The playful experimentation with wind harps took place at the same time as a great deal of scientific research into the properties of sound in the eighteenth and nineteenth centuries. Much important work on the theory and mathematics of harmony

---

[16] See the entry, "Aeolian harp," *The New Grove Encyclopedia of Music*, 1: 173–175; Geoffrey Grigson, *The Harp of Aeolus* (London: Routledge, 1947) 24–31; Sachs, 402.

[17] Thompson's poems are treated as precursors to Coleridge's by James H. Averill in "Coleridge's 'The Eolian Harp' and James Thomson's 'An Ode on Aeolus's Harp'," *English Language Notes* 16 (1979): 223–227. For more historical genealogy, see C.G. Martin, "Coleridge and Cudworth: A Source for 'The Eolian Harp,'" *Notes and Queries* 13 (1966): 173–176.

was done in the eighteenth century by Jean le Rond d'Alembert, Jean-Philippe Rameau and others.[18]

The Eolian harp presents a kind of ambivalence between *techné* and nature that points to the persistence of a dual agency. On the one hand, there is a wish to submit to the tones of nature; in this sense, the inspired poet can be compared to the Eolian harp, the passive conductor of a force beyond himself. On the other hand, the technology required to allow the nature tones to resound gives control back to human agency as the necessary means by which the "harmony of the spheres" can become audible.[19] This ambivalence has been developed with wonderful clarity in the writings of E.T.A. Hoffmann, sometimes considered the first to write music criticism in the contemporary sense. Hoffmann talks about this dualism in terms of a "higher mechanics," contrasting normal sense with "higher" sense:

> Can the music which dwells within us be any other than that which lies buried in nature as a profound mystery, comprehensible only by the inner higher sense, uttered by instruments, as the organs of it, merely in obedience to a mighty spell, of which we are the masters?[20]

But insofar as "we" are masters of these tones, they are mediated by instruments and technique and only resound in analogy with the tones of nature. These can be generated only in the realm of dream, where mechanics, technology and cause and effect are obliterated. The text, "Die Automate,"

---

[18] See Jean-Philippe Rameau, "Traité de l'Harmonie reduite à ses Principes Naturels," *Complete Theoretical Writings*, ed. Erwin R. Jacobi, vol. 1 (American Institute of Musicology, 1967); Jean le Rond d'Alembert, "Discours Préliminaire de l'Encyclopédie," *Oeuvres Complètes*, vol. 2 (Paris, 1821) 17–99; d'Alembert, *Elemens de Musique theorique et pratique* (1799; New York: Boude Brothers, 1966). Ernest F. Chladni published his research on "Die Akustik" on the velocity of the transmission of sound through solid bodies in 1802. This research generated the phenomenon of "Chladni figures," or in German *Klangfiguren*. Chladni's text includes popularized instructions, apparently suitable for the home, about how to set up a metal plate and transmit tones to produce the corresponding figures in sand. The interest in technological games connected with sound and strings takes place contemporaneously with developments of automata, including Jacques de Vaucanson's famous flute-player and other musical automata in France, as well as phenomena of electricity. Magnetism, too, becomes a parlor game around the same time. For thorough historical treatments of these sciences and their relationship to music, see Winters, Weliver, Zon; and Jamie C. Kassler, *Music, Science, Philosophy* (Aldershot: Ashgate, 2001).

[19] Grigson points this out but doesn't make much of the contradiction: "Man, by artifice, if not art, arranges several strings on a rectangular pine-wood box, the wind moves the strings; and the man-arranged music is not man-made, but made from Nature, is Nature's music, made audible. A self-deception, but how useful in image, how delightful a toy for the next seventy years!" (29).

[20] E.T.A. Hoffmann, "Die Automate," (1814), *The Best Tales of Hoffmann* (New York: Dover, 1967) 98. The German text reads: "Kann denn ... die Musik, die in unserm Innern wohnt, eine andere sein als die, welche in der Natur wie ein tiefes, nur dem höhern Sinn erforschliches Geheimnis verborgen, und die durch das Organ der Instrumente nur wie im Zwange eines mächtigen Zaubers, dessen wir Herr worden, ertönt?" *Die Serapionsbrüder* (Frankfurt am Main: Insel Verlag, 1983) 2: 463.

continues to follow the conversation between the two characters, Ludwig and Ferdinand:

> "But in the purely psychical action and operation of the spirit – that is to say, in dreams – this spell is broken; and then, in the tones of familiar instruments, we are enabled to recognize those nature tones as wondrously engendered in the air, they come floating down to us, and swell and die away."
> "I am thinking of the Aeolian harp," said Ferdinand. (98)[21]

The relation between conventional music and "nature tones" is one of metaphoric doubling. The "inner" or "higher" music is an elevated and rarified duplicate of the first. Once the rules of technology are broken, the "higher" music is reinscribed in conventional music where it then resonates. One might understand it as a "multiple" of the first sound wave and read it as a kind of Fourier analysis. This model would fall in with an expanded notion of the "music of the spheres."

For Hoffmann, the experience of this kind of music decenters the self while connecting it with foreign elements. Here is one of the many descriptions he gives of musical ecstasy:

> As it [the music] rose in simple phrases, the clear upper notes like crystal bells, and sank till the rich low tones died away like the sighs of a despairing plaint, a rapture which words cannot describe took possession of me – the pain of a boundless longing seized my heart like a spasm. I could scarcely breathe, my whole being was merged in an inexpressible, superearthly delight. I did not dare to move; I could only listen; soul and body were merged in ear. ("Die Automate," 85)[22]

In this musical experience, the "I" contracts in a spasm, and body and soul are joined in the external organ of the ear.[23] It moves along with the wave of the swelling tone, rising and falling over time; its breath is suspended. The subject is like a vibrating string.[24] Like the tone of a string, its waves pass from outside

---

[21] "'Aber im reinpsychischen Wirken des Geistes, im Traume ist der Bann gelöst, und wir hören selbst im Konzert bekannter Instrumente jene Naturlaute, wie sie wunderbar, in der Luft erzeugt, auf uns niederschweben, anschwellen und verhallen.' 'Ich denke an die Äolsharfe,' unterbrach Ferdinand" (2: 463).

[22] "wenn sie den Gesang in einfachen Melismen bald in die Höhe führte, daß die Töne wie helle Kristallglocken erklangen, bald in die Tiefe hinabsenkte, daß er in den dumpfen Seufzern einer hoffnungslosen Klage zu ersterben schien, dann fühlte ich, wie ein unnennbares Entzücken mein Innerstes durchbebte, wie der Schmerz der unendlichen Sehnsucht meine Brust krampfhaft zusammenzog, wie mein Atem stockte, wie mein Selbst unterging in namenloser, himmlischer Wollust. Ich wagte nicht, mich zu regen, meine ganze Seele, mein ganzes Gemüt war nur Ohr" (2: 443).

[23] The notion of existence as spasm is important in Avital Ronell's analysis of epilepsy, poetic language and irony in *Stupidity* (Urbana: University of Illinois Press, 2002).

[24] See Kimiyo Ogawa for a detailed comparison of the medical discourse on nerves in relation to musical instruments. I have analyzed a similar figure in Baudelaire in *Virtuosity of the*

to inside, from object to subject, through the organ of the ear. But what is the ear? It remains, like a frame, as a physical limit or condition that cannot ascend into the experience it makes possible. As it draws up, it also leads down. Likewise, as the text above continues, the poetic dream figure is interrupted by an obvious prosaic device. The narrator eventually falls asleep, and is awoken by "the shrill notes of a posthorn" (2: 444–445). The same organ takes apart what it joins. The posthorn, a feature that occurs frequently in Hoffmann's prose, heralds the persistent return of the prosaic sphere of letters – of the technology of communication over time and space, delayed by delivery, distance and difference.

I begin with an exposition of these problems in Hoffmann because he is a prolific guru on the subject of musical experience as a loss of self in the medium of synaesthesia. Synaesthesia of course joins the senses, just as self and other, inside and outside, body and soul, are fused in the passages I have quoted.[25] Hoffmann's interest in the uncanny provides the interesting double of this musical experience. The uncanny duplicates the structure of possession by an other, suspension of time and space and self-loss with the opposite values. The relation between music and the uncanny articulates the ambivalence around the exposure of the "I" to an other – a contact that is both the consummation of the desire for union with an other and the fear of self-loss or death.[26]

While musical instruments in general often figure this ambivalence, the image of the Eolian harp exacerbates the tension outlined above since it puts the agency of the human subject and the "other" called Nature into direct rivalry. In an important essay, "Apostrophe, Animation, and Abortion," Barbara Johnson has analyzed this rivalry in terms of the very structure of the Romantic lyric "I" in Shelley's "Ode to the West Wind."[27] The relation between the "I" and the wind, enacted through direct address and the personification of the wind it implies, presents the desire for fusion in a figure of speech that makes that identity impossible. For as the calling voice brings the wind near, it also holds it forever separate by positing and repositing it as an addressee, a structural "other" without whom the "I" cannot call. The

---

Nineteenth Century, especially in Chapter 8, "Music, Painting and Writing in Baudelaire's *Petits poëmes en prose*."

[25] Baudelaire, for example, quotes Hoffmann's *Kreisleriana* in his *Salon de 1846* to illustrate the principle of synaesthesia. See E.T.A. Hoffmann, "Höchst zerstreute Gedanken," *Kreisleriana* (Stuttgart: Reclam, 1983) 39–40; Charles Baudelaire, *Oeuvres Complètes* (Paris: Bibliothèque de la Pléiade: 1975) 2: 425–426.

[26] See Sigmund Freud's essay, "Das Unheimliche," *Gesammelte Werke* XII (S. Fischer Verlag), in which Freud analyzes Hoffmann's story, "The Sandman." On Freud's essay and literary aspects of the uncanny, see Samuel Weber, "The Sideshow, or: Remarks on a Canny Moment," *MLN* 88 (1973): 1102–1133; Neil Hertz, "Freud and the Sandman," in *The End of the Line: Essays on Psychoanalysis and the Sublime* (New York: Columbia University Press, 1985); and Barbara Johnson, "Frames of Reference." See Wallen and Weliver for further discussions of magnetic influence, the loss of self, and questions of gender.

[27] Barbara Johnson, *A World of Difference* (Baltimore: Johns Hopkins University Press, 1987) 184–199.

mutual interdependence of the two positions is most poignant in the repeated demand, "hear, oh hear!" The speaker asks for recognition and response from an agent that it has itself named, personified and called forth. The figure of apostrophe (address) holds the positions apart and maintains the fiction that the wind addressed is not identical with the speaker, not simply its instrument or extension.

The speaker in the "Ode" calls upon the wind to be its means of extension, of connection with the world. It wants to be carried away by the wind, to give itself over and rise to the heights of a power beyond itself:

> If I were a dead leaf thou mightest bear;
> If I were a swift cloud to fly with thee;
> A wave to pant beneath thy power, and share
>
> The impulse of thy strength, only less free
> Than thou, O Uncontrollable![28]

To extend the analogy of Fourier's wave terminology, we might say that the voice is trying to adjust itself to be in harmonic resonance with the wind, to be a simple multiple that can fuse and rise with the stronger tone. Fourier demonstrated that a wave – a periodic motion – can be decomposed into a series of simple harmonic motions. If each agent is figured as a resonant wave, the "I" becomes identical to the wind as they resound in a common frequency – or, *almost* identical, but not quite. Perhaps their relation is better understood as a beat, a moment of amplification and punctuation that seems to imply identity but actually marks only coincidence between two waves of differing frequencies.[29] At the moment where their periods coincide, the volume goes up: the leaf flies around, the cloud blows by. No wind, no "I."

But the "I" here is not able to give itself up, for its speech – direct address – forms the very structure or frame of the poem. Its very statements, in the contrary-to-fact subjunctive, prevents identification or fusion; the form of speech itself asserts difference even while wishing for unity: "A heavy weight of hours has chained and bowed / One too like thee: tameless, and swift, and proud" (55–56). The I's resistance to the wind keeps it separate and apart: "One too like thee": that is, as we move through the poem, through time and space, through the wind, the I utters itself as One; passes over into relationship with another – two. I is one, two: not only I, but also (too), like thee. I and thee, self and other, one, two, are never reducible to a single point. In the final section of the ode, the desired relationship of unity is expressed in another imperative: "Make me thy lyre, even as the forest is: / What if my leaves are falling like its own!" (57–58). The "I" sees its identification with nature as a

---

[28] P.B. Shelley, *Shelley's Poetry and Prose*, eds Donald H. Reiman and Sharon B. Powers (New York: Norton, 1977) 43–47. All subsequent citations of Shelley's poetry are from this edition and are given in the text using line numbers.

[29] For a definition of "beat" in work by Mersenne, Sauveur and Thomas Young, see Beyer 9–10.

kind of death, a loss. But as long as it speaks, it forestalls this fusion. While it names the Eolian harp, it cannot become an Eolian harp; for then the "I" would simply resonate, like a string, and lose itself. The articulation of the wish of unity itself holds separate the very terms it would unite: "Be though, Spirit fierce, / My spirit! Be thou me, impetuous one! / ... / And, by the incantation of this verse, / Scatter, as from an unextinguished hearth / Ashes and sparks, my words among mankind!" (61–62, 65–67). The "I" calls upon the wind to "deliver" the text in its own future absence: in its writing, as the metaphor of voice takes its place on the leaf of the page.

The structure of address in this poem, extending from beginning to end, is its condition of possibility; it prohibits the erasure of the "I" that it calls for or its fusion with the wind, nature, other, etc. As a rhetorical technique, apostrophe frames the points of contiguity between leaf and wind, cloud and wind, and duplicates the structure of the Eolian harp: a stringed frame. If we focus only on the resonance of the strings, we can fictionalize a fusion between subject and nature through the image of music. But in the end, it is the linguistic framing device that creates this image of a unity never present or possible, never actualized or represented. Shelley's text teaches us about this difference, the persistence and necessity of the frame, even as it delivers a kind of ideology of unity in the figure of a resounding tone. But – time passes and phases diverge.

The dualism of subjectivity recurs both thematically and structurally in Shelley's longer poem, *Alastor*.[30] This poem, published in 1816, tells the story of a poet-figure, his experiences of inspiration and vision, and his ultimate failure. In search of a vain ideal, the poet-figure dies an untimely death. This story is framed by an explicit narrative, including an opening invocation and intermittent asides by the narrating voice, which recounts the Poet's travels, visions and end. Thus the lyric subject position is split between a narrative frame and the figure of Alastor, or the Poet. The inner figure acts out the failed desire for unity with another (figured in a Vision), while the framing voice tells of the poet's history and demise. The outer voice, let us call it, takes on the passive stance of a historian who merely records what is presented to it. It stakes out no originary position or action of positing, but instead calls upon Nature to animate it: "Mother of this unfathomable world! / Favour my solemn song" (18–19). The narrator awaits inspiration, awaits the delivery of his text, likening himself to an Eolian harp:

> serenely now
> And moveless, as a long-forgotten lyre
> Suspended in the solitary dome
> Of some mysterious and deserted fane,
> I wait thy breath, Great Parent, that my strain
> May modulate with murmurs of the air,

---

[30] Again, see Ogawa's essay in this volume for an excellent and thorough reading of figures of the harp not only in *Alastor*, but throughout Shelley's writing.

> And motions of the forests and the sea,
> And voice of living beings, and woven hymns
> Of night and day, and the deep heart of man. (41–49)

This feint of humility and self-erasure allows the figure of Alastor to come upon the stage and his story to be told; intermittently, his very voice speaks in the first person. In contrast to the opening narrator (and beyond that, there is also a preface by "Shelley," so potentially an infinite regress of positions), Alastor is rather a figure of hybris, never satisfied, striving for self-origination, like the "I" of the "Ode to the West Wind." Alastor fails in his project to create and fuse with his imagined other and finally dies in his search. Just as the "I" of the Ode is given over to the wind to disperse, Alastor lives on only in the narrator's frame. "Nor, when those hues are gone, / And those divinest lineaments, / Worn by the senseless wind, shall live alone / In the frail pauses of this simple strain" (703–706). These lines are uttered from the perspective of the framing device. That position cannot and does not duplicate or repeat the absent moment of lyric presence; rather, it shows the shadow side of the instrument whose strings have snapped: "But pale despair and cold tranquility, / Nature's vast frame, the web of human things, / Birth and the grave, that are not as they were" (719–720). Frames converge here in an image of death, a frame like the skeleton of the Poet that was. Framing means finitude; it means a limit, a boundary, an end.

I would like to turn now to Coleridge's poem, "The Eolian Harp," which Grigson calls the *locus classicus* of the poetic image of the Eolian harp.[31] In this poem, the Eolian harp lays the ground for an ambivalent tension, but its function is not strictly identical to what I have analyzed in Shelley. Like "Ode to the West Wind," "The Eolian Harp" begins with a direct address, but one that is very concrete: "My pensive Sara! Thy soft cheek reclined / Thus on mine arm, most soothing sweet it is / To sit beside our Cot" (1–3).[32] Readers tend to focus on this as an address to Coleridge's wife written shortly before their marriage. This biographical angle, however, does not fully interpret the formal aspects of the poem. At the opening, "I" and "thou" sit intertwined, securely framed by a cottage scene in the opening lines. At line 13, the voice begins to digress from the concrete setting and the focus is on the here and now in the opening domestic scene. These lines read:

> And that simplest Lute,
> Placed length-ways in the clasping casement, hark!
> How by the desultory breeze caress'd,
> Like some coy maid half yielding to her lover,

---

[31] Shelley's *Alastor* was published in 1816; his "Ode to the West Wind" in 1820. Coleridge's harp poem was first composed in 1795, but underwent a significant addition in 1817. Thus the dates of the various poems are interspersed; but I make no pretense of historical genealogy here.

[32] Coleridge's text is quoted from *English Romantic Writers*, ed. David Perkins (New York: Harcourt Brace Jovanovich, 1967) 399–400.

> It pours such sweet upbraiding, as must needs
> Tempt to repeat the wrong! And now, its strings
> Boldlier swept, the long sequacious notes
> Over delicious surges sink and rise,
> Such a soft floating witchery of sound
> As twilight Elfins make, when they at eve
> Voyage on gentle gales from Fairy-land, (13–22)

The poem undergoes a kind of rupture away from reference towards "fantasy" here; the shift is marked by the fragmentary syntagm of the exclamation, "that simplest lute!" Typically placed in the casement, the harp literally marks the passage-way between inside and outside in the material terms of an architectural window. The domestic gives way, at this threshold, to the fanciful elaborations that follow. The passage of the wind over the harp is compared to the advances of a lover; the tones the woman or the harp emit are contradictory, both urging on and resisting. The sexuality here suggests the physical nature of the Eolian harp as a foundation, the concrete origin of the various figurative elaborations that develop in the poem. The drift of the poem's tone away from the concrete setting of the instrument in the casement is transgressive; at the end of the poem, of course, it is disapproved and dissolved by the real moralizing woman (in contrast to the seductive figure coming out of the harp image). Clearly some kind of guilt or shame is associated with the flight of fancy into figurative language. In the next section of the poem, the "I" himself becomes identified with the harp; in some sense, he changes places with the coy maid and now becomes the passive member of the relationship. This self-abandonment relinquishes control and allows arbitrary signs to proliferate, independently of any agent or meaning. "Full many a thought uncall'd and undetain'd, / And many idle flitting phantasies, / Traverse my indolent and passive brain, / As wild and various as the random gales / That swell and flutter on this subject Lute!" (39–43).

The swelling and fluttering subject here can't float on much longer without becoming "You" – without becoming a woman, an other. The image of the Eolian harp has drifted from its literal sense to the figurative sense in which it is equated with the subject. As the metaphor is uprooted, the subject begins to float away. The experience is then framed with the famous lines that have been the subject of extensive commentary: "And what if all of animated nature / Be but organic Harps diversely fram'd, / That tremble into thought, as o'er them sweeps / Plastic and vast, one intellectual breeze, / At once the Soul of each, and God of all?" (44–48). I will not attempt here a full exegesis connecting these lines to Coleridge's "doctrine," but will limit this discussion to some comments about the role of the harp.[33]

---

[33] There are many thorough readings of this kind. In addition to Abrams, see for example Paul Magnuson, "'The Eolian Harp' in Context," *Studies in Romanticism* 24 (Spring 1985): 3–20; Ronald C. Wendling, "Coleridge and the Consistency of 'The Eolian Harp,'" *Studies in Romanticism* 8 (1968): 26–42; William H. Scheuerle, "Reexamination of Coleridge's 'The Eolian Harp,'" *Studies in English Literature 1500–1900* 15 (1975): 591–99; Ronald A. Sharp,

The ecstatic experience of the previous lines is contained, framed, by a further generalization and metaphorization that continues to drift away from the frame of the harp figure. The generalizing remarks posit a unity to all things that justifies the resonant indulgence of the earlier sections of the poem; the full metaphor of the harp redeems the erotic and partially aberrant – i.e., uncontrollable excess – of the literal Eolian harp which prefigures it. I would suggest the same motive for the addition of the lines of 1817. These break from the fairy-vocabulary – "footless and wild," i.e., uncomposed, unmetered, uncontrolled – to make a general explicit statement about the unity of all things:

> O! the one Life within us and abroad,
> Which meets all motion and becomes its soul,
> A light in sound, a sound-like power in light,
> Rhythm in all thought, and joyance every where –
> Methinks, it should have been impossible
> Not to love all things in a world so fill'd;
> Where the breeze warbles, and the mute still air
> Is Music slumbering on her instrument. (27–33)

"Music" is erected as a figured subject unifying the various sensations and events described; we are given an explicit statement of unity that does nothing to bring this unity about, but rather states it in a relatively prosaic way, hoping to simulate unity through chiasma: "A light in sound, a sound-like power in light". In this line, though, the elements remain clearly separated from each other; no illusion of unity sweeps over us.

Returning to the mechanics of the Eolian harp, we recall that it is the nature of the tones to drift away from their source, into the ear and the mind. So the generalization away from the concrete is in fact prescribed by and dependent upon the concrete image it is supposed to replace. The "trembling into thought" connects body and mind in the vibrations of the body. Mind, generality, thought – emerge only as the cracks, the pauses, the spasms, in the body, the vibrations of the harp which move nature's voice from "out there" to "in here." Can it be that thought is material in nature, "of the body," nothing but difference, even erotic in nature?

Significantly, the swollen image of the Harp is framed by a question: "And what if all of animated nature / Be but organic Harps diversely fram'd, / That tremble into thought, as o'er them sweeps / Plastic and vast, one intellectual breeze, / At once the Soul of each, and God of all?" (44–48). That is, Coleridge has set up the possibility for a resounding "No!" The figure of Sara returns to censure this "trembling into thought": "Well hast though said and holily disprais'd / These shapings of the unregenerate mind; / Bubbles that glitter as

---

"The Structure of Coleridge's Nature Poetry," *Papers on Language and Literature* 21 (Winter 1985): 28–42; John A. Hodgson, "Trembling into Thought: Approaching Coleridge through 'The Eolian Harp,'" *Approaches to Teaching Coleridge's Poetry and Prose*, ed. Richard E. Marlak (New York: Modern Language Association of America, 1991) 69–75.

they rise and break / On vain Philosophy's aye-babbling spring. / For never guiltless may I speak of him, / The Incomprehensible!" (54–59). The scene returns to a simple dialogue, piously referential. The guilt of passivity, of the eroticizing of thought and the feminization of the poetic position, is atoned for as it is translated into theological debate. The dialogue between the speaker and Sara, occurring in the opening and the ending of the poem, clearly frames the flight of fancy in its interior. But this frame is itself framed by the title: "The Eolian Harp," whose tension and ambivalence remain, despite the closure offered by the humility of the final lines. These again speak of "the Incomprehensible": "Who with his saving mercies healed me, / A sinful and most miserable man, / Wilder'd and dark, and gave me to possess / Peace, and this Cot, and thee, heart-honour'd Maid!" (61–64). The frame of the harp holds fast the sinful excursion into erotic fancy, transgressive figuration, seductive passivity.

I have focused here on a formal approach to the problem of the Eolian harp to show how the instrument itself gives rise to its own figurative deviations. We might say that poetic language, here, operates on a principle of vibration, a self-differentiation that doubles and returns. The terminology of acoustics structuring my exposition itself returns us to the musical sphere from which it departed. The sciences and popular practices experimenting with resounding instruments surround and condition this poetry; yet it is not reducible to it. We can still observe a sort of historical detritus, "Nature's great frame," in the tradition of the Eolian harp, a tradition in itself divided, divergent and structured by difference.

Chapter 4

Music and Inspiration in Blake's Poetry

John Hughes

In both obvious and subtle ways William Blake's work remains to this day an abiding source of musical inspiration, though his own inveterate and life-long music-making remains regrettably only a matter of report. Allen Cunningham described Blake's musical facility and spontaneity as he worked at his engraving: "As he drew the figure he meditated the song that was to accompany it, and the music to which the verse was to be sung, was the offspring too of the same moment."[1] Another contemporary, J.T. Smith, described in a similar way how he had:

> often heard him read and sing several of his poems. He was listened to by the company with profound silence, and allowed by most of the visitors to possess original and extraordinary merit.

Though Smith reported that "musical professors" would write down the "singularly beautiful" melodies with which Blake would accompany his poetry no such transcriptions have survived, and Blake himself was "wanting," as Cunningham wrote, "the art of noting it down."[2]

Instead, it has fallen to generations of musicians to develop the musical traces and intimations of Blake's work, in a variety of genres and modes;[3] Donald

---

[1] Allan Cunningham, *Lives of the Most Eminent British Painters, Sculptors, and Architects* (1830), rpt. in *William Blake: The Critical Heritage*, ed. G.E. Bentley, Jr (London: Routledge and Kegan Paul, 1975) 175.
[2] Smith's comments are extracted respectively from *A Book for a Rainy Day* (1845) and *Nollekeens and his Times* (1828), rpt. in G.E. Bentley Jr, *William Blake: The Critical Heritage*, 48.
[3] B.H. Fairchild gives a detailed account of some of the most illustrious of these, bringing out their generic variety: "Many of Blake's songs have been set to music, ranging from Benjamin Britten's *Songs and Proverbs of William Blake* to Allen Ginsberg's recent 'tuning' of the *Songs of Innocence and Experience*. And I cannot avoid also mentioning Ellen Raskin's inspired settings for the *Songs*, which my children have sung to me. But Blake's larger works have received settings as well, including Dennis Arundell's opera, *The Ghost of Abel*; William Alwyn's oratorio, *The Marriage of Heaven and Hell*; and John D. White's setting of the "Praeludium" of *America*. Blake's illustrations to Job have inspired Ralph Vaughan Williams's

Fitch charts over two and a half thousand musical settings between the mid 1870s and the late 1980s, although even his bibliography is by no means comprehensive.[4] Certainly, even the briefest survey soon begins to expand, as one indicates how musical workings of Blake range from those of classical composers like Benjamin Britten, Hubert Parry, Dennis Arundell, and Ralph Vaughan Williams, to those of more contemporary jazz and ragtime-influenced writers like Mike Westbrook or William Balcom, or to the contributions of the many rock artists, like the Fugs and the Doors, or performance artists such as Mikhail Horowitz, who have taken Blake as their inspiration. (This, of course, is not to mention, in Mary Lynn Johnson's words, "all the poets, novelists, and culture critics who have come under Blake's spell.")[5] Perhaps most celebrated of all is the case of Allen Ginsberg's auditory visitation. "Inspired by Blake's own voice, heard spiritually" Ginsberg "tuned the *Songs* for voice, pump organ, kazoo, and other instruments."[6] *Sui generis* as this last case may seem on the face of it, it can appear from another angle as merely the most clearly developed case of a common response to Blake's work, whereby musicians find themselves engaged at some level in an act of visionary transport or reclamation, similar to that which Blake himself undertook when, at the point of death, he began to sing the music of heaven:

> "My beloved, they are not mine," he told his wife as she listened to what she later called "songs of joy and Triumph", "– no – they are not mine."[7]

Peter Ackroyd cites George Richmond's words to Samuel Palmer a little while afterwards,

> He died on Sunday night at 6 O clock in a most glorious manner. He said He was going to that Country he had all His life wished to see & expressed Himself Happy, hoping for Salvation through Jesus Christ – Just before he died His Countenance became fair. His eyes

---

Job: A Masque for Dancing, a ballet with full orchestration". See B.H. Fairchild, *Such Holy Song: Music as Idea, Form and Image in the Poetry of William Blake* (Kent, OH: Kent State University Press, 1980) 8.

[4] Donald Fitch, *Blake Set to Music: A Bibliography of Musical Settings of the Poems and Prose of William Blake* (Berkeley: University of California Press, 1996).

[5] Mary Lynn Johnson in *The English Romantic Poets: A Review of Research and Criticism*, eds John Clubbe, Stuart Curran, Mary Lynn Johnson, Frank Jordan, Karl Kroeber, Max F. Schulz and Jack Stillinger (New York: MLA, 1985) 189–190. Johnson writes that a "list of all the poets, novelists, and culture critics who have come under Blake's spell would be tedious to compile". Nonetheless, including some of her examples, one could offer as a preliminary list, the following, D.H. Lawrence, George Bernard Shaw, Dylan Thomas, Theodore Roethke, Joyce Cary, Allen Ginsberg, Algernon Swinburne, Dante Gabriel Rossetti, W.B. Yeats, Arthur Symons, W.H. Auden, Michael Horowitz, Howard Nemerov, Kenneth Rexroth, Robert Duncan, Ted Hughes, Sylvia Plath, Colin Wilson, R.D. Laing, Bob Dylan, and so on.

[6] Johnson, *The English Romantic Poets*, eds Clubbe et al, 189.

[7] Peter Ackroyd, *Blake* (London: Quality Paperbacks Direct, 1995) 367.

Brighten'd and He burst out into Singing of the things he saw in Heaven. (*Blake*, 367)

This chapter explores Blake's poetry in relation to this topic of musical inspiration. It argues that musical responsiveness is at the heart of his work, not merely in these ways as an effect (whereby the writing provokes the reader to musical imaginings of his or her own), or as an aspect of his own visionary creativity (whereby a musical visitation possesses Blake himself). Beyond and beneath these manifestations, musical pleasure operates in many interconnected ways. Above all, it works as a recurrent figure, within the scenarios of the poems, for those capacities of affective and imaginative expression that lie at the core of Blake's work. Blake's anti-rationalist stance, his affirmation of an ethics and politics of joyful autonomy and relatedness over a morality of obligation and separated cognition, is inseparable from an affirmation of individuality that is itself premised on the primary, associative, powers of body and mind, and that is often configured or dramatized in terms of musicality. Musical experience, that is, offers Blake both a means and a dramatic equivalent of individuality, and the redemptive kinds of inspiration and innocence with which it is linked.

Of course, to broaden the discussion briefly, this image of musical inspiration in Blake can be identified with many ideas of music and aesthetic experience that were evident or emerging in European thought from the turn of the nineteenth century, perhaps most decisively and influentially in the work of philosophers such as F.W.J. Schelling, and later Friedrich Nietzsche and Arthur Schopenhauer. For all their differences, these writers were united by a concern to relate rational experience to what are seen as its unconscious, physical and affective conditions.[8] Accordingly, music is privileged in their work as the art, *primus inter pares*, that expresses this dependence of the spiritual upon sensation, and that contradicts the idealist assumption that all meaningful experience can be assimilated to the representative work of reason and cognition. However, one can trace through the century in their work, and beyond, into the twentieth century (for instance, in Theodor Adorno and Ernst Bloch's dystopian thinking about music), an increasingly pessimistic, even tragic, sense of a disjunction between subjectivity, on the one hand, and passion and perception, on the other. Such a breach, it scarcely needs saying, is contrary to Blake's fundamental belief in the immanence of God in nature and the human mind.[9] In this context, his work offers a conception of creativity, and of music, that shares this anti-rationalist orientation, but while offering a different conception and evaluation of the possibilities of human thought and society. For Blake, the divine is neither transcendent to, nor absent from, the material world, but is its inmost expressive possibility, and he employs music

---

[8] Of course, there is a correspondence here with the notions of sympathy and sensation which provide an empiricist writer like Hume with the foundations of subjectivity.
[9] In respect of this identification of the world with God he is closer to earlier thinkers like Leibniz, and Spinoza especially.

continually in his work as a motif to reveal continuities between the human, the natural and the divine. The gulfs in the self and the cosmos, that become increasingly the stock in trade of these philosophers (and their poetic counterparts who meditate profoundly on musical experience – in England poets like Keats, Shelley, Swinburne, Arnold, Tennyson and Hardy), are then alien to Blake, who shows no such nostalgia for transcendence, and whose basic viewpoint is that the material can express the infinite because it is itself infinite.[10]

If music can be a privileged vehicle and analogue for this visionary outlook, it is because Blake discerns in musical events ontological and temporary possibilities that eclipse the determinations of consciousness and chronology. Musical experience as a paradigm of artistic inspiration offers him visitations of the divine, opening up the mundane and the prosaic to the infinite and the eternal as immanent, creative powers of thought. In such moments, Blake reveals his idea of human individuality as an essential and abiding power of selfhood, like a theme hidden in variations, and capable of an infinite number of different manifestations. The following section explores these ideas in *Songs of Innocence and Experience*, concentrating particularly on the links between innocence and music, and the redemptive ethical aspects of these transfiguring presentiments. Musical events in the *Songs* reveal the heart of Blake's vision: aesthetic experiences recover our true imperatives and potentials, in accordance with Northrop Frye's words that in Blake "Eternity is not endless time, nor infinity endless space: they are the entirely different mental categories through which we perceive the unfallen world."[11] Finally, the last section of the chapter examines broader contexts and aspects of these links between music and eternity, particularly the ways in which the eternal is evident for Blake in history itself. To put it another way, Blake writes epic and prophetic narratives as well as lyric poems. In the prophetic books, for instance, he identifies music with the actuality of a lost, mythologized, prelapsarian past, and with the new worlds of the future, the work itself essentially occupying a moment of critical transition. Accordingly, this closing section surveys these features of the historical and political aspects of musical inspiration in Blake. Throughout, as a way of further illuminating this argument, the essay will intermit references to further biographical, critical and musicological contexts.

---

[10] So, by the turn of the twentieth century, we find ourselves, like Hardy's speaker in "The Darkling Thrush" tormented by the hopes which music signals and inspires, and which seem to have a vanishing sense of correspondence with the natural world:
>   An aged thrush, frail, gaunt, and small,
>   In blast-beruffled plume,
>   Had chosen thus to fling his soul
>   Upon the growing gloom.

See Thomas Hardy, "The Darkling Thrush," *The Complete Poems*, ed. James Gibson (London: Macmillan, 1976) 21–24.

[11] Northrop Frye, *Fearful Symmetry* (Princeton: Princeton University Press, 1969) 46.

Inspiration and innocence

In this opening section, I want to trace some of these related ideas of music, individuality and inspiration through a discussion of the ideas of innocence and experience in Blake's *Songs of Innocence and Experience*. Clearly, in straightforward ways, within *Songs of Innocence*, we can see how the joyful expression and reciprocity which are the main manifestations of innocence are repeatedly staged in terms of, and sustained by, a general giving and receiving of sound that is often explicitly musical, and that always embodies spiritual qualities. The Shepherd whose "tongue shall be filled with praise" "hears the lambs' innocent call" and "the ewes' tender reply."[12] "The Echoing Green," similarly, is a poem that celebrates the eternal values of its initial scene, and conveys these in terms of the affects and sensations, the physical capacities for play and pleasure, that are released and circulate by means of the sunshine, the bells, the birds' singing:

> The sun does arise,
> And make happy the skies;
> The merry bells ring
> To welcome the spring;
> The skylark and thrush,
> The birds of the bush,
> Sing louder around,
> To the bells' cheerful sound,
> While our sports shall be seen
> On the Echoing Green. (1–10)

Of course, as it closes, the poem comes to accommodate, at its margins, the counter-knowledge of experience, hinting at the scene's transience, and the inevitable encroachments of sadness, death, and darkness. However, to acknowledge this is not to deny the happy reality of the moment, but merely to indicate that innocence and experience are two inseparable tendencies, or viewpoints, or moments, of being for Blake. Innocence may be ignorant of the knowledge of experience, but that does not mean that it does not express essential values, forgotten in their turn by experience. In "The Little Girl Lost," Lyca goes astray after wandering "long, / Hearing wild birds' song" (15–16), but despite her parent's terrors, she discovers an unsuspected tenderness in the wild beasts that care for her. The music of the wild birds reveals innate tendencies of response and compassion that the animal kingdom share, and that are at odds with our socially conditioned fear and distrust. A similar idea is the

---

[12] William Blake, "The Shepherd," *The Complete Poems of William Blake*, ed. W.H. Stevenson, with text by David V. Erdman (London: Longman, 1971) 4, 5, 6. All subsequent citations of Blake's poetry are from this edition and are given in the text with line numbers. The *Songs of Innocence* and *Songs of Experience* were first published separately in (respectively) 1788–1789 and 1793, and jointly as *Songs of Innocence and Experience* in 1794.

burden also of "On Another's Sorrow," which seeks to revive in us such lost, protective impulses of pity and love.

In this connection, it is clearly a commonplace to say that ethical value for Blake resides not in law but in response (as in his statement in *The Marriage of Heaven and Hell* that "Jesus was all virtue, and acted from impulse, not from rules" [282–283]). However, I need to demonstrate further the extent to which musical experience, as primarily responsive and expressive, is pervasively entwined in the ethical dramas and effects of his verse, particularly in the *Songs of Innocence*. This is clearly so, for instance, as at the end of the first "Holy Thursday" poem where we are counseled to "cherish pity, lest you drive an angel from your door", after hearing of how the "[t]housands of little boys and girls" "like a mighty wind ... raise to heaven the voice of song" (12, 8, 9).[13] And so, time and again, as has been suggested, we find musical experience in these songs by-passes conditioned morality and the will, and promotes involuntary, automatic, essential, expressions of the self. In "The Echoing Green," the scene is, for an indefinite interval, joined by sound and echoes, and life incarnates the values of innocence, as at the end of "Nurse's Song," where we read of how "[t]he little ones leaped and shouted and laughed, / And all the hills echoed" (15–16). One could multiply examples of such harmonious incidents, involving the animating powers of sound, from the *Songs of Innocence*, but here are two further examples:[14]

> Sound the flute!
> Now it's mute;
> Birds delight
> Day and night;
> Nightingale
> In the dale,
> Lark in the sky,
> Merrily
> Merrily, merrily, to welcome in the year. ("Spring," 1–9)

and:

> I love to rise in a summer morn,
> When the birds sing on every tree;
> The distant huntsman winds his horn,
> And the skylark sings with me.
> Oh, what sweet company! ("The Schoolboy," 1–5)

---

[13] There are many cases where a poem in *Songs of Innocence* has a counterpart poem in *Songs of Experience* with the same title, such as the pairs of poems entitled "Nurse's Song," "The Chimney-Sweeper," "Holy Thursday" and so on.

[14] "The Schoolboy," of course, though initially placed in *Songs of Innocence* is often placed in *Songs of Experience*.

This brings us again, though (as with "The Echoing Green") to the need to point out the more disturbing, violent, implications or intimations of a line like, "The distant huntsman winds his horn." Typically, at such moments, the poem accommodates contrary attitudes – our unreflective responsiveness to the exuberance of this opening scene is troubled by a contrary, momentary, disquiet as to the predatory relation of man and nature.

This raises the question, of course, of how we read such disturbing undercurrents of *Songs of Innocence*, and the apparent duplications and ramifications of sense that can seem to cloud their seemingly clear surface. In this aspect, the texture of the writing appears itself at such moments to be woven out of divergent attitudes of innocence and experience, of enthusiasm and reflective suspicion. Critics like David Punter, Edward Larrissy and Michael O'Neill have all concentrated on this counterpoint of viewpoint in the poems, and with fascinating results.[15] What seems common, crudely, to these writers is a view that the poems should be read as holding these different readings in suspension, as a self-ironizing mark of the poet's consciousness about their incommensurability. Larrissy writes:

> The question that is posed by *Songs of Innocence and Experience* as a whole is: what is true innocence? And this true innocence cannot be spoken of in the terms set by most of the poems in either of the two series. Blake was not sufficiently confident that it was possible to conceive of a world or a discourse without limitation and "imposition", which is what true innocence would mean.[16]

In so far as this impossibility of true innocence is a feature of the complications of the poems themselves, Larrissy is surely correct that the poems all to some degree register the ineradicable connections of innocence with experience, and refuse the reader stable positions of knowledge and mastery. In the process, he argues, one is jolted out of customary assumptions of the work as "an object of consumption," and enjoined to a suspicion of ideological and discursive fictions (156). So his striking and subtle reading of the first "Chimney Sweeper" poem in *Songs of Innocence*, for instance, turns on the way the boy-speaker reveals, without knowing it, the ideological framework that both comforts and subjects him, and that has brainwashed him into religiose compliance with the economic necessities of capitalism. At the end of the poem, he tells us how a fellow-sweep, little Tom, wakes from a dream in which an angel had set the sweeps free to "wash in a river and shine in the sun." and to "rise upon clouds and sport in the wind" (16, 18):

---

[15] Michael O'Neill, *Romanticism and the Self-Conscious Poem* (Oxford: Clarendon Press, 1997) and David Punter, ed., *Blake: The New Casebook* (London: Macmillan, 1996). It is important also to mention here the fascinating deconstructive work of the Santa Crúz collective, in scrupulously delineating Blake's textual aporias: see *Unnam'd Forms: Blake and Textuality*, eds Nelson Hilton and Thomas A. Vogler (Berkeley: University of California Press, 1986).
[16] Edward Larrissy, *William Blake* (Oxford: Blackwell, 1985) 67.

> And the angel told Tom, if he'd be a good boy,
> He'd have God for his father and never want joy.
>
> And so Tom awoke, and we rose in the dark,
> And got with our bags and our brushes to work.
> Though the morning was cold, Tom was happy and warm;
> So if all do their duty, they need not fear harm. (19–24)

Accordingly, as readers we take up a position that combines sympathy with penetration. We respond with feeling to the speaker while preserving an insight into his predicament that is beyond his false moralizing. Reading is thus configured as a double process that oscillates, in an indefinitely preserved present tense, between empathetic inwardness with the boy's perception, and a detached adult view into its limitations and economic determinants. The poems are designed to uncover ideological mystification not merely by what they represent, but by what they *do*, and what they do is to provoke modes of reading that run counter to an eighteenth-century aesthetic ideology predicated, Larrissy argues, on an assumption "whereby the subject is held to perceive the work of art either in a state of perfervid intuitive empathy or in one of passive contemplation" (155). Instead, the affective power of the poems lies in their capacity to maximize the reader's confrontation with these heterogeneous elements and levels of reading.[17]

While acknowledging the cogency of Larrissy's reading, it is also possible to feel that his view of the openness of meaning in the poems is itself a partial and negative one, predicated as it is on the priority of the cognitive over the affective dimensions of the text. So Larrissy and these other critics brilliantly display how Blake intricately reveals the political and epistemological limits of positions of understanding. They show how the appearance of truth is a cover for an assumption of mastery that conceals all kinds of hidden political interests and violent desires, as well as being constituted out of irreducible contradictions and aporias. However, this negative critique of the human mind neglects, I would argue, to give an adequate account of its positive counterpart – what I am calling Blakean inspiration. Beyond rage and indignation, Blake is also motivated by his affirmative, visionary, political and ethical enthusiasm, and importantly mobilizes a kind of thought that is based not on identity as interiority and reflection, but on individuality as response. Here music becomes particularly important, because Blake uses it to show how the exteriorized powers of passion, sensation, imagination break out from the integral, centripetal, identities of the self, of meaning, and of the moment. So in their nature, they resist the critic's will to paraphrase and close-off meanings.

---

[17] Larrissy concludes that the pleasure of reading Blake lies in an association of the political power of the poems with the specific pleasures of their resistance to straightforward consumption: "what you 'enjoy' is inseparable from the activity of *reading the poem*" (156).

While the *Songs* bare the poverty and contradictions of socially determined subjectivity, then, they also solicit and represent, through musical scenes and effects, the connective powers of feeling and thought. At this point, it is possible to draw some broad parallels between these features of Blake's writing and Romantic music, as it turns from the generic lines and patterns of Classical convention, to multiply the radiant, associative possibilities of sound. Edward Lippman has identified the tonal values of Romantic music with a vibrant blending of different tones, instruments and performers that makes the musical source into a tool of individual, and collective, expression:

> The very appearance of the conductor upon the scene meant that the orchestra was no longer a collection of individual performers, but a single tonal source, extensive and fused, and now capable of those inner effects that would seem to have the personality of a single executant as their prerequisite. With inexhaustible inventiveness, Romantic instrumentation ceaselessly mixes and blends tone-colours.[18]

Individuality here is a function of relatedness, as it is for Blake. The conductor, like the composer, takes on a different, and new kind of inaugural responsibility in the nineteenth century. He addresses the individuality of his musicians and listeners as he expresses his own. Again, as Blake's work breaks down the separations between poetry, music and the visual arts, so the nineteenth-century composer was often concerned to use music to evoke or incorporate all kinds of pictorial, narrative, mythological, political, natural and metaphysical material. Orientalism, medievalism, myth and legend liberate the musician from the constraints of culture, time and space, in accordance with Lippman's observation that visionary transport is a prevalent effect in Romantic music, as it ranges over, even transcends, time and space. The "essence of Romanticism," he writes, "is taken to be expanse and lack of confinement" (128). So this ambition extends also to the cosmic evocations of Liszt and Wagner, for Lippman, as in the latter's "*Ring des Nibelungen,* where music gives voice to the being of all inanimate and animate nature, very much in accordance with Schopenhauer's philosophical conception" (128). Further, it needs emphasizing how this new sense of the visionary dimensions of music led many of these composers also to override the division between the musical and the philosophical, so that as Lippman indicates, the music offered images of the universe, and drew composers like Schumann and Wagner into endless reflections as to what was involved in music itself.

Returning to Blake's *Songs,* we can certainly find many examples of scenes where music is associated with such kinds of inspiration and origination. There musical joy reiterates possibilities of thought and experience, and experiences of relatedness, at odds with the more static

---

[18] Edward A. Lippman, "The Tonal Ideal of Romanticism," *The Philosophy and Aesthetics of Music* (Lincoln: University of Nebraska Press, 1999) 124.

positionings of understanding. The famous "Introduction" from the *Songs of Innocence* is a case in point:

> Piping down the valleys wild,
> Piping songs of pleasant glee,
> On a cloud I saw a child
> And he laughing said to me: (1–4)

In these opening lines, the piper inspires the child who in turn encourages him to "Pipe a song about a lamb," to "Sing thy songs of happy cheer" and to "sit thee down, and write / In a book that all may read" (5, 10, 13–14):

> So he vanished from my sight:
> And I plucked a hollow reed,
>
> And I made a rural pen,
> And I stained the water clear,
> And I wrote my happy songs
> Every child may joy to hear. (15–20)

The poem's scene of inspiration is certainly a complex one to understand: is it the child who inspires the piper, or vice versa, or a combination? However, the piper is certainly commanded to pipe, then to sing, then to write, in a sequence that becomes in its turn complicated in a new way, as many critics have commented, with the word "stained." This word marks the transition from hearing to reading, from music to text, from feeling to understanding, and suggests in one aspect that this can be conceived of only as a polluting, a "staining" of the natural fluidity, and vitalizing clarity of water. This process, the poem also suggests, can only be reversed when the poem itself recovers its effect of transparency and turns back towards the condition of music, as in the final words which emphasize that these are "happy *songs* / Every child may joy to *hear*." With these closing lines, the interanimation of musical expression plays once more between piper, poet, child and reader.

The contagious, revitalizing, power of music is similarly to be found in "Laughing Song," which celebrates the power of music to exceed stable positions and contents of communication. Indeed, the poem demands that we do not so much read it as participate in it. The poem works outside the adult consciousness, with all its preoccupations of knowledge and possession, to recover the creative joy of innocence:

> When the green woods laugh with the voice of joy,
> And the dimpling stream runs laughing by;
> When the air does laugh with our merry wit,
> And the green hill laughs with the noise of it;
>
> When the meadows laugh with lively green,
> And the grasshopper laughs in the merry scene,

> When Mary and Susan and Emily
> With their sweet round mouths sing *Ha, ha, he!*
>
> When the painted birds laugh in the shade,
> Where our table with cherries and nuts is spread,
> Come live and be merry and join with me,
> To sing the sweet chorus of *Ha, ha, he!*

This poem describes a world where innocent joy and laughter pass back and forth between the woods, the streams, the air, the hill, the meadow, the birds, and Mary and Susan and Emily. What counts in this poem is not what it means (since it defies paraphrase), but what it *does*: the mood of youthful and natural spontaneity and vitality that it expresses and seeks to pass on to the reader. Enjoyment has precedence over thought and reflection here, as in the syntax that manifests the sense of connectedness given by nature and laughter. The poem does not employ sentences as such, and there are no full stops. Instead it uses semi-colons, commas and exclamation marks to pass on this world of echo, music, harmony. It creates expressive flows and phrases of sound, rather than closed statements, and adopts a simple repetitive, echoing, structure of clauses, simply adding these together by repeating the simple connectives, "When" and "And."

Against this positive conception of mind, one can contrast the corresponding poem – also entitled "Introduction" in *Songs of Experience* – where the Bard's injunction to "Hear" is not musical, and where he speaks with the voice of moralizing obligation and omniscience:

> Hear the voice of the bard,
> Who present, past, and future sees –
> Whose ears have heard
> The Holy Word
> That walked among the ancient trees,
>
> Calling the lapsed soul
> And weeping in the evening dew – (1–7)

The Bard summons the hearer/reader by identifying him or her as a responsible subject, like the "weeping" and "lapsed soul" who is similarly bound by remorse to a socialized form of identity. Subjectivity in Blake, as a socialized form of identity is always in this way subjection, a belated and mutilating reduction of the mind's innate powers of improvisation and provisionality. The "mind-forged manacles"[19] of London are both those produced by society, but also clearly those which we come to impose on ourselves in so far as we passively accept and resentfully internalize its repressive dictates:

---

[19] Blake, "London," 8.

> Struggling in my father's hands,
> Striving against my swaddling bands,
> Bound and weary, I thought best
> To sulk upon my mother's breast. ("Infant Sorrow," 5–9)

Blake's analysis of the social formation of self-consciousness resembles Althusserian "interpellation," or Nietzsche's analyses of *ressentiment* in *The Genealogy of Morals*.[20] Certainly, like Nietzsche, Blake's work is concerned with the passages and gulfs between these two inseparable powers of thought: on the one hand, the unbound exuberance of self-delighting, unreflective, physically conditioned self-expression, and on the other, the bounded, grief-stricken, resentful alienation of the ruminative consciousness. Each has a power of relatedness, though opposed in tendency. The contagious and fluent empathies and inspirations of innocence have their opposing terms in the contaminating and isolating transfers of resentment and fear staged throughout Blake's work. The *Songs of Experience* clearly draw much of their mesmerizing power from the ways in which they diagnose such affective violence or infection, and the different types of emotional bondage which result for the victim who finds him or herself divided from others, and his own innate powers, imprisoned by guilt, fear, jealousy, hatred .... In Blake's work, the inspiration and visitations of *Milton* find their flip-side in this recurring nightmare, of characters who participate as judge, jury and jailer in their own self-condemnation while the real perpetrators of their subjection are elsewhere:

> But when they came to the dark rock & to the spectrous cave,
> Lo! the young limbs had strucken root into the rock, & strong
> Fibres had from the Chain of Jealousy enwove themselves
> In a swift vegetation round the rock & round the cave
> And over the immortal limbs of the terrible fiery boy. (*The Four Zoas*, 155–159)

Most broadly, one can say that participation and retreat are the two modes, open and closed, expansive and contractive, of the self, but this is not a distinction between body and mind, since both are involved in each mode, but between two qualities, potentials, or types of existence. From another angle, they can be seen as two distinct but ultimately inseparable moments of the soul, diastolic contraries, in Blake's terms, locked in eternal opposition and recurrent oscillation, and corresponding, roughly to Blake's states of innocence and experience.

So throughout the *Songs*, Blake explodes the moralizing and socialized fiction whereby mind and freedom are identified with the self-conscious subject, with reason and will. To give more detail to this contrast, in relation to music, a poem like "The Little Vagabond" is again clearly relevant:

---

[20] Friedrich Nietzsche, The Birth of Tragedy *and* The Genealogy of Morals, trans. Francis Golffing (New York: Doubleday, 1956).

> Dear mother, dear mother, the church is cold;
> But the ale-house is healthy and pleasant and warm.
> Besides I can tell where I am used well;
> Such usage in Heaven will never do well.
>
> But if at the church they would give us some ale,
> And a pleasant fire, our souls to regale,
> We'd sing and we'd pray, all the livelong day,
> Nor ever once wish from the church to stray.
>
> Then the parson might preach and drink and sing,
> And we'd be as happy as birds in the spring;
> And modest dame Lurch, who is always at church,
> Would not have bandy children nor fasting nor birch.
>
> And God, like a father rejoicing to see
> His children as pleasant and happy as he,
> Would have no more quarrel with the Devil or the barrel,
> But kiss him and give him both drink and apparel.

If the church could incorporate the communal warmth and pleasure of the ale-house, it would have no need of those punitive devices that it uses to mould the behavior and consciousness of its childish subjects, and to prevent the little vagabond from straying. So for all his destitution, the child incarnates values of movement and affectivity that again counter social identification. The poem begins with the address, "Dear mother, dear mother," but its title and narrative, and its mood of longing, strongly suggest that the child has neither home nor shelter. David Punter suggests (like Larrissy did of the first "Chimney Sweeper" poem) that the end of the poem projects merely the child's own saving, compensatory fantasy:

> there seems to be something plaintive, almost hopeless, in the tone of the poem; it is as if the little vagabond can see what the shape of a better life might be like, but this figures for him only as a fantasy, a dream ... in this fallen world of experience.[21]

Fantastic or not, the pathos of the child's vision is that it incarnates essential values of innocence from which he is estranged within the social world of the poem.

In the same way, in the "Holy Thursday" and "The Chimney-Sweeper" poems in *Songs of Experience*, the children's plight is expressed through the loss not of music, but of the personal context in which musical spontaneity can be associated with joy. In these poems too, musical expressiveness is at best a necessary shield against real and affective destitution. In "Holy Thursday" the poet asks:

---

[21] David Punter, *William Blake: Songs of Innocence and Experience* (London: Longman, 1998) 37.

> Is that trembling cry a song?
> Can it be a song of joy –
> And so many children poor? (5–7)

In "The Chimney-Sweeper," the boy recounts how his pious parents "taught me to sing the notes of woe." (8) They perpetuate his injury, and their wrong, by persevering in their illusion that he is content because he retains an appetite for life:

> "And because I am happy and dance and sing,
> They think they have done me no injury –
> And are gone to praise God and his priest and king,
> Who make up a Heaven of our misery." (9–12)

In all three poems, an impoverished form of music-making indicates the child's pitiable affective dislocation, and the ideological fictions and barriers that imprison him and those around him. At the same time, it also testifies to the ineradicable nature of the desire for happiness. This is even true of "The Garden of Love" which, like many in *Songs of Experience*, has no explicit reference to music, yet which clearly dramatizes this conversion of the vibrant world of innocence, the open space of the green, into the enclosing and predictable routines of experience:

> And priests in black gowns were walking their rounds,
> And binding with briars my joys and desires. (11–12)

In these lines sound conveys not musical mobility but an amusical and mechanical insistence. Alliteration, syntactical repetition and rhythmical regularity pass on to the reader the impositional force of this deathly, repressive world where the supreme value is obedience.

In such ways, innocence in the *Songs* involves a trusting responsiveness to another that is itself nonetheless always vulnerable to the designs of the world of experience. The "little clod of clay" that "sang" that "Love seeketh not itself to please"[22] is sometimes taken as merely foolishly utopian and self-abnegating, as if its attitude were merely credulous alongside the knowingness of the pebble who has the last word with the statement that "Love seeketh only self to please" (9). Blake's poem certainly indicates the inevitability of such reflections given the nature of human dealings, yet he can scarcely be read as endorsing such cynicism. Instead, it is possible to read the poem as putting these two attitudes into circulation once again, while exposing the cruelty and poverty of the pebble's worldly calculations. So the poem implies that life is unimaginable without the belief that the pleasure of love for the self is based on the pleasure of the other. Once again, self-expression and "joy" in Blake's world is inseparable from response and relatedness to the other, a state of the

---

[22] Blake, "The Clod and the Pebble," 5, 1.

self associated with music, and opposed to that given by the pebble, whose attitude is one of pained and guarded retreat, and which issues ultimately in cruelty, jealousy and a compensatory self-elevation. On this view, then, Blake can be read as subscribing to a view of Innocence that indicates all the forces – cultural, psychological, affective – that interfere with it, and that ensure that its manifestations in life are often transitory intermissions or passages between the closed moments of chronology and the lowering reflections of subjectivity. However, Blake's work uses music, as we have seen, to indicate his beliefs that innocence is an essential disposition of the soul, and that life demands an unceasing dedication to maximizing those visionary potentials with which it is associated.

Music and vision

This second part of the chapter will seek to broaden and substantiate the discussion of these connections between music and imaginative experience in Blake's poetry by referring to his work as a whole and some of its key contexts. In very obvious and literal ways, as we have seen with the piper in *Songs of Innocence*, music often does come first within Blake's work as a fundamental, animating component of the visionary inspiration. So, often, a musical prelude introduces the main scenario of the prophetic poems and configures the poem itself as originating in the responsive capacities of the poet or central figure. Time and again, the poem unfolds within an encompassing song, as in "The Song of Los" which begins with Los singing, "*I will sing you a song of Los, the eternal prophet*" (original emphasis) and in "Europe" which begins with the song of the fairy, a visitant who celebrates the capacities of the senses to access the eternal:

> "Five windows light the caverned man: through one he breathes the
>   air;
> Through one, hears music of the spheres (1–2)

As the poet questions him, the fairy offers to dictate the poem, if the poet is able to feed him "on love-thoughts, and give me now and then / A cup of sparkling love fancies" (15–16):

> ["]So when I am tipsy,
> I'll sing to you to this soft lute and show you all alive
> The world, when every particle of dust breathes forth its joy."
> I took him home in my warm bosom. As we went along
> Wild flowers I gathered, and he showed me each eternal flower; (16–20)

In a comparable way, in "Thel" the young girl's initial "gentle lamentation" and "soft voice" (5, 4) provoke the answering voices of the lily, the cloud, the worm and the piece of clay to their redemptive messages of reciprocity. In *Milton*, there are several plates dedicated at the beginning of the poem to the Bard's "prophetic song" (2.22) by which Milton is confronted with his errors of vision, and enjoined recurrently to *"Mark well my words; they are of your eternal salvation"* (2.25; original emphasis).

The central emphasis here is that such musical annunciations inaugurate a virtual community that is both anticipated in the future and recovered from the past, and whose liberating effects are held to extend to the reader.[23] John Beer takes the lark that sings at the close of the Second Book of *Milton* as an example of this radiating musical power in its most energizing and visionary aspects:

> The straining of the eye to follow it into the heavens is matched by an unorganized expansion of the physical senses produced by its song. This again is no quantitative response: to measure the distance of the bird's flight would be absurd. The "infinite" dimension here is measured by the impulse in the bird, not by its capability of ascending to this or that particular height in the sky.[24]

The lark depicts the inspiration that the poem passes to the reader as an affect, which is to say that the social and aesthetic vision of this poem, like many others, is conveyed by feeling as well as by content. Blake's verse depends on such transmissions whereby the reader shares in the sense of imaginative emancipation, of joy and communality. In fundamental ways, this is a feature of the materiality of the poem's language. But what is meant by "materiality" here? (It is important briefly to explicate this, since the idea is a key one for my larger argument, and for describing the proximate, criss-cross relations of music and language in Blake.) Fundamentally, a Blake poem creates productive passages between its forms of expression and of content in two important ways: meaning becomes productively indeterminate, stimulating the reader's mind; and sound becomes significantly determined, as in music, as if it were sense in a virtual, transcendent form, yet to issue in the finite actuality of a statement.[25] These materially organized but productively indefinite

---

[23] Following Gilles Deleuze's uses of the term in his books on Proust and Bergson, I use the word "virtual" in a philosophical sense to refer to something potential, something that is real but not actual (while it can become so): in this case, of a community-in-becoming of listeners and readers whose responses accord with, and are presupposed by, the shaping vision of the artist. The books are *Proust and Signs*, trans. R. Howard (New York: Braziller, 1972) and *Bergsonism*, trans. H. Tomlinson and B. Habberjam (New York: Zone, 1988).

[24] John Beer, *Blake's Visionary Universe* (Manchester: Manchester University Press, 1969) 7.

[25] The open-ended accommodation of different readings, maximized in Blake's poetic practice, retains, then, an inwardness with the expansive possibilities of the musical scenes. To draw out a further type of indetermination here, we can consider the commutability, the transfer or oscillation, that can take place in the scene of reading itself, as in Michael Simpson's account of the "the possible transpositions of subject and object" that can take place in reading Blake, so that we don't know if it is we who are reading the poem, or the poem that is reading us. In a similar vein, one could read "The Sick Rose," for example (to return to the *Songs* for a

features of Blake's language open up passages between reader and artist, so that the reader is introduced (however modestly) into the visionary dimension of Blake's verse. That is to say the reader is someone here who must create and imagine meaning. As the poet is seized by the muse, then, so the reader cannot dissociate him or herself from the verse and poet who introduce him or her into what John Beer has described, as Blake's "universe," where "the artist is king," and where the poet's "true purpose ... is to transform the reader's vision of the universe" (2, 5).

Thus those particular, communal musical scenes which we have noted in Blake's work are of a piece with these general effects of his work, as well as of those more overt and high prophetic moments in Blake's work, wherein the human being is conceived as delivered "into a state which is expansive and sublime" (Beer, 7). In terms of the ideas of mind and individuality that lie behind this, and their essentially creative and transpersonal conditions, my argument intersects at this point with that of Leonard W. Deen who argues that in Blake's work one finds a notion of identity and mind counter to that of eighteenth-century rationalists and empiricists who seek to locate it in the inviolable core of the separated, conscious self.[26] Deen argues that the self in Blake, and the other English Romantic poets, is productive and collective. I am because I make, and what I make or recreate is communal, in its effects and conditions:

> Unlike the philosophers, who are interested in logical problems of whether it is the same or "identical" person who remembers or survives or who is resurrected after death, they look at the active powers of memory, vitality, awakening. They are less interested in the personal identity that exists as an ideal datum of conscious and

---

moment), as a poem that dramatizes reading itself in the destructive, invisible, invasive attentions of the worm:
O rose, thou art sick:
The invisible worm
That flies in the night,
In the howling storm,

Has found out thy bed
Of crimson joy;
And his dark secret love
Does thy life destroy.

The critic's desire to understand the poem here would thus contravene his response to it, those complexities and intensities of imaginative passion that the poem produces, and that correspond to the threatened life and secret joy of the Rose. To the extent that this is true, the poem offers an allegory or scene of reading, and the divisions within the reader who exists on the threshold, and in constant transition or circulation, between the unconscious life of physical expressiveness and the centripetal directives of rational subjectivity.

[26] See, for instance, the introduction to Leonard W. Deen, *Conversing in Paradise: Poetic Genius and Identity-as-Community in Blake's Los* (Columbia: University of Missouri Press, 1983).

> inward-turning memory than in the identity that is implied in the source and emerges as working or interaction. (Deen, 3)

Individuality is a function of imagination, and aspires to a reintegration of the self through a regeneration of human relations and time itself. Blake is one of those poets who "turn back to a state they image as before established society in order to re-envision and renew the nature of man and, in this way, recreate community. The turning back seeks the future" (Deen, 9): Jerusalem is both a myth of origin and a political utopia. My main point again, though, is simply that it is music, as motif or effect, that often induces the enhanced state of mind by which Blake's poetry, as Michael O'Neill has put it, "rouse[s] the reader's faculties to act," and becomes adequate to the democratic imperative that O'Neill identifies in Blake and associates with Michael Ferber's remark that the poet-artist "wants us all to become artist-artisans ourselves." (O'Neill, xxxvii) On a biographical note, too, one can describe how similarly throughout Blake's life music retained for him the power to express the abiding spiritual potentials that inhabit the world of the senses. Musical events provided both an image and an inspiring means for regenerative, individuating events of association and projection, as in his youthful, even formative, vision in Westminster Abbey when he saw the spirits of "a great procession of monks and priests, choirsters and censer-bearers, and his entranced ear heard the chant of plain-song and chorale, while the vaulted roof trembled to the sound of organ music."[27] For Blake, as Peter Ackroyd has speculated, this musical moment retained the status of a sublime summons to art.

As creativity in this way involves an overcoming of the limits of self and other, it also involves accepting the otherness within the self. The individual for Blake is defined by his capacity for becoming and self-differentiation, in a way comparable to the way in which a musical theme can be manifest in its successive variations and their different performances. Blake annotated an Emanuel Swedenborg passage with an affirmation of the divine as an ideal essence capable of infinitely various actualizations: "Essence is not Identity but from Essence proceeds Identity & from one Essence may proceed many Identities as from one Affection may proceed many thoughts."[28] Such ideas of originality and individuality connect up at many points with John Barrell's discussion of these and the related notion of the eternal as underlying Blake's thinking on art. Blake, Barrell argues, held to a view of the poet's originality as working to copy not Nature, but "vision, imagination and inspiration" where these faculties reveal the underlying typology, the eternal varieties and possibilities, of spiritual existence:

---

[27] These are Blake's words from *Blake Records*, ed. G.E. Bentley (Oxford: Clarendon Press, 1988) 512. Cited by Ackroyd, 55.
[28] Cited by E.P. Thompson, *Witness Against the Beast* (Cambridge: Cambridge University Press, 1993) 154–155.

> Originality does not consist in any quality or novelty that the best artists may display, but in their ability to penetrate through the accidents of time and place to the substance of things, which are discoverable only by imaginative vision. The difference between Reynolds's notion of originality and Blake's does not reside in any greater power in Blake's artist to produce inventions out of nothing, or inventions which originate in his individual self; it depends entirely on the fact that, for Reynolds, substance is discoverable by the imagination working empirically; for Blake, by the imagination working intuitively, seeing into things, through to their original forms.[29]

"Genius and Inspiration", Barrell argues, are not merely the artist's mode of access to these "'original conceptions' of the eternal forms of things," but "are also, according to Blake, 'the Great Origin and Bond of Society': their function is to create, and to confirm a society, which is also, as we shall see, a public" (106). Art's function is not directly to delineate the character of the artist, as such, but to penetrate appearances to reveal the eternal types of humanity, like Chaucer's pilgrims, who recur and subsist through the ages beneath all the acts and contingencies of history.

Of course, within the prophetic books, an individual reaches his fullest expression, in the time of eternity, when he transcends the limits of the empirical self, and encompasses within himself all his different forms or emanations. Thus the individual becomes an ensemble, and reiterates the infinite and collective values of the eternal community itself. As Leonard Deen has argued, Los is a principle of community, both that community which he embodies, and the related one which he produces, and anticipates. He is a microcosm and metonym, of the whole of redeemed humankind that he projects:

> We have followed the course by which Los as demiurge and artist, poet and prophet, awakener and redeemer, becomes in Blake's last, long prophecies the creative powers of all men acting through the individual person to create a human world. We have seen that Los ends as the single identity that stands metonymically for the whole community of men: it is in and through Los that Blake works out the prophetic words of "There is No Natural Religion" of 1788: "God becomes as we are, that we may be as he is." (Deen, 260)

Each book narrates the relation between this prior and future state and the divisions and conflicts that characterize the fallen world of time, where the community of the self has become conflictual, atomized into its divided elements. In eternity, one might say, there is no important distinction between

---

[29] John Barrell, "Original," "Character" and "Individual," from *The Political Theory of Painting from Reynolds to Hazlitt* (London: Yale University Press, 1986) rpt. in *William Blake*, ed. John Lucas (London: Longman, 1998) 104.

identity and community, because the individual celebrates the community of which he is a part through the expansive, inclusive, expression of the community that he himself essentially is. Microcosm and microcosm exist in counterpoint, indivisible in themselves and in their correlation, like an individual line or phrase of music and the larger whole that it introduces or into which it is interwoven. As music often in Blake, as we have seen, provides a trigger or means for individual and collective expression, so in this case it provides at the same time a useful analogue for thinking of the relations between, and constitution of, the individual and community. In this connection, B.H. Fairchild cites Blake's dictum, "Music as it exists in old tunes or melodies ... is Inspiration, and cannot be surpassed; it is perfect and Eternal" (19).[30] He then elaborates an account of the redemptive function of music within *Job* by which the lost potentials of the past are repeated in the present:

> For Blake, as for Milton, music became a symbol of transcendence, an image of innocence as well as of spiritual unity, as symbolized in the first and last plates of Job and in the poetry. Blake's Job is perhaps his clearest and most dramatic expression of music as a symbol of the creative life indispensable to salvation. As Job comes to realize his errors and, with his family, is reintegrated into the imaginative life of the spirit, the musical instruments are taken down from the tree and Job's daughters (the sister arts) are joined in an instrumental and vocal expression of paradise regained. (Fairchild, 19)

Fairchild's invocation of Milton, in respect of this prophetic temporality, accords with Morton D. Paley's remark that *Jerusalem* is "At once Blake's Paradise Lost and his Divine Comedy," since it "presents both the mythic history and the visionary future of mankind, all devolving upon the present moment."[31]

Indeed, the prophetic features of Blake's verse can be related in other ways to the sonic features of his verse. Critics differ in their readings of the purposes of Blake's metrics, but they tend overwhelmingly to agree that his versification is radical and oppositional in intent, as it works, like his diction, against the conventions of eighteenth-century notions of form. So while interpretations may differ as to the purposes of Blake's prosody, they rarely conflict, and in most cases offer complementary indications of the different facets of Blake's sound-world.[32] John Beer, for instance, has written that *Jerusalem* proclaims a

---

[30] The full reference is William Blake, "Blake's Exhibition and Catalogue of 1809, Number V," *The Complete Poetry and Prose of William Blake*, 544.

[31] Morton D. Paley, *"The Continuing City": William Blake's "Jerusalem"* (Oxford: Clarendon Press, 1983) 1. The titles are not italicized in the original.

[32] Two important further discussions are those of John Hollander and William Kumbier. Hollander writes of the subversive and innovative features of Blake's metrics, as the poet overturns existing forms to anticipate the viewpoints of Whitman and others. See John Hollander, "Blake and the Metrical Contract," *From Sensibility to Romanticism*, eds Frederick

"new theory of prosody," one "occupied with the development of an 'instinctive' rhythm,

> one which will act like the powers of digestion or sleep in the human body. He is resolved to break the bonds of blank verse, even the developed forms used by Shakespeare and Milton, and to use instead a method by which variety of cadence will occur in every line. In point of fact the rhythm used is very like that of the Old Testament in the Authorized Version: it clearly owes much to reiterated reading of visionary passages such as those in the Book of Isaiah." (*Blake's Visionary Universe*, 240)

Few critics would argue with this picture of the Biblical inflections and the somatic features of Blake's versification in his prophetic books, though they may choose to make other emphases. John Lucas, for instance, argues that adoption of balladic and hymnal modes, in the *Songs* and elsewhere (that is, the use of the "common measure" of alternating four and three beat lines) locates Blake with the counter-traditions of the ballad, and the hymn writers who preceded him, like Isaac Watts (1674–1748), Charles Wesley (1707–1788) and William Cowper (1731–1800).

Finally, one can follow the musical threads of this discussion to the final context that I am going to mention here, and suggest that the song form in particular was the vehicle by which Blake sought to pass on his radical antinomianism, his vision of a regenerative spiritual inspiration that could be directly expressed and disseminated, and that entailed new forms of political and aesthetic association which essentially contested the prescriptions of Church and State. Jon Mee's emphasis is on the vibrant and communal aspects of such eighteenth-century heterodoxy:

> The point is that antinomianism and millenarianism of varying degrees of extremism remained available in the popular culture of the eighteenth century. If this is accepted Blake seems less the mystic who reproduced beliefs that had generally disappeared than someone whose radicalism was the product of a dialogue with the complex nexus of popular enthusiasm.[33]

W. Hilles and Harold Bloom (New York: Oxford University Press, 1965). William Kumbier experiments with musical notations to convey the tendency of Blake's "rhythmic units and phrases to define themselves over a sequence of lines, rather than in any [single] line". See Kumbier, "Blake's Epic Meter," *Studies in Romanticism* 17 (1978): 163–192. Mary Lynn Johnson surveys a range of accounts of Blake's in *The English Romantic Poets*, 177.

[33] Jon Mee, "Is there an Antinomian in the House? William Blake and the After-Life of Heresy," *Historicizing Blake*, eds Steve Clark and David Worrall (London: Macmillan, 1994) 55. See also Mee, *Dangerous Enthusiasm: William Blake and the Culture of Radicalism* (Oxford: Clarendon, 1992); A.L. Morton, *The Everlasting Gospel: A Study of the Sources of William Blake* (London: Lawrence & Wishart, 1958).

As E.P. Thompson put it, "Antinomianism, indeed, is not a place at all, but a way of breaking out from received wisdom and moralism, and entering upon new possibilities" (93). Thompson's further arguments and speculations as to Blake's specifically Muggletonian heritage, within this broad and variegated counter-tradition, are perhaps of particular interest here. Thompson provides enormous evidence as to how music functioned for the Muggletonians (as a particular grouping, what Mee calls one of the "variants," within the larger "tendency" or movement of antinomianism) (45). Music operated as an essential rehearsal of collectivity, and an affective sign of the sect's necessary orientation to futurity, their virtual anticipation of new communities, and celebration of the eternal within the moment. Thompson points out that songbooks are a fundamental part of the secreted archive, and that "divine songs" and ecstatic singing were the means by which this group would maintain their dynamic and mobile, antagonistic existence: "They met for discourse, readings and songs in each other's homes" (67). Music was thus in a very real way the connective medium of the sect. In closing here, aside from the doctrinal correspondences between Muggletonian doctrine and Blake's thought, one can point out briefly here, too, Thompson's conclusion that "it was clearly a devout ambition of each believer to add an acceptable song to the common stock" (89), and his speculation that the song-writing George Hermitage may have been closely related by marriage to Blake's mother. Of one of Hermitage's (very Blakean) songs, he writes: "It is at least a pleasant fiction to think of Blake's mother crooning that song to baby William on her lap" (Thompson, 105).

In conclusion, then, musical experience is associated by Blake with inspiration as a mode of relatedness that individuates those who listen, reviving their expressive potentials, so that all kinds of communal possibilities, real but yet to be translated into actuality, are in the air. Temporally, too, musical inspiration ties together disparate elements – of past and future which are synthesized in its movements and passages; and of the present and eternity, as the former becomes opened again to the latter's abiding potentials of expression and relatedness. Further, music as an art of sensation proves for Blake the basis of the mind in the body; and of ethics and religion in joyful enactment. As such, musical experience offers a model for thought itself, where thinking as a radical power is considered not primarily as a function of the mind's interiority, or of volition, but as an inventive counterpart of sensation and feeling. Thus music, we have seen, works in many ways in Blake as a figure and stimulus for unreflective and joyful responsiveness, so that the poems and songs express what they dramatize, even while they retain their essential openness of meaning.

Chapter 5

"Music their larger soul":
George Eliot's "The Legend of Jubal" and Victorian Musicality

Ruth A. Solie

> And Lamech took unto him two wives: the name of the one was Adah, and the name of the other Zillah.
> And Adah bare Jabal: he was the father of such as dwell in tents, and of such as have cattle.
> And his brother's name was Jubal: he was the father of all such as handle the harp and organ.
> And Zillah, she also bare Tubalcain, an instructor of every artificer in brass and iron: and the sister of Tubalcain was Naamah.[1]

And so, in the land of Nod, east of Eden, human culture was born. It is customary to interpret the dominions of Jabal and Tubal Cain very broadly, to hold the one responsible for all settled agriculture and animal husbandry, the other for the full extent of human industry and manufacture. But Jubal's contribution has always been oddly contested: on the one hand, religious conservatives from medieval times to the present day have querulously confined him to the invention of instrumental music (singing, they insist, was given directly by God to Adam – thus an endlessly reiterating controversy over the appropriateness of instrumental music in worship); on the other, literary and scriptural critics have tended to read his as a brief for all of the arts, for human creativity in general.[2]

In her long poem retelling the story of Jubal and some of its consequences, George Eliot opts for a very straightforward and centrist interpretation. Although her critics, as we shall see, still strain to read Eliot's Jubal as a figure

---

[1] Genesis 4: 19–22, KJV.
[2] On the former, see the general discussion in Chapter 2 of Warren Dwight Allen's *Philosophies of Music History: A Study of General Histories of Music 1600–1960* (New York: Dover, 1962), originally written in 1939 but never surpassed or even matched in intellectual scope. In a characteristic sentence summarizing the argument of many early treatises, Allen concludes that "in other words, it must be admitted that man invented instruments, but not that man invented music" (56).

of "the artist," I will argue that he, along with the protagonists of many of her other poems, embodies a much more restricted focus on music itself; this focus is readily understood not only in terms of Eliot's own biography and her deep attachment to music, but also as a feature of Victorian culture with a centrality and a particularly resonant set of meanings of its own.

Music in George Eliot's poetry

The story of George Eliot's devotion to music is well known and has been frequently recounted. Her biographers uniformly provide information about her childhood music study, her lifelong piano playing, and her regular and eager concert and opera attendance; her diaries and correspondence richly round out our sense of a woman both dedicated to music and quite knowledgeable about it. Before meeting George Henry Lewes (1817–1878) she had gone regularly to the opera with her friend Herbert Spencer (1820–1903), and afterwards she and Lewes were frequent presences at London and continental musical events. Later in her career, when her literary reputation had begun to outweigh the social opprobrium she suffered for living unmarried with Lewes, guests came to their home for regular afternoon musicales.[3] Music is a nearly constant presence in her writing as well, and its deployment in the novels (Eliot's most intensively studied body of writing, of course) has been the focus of a significant amount of criticism.[4]

There is – and has been since its original publication – widespread critical consensus that George Eliot's poetry is not of the quality of her fiction, even that it is frankly poor; accordingly, there is little critical writing about it from recent decades, given her status as a literary figure. And yet some critics have

---

[3] For a compact version of the story, see Beryl Gray's entry on "music" in the *Oxford Reader's Companion to George Eliot*, ed. John Rignall (Oxford: Oxford University Press, 2000). Another brief sketch is offered by Alice Lynes, "George Eliot and Music," *George Eliot Fellowship Review* 1 (1991): 2–3.

[4] Studies on the general topic include Alison Byerly, "'The Language of the Soul': George Eliot and Music," *Nineteenth-Century Literature* 44 (1989): 1–17; Beryl Mary Gray, *George Eliot and Music* (New York: St Martin's 1989); Robert L. Jacobs, "The Role of Music in George Eliot's Novels," *Music Review* 45 (1984): 277–282. On the most musical of all her novels, criticism that also sheds light on the larger question includes Marghanita Laski, "The Music of *Daniel Deronda*," *The Listener* 96 (1976): 373–374; Shirley Frank Levenson, "The Use of Music in *Daniel Deronda*," *19th-Century Fiction* 24 (1969): 317–334; E.A. McCobb, "The Morality of Musical Genius: Schopenhauerian Values in *Daniel Deronda*," *Forum for Modern Language Studies* 19 (1983): 321–330; Phyllis Weliver, "Music as a Sign in *Daniel Deronda*," *George Eliot Review* 27 (1996): 43–48 and her *Women Musicians in Victorian Fiction, 1860–1900: Representations of Music, Science and Gender in the Leisured Home* (Aldershot: Ashgate, 2000); and my own "'Tadpole Pleasures': George Eliot's *Daniel Deronda* as Music Historiography," in *Music in Other Words: Victorian Conversations* (Berkeley: University of California Press, 2004). Also of interest is Karen B. Mann, "George Eliot and Wordsworth: The Power of Sound and the Power of Mind," *SEL* 20 (1980): 675–694. Naturally, a very considerable amount of other critical writing about Eliot also deals with music, even though not taking it as a principal focus.

found good reasons for studying it, apart from sheer literary merit. Barbara Hardy puts it well:

> George Eliot's poems are indifferent wholes but treasure-houses of detail, as Henry James might have said. The very failures in particularity of feeling and language make her verse an awkward and accidental anthology of good ideas. All the things which make it bad as poetry – its illustrativeness, its explicitness, and its abstraction – highlight generalization.[5]

What Henry James did in fact say was much along the same lines:

> Our author's verse is a mixture of spontaneity of thought and excessive reflectiveness of expression, and its value is generally more in the idea than in the form. In whatever George Eliot writes, you have the comfortable certainty, infrequent in other quarters, of finding an idea.[6]

Just so, I have found the poems, and "The Legend of Jubal" (1870) especially, a rich source of understanding of the ways in which musicality can signify and resonate, not only through George Eliot's writing but through Victorian culture generally.

A striking number of her poems are about music or musicians – six out of the ten published in the original *Jubal* volume,[7] if one counts the metaphoric "choir invisible" in the poem that is routinely referred to as Eliot's "anthem" to the Positivist goal of achieving immortality by living effectively and generously in the world, "So to live is heaven: / To make undying music in the world,"[8] and at least one unpublished poem, "Erinna," whose heroine sings her way through her bondage to the "insect labor" of her spindle (11).[9]

---

[5] Barbara Hardy, *Particularities: Readings in George Eliot* (London: Peter Owen, 1982) 183.
[6] Henry James, "George Eliot's *The Legend of Jubal*," *North American Review* 119 (October 1874): 484–489; rpt. in *A Century of George Eliot Criticism*, ed. Gordon S. Haight (London: Methuen, 1965) 87–92.
[7] The original volume, entitled *The Legend of Jubal and Other Poems*, appeared in May 1874 and contained ten poems: the title poem, "Agatha," *Armgart*, "How Lisa Loved the King," "A Minor Prophet," "Brother and Sister," "Stradivarius," "Two Lovers," "Arion," and "O May I Join the Choir Invisible." When the Cabinet Edition of her works was prepared in 1878, four more poems were added: "A College Breakfast-Party," "Self and Life," "Sweet Evenings Come and Go, Love," and "The Death of Moses." Also in her poetic canon, of course, is the novel-length verse drama *The Spanish Gypsy*.
[8] "O May I Join the Choir Invisible," lines 10–11. On the hermeneutic significance of music in this poem, see Martha S. Vogeler, "The Choir Invisible: The Poetics of Humanist Piety," *George Eliot: A Centenary Tribute*, eds Gordon S. Haight and Rosemary T. Van Arsdel (Totowa, NJ: Barnes & Noble, 1982) 64–81. Unless otherwise indicated, the text I am using for the poems is the Cabinet Edition, whose production Eliot supervised. See George Eliot, *The Legend of Jubal and Other Poems, Old and New*, Cabinet ed. (1874; Edinburgh: Blackwood, 1879).
[9] Margaret Reynolds is almost alone in having noted the pervasive thematics of music in Eliot's poetry. See her entry on "poetry of George Eliot" in the *Oxford Reader's Companion to*

The verse drama *Armgart*, which recently has been much studied by feminist critics for its apparent ambivalence about the artistic career of a strong and creative woman, is rather like a sketch for the later character of the Princess Halm-Eberstein, the problematic opera diva who was Daniel Deronda's mother.[10] Armgart is a successful and bouquet-decked singer whose delight and confidence in her musical power tend to express themselves as contempt for ordinary women and the satisfactions of family and service – values that we know very well her creator held dear despite the irregularity of her own life and career. After an illness, Armgart discovers (or fancies) that her voice has been ruined; her rage and terror at the prospect of ordinariness grow even more consuming.

> I read my lot
> As soberly as if it were a tale
> Writ by a creeping feuilletonist and called
> "The Woman's Lot: a Tale of Everyday:"
> A middling woman's, to impress the world
> With high superfluousness; (V: 126–131)

By the end, though, Armgart's companion Walpurga has helped her to become resigned to a less spectacular career in which she might be made useful by teaching the delights of music to others.

"Arion," a verse retelling of a story from Herodotus, concerns a figure somewhat like Jubal himself. In the original, he is described as "Arion of Methymna, who as a player on the harp, was second to no man living at that time, and who was, so far as we know, the first to invent the dithyrambic measure, to give it its name, and to recite in it at Corinth".[11] Victim of a thieving crew while sailing from Tarentum to Corinth, Arion promises to leap into the sea (saving the sailors the trouble of murdering him) if they will allow him to play and sing one song first; unbeknownst to the nefarious sailors, a

---

George Eliot. For the text of "Erinna," see *George Eliot: Collected Poems*, ed. Lucien Jenkins (London: Skoob, 1989).

[10] See Wendy Bashant, "Singing in Greek Drag: Gluck, Berlioz, George Eliot," *En Travesti: Women, Gender, Subversion, Opera*, eds Corinne E. Blackmer and Patricia Juliana Smith (New York: Columbia University Press, 1995) 216–241; Kathleen Blake, "*Armgart* – George Eliot on the Woman Artist," *Victorian Women Poets: A Critical Reader*, ed. Angela Leighton (Oxford: Blackwell, 1996) 82–87; Rebecca Pope, "The Diva Doesn't Die: George Eliot's *Armgart*," *Embodied Voices: Female Vocality in Western Culture*, eds Leslie C. Dunn and Nancy A. Jones (Cambridge: Cambridge University Press, 1994) 139–151; and Susan Rutherford, "The Voice of Freedom: Images of the Prima Donna," *The New Woman and Her Sisters: Feminism and Theater 1850–1914*, eds Vivien Gardner and Susan Rutherford (Ann Arbor: University of Michigan Press, 1992) 95–113. Daniel's mother's given name is Leonora, and Armgart realizes the terrible results of her illness precisely in her failed attempt to *sing* Leonora.

[11] Herodotus, *History*, book 1, *The Internet Classics Archive*, ed. Daniel C. Stevenson, 1994–2000, Massachusetts Institute of Technology, November 2002 <http://classics.mit.edu/index.html>.

dolphin responds to Arion's song and carries him to safety on its back. Eliot's version, oddly enough, omits the celebrated dolphin altogether in favor of a different denouement:

> The last long vowels trembled then
> As awe within those wolfish men:
> > They said, with mutual stare,
> > Some god was present there. (57–60)

With George Eliot, the issue is always music and its power. One of the more charming versions of this insistent theme is "Stradivarius," in which the painter Naldo taunts old Antonio with his subservient and unromantic craftsman's identity, not creating like a real artist but only mechanically "turning out work" over and over. But Antonio is unperturbed, fully understanding the value of his contribution. Stressing that it takes three separate geniuses to make the music live, the author's voice frames the story with a direct address to a startlingly contemporary reader:

> Your soul was lifted by the wings to-day
> Hearing the master of the violin:[12]
> You praised him, praised the great Sebastian too
> Who made that fine Chaconne; but did you think
> Of old Antonio Stradivari? (1–5)

From Boccaccio Eliot took the story of "How Lisa Loved the King."[13] A young Sicilian girl spies King Pedro of Aragon from a window during a procession, and sickens near to death for lack of an opportunity to tell him of her reverence and love for him. When her distraught parents promise any favor she might choose to tempt her back to life, Lisa summons the musician Minuccio and in effect commissions from him a song that will communicate her feelings to the King. So successful is the musical emissary that Pedro himself comes to visit her sickbed, cajoling her back to health with a kiss and promises of an extravagant future.

Eliot retells the story very faithfully, though adding frequent incidental mentions of music throughout and one extensive and characteristic paean to the power of Lisa's song.

> > It seemed a pleading cry,
> And yet a rounded perfect melody,
> ...
> Trembling at first, then swelling as it rose,
> Like rising light that broad and broader grows,

---

[12] Later in the poem the violinist is identified as Joseph Joachim.
[13] Giovanni Boccaccio, *The Decameron*, 10th day, 7th novel, trans. J.M. Rigg (1903; London, 1921), *Decameron Web*, eds Massimo Riva and Michael Papio, Brown University, 7 December 2002 <http://www.brown.edu/Departments/Italian_Studies/dweb/dweb.shtml>.

> It filled the hall, and so possessed the air
> That not one breathing soul was present there,
> Though dullest, slowest, but was quivering
> In music's grasp, (363–364, 367–372)

Jubal's story

It is, however, in the title poem "The Legend of Jubal" that George Eliot's passion for music and her beliefs about its importance in the human world come through most clearly and are elaborated most vividly. The circumstances of its composition are poignant, and may well account in part for her decision at that moment to develop a theme that was so emotionally meaningful to her; they account as well for a gap in immediate documentary evidence about the poem's composition that is nearly unique in her body of work. In a diary entry for 5 October 1869 Eliot wrote, "*I have begun a long-meditated Poem: 'The Legend of Jubal,'*" but have not written more than 20 or 30 verses."[14] It was just during the period in which her companion G.H. Lewes's son Thornton had come home very ill from South Africa, and was evidently dying. Eliot had become close to the boy and exhausted herself in caring for him and hoping somewhat unrealistically for his recovery. On October 19 we read, "This evening, at half past six o'clock our dear Thornie died," after which there are no further diary entries until the following May.[15]

Letters too are very sparse during the period immediately following Thornie's death, and in those that exist there is hardly any mention of "Jubal" except for a March 1870 letter to her publisher, John Blackwood, indicating that she had sold the poem to Macmillan.[16] The research notebooks reveal an equivalent reticence; the editors of those from the immediate period observe that, after Thornie's death, Eliot abandoned her normal note-taking habits and resumed them only in the following spring.[17] A table listing the genealogy from Cain through Lamech to Jubal and his brothers is laconically given, and "Vision of Jubal" is included in a list of "themes for poems" – another on "The Death of Pan" is also projected, though never written – but otherwise there is silence (Pratt and Neufeld, 78, 72).

If we do not have as much evidence about her compositional procedures or her aesthetic intentions for "Jubal" as is so richly available for many of her

---

[14] George Eliot, *The Journals of George Eliot*, eds Margaret Harris and Judith Johnson (Cambridge: Cambridge University Press, 1998) 138. The emphasis is Eliot's.

[15] Cynthia Ann Secor reports that there is some evidence that the idea for the poem came to Eliot while reading Hermann Helmholtz's *Lehre von dem Tonempfindungen*, which her diary reports her doing on 24 February of that year. See Cynthia Ann Secor, "The Poems of George Eliot: A Critical Edition with Introduction and Notes," diss., Cornell University, 1969, 16.

[16] For these letters, see volume 5 (1869–1873) of *The George Eliot Letters*, ed. Gordon S. Haight (New Haven: Yale University Press, 1955). George Eliot's letter to John Blackwood is dated 7 March 1870.

[17] *George Eliot's* Middlemarch *Notebooks*, eds John Clark Pratt and Victor A. Neufeld (Berkeley: University of California, 1979) xxiii.

other works, we do have an intriguing letter to Blackwood from March of 1874, proposing the publication of some of her poems in the volume that became *The Legend of Jubal and Other Poems*. She tells him that "every one of those I now send you represents an idea which I care for strongly and wish to propagate as far as I can."[18] Triangulating, so to speak, from her fiction and from the body of contemporary writing about it that was already considerable, it is not difficult to understand the moral and aesthetic messages of the poem and their reception by her readers.

The story itself is simple enough: after his banishment from Eden for murdering his brother, Cain wanders eastward and settles in a land where he and his descendants live happily and without the knowledge of death. "Thus generations in glad idlesse throve" (40) until one day Lamech accidentally kills a young man with a thrown stone, "And a new spirit from that hour came o'er / The race of Cain" (82–83).[19] In this "new spirit" Lamech's sons develop ambition and determine to discover means of human immortality. When Jubal has achieved his invention of music and taught it to the people, he leaves home and travels the earth, collecting new sounds and "sowing music" (506). Returning home years afterward, he finds his own people steeped in music and in ceremonial celebration of his name; alas, they do not recognize him or connect him with the "Jubal" of their mythic memory. "[S]coffing at a madman's lie" (695), they run him off to die solitary and unappreciated.

Most of the poem's nearly eight hundred lines are spent, typically enough for Eliot, ruminating on the implications of the characters' actions, and in particular of Jubal's discovery. This outcome of Cain's wandering into the land "east of Eden" is adumbrated in an earlier Eliot poem, "Ex Oriente Lux" (1866), whose poetic conceit is the birth, not only of light but of music as well, in an appropriately cosmic and apparently natural process. As "Asia was the earliest home of light", so

> Ever wandering sound
> That dumbly throbbed within the homeless vast
> Took sweet imprisonment in song and speech –
> Like light more beauteous for shattering,
> Parted melodious in the trembling throat
> Of the first matin bird; made utterance
> From the full-rounded lips of that young race[20]

---

[18] George Eliot to John Blackwood, 6 March 1874, *George Eliot Letters*, 6: 25–26.
[19] The immediately following verses in Genesis tell this part of the story:
> And Lamech said unto his wives, Adah and Zillah, Hear my voice; ye wives of Lamech, hearken unto my speech: for I have slain a man to my wounding, and a young man to my hurt.
> If Cain shall be avenged sevenfold, truly Lamech seventy and sevenfold.
> (Genesis, 4: 23–24)

[20] George Eliot, "Ex Oriente Lux," *George Eliot: Collected Poems*, ed. Lucien Jenkins (London: Skoob, 1989) 12–18. All subsequent citations from this poem are from this edition.

But in "The Legend of Jubal" it is the experience of death, stirring the people out of their "idlesse" with "the stings / Of new ambition" (112–113), that prompts and perhaps necessitates the birth of music.

The poet considers what mankind has gained from the inventions of each of the three brothers, and one can almost feel her effort not to give Jabal and Tubal Cain too short shrift in her eagerness to celebrate the invention of music. In Jabal's case she is tender about the "star-browed calves" (160) and "silly sheep" (164) and even "sharp-nosed" (180) wolf cubs, and lets us know the ultimate value of home life and family:

> This was the work of Jabal: he began
> The pastoral life, and, sire of joys to be,
> Spread the sweet ties that bind the family
> O'er dear dumb souls that thrilled at man's caress,
> And shared his pains with patient helpfulness. (185–189)

In Tubal Cain's case there is more skepticism, although the romance of the roaring furnace and of the hard metals subdued by the sheer force of creative will is stirringly depicted; but there is a sinister side to his inventions, which

> were as seeds instinct with hidden power.
> The axe, the club, the spikèd wheel, the chain,
> Held silently the shrieks and moans of pain;
> …
> Thus to mixed ends wrought Tubal; (217–219, 224)

and the poor blacksmith is even taxed with the forging of thirty portentous pieces of silver (226).[21]

Jubal, too, comes upon the first glimmerings of his invention in the smithy, hearing potential music in the clang of hammer on anvil – just as Pythagoras did in an alternative originary myth that had, ever since Boethius, been entangled with Jubal's story.[22] The recounting of Jubal's auditory "vision," however, cannot be contained in a few brief stanzas but goes on for pages; although some contemporary critics found fault with her inability or unwillingness to describe the actual act of invention with her customary

---

[21] Long tradition holds that Tubal Cain used his technological inventions to further the murderous schemes of his namesake ancestor; Rudyard Kipling's poem "Jubal and Tubal Cain" is a case in point.

[22] See Gaudentius, "Harmonic Introduction," Section ii (n.d., but before 6th century C.E.) in *Source Readings in Music History*, ed. Thomas J. Mathiesen, vol. 1 (New York: Norton, 1998) 74: "They tell the story that Pythagoras took the beginning of his discovery of these ratios from the chance that while passing by a smithy, he sensed that the strikings of the mallets upon the anvil were dissonant and consonant" (translated by the editor). Because there were many manuscript sources for Gaudentius all the medieval theorists knew the story, and as classical learning began to collide with Christian, Pythagoras's name and Jubal's became very widely confused. Treatises began to ponder whether Jubal or Pythagoras was the inventor of music, and the tradition of Pythagoras in the smithy was eventually transferred to Jubal.

obsessive realism, that invention is, nonetheless, the point, and readers are given no opportunity to miss it.[23] Taken together, the stories of the three brothers present an entire cosmology, complete with relative valuations that richly exemplify themes and attitudes well known from Eliot's fiction and familiar in criticism since her own day – her reverence for family ties and home life, her mixed curiosity about and suspicion of technology, and her pure worship of music.

Finally, and most shatteringly, the poem explores Jubal's disillusionment when he returns home from filling the world with music –

> "No farther will I travel: once again
> My brethren I will see, and that far plain
> Where I and Song were born." (535–537)

– and his own people do not recognize him. Jubal has aged, changed, worn out, and by now is remembered only by reputation and as a mythic figure, "the tune-writ story of a man" (568).[24]

> Jubal was but a name in each man's faith
> For glorious power untouched by that slow death
> Which creeps with creeping time; (691–693)

In the end, Jubal himself has to learn the most painful lesson: his discovery, music, counts for more than the ignominy he now suffers, and its immortality is of greater import than his own. Jubal accepts his lesson and expires in a kind of *Lieder-Tod*, a musical death:

> The words seemed melting into symphony,
> The wings upbore him, and the gazing song
> Was floating him the heavenly space along,
> Where mighty harmonies all gently fell
> Through veiling vastness, like the far-off bell,
> Till, ever onward through the choral blue
> He heard more faintly and more faintly knew,
> Quitting mortality, a quenched sun-wave,
> The All-creating Presence for his grave. (783–791)

Jubal's musical morality

There is no doubt that this poem, like the others, teaches moral lessons larger than their specific messages about music, and these are the ones Eliot's

---

[23] W. Minto writes about this absence at length. See his review in *The Examiner* 16 (1874): 513–514; rpt. in *George Eliot: Critical Assessments*, ed. Stuart Hampshire, 4 vols (East Sussex: Helm Information, 1996) 1: 341–345.

[24] The Cabinet edition has "rune-writ," corrected in the Skoob edition to "tune-writ," which makes better sense in the context.

Victorian contemporaries and near successors tended primarily to see. "The idea here is a fine one," wrote Elizabeth Haldane in 1927, "and it expresses the doctrine George Eliot was so fond of enunciating, that the important thing is to have the consciousness that we have tried to do our duty in life, and that reward or fame as such are of little or no account."[25] This interpretation, focusing on duty and self-sacrifice, had a long pedigree, and it is an interpretation that the book's earliest reviewers tended to draw out to an almost excruciatingly moralizing extent. Eliot's first biographer, Mathilde Blind, summed up the message of the poetry in this way:

> Nowhere do we perceive so clearly as here the profound sadness of her view of life; nowhere does she so emphatically reiterate the stern lesson of the duty of resignation and self-sacrifice; or that other doctrine that the individual is bound to the social good, that he has no rights save the right of fulfilling his obligations to his age, his country, and his family.[26]

Another reviewer entirely concurred:

> The scientific truth that the welfare of the individual must yield to that of the race is true in a higher sense as an ethical and political precept. No modern writer has seen more clearly than George Eliot the necessity of insisting on this doctrine.[27]

It was, to be sure, a "doctrine" given ample warrant in her fiction, although she seldom put it quite so baldly. The question thus arose whether the poem was ultimately optimistic or pessimistic. Most of its contemporaries saw it as fairly grim – Henry James called its denouement "the expression of a pessimistic philosophy which pivots upon itself only in the face of a really formidable ultimatum" (90) – and certainly the disillusionment and solitude of Jubal's end support that reading. The impression was intensified by critics' fascinated focus on the poem's way of positing death as the spur to creativity. "The glorification of Death is of course the burden of 'Jubal,'" wrote G.A. Simcox in a review of the published volume of poems, and R.H. Hutton suggested that the poem "might ... have been more fitly termed a hymn in praise of death."[28]

Such a reading of "Jubal" did not necessarily give reason for disapproval, of course; on the whole Victorian critics liked the poem – it was the runaway

---

[25] Elizabeth S. Haldane, *George Eliot and Her Times: A Victorian Study* (New York: Appleton, 1927) 225.

[26] Mathilde Blind, *George Eliot* (London: Allen, 1883) 169. Her husband John Cross's biography – *George Eliot's Life as Related in Her Letters and Journals* – did not appear until 1885.

[27] Anonymous review of "George Eliot's Poems," *Saturday Review* 37.972 (13 June 1874): 756.

[28] G.A. Simcox, untitled review in *Academy* 5 (May 1874): 533–534; rpt. in *George Eliot: Critical Assessments*, 348; Richard Holt Hutton, "George Eliot," in *Essays Theological and Literary* (London: Strahan, 1871) 2: 347.

favorite among those in the volume – and seemed to enjoy being challenged by what they saw as Eliot's gloomy philosophy, and by 1870 they were predisposed to admire her extravagantly in any event.[29] With a kind of morbid glee Margaret Oliphant (1827-1897) referred to it as a poem in which "George Eliot has demonstrated, or attempted to demonstrate, the wonderful uses of the fact of death; the quickening of feeling, the growth of mental energy which proceeded from its first realization."[30] But somehow the characteristic Victorian faith in human progress balked at the idea that invention and creativity depended on so heavy a cost, even as it worried obsessively over it. Only a few decades afterward, Leslie Stephen objected: "The moral that, as we have got to die, we should be content with the consciousness of having played our part, without expecting reward or bothering ourselves about posthumous fame, is more to the purpose."[31] And indeed, to go farther, if we take the music seriously, Jubal's rhapsodic death may strike us altogether differently: "as we have got to die," as Stephen says, what music-lover could wish for better?

But taking the music seriously is just what is seldom done, even by modern critics who, needless to say, have utterly different interests from those common among the poem's contemporaries. Cynthia Secor offered an early instance of what has become the principal interpretive trope of this criticism by calling attention to "Jubal's" exploration of the role of the artist, characterizing it as a "justification of the poet's trade" and, vis-à-vis the other poems in the volume, the introduction to a whole series of artist-poems (67, 71). To pursue this kind of interpretation, it is necessary to read the musician as a kind of metaphor for the poet, or for the artist in general, a reading that very quickly became standard. Bonnie Lisle, for example, suggests that "Jubal" and *Armgart* "explore the origins, nature, and responsibilities of artistry"; Eliot's conclusion, she suggests, is that the artist's privilege "must be redeemed by suffering and self-annihilation." [32]

The trope can be further refined, as it has been by several critics with feminist principles in mind, as a somewhat anxious exploration of the role of the woman artist in particular. Gillian Beer has noted that "her chosen figure for the creative woman is not the writer, who might too much draw attention to George Eliot's own activity in her work. Instead it is the musician, and in particular the singer."[33] Beer is thinking of the fictional characters, from Caterina Sarti in "Mr Gilfil's Love-Story" (*Scenes of Clerical Life*) straight through to Alcharisi and Mirah in *Daniel Deronda*, but her observations are

---

[29] "The Legend of Jubal" was composed between *Middlemarch* (1874) and *Daniel Deronda* (1876); both the individual poem and the subsequent volume of poems were thus presented to a public already in awe of George Eliot and, what is more, inclined to view her as a sibyl or wisdom figure.
[30] Margaret Oliphant, "William Smith," *Blackwood's Edinburgh Magazine* 112 (October 1872): 434. Quoted in Secor, 65.
[31] Leslie Stephen, *George Eliot* (New York: Macmillan, 1909) 171.
[32] Bonnie J. Lisle, "Art and Egoism in George Eliot's Poetry," *Victorian Poetry* 22 (1984): 263, 265.
[33] Gillian Beer, *George Eliot* (Bloomington: Indiana University Press, 1986) 202.

also obviously relevant to Armgart, Erinna, and perhaps Lisa; from there it is not far back to the supposition that Stradivarius, Arion, and Jubal himself stand in for the poet's own intense ambivalence about the rights and prerogatives of the gifted creative individual, the musician's identity being a psychically-defensive displacement of the poet's. Rosemary Ashton identifies this process precisely, suggesting that "'The Legend of Jubal' ... seems to be a displaced expression of her anxiety about her writing past, present, and future," and Angela Leighton and Margaret Reynolds agree that her poetry in general can "reveal something of her attitudes to art and womanhood which the novels conceal".[34] Even Rosemarie Bodenheimer, who protests against the over-simple notion of such a displacement, summarizes the musical poems with a generalization of her own: "'The Legend of Jubal' (1869[sic]) and the minor poem 'Stradivarius' (1873) specifically pursue aspects of the relationships among ambition, fame, and artistry."[35]

It may seem naive, in the face of this nearly unanimous onslaught of interpretation, to assert that the poem is really (or, at the very least, is also) about *music* – but so, I will insist, it is. Let me stress that I have no particular disagreement with the customary line of interpretation; there is good evidence that the poet herself did indeed suffer from just such sorts of ambivalence and uncertainty, accusing herself repeatedly of egoism and unseemly ambition. But can it be possible, really, that George Eliot tells so many stories about music and musicians *only* to point us in the general direction of "the artist" or of ambitious people altogether? This strikes me as more an artifact of the thematic concerns of late-twentieth-century literary criticism than a trait of Eliot's interests as a poet. What I wish is only to suggest that there is more still to be gleaned, more that will not be clearly seen unless Eliot's purposeful focus on *music as such* is faced directly.

What could make music so especially important, and what might those "ideas" be that she wished to "propagate" in her poetry? There is throughout the poetry an interesting suggestion that "the dancer and the dance" are not only distinguishable but are in fact rivals, and in ways that seem peculiar to music, that art in which so many different creative roles are entailed.[36] Stradivarius, as we have seen, reminds us of the crucial role played by the humble maker of instruments, without which there would be no music regardless of either composer's or performer's genius. Armgart runs afoul of her mentor's artistic disapproval by overstepping the bounds of her interpretive

---

[34] Rosemary Ashton, *George Eliot: A Life* (London: Hamilton, 1996) 302; Angela Leighton and Margaret Reynolds, eds, *Victorian Women Poets: An Anthology* (Oxford: Blackwell, 1995) 221.

[35] Rosemarie Bodenheimer, "Ambition and Its Audiences: George Eliot's Performing Figures," *Victorian Studies* 34 (1990): 7–34.

[36] An imagined combat for the aesthetic laurels was a standard trope of earlier nineteenth-century music criticism. See, for instance, Lydia Goehr, *The Imaginary Museum of Musical Works: An Essay in the Philosophy of Music* (Oxford: Clarendon Press, 1992); David Gramit, *Cultivating Music: The Aspirations, Interests, and Limits of German Musical Culture, 1770–1848* (Berkeley: University of California Press, 2002).

role and adding musical details that should be the sole prerogative of the composer:

> O I trilled
> At nature's prompting, like the nightingales.
> Go scold them, dearest Leo. (I: 102–104)

For Jubal, the moral crisis is his ego-destroying discovery that while humankind celebrates the mythic memory of "Jubal" and their devotion to his invention, it entirely fails to recognize him in the flesh. This pattern reminds us – again – that for Eliot it is always the *music*, not the individual musician, whose meaningfulness supersedes other concerns. All of these poetic characters, and we as well, must learn to subordinate ourselves to its requirements. But why should it have this paramount importance?

Beryl Gray observes that, for Eliot, music – rather than any other form of art – was "the delicate messenger to the utmost sanctuary of the soul," and that for her there was a paramount relation "between feeling ... and auditory sensibility" that was "integral to the idea of moral development."[37] It is not simply that music expresses or stimulates feeling – a Victorian, as well as a Romantic, commonplace; rather this "messenger" is a diagnostic sign that lets us know the moral condition of an individual. It is a familiar trope of criticism to identify the role of sympathy in Eliot's writing.[38] Well known to have abandoned the evangelical religion of her upbringing, she had replaced its teachings with a humanist creed strongly inflected by the Positivism of her friends of early adulthood, a creed that included dicta like Ludwig Feuerbach's assertion in *The Essence of Christianity* that "God is a feeling being ...: feeling is absolute, divine in its nature."[39] As Suzy Anger has written, "Eliot's fundamental moral principle is that the capacity for sympathy is a necessary condition for a moral agent, since morality grows from the ability to imagine another's state of mind."[40] And the musicality of a character's nature is a direct symptom of his or her capacity for sympathy.

She had a particularly thoroughgoing, though not otherwise unusual for the time, near-literal belief in an ideal development of personality aspiring, as Tennyson put it in the prologue to *In Memoriam* (1850), "That mind and soul

---

[37] This quotation from Eliot's story "The Lifted Veil" is given, and discussed, in Beryl Gray, *George Eliot and Music*, ix.

[38] For a general discussion of this very important aspect of George Eliot's writing, see Elizabeth Ermarth, "George Eliot's Conception of Sympathy," *Nineteenth-Century Fiction* 40 (1985): 23–42. Virtually all of the authors named in note 3 explore this topic, so closely connected to music in Eliot's mind, as do many other critics of Eliot's writing in great variety of contexts.

[39] Ludwig Feuerbach, *The Essence of Christianity* (1841), trans. Marian Evans (Chapman, 1854) 61–62. Quoted in Joseph Wiesenfarth, *George Eliot's Mythmaking* (Heidelberg: Carl Winter, 1977) 38.

[40] Suzy Anger, "George Eliot and Philosophy," in *The Cambridge Companion to George Eliot*, ed. George Levine (Cambridge: Cambridge University Press, 2001) 80.

according well / May make one music".[41] This musical personality, both emerging from and nurturing a higher sensibility, became a recurring aspect of characterization in Eliot's writing, from Arion, whose "melodic soul" makes its appearance in the first line of his eponymous poem, to Daniel Deronda, who is likened to "a cunningly-wrought musical instrument, never played on, but quivering throughout in uneasy mysterious moanings of its intricate structure that, under the right touch, gives music."[42] Daniel's moral earnestness and human sympathy are certified for us in this description, Eliot's highest accolade; though his musicality is as yet untried, we can rest assured that he will rise to the occasion when it is.

And just similarly here: despite the poem's attempt to be fair to the three creative sons of Lamech, nonetheless

> Jubal had a frame
> Fashioned to finer senses, which became
> A yearning for some hidden soul of things, (148–150)

that he found in music.

There is a reciprocal implication as well: not only do musical souls exhibit a kind of special sympathy and sensibility, but music itself is to be understood as having an especially intimate relationship to the soul and thus serving as a kind of model for abstract thought and human understanding of all sorts. At the end of "Ex Oriente Lux" the poet hints at the startling outcome of the birth of human singing: song "[f]rom the full-rounded lips of that young race" (18) like the light fracturing in a continual process of differentiation and speciation (as prescribed by current evolutionary theory), "Clove sense and image subtilly in twain, / Then wedded them, till heavenly Thought was born." (21–22) We conclude that song not only precedes thought in human development, but may indeed be an ontological precondition for it.

One of the characters in Eliot's "A College Breakfast-Party" makes a similar point:

> God, duty, love, submission, fellowship,
> Must first be framed in man, as music is,
> Before they live outside him as a law. (536–538)

Like so many of her musical articles of faith, this one too finds its echo in *Daniel Deronda*. Her poetic epigraph for Chapter 44 insists that

---

[41] George Eliot herself quoted these lines at the end of her scathing review of the evangelical writings of John Cumming, emphasizing her preference for this harmonious personality over the small-minded and crabbed one Cumming advocated. See her "Evangelical Teaching: Dr Cumming," *Westminster Review* 44 (October 1855): 436–463; rpt. in *Essays of George Eliot*, ed. Thomas Pinney (New York: Columbia University Press, 1963) 158–189.

[42] George Eliot, *Daniel Deronda*, Cabinet ed., vol. 3 (1876; Edinburgh: Blackwood, 1878) 315.

> Thus all beauty that appears
> Has birth as sound to finer sense
> And lighter-clad intelligence. (3:3)

But music also has the closest of ties with the moral sense for another reason: because of its saturation with canons of correct measurement and rule. As Eliot writes of Jubal, he gradually learned that music-making required and in turn reinforced this sense,

> Teaching to ear and hand the blissful Right,
> Where strictest law is gladness to the sense
> And all desire bends toward obedience. (347–349)

Again, as in Tennyson, mind and soul – conscience and desire, obedience and pleasure – harmonize.

I would suggest, following this lead, that perhaps the real lesson of Armgart's story is that it is possible to go on being "musical" after the music is gone; indeed, put more strongly, that her real musicality is not in her singing at all but in her moral growth. Having transgressed music's ethical demands by her artistic egotism, she becomes *more* truly musical when, after the crisis in her career, she decides to devote herself to the musical needs of others. The lesson is reminiscent of the sharp contrasts Eliot draws in *Daniel Deronda* between the two flawed (though very differently so) musicalities of Gwendolen Harleth and the diva Alcharisi and the genuine, earnest, and harmonious musical personality of Mirah Lapidoth, with its artistically self-effacing ambition and its readiness to teach and serve others.

Finally, music's rule-governed nature, its intimate association with number and measure, also equips it well to serve as both a reminder of and an antidote to the passage of time. Although all of human culture, the endeavors of the descendants of all three sons of Lamech, serve as means to defeat death and offer human hostages to fortune, it is music that most intimately embodies that foreboding awareness of time, that irruption into antediluvian "idlesse." After the death of Lamech's boy

> Time, vague as air before, new terrors stirred,
> With measured wing now audibly arose
> Throbbing through all things to some unknown close. (89–91)

Perhaps music's own manipulations of time can transform it from fearsome enemy to source of transcendent pleasure.

For George Eliot, as for other Victorians, music also represented a potent community-building force, precisely by virtue of its ability to magnify the human capacity for sympathy. A contemporary writer called it "the panegyric among the fine arts,"[43] an image much reinforced for us by our familiarity with the enormous choral festivals that marked the era and that are so aptly described by the phrase. Jubal too finds that his ecstasy in solitary music-making soon pales, and resolves that

> This wonder which my soul hath found,
> This heart of music in the might of sound,
> Shall forthwith be the share of all our race
> And like the morning gladden common space: (359–362)

Moving outward from his own community into the world, Jubal roams, "listening" – the poet insists – to all the sounds of the earth that could be woven into the playing of his lyre.

> He lingered wandering for many an age,
> And, sowing music, made high heritage
> For generations far beyond the Flood –
> For the poor late-begotten human brood
> Born to life's weary brevity and perilous good. (505–509)

Jubal's context: Music as a site of Victorian moral teaching

A central part of my argument here is that evidence for music's centrality and about the primary meanings that it held for Victorians can be gleaned from just about any source available; musical tropes and metaphors, and even rather serious discussions about music and its effects, are ubiquitous. To illustrate my case I will not invoke the writings of professional musicians or scholars of music, whose particular orientation would certainly be misleading, but will refer instead to sources more prone to take the general pulse accurately: first, numerous articles in *Macmillan's Magazine*, the widely-circulating "shilling monthly" in which Eliot's poem itself first appeared[44] (and thus its own intertextual milieu); second, a variety of writings by those celebrated "Victorian sages" who published to inform and edify their contemporaries and who were widely quoted by them,[45] including the most celebrated book on the

---

[43] "For us in England just now music seems to be what the drama was in the Elizabethan age – the panegyric among the fine arts ... the art that can bring the largest gathering of people into conscious and intelligent sympathy, increasing the pleasure of everyone by the sense that many other persons are sharing it at the same time." Anon., "Notes on Mr. Tennyson's 'Queen Mary'," *Macmillan's Magazine* 32 (1875): 434.

[44] "The Legend of Jubal" made its first appearance in volume 22 of *Macmillan's*, in the first eighteen pages of the issue for May 1870; in the United States it appeared simultaneously in the *Atlantic Monthly* 25 (May 1870): 589–604. For a broader study of musical references and meanings in *Macmillan's* during the editorship of George Grove, see Chapter 2 of my *Music in Other Words: Victorian Conversations*.

[45] George Landow says of the genre of these writings that it "variously combines the attributes of the sermon, Jeremiad, and neo-Classical satire." See *Victorian Types, Victorian Shadows:*

subject, *Music and Morals* (1871) by the Reverend H.R. Haweis, whose title makes explicit the connection at the crux of the matter.

A good first step in understanding the centrality of music and musicality for the Victorians is to take seriously Walter Pater's famed dictum that "all art constantly aspires towards the condition of music" together with the reciprocal observation of which so many apologists for music were fond: as Edward Dannreuther (1844–1905) expressed it, "music has become *the* modern art."[46] There was a widespread sense that developments in European music since Romanticism – its growing technical sophistication, its highly nuanced abstraction, its increasingly powerful expression of feeling, its sometimes self-conscious spirituality – suited the temper of the times particularly precisely. As a result the casual invocation of musical metaphors became rampant; occasionally they took surprisingly concrete and specific form, as in Francis Palgrave's preface to the first edition of *The Golden Treasury* of 1861:

> In the arrangement, the most poetically effective order has been attempted .... within each book the pieces have therefore been arranged in gradations of feeling or subject. The development of the symphonies of Mozart and Beethoven has been here thought of as a model, and nothing placed without careful consideration.[47]

Accordingly, there was some effort in the press to argue that musicality in general was on the rise; given the high prestige that music enjoyed at the time, England was beginning to smart under its continental reputation as *das Land ohne Musik* and, even if not much could be done to produce indigenous Handels and Mendelssohns, at least a proper national susceptibility to the art could be asserted. An anonymous and typical author insisted that a taste for music was developing among the undergraduates at Oxford:

> Not the least of the influences which are at work upon Oxford social life at the present day is the growing appreciation for music which most men have. Every undergraduate "goes in" for music in one shape or another. If he cannot play a fugue, he can sing a comic song; if he does not understand Mozart, he can "interpret" Offenbach ....

Biblical Typology in Victorian Literature, Art, and Thought (Boston: Routledge & Kegan Paul, 1980) 110.
[46] Walter Pater, "The School of Giorgione," in his *Studies in the History of the Renaissance* (1873); rpt. in *Walter Pater: Three Major Texts*, ed. William E. Buckler (New York: New York University Press, 1986) 156. Edward Dannreuther, "Beethoven and His Works," *Macmillan's Magazine* 34 (July 1876): 193.
[47] Quoted in Anne Ferry, *Tradition and the Individual Poem: An Inquiry into Anthologies* (Stanford: Stanford University Press, 2001) 46. The simile was dropped in later editions. Many thanks to Paul Alpers for sending this pertinent quotation to me. As to the widespread use of musical metaphors in other fields of endeavor and in general conversation, see my *Music in Other Words: Victorian Conversations*.

> Many men have pianos in their rooms, and not a few play really well.[48]

And the ubiquitous Arthur Helps (1813–1875) – social commentator, member of the Cambridge "Apostles," and back-pocket moralizer – agreed, remarking, "I say, for one, that the greatest amusement in the world, namely, music, has largely increased, and has judiciously increased."[49] Even Thomas Carlyle's satirical report on the present condition of the opera, with its facetious alarm at the degradation of the divine art that represents the "speech of angels" and its apparent denial of such cheerful reports of increasing British musicality, reminds us through its rhetoric of the high degree of importance that was often attributed to music around mid-century:

> Serious nations, all nations that can still listen to the mandate of Nature, have prized song and music as the highest; as a vehicle for worship, for prophecy, and for whatsoever in them was divine ....
> Reader, it was actually so in Greek, in Roman, in Moslem, Christian, most of all in Old-Hebrew times: and if you look how it now is, you will find a change that should astonish you.[50]

The power of music, and more specifically its moral power, was in truth a creed almost universally subscribed to. The distinguished clergyman and Dean of Westminster, A.P. Stanley (1815–1881), wrote frequently for *Macmillan's* on topics of religion, morality, and Church history. In a piece on the various American Protestant churches he admiringly quotes the beloved Unitarian minister and abolitionist William Ellery Channing (1780–1842) of Boston:

> I am conscious of a power in music which I want words to describe. Nothing in my experience is more inexplicable. An instinct has always led me to transfer the religious sentiment to music; and I suspect that the Christian world under its power has often attained to a singular consciousness of immortality.[51]

The familiar nineteenth-century "sacralization" of the arts is here raised beyond metaphoric status to that of moral truism, combining handily with crude evolutionary assumptions about both Christianity and Western music as ultimate human achievements. As Stanley suggests in the essay, the sentiment expressed here is akin to ones familiar from Cardinal Newman's writings – and, indeed, to a plethora of others that would have been ready to hand for any Victorian reader.

---

[48] Anon., "Oxford Reform," *Macmillan's Magazine* 20 (May 1869): 128.
[49] Arthur Helps, *Social Pressure* (1874; Boston: Roberts Brothers, 1875) 132.
[50] Thomas Carlyle, "The Opera," rpt. in his *Critical and Miscellaneous Essays* (Chicago: Belford, Clarke, n.d.) 115–120.
[51] Quoted in A.P. Stanley, "The Historical Aspect of the American Churches," *Macmillan's Magazine* 40 (June 1879): 105.

J.R. Seeley (1834-1895) went further. His *Natural Religion*, one of many books of the period to explore the cultural implications of evolutionary thought and to hypothesize about the "religion of the future" – the Wagnerian (or, more properly perhaps, Feuerbachian) catchphrase was ubiquitous – was serialized in *Macmillan's* between February 1875 and October 1876. The "natural religion" he advocated bore some resemblances to George Eliot's own Positivist-inflected form of humanism, and one of its most striking elements was to be the reinterpretation of the divide between sacred and secular. Future historians, he suggests, will recognize the present age as "the period when the English mind first clearly grasped the ideas of Art and Science," both of which were now in the process of taking on a "religious character."[52] The arts, with Oratorio as the first pioneer in "a really fruitful alliance between religion and music," would cease to be "captives" of the Church and "in perfect independence ... co-operate with Christianity in that work in which, whatever may be their quarrel with Christianity, they are her natural allies, namely, the work of stemming worldliness and fostering the higher life" (187).

Grappling with aestheticist currents that challenged the more traditional association of art and morality, mainstream critics tried to insist that excellence in both still went hand in hand. "In truth," wrote G.A. Simcox (1837–1900), "the question within what limits it is safe to pursue 'art for art' is hardly one that could be asked in an ideal state of things." He is patently relieved to be able to note that "in music there are hardly any limits [to moral toleration] at all; we can hardly imagine such a thing as a melody immoral in itself, though there are melodies which do not seem profaned when fitted to immoral words."[53] The problem of aesthetic pleasure was one taken up with gusto by the dissident and unmusical Samuel Smiles (1812–1904), popular ethicist and author in 1859 of the portentously-named *Self-Help* along with such other equally inviting titles as *Character* (1871), *Thrift* (1875), and *Duty* (1880). Smiles was at heart a businessman and engineer, and saw no particular merit in aesthetic experience; but his warnings about its dangers are instructive in our context because they rely on exactly the same set of associations.

> It is indeed doubtful whether the cultivation of art – which usually ministers to luxury – has done so much for human progress as is generally supposed. It is even possible that its too exclusive culture may effeminate rather than strengthen the character, by laying it more open to the temptations of the senses .... The gift of the artist greatly differs from that of the thinker; his highest idea is to mould his subject – whether it be of painting, or music, or literature – into that perfect grace of form in which thought (it may not be of the deepest) finds its apotheosis and immortality.[54]

---

[52] Unsigned [J.R. Seeley], "Natural Religion," part x, *Macmillan's Magazine* 37 (January 1878): 186. A similar sort of project is Charles Kingsley's "The Natural Theology of the Future," in volume 23 (March 1871): 369-378.

[53] G.A. Simcox, "Art and Morality," *Macmillan's Magazine* 26 (October 1872): 489.

[54] Samuel Smiles, *Character* (1871; New York: Harper, 1904) 265.

But the general topic of music and morality is one which the Reverend Hugh Reginald Haweis (1838–1901) made singularly his own in his wildly popular *Music and Morals* (1871), which went through at least fifteen editions in its author's lifetime and still more in subsequent decades. The book's influence, which was apparently very great, no doubt stemmed from the resonance of Haweis's argument with beliefs about music that had become familiar and mainstream in Victorian England by this historical moment, just the same moment in which George Eliot's "Legend of Jubal" first appeared.

Music and Morals opens, strikingly, with the same image that George Eliot used in "Ex Oriente Lux," the fracturing of light into many colors; but here the figure is used as the basis for an unusual argument: that the composer has far more work to do, from far less raw material given in nature, than his counterpart in the visual arts. It is one of the aspects of Haweis's insistence upon the very special and quasi-divine nature of musical art. He considers its role as "the language of the emotions" and then, still unwittingly following Eliot, expands upon the way in which thought follows from more immediate emotional experience; this link is fortified by the assertion that the physical properties of music resemble those of emotional experience. "Music will then emerge, like a new Venus from a sea of confused murmur, and announce herself as the royal Art-medium of Emotion,"[55] apparently on inarguable psychological and physiological grounds.

But, of course, this is only the first step on Haweis's path. Given music's centrality in human life, and especially given the fact – here he echoes many another Victorian commentator, as we have seen – that "music is pre-eminently the art of the nineteenth century" (43), it is clearly of great importance to explore its moral force and its role in human moral life, for "who will deny the experience of such Soul-atmospheres must leave a definite impress upon the character?" (51) Ultimately, "if, as we have maintained, music has the power of actually creating and manipulating ... mental atmospheres, what vast capacities for good or evil must music possess!" (52).

Haweis organizes the burden of his moral argument by categories of musical participation, addressing separately the composer, the "executive musician" and, most interestingly, the listener. He is unusual in considering the musical experience of listeners (and, later in the book, of amateur players), although the logic of the cultural situation confirmed him in assuming its centrality from a moral point of view; musical susceptibility being on the rise, and the size of musical audiences likewise, it surely behove any churchman to consider its long-term effects on the spiritual health of the flock. Haweis's argument is thoroughly saturated with the ideology of gender (his was a progressive, although still thoroughly essentialist, view); he scorns the argument that musicians, especially female ones, must be wanting in conventional morals, even though he is persuaded that

---

[55] H.R. Haweis, *Music and Morals* (New York: Harper, n.d.) 31.

> the emotional force in women is usually stronger, and always more delicate, than in men. Their constitutions are like those fine violins which vibrate to the lightest touch. Women are the great listeners, not only to eloquence, but also to music. (102)

But it is clear that everyone, male and female alike, is vulnerable to the powers of music that he is detailing.

What I most want to stress, however, is the moral and emotional seriousness of Haweis's argument and, we can only assume from the book's ubiquity, its resonance with his readers. His (and their) sense of music's power emerges from the text not so much in terms of the logic he pursues as of his rhetoric, sufficiently purple in places but always eloquent in its ultimate failure to achieve its task: language repeatedly pales, simply gives up, before the strength of musical experience:

> Like the sound of bells at night, breaking the silence only to lead the spirit into deeper peace; like a leaden cloud at morn, rising in gray twilight to hand as a golden mist before the furnace of the sun; like the dull, deep pain of one who sits in an empty room, watching the shadows of the firelight, full of memories; like the plaint of souls that are wasted with sighing; like paeans of exalted praise; like sudden songs from the open gates of Paradise – so is Music. (88–89)

Charles Kingsley (1819–1875), another well-known clergyman who clearly shared many of Haweis's attitudes, preached many of these same themes in an extraordinary Christmas Day sermon he titled "Music."[56] He attributes its close relation to morality to its legendary rule-governed nature, just as Jubal came to understand it:

> There is music in heaven, because in music there is no self-will. Music goes on certain laws and rules. Man did not make those laws of music; he has only found them out: and if he be self-willed and break them, there is an end of his music instantly: all he brings out is discord and ugly sounds (166)

Kingsley draws this lesson out to make the Tennysonian point about the harmonious balance of duty and pleasure: "Music, I say, is a pattern of the everlasting life of heaven; because in heaven, as in music, is perfect freedom and perfect pleasure; and yet that freedom comes not from throwing away law, but from obeying God's law perfectly" (167). There is a sense, of course, in which his usage is "merely" metaphoric – "music is a pattern and type of heaven," he says (167), going on to draw the obvious conclusions about the way his listeners should conduct their lives in sweetness and in harmony. But Kingsley also explains to his flock the definitions of both melody and

---

[56] Charles Kingsley, *The Good News of God: Sermons* (London: Parker, 1859) 164–172. I have not been able to discover in what year this sermon was delivered.

harmony, and how they work together, and it is clear that he also has quite a literal reference in mind in citing "the everlasting harmony and melody by which God made the world and all that therein is, and behold it was very good, in the day when the morning stars sang together, and all the sons of God shouted for joy over the new-created earth" (169).

Humor can be just as informative. Charles Lamb confesses, in an essay he calls "A Chapter on Ears," to having no ear for music, and to suffering greatly from this handicap during an era so copiously saturated with it:

> It is hard to stand alone in an age like this, (constituted to the quick and critical perception of all harmonious combinations, I verily believe, beyond all preceding ages, since Jubal stumbled upon the gamut,) to remain, as it were, singly unimpressible to the magic influences of an art which is said to have such an especial stroke at soothing, elevating, and refining the passions.[57]

It is striking, and symptomatic, that Lamb attributes his difficulties to an *excess* of susceptibility – to the "sheer pain" and "inexplicable anguish" musical sound causes him – rather than to any deficiency of sensibility, which would be admitting rather too much. For the widespread belief that Englishmen were becoming more musical entailed, indeed rested upon with considerable optimistic faith, the certainty that they were becoming more sensitive and more sympathetic. Helps wrote that "the ear is an organ of finer sensibility than the eye, according to the measurement of philosophers" and that, furthermore, "strong feelings are generally allied to strong intellects, and both together form the truly great character …. The great man is one of boundless love and extended sympathies."[58] No less a scientific authority than Alfred Russell Wallace (1823-1913) concluded that "the emotions excited by colour and by music, alike, seem to rise above the level of a world developed on purely utilitarian principles."[59]

The same belief, that musicality is associated with a certain emotional vulnerability, is drawn upon in one of the most notorious books of the era, James Anthony Froude's so-called "novel" – really a thinly-disguised combination of autobiography and polemic – *The Nemesis of Faith* of 1848, which retained its unsavory reputation for so long that even the eleventh edition of the *Encyclopedia Britannica* (1911) calls it "an heretical and unpleasant book."[60] Froude had been an associate of Newman and a member of the Oxford movement, ordained in 1845, but then experienced severe religious

---

[57] Charles Lamb, "A Chapter on Ears," *Life, Letters, and Writings of Charles Lamb*, ed. Percy Fitzgerald, vol. 3 (London, 1825) 192. I am grateful to my colleague Craig Davis for suggesting this text to me.
[58] Arthur Helps, *Essays and Aphorisms* (London: Walter Scott, [1871]) 265, 166.
[59] Alfred R. Wallace, "The Colours of Animals and Plants," *Macmillan's Magazine* 36 (October 1877): 471.
[60] This unsurpassed wonder of the reference world is now available online. *Encyclopedia Britannica* (1911), 7 December 2002 <http://1911encyclopedia.org/index.htm>.

doubts which he immediately began to promulgate in publications. Very much a young man's book, tortured and self-absorbed, *Nemesis* follows the mental and spiritual journey of its author's *alter ego* Markham Sutherland in excruciating detail. After Markham has managed to reach a precarious peace in his self-imposed rustication, he begins to play a flute because "music was able to do for him what language could not" for, the narrator assures us, "After all, it is no sign of ill-health of mind, this power of self-surrender to the emotions which nature breathes upon us."[61] But the emotions so richly called forth by the music are unleashed from a troubled and unbalanced personality, and readers soon learn what would not surprise any Victorian: his flute-playing draws Markham into a liaison with a married woman, and eventually spells the doom of both.

For healthy and happy people, though, sympathy remained a positive virtue – indeed, the preeminent one in a culture so reliant upon the development of social interactions of great variety and subtlety. In his best-known book, Arthur Helps advises that

> Sympathy is the universal solvent. Nothing is understood without it.
> The capacity of a man, at least for understanding, may almost be said
> to vary according to his powers of sympathy.

Without sympathy, even given the highest development of every other Christian virtue, he says, "we have had splendid bigots or censorious small people."[62]

These images – and related ones having to do with individual "well-tuned" personalities – are perhaps the Victorian descendants of the ancient *musica humana*, part of the medieval tripartite division of music. Sympathy was a significant binder of the social fabric, and music a major stimulus to that sympathy, so music began to be seen just as Jubal learned to see it, as a fundamental catalyst to the formation of community. Even Samuel Smiles understood the connection, conceding (or perhaps bragging) that

> The English are inartistic for the same reason that they are unsocial.
> They may make good colonists, sailors, and mechanics; but they do
> not make good singers, dancers, actors, or modistes .... What they
> have to do they do in a straightforward manner, but without grace.
> (*Character*, 263)

Smiles's own opinion about the relative merits of these character types is not far to find.

One of the most intriguing contexts in which these assumptions about music and community emerge is the many discussions of the proper role of

---
[61] James Anthony Froude, *The Nemesis of Faith: Or, the History of Markham Sutherland*, 2nd ed. (London: Routledge, 1903) 107.
[62] Helps, *Friends in Council: A Series of Readings and Discourse Thereon* (Boston: Munroe, 1849) 76.

government that regularly appeared in the Victorian press. Ideas about the social role of state and municipality were utterly different from more recent expectations, and every philanthropic intervention (especially those that violated the received understanding of the somewhat brutally misnamed "social Darwinism"[63]) was highly controversial and received by the ruling class with indignation, from the provision of poor relief to the establishment of public schools. Music could serve as an argument in favor, since writers were confident that an investment in musical training would be manifestly repaid in safer streets. Arthur Helps made such an argument:

> There is another mode in which Government may indirectly favour and further one of the best and safest means of recreation. This is by making music one of the subjects for education in all Elementary Schools. It is almost impossible to overrate the effect upon the manners, the morals, and the enjoyments of the people, which may be produced by the encouragement of an art which especially lends itself to the best kind of social recreation .... [In many continental towns] there is music of an excellent kind, and ... the townspeople may be seen ... enjoying with their families the delights of music and of dancing; the time thus spent occupying a large portion of that leisure which is so dangerous when no means are provided for employing it.[64]

On the other hand, the same musically-induced community spirit was widely understood to encourage and whip up religious enthusiasm; Haweis attributes to Henry Ward Beecher sentiments that he surely shared:

> Singing is that natural method by which thoughts are reduced to feeling, more easily, more surely, and more universally than by any other. You are conscious when you go to an earnest meeting, for instance, that while hymns are being sung and you listen to them, your heart is, as it were, loosened, and there comes out of those hymns to you a realization of the truth such as you never had before. (106)

At any rate, such expectations of social harmony – and effective management of the underclasses – offer another perspective on the potential importance of Jubal's discovery. Sincerity, emotional genuineness, truth, community: it is no wonder that interest in the "panegyric" of Victorian society should run high and its images appear so persistently in the discourses of the era.

---

[63] This congeries of doctrines advocating the "survival of the fittest" in human society might more aptly have been called "social Spencerianism," and was in any event largely based on pre-Darwinian models of evolutionary process.
[64] Unsigned [Arthur Helps], "Thoughts upon Government," *Macmillan's Magazine* 26 (July 1872): 220.

Conclusion

Given the dearth of documentary evidence around George Eliot's composition of "The Legend of Jubal," we may never know how she came to choose this particular biblical personage as the subject of a poem. Such a legendary figure – indeed, poetry-writing in general – seems an enigmatic choice for an author as celebrated as she was for an especially meticulous contribution to the nineteenth-century realist project. A number of critical writers have worked to encapsulate her brand of realism under the aspect of widespread nineteenth-century practices of mythmaking and biblical typology, and Felicia Bonaparte has even said that "the failures of Eliot's realism are, in fact, the triumphs of her poetry":[65] that is, the philosophic habit of thought and the strong character of moral teaching that mark all her writing may sometimes wish to escape the bonds of realistic portrayal and reach for the abstract universalizing power of myth. (That ambition is marked, perhaps, by the realization that "Jubal" may be the Babylonian or Sumerian word for "musician," just as "Klesmer" is the Yiddish.[66])

If so, that power is exercised here on behalf of a set of musical values that Eliot held dear, and also held in common with contemporary Victorian society. Taking together all the strands of meaning that cluster around it, it is not surprising how extravagantly she characterizes the great gift of music, "And thus did Jubal to his race reveal / Music their larger soul" (468–469), resonating with the stirring closing lines of her Positivist anthem: "So shall I join the choir invisible / Whose music is the gladness of the world" (44–45).

---

[65] Felicia Bonaparte, *The Triptych and the Cross: The Central Myths of George Eliot's Poetic Imagination* (New York: New York University Press, 1979) 5. See also George P. Landow, *Victorian Types, Victorian Shadows*; Wiesenfarth, *George Eliot's Mythmaking*.

[66] See, for example, the discussion of "Jubal" on *Jewish Encyclopedia* (1901–1906), 7 December 2002 <http://JewishEncyclopedia.com>.

Chapter 6

Musical Reactions to Tennyson: Reformulating Musical Imagery in "The Lotos-Eaters"

Michael Allis

This chapter highlights the significance of Tennyson's use of musical imagery.[1] Although several musical references in the poems could be explored,[2] one work which has particular potential for detailed study is "The Lotos-Eaters." Not only is the musical imagery striking in itself, but the way in which this is connected with themes of sensuality, the siren and the unconscious reflects general concerns within nineteenth-century culture. The importance of Tennyson's poem is suggested by the fact that two eminent British composers, Hubert Parry (1848–1918) and Edward Elgar (1857–1934), chose to use this text as the basis of a musical setting. More significantly, these settings allow us to explore the ways in which composers could reformulate the musical images of the poem in their own compositions – in effect, how they chose to represent the musical representation of the poem. As critical readings of Tennyson's text, the settings also represent a significant contribution to the literary debate over the meaning of the poem. Although studies of musical imagery in British novels and poetry in the nineteenth century have identified a close relationship between the arts,[3] references to

---

[1] An earlier and shorter version of this chapter was presented at a study day on The Idea of Music in Fiction at Reading University in May 2000. I am grateful to those who participated in the discussion at this event, and to Amanda Glauert, Sarah Callis, Bennett Zon and Phyllis Weliver for several helpful suggestions.

[2] Significant musical imagery in Tennyson's poems includes bell imagery, hymn-like or religious music, references to "ancient" music, music and excess, music and Nature, or music and the strange. Of particular interest are the frequent references to song throughout the poems and the embedding of songs within the poetic form. For a brief discussion of auditory images in Tennyson, including music, see Asha Viswas, *Tennyson's Romantic Heritage* (Meerut: Shalabh Prakashan, 1987) 141–146.

[3] See, for example, Allan W. Atlas, "Wilkie Collins on Music and Musicians," *Journal of the Royal Musical Association* 124 (1999): 255–270; Mary Burgan, "Heroines at the Piano: Women and Music in Nineteenth-Century Fiction," *The Lost Chord: Essays on Victorian Music*, ed. Nicholas Temperley (Bloomington: Indian University Press, 1989) 42–67; Beryl Gray, *George Eliot and Music* (London: Macmillan, 1989); Nicky Losseff, "Absent Melody

contemporary British composers in the literary works under discussion have been significant by their absence; this study therefore also helps to reassess perceptions concerning the role of British composers in any connections between music and literature.[4]

Tennyson's poem "The Lotos-Eaters" is, of course, loosely based upon Homer's *Odyssey*, canto nine, lines 82–104. In Homer's tale, Ulysses and his mariners land on an island where the mariners eventually succumb to the pleasures of the lotos fruit. The effects of the fruit create an unwillingness to set sail again, and Ulysses has to drag his crew back to the ship by physical force. However, Tennyson's poem, an introductory narrative followed by a Choric Song, makes no mention of a return to the ship; instead, as John Croker puts it, the poet "leaves the mariners in full song."[5] It was originally incorporated into the set of *Poems* published in December 1832, but was then heavily revised for its reappearance in the *Poems* of 1842.[6] The gap between the two sets represented Tennyson's famous literary silence – a period in which the poet eschewed publication of any significant works. Of the several explanations that have been suggested (including mourning Arthur Hallam's death, or concern over the health of Tennyson's brothers Charles and Septimus), one of the most convincing is Tennyson's reaction to the critical reception of the 1833 *Poems*. All six poems republished in 1842 from the 1833 set ("The Lotos-Eaters," "The Lady of Shallott," "The Miller's Daughter," "Œnone," "The Palace of Art" and "A Dream of Fair Women") were rewritten or rearranged, apparently as a response to detailed criticisms of specific lines. John Croker's hostile review is often cited as being of particular significance, eventually leading to Tennyson's decision, noted in a letter to James Spedding, not "*to be dragged forward again in any shape before the reading public at*

---

and *The Woman in White*," *Music and Letters* 81 (2000): 532–550; Rebecca A. Pope, "The Diva Doesn't Die: George Eliot's *Armgart*," *Embodied Voices: Representing Female Vocality in Western Culture*, eds Leslie Dunn and Nancy A. Jones (Cambridge: Cambridge University Press, 1994) 139–151; Phyllis Weliver, *Women Musicians in Victorian Fiction 1860–1900: Representations of music, science and gender in the leisured home* (Aldershot: Ashgate, 2000).

[4] For a study of another British musical response to the poetry of Tennyson which represents a significant reading of the text, see Linda K. Hughes, "From Parlour to Concert Hall: Arthur Somervell's Song-cycle on Tennyson's *Maud*," *The Lost Chord*, ed. Temperley, 102–118. Somervell's reading of Tennyson inverts aspects of the poetic sequence and eliminates "the least attractive utterances of Tennyson's hero" (116). The composer's prefatory notes to the cycle in the published score also represent a striking contextual commentary upon the poem.

[5] See Croker's review of the 1833 *Poems*, rpt. in *Tennyson: The Critical Heritage*, ed. John D. Jump (London: Routledge and Kegan Paul, 1967) 78. Croker's unsigned critique originally appeared in *Quarterly Review* xlix (April 1833): 81–96.

[6] See Edgar Finley Shannon, Jr, *Tennyson and the Reviewers: A Study of His Literary Reputation and of the Influence of the Critics upon His Poetry 1827–1851* (Cambridge, MA: Harvard University Press, 1952), particularly 36–45. For details of the alterations, manuscript variants and possible textual influences (including Tasso's *Gerusalem Liberate* and Washington Irving's *Columbus*), see Christopher Ricks, ed., *The Poems of Tennyson*, 2nd ed., 3 vols (London: Longman, 1987) 1: 467–477.

present" (original emphasis).⁷ Croker's sarcastic tone, in evidence throughout his critique, is apparent in his discussion of "The Lotos-Eaters":

> The "Lotos-Eaters" – a kind of classical opium-eaters – are Ulysses and his crew. They land on a "charmèd island", and eat of the "charmèd root", and then they sing –
> > Long enough the winedark [wave] our weary bark did carry.
> > This is lovelier and sweeter,
> > Men of Ithica, this is meeter,
> > In the hollow rosy vale to tarry,
> > Like a dreamy Lotoseater – a delicious Lotoseater!
> > We will eat the lotos [*sic*], sweet
> > As the yellow honeycomb;
> > In the valley some, and some
> > On the ancient heights divine,
> > And no more roam,
> > On the loud hoar foam,
> > To the melancholy home,
> > At the limits of the brine,
> > The little isle of Ithica [*sic*], beneath the day's decline.
>
> Our readers will, we think, agree that this is admirably characteristic, and that the singers of this song must have made pretty free with the intoxicating fruit.⁸

It is significant that the original final verse, quoted here by Croker, was completely rewritten in the 1842 version (lines 145–173); the other major alteration was the addition of stanza six.

Music and "The Lotos-Eaters"

"The Lotos-Eaters" begins with forty-five lines of introductory narrative, which recounts how Ulysses and his mariners reached the enchanted island, and, greeted by the "mild-eyed melancholy Lotos-eaters",⁹ were offered the lotos fruit. Musical imagery is introduced as Tennyson describes the effects of the fruit:

> but whoso did receive of them,
> And taste, to him the gushing of the wave
> Far far away did seem to mourn and rave
> On alien shores; and if his fellow spake,

---

⁷ Hallam Lord Tennyson, *Alfred Lord Tennyson: A Memoir by his Son*, 2 vols (London: Macmillan, 1897) 1: 145.
⁸ Croker, rpt. in Jump, *Tennyson: The Critical Heritage*, 78.
⁹ Tennyson, "The Lotos-Eaters," *The Poems of Tennyson*, ed. Ricks, vol. 1, 27. All subsequent citations from Tennyson's poems are taken from this edition and are given in the text using line numbers.

His voice was thin, as voices from the grave;
And deep-asleep he seemed, yet all awake,
And music in his ears his beating heart did make. (30–36)

The effects of the fruit induce a dream-like state and a sense of weariness in relation to their former lives, and one of the mariners proclaims that "We will return no more" (43). This leads to a transformation from speech to song as "all at once they sang, 'Our island home / Is far beyond the wave; we will no longer roam'" (44–45). The eight stanzas which follow represent this Choric Song (simply, a song sung by a choir of voices), and again, music is at the heart of the sense of languor engendered by Lotosland:

There is sweet music here that softer falls
Than petals from blown roses on the grass,
Or night-dews on still waters between walls
Of shadowy granite, in a gleaming pass;
Music that gentlier on the spirit lies,
Than tired eyelids upon tired eyes;
Music that brings sweet sleep down from the blissful skies. (46–52)

Stanzas two to seven alternate between a sense of debate concerning the mariners' former lives and increasingly rich descriptions of the delights of Lotosland ("The full-juiced apple, waxing over-mellow, / Drops in a silent autumn night" [78–79]). The eighth and final stanza reiterates the mariners' decision to leave their former world behind, but again musical imagery is significant, whether in relation to the seductive beauties of the island ("All day the wind breathes low with mellower tone" [147]) or to the contrast with the world of responsibilities and toil, characterized by "a music centred in a doleful song" (162).

Whilst the way in which the subject of music is depicted (and subsequently responded to in musical terms) is the focus of this study, there is of course a separate tradition of using musical metaphors in discussions of poetry, and "The Lotos-Eaters" is no exception. William Buckler, for example, has highlighted the transformation of "narrative poetry (past tense 'they') into dramatic poetry (present tense 'we') that is so profoundly intensified lyrically that it aspires to the condition of music" as a quality which ultimately attracts.[10] R.H. Horne's suggestion that Tennyson "will write you a poem with nothing in it but music, and as if its music were everything, it shall charm your soul,"[11] also highlights the importance of the sound of the poem in musical

---

[10] William E. Buckler, *The Victorian Imagination: Essays in Aesthetic Exploration* (Brighton: Harvester, 1980) 103. See also F.E.L. Priestley, *Language and Structure in Tennyson's Poetry* (London: Andre Deutsch, 1973) 57; J.F.A. Pyre, *The Formation of Tennyson's Style: A study, primarily, of the versification of the early poems* (Madison: University of Wisconsin, 1921) 52–53.
[11] R.H. Horne, "Alfred Tennyson," *A New Spirit of the Age* 2 (1844): 3–32. Partially rpt. in Jump, *Tennyson: The Critical Heritage*, 155.

terms. Tennyson was particularly interested in the vocal nuances connected with performances of his poetry. In relation to "Boädicea," for example, "he [Tennyson] feared that no one could read it except himself, and wanted someone to annotate it musically so that people could understand the rhythm," and yet felt that "If they would only read it straight like prose, just as it is written, it would come all right."[12] Eric Griffiths has suggested that Tennyson's dilemma was due to his poems being written "in the rhythm of the breath" with Tennyson's own "respiration, and other physical motor-rhythms" representing a central aspect of his work: "Tennyson thought *in* melody, and did so because his preoccupation with self-identity over time and beyond time drew him down repeatedly to an encounter with the human body itself as the crucial location of his thinking."[13] With this in mind, it is significant that "The Lotos-Eaters" was created as a complete verbal structure, and was therefore performance/sound-led rather than text-led, before being transferred to written form:

> Once he [Tennyson] was sitting smoking with his feet on the chimney-piece as he spouted "The Lotos Eaters" in its first form; unknown to him, [Arthur] Hallam darted around to a table behind him and took it all down as fast as he could to rescue it from oblivion.[14]

To return to Tennyson's poetic representation of music, however, in terms of wider issues it is striking that Tennyson's musical imagery is associated with other elements which were major concerns in nineteenth-century culture. One of these is the link between music and the unconscious mind.[15] Experiments in mesmerism had highlighted the fact that subjects were often able to display musical skills that were not accessible to them in their conscious state,[16] a feature explored in George Du Maurier's novel *Trilby*

---

[12] Hallam Lord Tennyson, 1: 459. See also William Allingham, *A Diary*, eds H. Allingham and D. Radford (London: Macmillan, 1907) which notes that Tennyson would "not admit that any one save himself can read aloud his poems properly" (95), and that Tennyson "spoke a good deal about the want of some fixed standard of English pronunciation, or even some fixed way of indicating a poet's intention as to the pronunciation of his verses. 'It doesn't matter so much', he said, 'in poetry written for the intellect ... but in mine it's necessary to know how to sound it properly.' I suggested that he might put on record a code for pronouncing his own poetry, with symbolized examples, and he seemed to think that this might be done" (344).
[13] Eric Griffiths, *The Printed Voice of Victorian Poetry* (Oxford: Clarendon, 1989) 107. This is part of a discussion of "Tennyson's Breath," 97–170.
[14] Robert Bernard Martin, *Tennyson: The Unquiet Heart* (Oxford: Clarendon Press, 1983) 92.
[15] See also Tennyson's "The Hesperides," where the singing of the daughters of Hesperus induces in Hanno a dream-like state. For a study of another altered state explored by Tennyson see Ann C. Colley, *Tennyson and Madness* (Athens: University of Georgia Press, 1983). In *Tennyson and the Text*, Gerhard Joseph also suggests that Tennyson often develops the sense of a "claustral state" in poems such as *Mariana*, "The Lady of Shallott," "Merlin and Vivien," and "Tithonus" (36).
[16] Phyllis Weliver discusses the work of John Elliotson (1791–1868) and Chauncy Hare Townshend (1798–1868) in relation to such matters (71–80). See also contemporary references to music and the unconscious in writings such as E.S. Dallas, *The Gay Science*, 2 vols

(1894), where the heroine's voice is transformed under the hypnotic spell of Svengali.[17] Several Victorian novels developed this idea, whether in terms of the recurring theme of music as unconscious memory in Wilkie Collins's *The Woman in White* (1860), or the way in which music shifts Maggie Tulliver's mind in George Eliot's *The Mill on the Floss* (1860) "to a dreamy, imaginative state which she experiences as a gateway to tasting the divine and also involuntarily succumbing to sexual temptation" (Weliver, 202). It was not only musical performance which was perceived to link with the unconscious, but also the element of inspiration in musical composition, as suggested by Hubert Parry:

> When they [composers] come back in a cool and normal state to look at what they have done they may almost laugh in wonder how they came to do it. It is almost as if it were somebody else who had temporarily taken possession, or some capricious spirit that only occasionally deigned to exercise its powers.[18]

The altered state created by the lotos fruit in Tennyson's poem, however, is also connected with the idea of music as a seductive, dangerous art. There are suggestions here of siren imagery (a subject developed more obviously by Tennyson via another Choric Song in "The Sea-Fairies")[19] as "sweet music" (46) represents one of the main temptations of Lotosland; however, one could also argue that the mariners are responding to a siren element within themselves, as it is they who conduct their arguments in favour of remaining on the island through the medium of song – a form of self-temptation. As Phyllis Weliver has illustrated, siren imagery was a recurrent feature in Victorian culture, particularly in the novel;[20] Nina Auerbach has also traced siren/mermaid imagery in the iconography of William Makepeace Thackeray, Edward Burne-Jones, John Everett Millais, Dante Gabriel Rossetti and Arthur Hughes, and the prose of Walter Pater.[21] However, as Weliver points out, "part

---

(London: Chapman, 1866) and Francis Power Cobbe, "Dreams as Illustrations of Unconscious Cerebration," *Macmillan's Magazine* 23 (March 1871): 512–523.

[17] For an interesting discussion of the complex area of music in relation to Trilby's conscious and unconscious state, see Weliver, 245–284.

[18] C. Hubert H. Parry, *Style in Musical Art* (London: Macmillan, 1911) 410. For a discussion of Parry's approach to composition as a whole, see Michael Allis, *Parry's Creative Process* (Aldershot: Ashgate, 2003).

[19] "The Sea-Fairies" represents a direct appeal by the sirens to the mariners: "O listen, listen, your eyes shall glisten / When the sharp clear twang of the golden chords / Runs up the ridgèd sea. / Who can light on as happy a shore / All the world o'er, all the world o'er? / Whither away? listen and stay: mariner, mariner, fly no more" (37–42).

[20] Examples include Rosamond Vincy in George Eliot's *Middlemarch* (1874), who uses her musical arts to ensnare Tertius Lydgate; Gwendolen Harleth in *Daniel Deronda* (1876); and Lady Lucy Audley in Mary Elizabeth Bradden's *Lady Audley's Secret* (1862).

[21] See Nina Auerbach, *Woman and the Demon: The Life of a Victorian Myth* (Cambridge, MA: Harvard University Press, 1982) 88–96, which contains reproductions of Thackeray's illustrations to *Vanity Fair* (1847–1848) and *Pendennis* (1848–1850), and Burne-Jones's painting, *The Depths of the Sea* (1887).

of the Victorian fascination with the image of the singing woman was the inherent difficulty of distinguishing whether she was a siren or angel,"[22] creating layers of subtlety in relation to characters such as Du Maurier's Trilby,[23] or Isabel Vane in Mrs Henry Wood's *East Lynne* (1861).[24]

The problem for Tennyson's critics was how to characterize the poet's position in relation to this siren element (if indeed a position was felt to have been adopted), and hence suggest what the "message" of the poem might be. The critical history of the poem reveals a divergence of opinion – whilst some writers have found the poem to convey effectively a condemnation of the life of the lotos eaters, interpreting the text along moral or didactic lines, others have suggested that such an explicit meaning of the poem is undercut by the sensual languor of the verse, therefore following an aesthetic line of argument. Those promoting the didactic argument have pointed to several factors. Some have focused upon the significance of the revisional process in terms of interpretation, rather than simple technical improvement.[25] Others have suggested that knowledge of Homer's original tale should directly impinge upon considerations of Tennyson's message,[26] or have invoked a number of internal features of the poem.[27] Biographical material has also been cited, with

---

[22] Weliver, 7. See also Weliver for a definition of angel and siren: angels are "pure, passive, a-sexual and unaware of their enchanting grace", whereas sirens "deliberately and independently made music which was seductive and potentially dangerous"(56, 57).

[23] Weliver notes that Trilby "is depicted simultaneously as siren and angel" (18).

[24] "Her [Isabel's] ensuing adultery shocks because Isabel is not portrayed to Archibald, the reader or herself as a powerful siren who knowingly enchants" (Weliver, 99–100).

[25] For Stopford A. Brooke, *Tennyson: His Art and Relation to Modern Life* (London: Ibister, 1894), the recasting of the final section suggests "the sense of a dreadful woe tending upon those who dream" (123). See also Viswas, *Tennyson's Romantic Heritage*, 122 and Alastair W. Thomson, *The Poetry of Tennyson* (London: Routledge & Kegan Paul, 1986) 46. According to James Spedding, the line "And eyes grown dim with gazing on the pilot stars" (part of new material added as stanza six indicated "the first effects of the physical disease upon the moral and intellectual nature." See Spedding, unsigned review, *Edinburgh Review* 77 (April 1843): 373–391, rpt. in Jump, *Tennyson: The Critical Heritage*, 144.

[26] See Priestley: "we are ironically aware throughout of the strong will of Ulysses, the spirit expressed in the trumpeting of the first word, 'Courage!' We know that when the time comes, that hard voice will ring out again and the mariners will troop back to the oars ... The word 'Courage' echoes ironically behind all the languid tones of the chorus" (*Language and Structure in Tennyson's Poetry*, 56). A similar suggestion is made by Jerome Buckley in *Tennyson: The growth of a poet* (Cambridge, MA: Harvard University Press, 1960) 48–49, and by Theodore Redpath, "Tennyson and the Literature of Greece and Rome," *Studies in Tennyson*, ed. Hallam Tennyson (London: Macmillan, 1981) 120.

[27] A. Dwight Culler, *The Poetry of Tennyson* (New Haven: Yale University Press, 1977), for example, points to "the symbolic topography of the isle", "a certain element of excess in the language of the poem which condemns itself", "the slowly increasing length of the stanzas, as if one were sinking lower and lower into lethargy", or the fact that the mariners "appeal to the careless life of nature and the careless life of the gods but to no human precedent" (54). See also Leonée Ormond, *Alfred Tennyson: A Literary Life* (London: Macmillan, 1993), who suggests that the sailors' "very emphasis upon ease is denied by the rhythmic vigour with which they profess its alternative"(46).

particular attention being given to a letter written by Tennyson to his friend William Brookfield, criticizing his opium habit:

> Hollo! Brooks, Brooks! for shame! what are you about – musing, and brooding and dreaming and opiumeating yourself out of this life into the next? ... I think you mentioned a renewal of your acquaintance with the fishermen, which may possibly occur if you will leave off the aforesaid drug, if you do not I can foresee nothing for you but stupefaction, aneurism, confusion, horror and death.[28]

Tennyson's brother Charles was also addicted to opium, leading Peter Levi to view the poem as representing "sadness for Tennyson's friends, and their sadness too as he [Tennyson] feels it to be ... an astonishing exercise in real sympathy."[29]

The aesthetic line of interpretation seems to have begun with Croker's association of poet and subject matter, that "Tennyson – himself, [was] we presume, a dreamy lotos-eater, a delicious lotos eater,"[30] and was perpetuated in the debate concerning Tennyson's suitability to represent the "poet of the age."[31] Critics have questioned the apparent authoritative position of Ulysses,[32] and have suggested that the poem should be read as an autonomous work.[33] Similarly, the relative significance of the internal evidence cited in the didactic argument has been refuted or reinterpreted:

> It is no accident that the most famous lines of this poem nearly all come either from the stanzas pressing the claims of the magical isle or from the conclusion, in which the mariners decide to remain there.

---

[28] Cecil Y. Lang and Edgar F. Shannon, Jr, eds, *The Letters of Alfred Lord Tennyson*, 3 vols (Oxford: Clarendon Press, 1982, 1987, 1990) 1: 70–71.

[29] Peter Levi, *Tennyson* (London: Macmillan, 1993) 92. For a brief discussion of Tennyson's attitude to opium, and the suggestion that several of his poems represented a voicing of concerns over opium use in England, see Roger S. Platizky, "'Like dull narcotics, numbing pain': Speculations on Tennyson and Opium," *Victorian Poetry* 40.2 (Summer 2002): 209–215.

[30] Croker, rpt. in Jump, 78.

[31] Leigh Hunt, for example, in an article in the *Church of England Quarterly Review*, xii (October 1842): 361–376 (rpt. in Jump, 128), characterized the poet as growing "lazy by the side of his Lincolnshire water-lilies" with a mind living "in an atmosphere heavy with perfumes"; similarly, George Gilfillan, in "Alfred Tennyson," *Tait's Edinburgh Magazine* ns xiv (April 1847): 229–234 (rpt. in Shannon, *Tennyson and the Reviewers*, 86–87), warned that "He [Tennyson] must not linger too much upon the memories of the past, neither must he eat of the lotos fruit nor stray in the gardens of the Castle of Indolence, in which we hear he takes more delight than becomes a man so gifted as he". See also Jump, 165; anon., "Alfred Tennyson," *Hogg's Weekly Instructor*, vi (25 December 1847): 281–284, rpt. in Shannon, 87–88; and Michael Thorn, who notes Arthur Hallam's complaint of Tennyson's hedonistic tendencies on their excursion up the Rhine in 1832 and that the poet had "not written a jot of poetry" (*Tennyson* [London: Abacus, 1993] 97).

[32] Christopher Ricks, *Tennyson*, 2nd ed. (London: Macmillan, 1989) 86.

[33] See Buckler: "the reader ... is not free, even in the light of Homer, to rewrite the Tennyson text" (107–108).

Tennyson is subtly loading the dice by the sheer mellifluousness with which he presents one side of the case, so that stern devotion comes out a poor second. This may not have been totally intentional, but whether or not it was is irrelevant; what matters is that Tennyson's best method of argument was not rational but sensual.[34]

The suggestion that such an interpretation may not have been the poet's intention has parallels with the position adopted by the other group of critics, who, perhaps more interestingly, have understood the poem's significance as representing an unsteady conjunction of didacticism and aestheticism, revealing a sense of conflict.[35] Santosh Nath, focusing upon Tennyson's treatment of Greek mythology in general, and the genre of the Choric Song in particular, develops this idea of tension. He notes a number of shared concerns in the three poems ("The Lotos-Eaters," "The Sea-Fairies" and "The Hesperides") that adopt the Choric Song genre,[36] which point to "a definite relationship between the poems" representative of "the conflict between Tennyson the pure artist and Tennyson the poet who is but lately made aware of his responsibility towards society" (16). Nath sees the Choric Songs as a developing metaphor, illustrating a gradual change in Tennyson's aesthetic – a move away from the idea of the social responsibility of the poet:

> The mariners signify the poet sailing on the sea of life. Their reaction to the music floating towards them from the shore in the three poems is a symbolic depiction of the gradual change in the poet's attitude towards art. In "The Sea-Fairies" he resists the magnetic attraction of the world of art under the influence of the Apostles, while in "The Hesperides" he is filled with wonder and admiration at the holy act of its creation. It is in "The Lotos-Eaters" that he willingly submits to art. (33)

---

[34] Robert Bernard Martin, *Tennyson, The Unquiet Heart: A biography* (Oxford: Clarendon, 1983) 164. See also K.C. Kanda, *The Two Worlds of Tennyson: A Reconsideration of Tennyson's Major Poems* (Delhi: Doaba House, 1985), who plays down the significance of internal features cited in the previous argument as being "too slight and subtle, likely to be lost in the abundance of images and harmonies that go to make the fairy land of 'The Lotos-Eaters,'" and hence the Epicurean gods represent no more than a "caveat against the resolution of luxurious detachment" (49–52).

[35] See, for example, J.B. Steane, *Tennyson* (London: Evans Brothers, 1966) who suggests that "Officially he [Tennyson] is writing a denunciation; creatively he is making a defence" (46), and Ricks who identifies the problematic aspect of the poem as "a tension between its existing moment and its unmentioned outcome" (*Tennyson*, 104).

[36] Santosh Nath, *Treatment of Greek Mythology in the Poems of Tennyson* (Aligarh: Printwell, 1992) 9–34. Similarities between the poems noted by Nath include the fact that they are based upon fragmentary episodes from their original sources, that they share an identical structure (a brief narrative opening leading to an embedded song), that the song itself in each case is not actually present in the original, and that they all depict a similar landscape (an island of enchantment) which suggests the abode of the Muses.

Conversely, Isobel Armstrong's more recent political reading of the 1842 version of the poem as "an extraordinary response to the worsening social conditions of the 1840s"[37] posits a greater sense of social responsibility on Tennyson's part. By drawing parallels between the mariners' desire for the lotos fruit and the need of Victorian workers "to allay the horrors of labour," Armstrong suggests a critique both of the impulse and its root cause:

> "The Lotos-Eaters" is both the *expression* of the addictive desire in which drug requires further drugging, and an analysis of the conditions under which the unhappy consciousness and the unhappy body come into being .... In one reading a passive consciousness is the *result* of eating the Lotos. In the second reading exhaustion *causes* the addictive need to forget, rather than being the result of consuming the magic fruit. Behind the second reading is the cruelty of work, brute, mindless labour. (87; original emphasis)

Given this literary debate, the musical settings of Parry and Elgar are of interest in relation to their individual readings of Tennyson's text. More significantly, however, they highlight the ways in which Tennyson's poetic imagery could be reformulated in musical terms.

Hubert Parry: *The Lotos-Eaters* (1892)

Despite the range of poetic texts set by Parry, selective criticisms by particular writers have led to his being associated with a narrower field of literature. These negative perceptions stem, for example, from Arnold Bax's assessment that "Parry set Milton and the safer and more demure Elizabethans,"[38] and Frederick Delius's famous dictum that Parry "would have set the whole Bible to music had he lived long enough."[39] My focus upon connections with Tennyson therefore helps to revise some of these unfortunate generalizations and to place Parry more firmly within the context of his own epoch. In terms of general parallels between the two men, Tennyson's status as official Laureate compares with Parry's status as the central figure in a perceived English Musical Renaissance (hence Elgar's reference to Parry in his Birmingham lectures as "the head of our art in this country");[40] both also explored national sensibilities in the subject matter of their work, whether Tennyson's Arthurian

---

[37] Isobel Armstrong, *Victorian Poetry: Poetry, poetics and politics* (London: Routledge, 1993) 94.
[38] Arnold Bax, *Farewell, My Youth* (London: Longmans, 1943) 27.
[39] Eric Fenby, *Delius as I knew him* (London: G. Bell, 1937) 124.
[40] See Edward Elgar, *A Future for English Music and Other Lectures*, ed. Percy M. Young (London: Dobson, 1968) 49.

poetry and references to historical characters and events,[41] or Parry's twelve sets of solo songs entitled *English Lyrics*, his *English Suite* for strings, and his identification of a national musical rhetoric ("an English directness of expression") in a theme from his symphonic poem *From Death to Life* (1914).

Parry's *The Lotos-Eaters* was the result of a commission from the Cambridge University Musical Society. Due primarily to the efforts of Charles Villiers Stanford (1852–1924), CUMS had already performed Parry's *Prometheus Unbound* in 1881, and commissioned his Second Symphony, "The Cambridge," premiered at the Cambridge Guildhall in 1883.[42] The commission was for a choral work, a type of composition which, with its possible scale, democratic nature, and prospect of frequent performances was eminently suited to a didactic tone. However, since there were no apparent restrictions from CUMS as to subject matter, Parry was able to exercise free choice over his text. This was in stark contrast to guidelines imposed by some of the Festival committees. In 1887, for example, Parry had received a choral commission from Birmingham for the 1888 Festival. He wrote to his mentor and former piano teacher, Edward Dannreuther (1844–1905):

> Now today comes another application from Birmingham for a work of the Oratorical order two hours long for *next year*'s festival. I think I ought not to let such a chance slip if I can do it. But it's very short time to find a subject, & get it into shape & write the stuff. Moreover, I don't like the Oratorio notion – though of course one can make a work on oratorio lines which shall be perfectly independent of ecclesiastical or so-called religious conventions. Do you think there is anything to be made of the poetical materials in the same neighbourhood as Parsifal? Do you think there are any stories of the Albigensians or some such types? It must be something with lots of chance for chorus – & just at the moment – when I haven't thought about it – it seems to me it might be worked by having a "Narrator" as in the early Oratorios & in the Passions & Resurrections, introducing the characters in propriâ personâ as well. (original emphasis)[43]

The reply from the Committee was predictable, and somewhat depressing for the composer:

> The Birmingham people stood out for a regular Oratorio. I hope you won't swear! After some correspondence in which they declined my alternative proposals I caved in. But with a mental reservation that

---

[41] For a more sophisticated discussion of some of the issues surrounding Tennyson's "Englishness," see John Lucas, *England and Englishness: Ideas of Nationhood in English Poetry 1688–1900* (London: Hogarth, 1990) 170–190.

[42] In 1883, links with Cambridge were developed further with the performance of Parry's incidental music to Aristophanes's *The Birds*, along with his being admitted to Trinity College and proposed for an Honorary Doctorate of Music.

[43] Parry to Edward Dannreuther, 2 September 1887; *GB-Ob* (Bodleian Library, Oxford) Eng.Letters e.117.

there shouldn't be much of religion or biblical oratorio beyond the name.[44]

Parry may therefore have seized the opportunity to choose a secular text for the Cambridge commission. But by setting Tennyson's poem for soprano soloist, chorus and orchestra (a large-scale combination which would be ideal for inclusion in any choral festival), this could still have been viewed as a suitable vehicle for an implicit moral message.[45] Such expectations are reinforced by Delius's reference to Parry's Biblical propensities, especially as this seems to confirm a generalized picture of Parry as a composer who associated himself with the concept of morality in art – music and morality, of course, being commonly associated in this period.[46] One could easily cite the influence of John Ruskin's lectures at Oxford,[47] or quote from a plethora of passages in Parry's published writings which promote the moral responsibility of the composer.[48] As Jeremy Dibble has suggested, Parry's published prose employs a Ruskinian vocabulary which stresses notions of honesty, earnestness, nobility and genuineness,[49] of which the following is a typical example:

> Trivial and false music debases the minds that take their pleasure in it. Real music appeals to the higher faculties and also enhances them. If it is to be effective in any wide social sense it must be of the very best quality …. For quality is that which justifies itself to countless

---

[44] Parry to Dannreuther, 20 October 1887; *GB-Ob* Eng.Letters e.117.

[45] Another secular work, for example, Parry's setting of Robert Browning's *The Pied Piper of Hamelin* (1905), promotes a clear moral message.

[46] The association of music and morality was usually made in the context of vocal music; for further discussion of this issue, see, for example, Charles Edward McGuire, *Elgar's Oratorios: The creation of an epic narrative* (Aldershot: Ashgate, 2002) 17–30, and Ruth Solie's essay in this volume, "'Music their larger souls': George Eliot's *The Legend of Jubal* and Victorian Musicality."

[47] After reading Ruskin's *The Queen of the Air*, Parry noted in his diary in October 1870 that "he [Ruskin] makes a good case for his art and morality doctrine". For an interesting discussion of the role of music in Ruskin's philosophy, see Delia da Sousa Correa, "Goddesses of Instruction and Desire: Ruskin and Music," *Ruskin and the Dawn of the Modern*, ed. Dinah Birch (Oxford: Oxford University Press, 1999) 111–130.

[48] Parry was aware of the power of music to influence emotion and thought processes, for example, as illustrated by a passage in his unpublished work, *Instinct and Character* (c. 1915–1918): "Music coincides with the motion of human life; it goes alongside of it, and if it is real music it insinuates itself into that life, and takes possession of it. It transports that life into the moods it represents. If it is noble and the hearer is worthy of it, music elevates him, if it is gay it makes the hearer gay. If it mourns it makes the hearer mourn" (287). Typescript copies of this study are housed in London at the British Library and the Royal College of Music, at the Bodleian Library, Oxford, and at Shulbrede Priory in Lynchmere. For the suggestion that nobler minds would be more receptive to compositional inspiration, and the reference to "reckless levity" in connection with perceived lower forms of music, see Parry, *Style in Musical Art*, 131, 411.

[49] See Jeremy Dibble, "Parry as Historiographer," *Nineteenth-Century British Music Studies*, ed. Bennett Zon, vol.1 (Aldershot: Ashgate, 1999) 38–41.

> various types of mind and endures, – by ideas that are true and sincere, by texture that is honest and characteristic, by style that is apt, by organization that is convincing, by individuality that is interesting, by diction that is pure, by gaiety that is not blatant, by melancholy that has hope in it, by consistency of thought, by scope of imagination, by humanity that is generous, and by strength that is kindly to weakness. (*Style in Musical Art*, 426–427)

Parry's series of ethical cantatas composed between 1902 and 1908 (*War and Peace, Voces Clamantium, The love that casteth out fear, The Soul's Ransom, The Vision of Life* and *Beyond these voices there is peace*), his work ethic, and descriptions by Parry's children of his spartan lifestyle, seem to complete the picture.[50] In addition, the Tennyson/Brookfield issue cited above in the literary debate section has resonances in Parry's comments concerning the distressing decline of his brother, Clinton, into dipsomania:

> His humours alternated between violence and swearing and crying, extravagant demonstrations of affection for me, and collapse ... I had to hold him always as he seized every opportunity to try and get after more drink. Altogether he was a piteous and sickening spectacle.[51]

Clinton died in 1883 aged forty-three.

Given this biographical context, one might therefore expect Parry to adopt the didactic line of interpretation outlined by literary critics such as Spedding, Levi, et al. However, closer scrutiny of Parry's musical setting makes these preconceptions difficult to sustain. The first striking feature of the work is the status of the poetic text. Although only the Choric Song is actually set to music, the introductory stanzas are also retained in performance by being recited.[52] When Elgar decided to include the work in a concert by the Worcester Philharmonic in 1902, Parry reminded him:

> I hope you have got a good reciter to recite the preliminary stanzas. That is a very important part of the business – and I always begin the soft clarinet bit directly the reciter finishes "we will no longer roam" – That is if people will let me. For they generally applaud the reciter very warmly. I think they like that part of it best.[53]

---

[50] Parry's daughter Dorothea, for example, described her father as having a "puritanical vein" and noted that "He was an ascetic and spent nothing on himself." See the Letter to the Editor subtitled "Hubert Parry" in *Musical Times* 97 (May 1956): 263.

[51] Hubert Parry's diary, 1 May 1879. I am grateful to Laura Ponsonby and Kate and Ian Russell for allowing me to quote from Parry's diaries, which are held at Shulbrede Priory, Lynchmere.

[52] Hubert Parry, *The Lotos-Eaters* (London: Novello, 1892). All subsequent references to the score refer to this edition.

[53] Parry to Elgar, 19 April 1902, Hereford and Worcester Public Records Office, 705.445.5247/8:2797.

Parry's decision to include these preliminary stanzas probably dated from his visit to Tennyson's home in January 1892, after the work was basically complete. Here Parry documented Tennyson's manner of reciting "The Lotos-Eaters" via a series of detailed annotations on his own copy of the poem,[54] although he was surprised by several aspects of the poet's approach:

> He [Tennyson] soon set to work reading, and began with the "Lotos Eaters". It soon struck me it was not at all a prepared or careful performance as he frequently ignored stops and ran phrases in[to] one another with little apparent sense; but he evidently enjoyed it himself. The manner of reading is most strange – I should think something after the manner of the ancient professional reciter of epics and songs among barbarous people. He poised his voice rather high for average intoning, and raised and dropped it for special words. Moreover he was much given to a rather commonplace lilt; a sing-song method of enforcing the accents which rather jarred with my sense of the rhythmic variety of the written verse. If I had heard him read before I read his works I never should have thought him capable of such exquisite effects of subtle variety or the treatment of his metres. But it was a most interesting experience.[55]

One can speculate as to the reasons for, and the effect of, the incorporation of this recitation in the musical work. Some might suggest that the general move from speech to song reflected Parry's strong interest in evolutionary development.[56] Others might point to the deliberate inclusion of Ulysses's

---

[54] The volume of poetry was given to Parry by his cousin Lewis Majendie in 1865, and is now housed at Shulbrede Priory. I am grateful to Laura Ponsonby and Kate and Ian Russell for allowing me to study this material.

[55] Diary, 2 January, 1892. The British composer Charles Villiers Stanford (1852–1924), who published his own reminiscences of Tennyson in *Studies and Memories* (London: Constable, 1908), suggested that Tennyson's reading was "a chant rather than a declamation", and that he used "a peculiarly thin and ghostly tone of voice" in the Choric Song of "The Lotos-Eaters." Stanford went on to describe the musical nature of Tennyson's poetry: "The secret of the harmony of his verse lay in his incomparable ear for the juxtaposition of vowels and the exact suitability of each consonant. This makes it difficult to set his poems adequately to music. The music is so inborn in the poetry itself that it does not ask for notes to make incompleteness complete, and music is set to it rather for additional illustration than from inherent necessity" (90–95, 97–98).

[56] This progression from speech (reason) to song (feeling) is the opposite to that described by Rousseau in his *Essai sur l'origine des langues* (1753), where the first language is said to be characterized by the melodic accent of the passions, and was therefore sung, not spoken; see Jean-Jacques Rousseau, *Essay on the origins of languages and writings related to music*, ed. John T. Scott, in *The Collected Writings of Rousseau*, eds Roger D. Masters and Christopher Kelley, vol. 7 (Hanover: University Press of New England, 1998) 293–295. However, the speech-music progression mirrors that proposed by Herbert Spencer; see Spencer, "The Origin and Function of Music," in *Essays: Scientific, Political, and Speculative* (London: Longman, 1858) 373. Parry was familiar with several works by Spencer, including *Social Statics* (1850), *The Study of Sociology* (1861), *First Principles of Philosophy* (1862), *Data of Ethics* (1879) and *System of Synthetic Philosophy* (1896), along with Darwin's *Origin of Species* (1859) and

initial cry of "Courage!" in the recitation as confirmation that Parry's message represented a denunciation of the blissful life, or might simply view the passage as an *aide-memoire* designed to help those members of the audience whose Classical education was a little shaky. The presentation of the complete literary text certainly adds to the sense of the musical work representing a considered reading of the poem, but the effect of the recitation on the listener has an additional significance which will be discussed presently.

Example 6.1: Hubert Parry, *The Lotos-Eaters* (1892), opening of stanza 1

The Descent of Man (1871), and Samuel Butler's *Erewhon* (1872); Parry also met Spencer in 1874 and later corresponded with him. The influence of these evolutionary interests can be seen particularly in Parry's approach to historiography, in *Summary of Music History* (1893) and *The Art of Music* (1893), the title of which was later altered to *The Evolution of the Art of Music* (1896). For a recent discussion of the importance of recitation in British musical works in the late nineteenth and early twentieth century, see Lewis Foreman, "A Voice in the Desert: Elgar's War Music," *Oh, My Horses! Elgar and the Great War*, ed. Lewis Foreman (Rickmansworth: Elgar Editions, 2001) 263–285. See also Frederic Corder, "Recitation with Music," and Stanley Hawley, "Recitation-Music," *Voice, Speech and Gesture*, ed. R.D. Blackmore (London: Deacon, 1904).

Example 6.2: Parry, *The Lotos-Eaters*, stanza 2

It is in the details of the musical setting where we can begin to formulate Parry's interpretation more clearly. Where texture, rhythm, tempo, harmony and orchestration are concerned, it is significant that the worlds of Lotosland and reality are contrasted heavily in favour of the former. To take one striking example: in the choral writing, the listener associates the concept of harmony with Lotosland and unison writing with human responsibilities. The initial choral description of the island paradise sets the tone (see Ex. 6.1), employing a rich three-part choral texture and an upper line full of expressive accented passing notes and appoggiaturas. In contrast, the first reference to the world of reality at the beginning of the second verse is characterized by stark unisons (Ex. 6.2) – significantly, a texture which is retained throughout the verse, apart from the line associated with the inner spirit, "There is no joy but calm!" (68).

Example 6.3: Parry, *The Lotos-Eaters*, orchestral introduction

Similarly, the orchestral accompaniment has a crucial role in Parry's setting. The introductory material, which contains motivic material for solo clarinet, muted horns and strings (Ex. 6.3), creates a seductive orchestral palette suggesting the indolent world of the lotos eaters. More importantly, the many subsequent allusions to this opening material throughout the rest of the work represent a constant reminder of the sensual world, particularly as the motives retain their original orchestration. Some references occur as part of introductory or concluding orchestral passages at the beginning and end of verses, illustrated by the return of the horn motif at the end of verses three and seven and before the section "Let us swear an oath" (153) in verse eight, and by the way in which the clarinet motif ushers in verse five.[57] Other references to the opening material comment on the text itself, giving weight to the argument in favour of remaining on the island; these include the horn motif at passages such as "Give us long rest or death, dark death, or dreamful ease" (98), or the return of the violin arpeggios in the final verse at "For they lie beside their nectar" (156). In terms of suggesting a final decision on the part of the mariners, a slightly modified reappearance of the whole orchestral introduction (again with the same evocative scoring) before the repetition of the final line of the poem is particularly significant.

This sensual orientation of the work is heightened by the tonal structure, which deliberately explores third-related keys. Third-relations (whether mediant or submediant) were a feature of several nineteenth-century musical compositions. These include the E major subsidiary theme (in the context of a

---

[57] In the final verse, the horns also play a transformed version of their motif which is employed as a transition from a choral section to the passage for solo soprano, "But they smile, they find a music centred in a doleful song" (62).

C major tonic) in the first movement of Beethoven's Piano Sonata Op. 53 (*Waldstein*), the modulation from C major to E flat major in the first-movement Exposition of Schubert's String Quintet in C major D956, the use of F sharp minor to introduce the subsidiary theme in the first movement of Brahms's Symphony no. 2 in D (producing a I – II – V progression), or the move from D major to F sharp major in the second song of Mahler's *Lieder eines fahrenden Gesellen, Ging heut' morgens übers Feld*. In the second half of the nineteenth century in particular, it is tempting to view such relationships in a more metaphoric context, whether in terms of transcendence in the symphonies of Mahler,[58] or in relation to musical imagery in the *Lieder* of Hugo Wolf; Eric Sams, for example, discussing Wolf's *Die ihr schwebt un diese Palmen* and *In dem Schatten meiner Locken* from the *Geistliche Lieder* of the *Spanisches Liederbuch*, suggests that the mediant modulations represent "changing effects of light," or even "brightening and fading smiles of intending and relenting, or in more general terms sleeping and waking."[59] One could argue that tertiary relationships are particularly suitable in representing siren imagery. The retention of one note as a harmonic pivot, gently leading from one key centre to another, suggests modulation by stealth, a covert shifting of perspective (or seduction) which subtly reformulates the initial tonality, establishing the world of the new key almost imperceptibly. David Brodbeck, for example, has interpreted aspects of the move from F to A major in the first movement of Brahms's Third Symphony as an explicit reference to the Chorus of Sirens, "Naht euch dem Strande! Naht euch dem Lande," in Wagner's *Tannhäuser und die Sängerkrieg auf Wartburg*;[60] Hermann Kretschmar has invoked images of the temptress Delilah in relation to this same subsidiary theme.[61]

---

[58] The Finale of Mahler's First Symphony, for example, moves from F minor to D major; in the first movement of the Second Symphony, Mahler contrasts a C minor funeral march with a more lyrical theme in E major; the first movement of the Third Symphony moves from D minor to F major; the Finale of the Fourth Symphony moves from G to E; and the Sixth Symphony explores the relationship between tonal centers of A minor and F major. For a discussion of Mahler's tonal frameworks in the symphonies, and the consequent interpretations by Mahler scholars (whether in relation to a breakdown of tonality or a "double-tonic complex"), see John Williamson, "Mahler, Hermeneutics and Analysis," *Music Analysis* 10.3 (1991): 357–373, particularly 363–366.
[59] Eric Sams, *The Songs of Hugo Wolf*, 2nd ed. (London: Eulenburg, 1983) 255, 265.
[60] David Brodbeck, "Brahms, the Third Symphony, and the New German School," *Brahms and his World*, ed. Walter Frisch (Princeton: Princeton University Press, 1990) 67–70. Brodbeck notes "Brahms did not idly choose this passage to echo. This seductive song of the sirens, this invitation to enter into the Venusberg realm, may well be emblematic of the temptation which Wagner's musical language must periodically have exerted on Brahms" (68–69).
[61] Hermann Kretschmar, "The Brahms Symphonies," trans. Susan Gillespie, in Frisch, 136. Both Brodbeck and Kretschmar are briefly discussed in Susan McClary, "Narrative Agendas in 'Absolute' Music: Identity and Difference in Brahms's Third Symphony," *Musicology and Difference: Gender and Sexuality in Music Scholarship*, ed. Ruth A. Solie (Berkeley: University of California Press, 1993) 326–344.

150   THE FIGURE OF MUSIC IN 19TH-CENTURY BRITISH POETRY

Example 6.4: Richard Wagner, *Parsifal* (1882), Act II

MUSICAL REACTIONS TO TENNYSON 151

Example 6.4 continued

152   THE FIGURE OF MUSIC IN 19TH-CENTURY BRITISH POETRY

Example 6.4 continued

Although Parry's interest in third-related keys was more abstract, reflecting the influence of Beethoven, Schubert and Brahms in several of his chamber works,[62] there is one particular composition which may have been influential

---

[62] See, for example, the A major – C sharp major juxtaposition in the first movement of Parry's Second Piano Sonata, the move from E flat major to B major (originally C major) in the finale of the String Quintet and from D minor to B flat major in the first movement of the D minor Violin Sonata, the tonal ambivalence in the second movement of the Cello Sonata (A minor/F major), tertiary relationships in three movements of the Piano Quartet (first movement A flat/C, slow movement Db/F, finale A flat/F), the finale of the Wind Nonet (D major – D minor – B flat major), the second recapitulation in the one-movement *Fantasie Sonate* for violin and

in terms of suggesting a connection between tertiary progressions and siren imagery. At Bayreuth in 1882, Parry had been particularly impressed with a performance of Wagner's *Parsifal*:

> The scenic management and tableaux were supremely effective, and all the difficult points I had dreaded – the swan, the Blumenmädchen, were all just perfect. As a work of art, it is at the very highest point of mastery.[63]

The scene with the *Blumenmädchen* in Kundry's flower garden in Act II of *Parsifal*, to which Parry refers, contains just such a tertiary progression (see Ex. 6.4). Here the refrain "Komm! holder Knabe!" ("Come! Gentle lover!"), introduced in A flat major some 94 bars earlier, returns in A major, then subtly shifts to C major as the attempted seduction of Parsifal is raised to new heights.

There are several examples of tertiary relationships in Parry's *The Lotos-Eaters*. The first of the soprano's three stanzas ("Lo! in the middle of the wood"), for example, outlines a tonality of G flat major/F sharp minor after the previous stanza's B flat major, helping to establish the soloist as the seductive voice. Similar modulations within stanzas develop the sense of covert seduction as the singers are gently led into new harmonic regions. The initial stanza, for example, which begins in the tonic, D major, and ends in the dominant, includes an extended passage in F major ("Than tired eyelids upon tired eyes; / ... / And through the moss the ivies creep" [51–54]).[64] These relationships culminate in the soprano's final solo promotion of the blissful life, "But, propt on beds of amaranth and moly" (133), which begins in G major and ends in B flat major; the latter key then forms the starting point for one of the most distinctive modulations in the whole piece, where the tonic returns in the final section, "The Lotos blooms below the barren peak" (145), as illustrated in Ex. 6.5. The seductive associations of the harmonic

---

piano (B/D), and particularly the Piano Trio in E minor, where the relationship E minor/C major is significant in the outer movements, and the A major scherzo is followed by a C major Trio. For a discussion of Parry's approach to harmony in the chamber music in particular, see Jeremy Dibble, "Structure and Tonality in Parry's Chamber Music," *Journal of the British Music Society* 3 (1981): 12–23. Tertiary relationships are also present in the orchestral works, such as the move from F sharp major to D major and F sharp major to B flat major in the outer movements of the Piano Concerto, the slow movement of the Third Symphony (A minor/C minor), the *Overture to an Unwritten Tragedy* (A minor/C major), the *Guillem de Cabestanh* overture (F major/D flat major), and the G minor – E flat major relationship in the Exposition of the *Concertstück*. Jeremy Dibble also suggests that the latter piece may have been a reworking of an earlier *Aurora* overture; Aurora, the goddess of the dawn, has links with Tennyson's poem "Tithonus," so this may be an early example of Parry adopting third-related keys in relation to Tennyson and song references. See Dibble, *C. Hubert H. Parry: His Life and Music* (Oxford: Clarendon, 1992) 151.

[63] Diary, 26 July 1882.

[64] Harmonic effects are also used to sustain the poetic argument in general. The first "human" stanza, with its question, "Why are we weigh'd upon with heaviness" (stanza two), represents a striking interruption to the world of Lotosland by the deliberate shattering of the reassuring dominant at the end of the first stanza.

relationships are made even more effective by the temporal context in which they occur – parameters of *Andante tranquillo* or *Andantino*, whereas references to the world of responsibility are associated with *Allegro, Allegro Moderato,* or *Moderato* tempi.[65]

Example 6.5: Parry, *The Lotos-Eaters*, opening of stanza 8

A further compelling feature is the musical characterization. In Tennyson's Choric Song, the singers are the mariners, hence the use of the first person plural "we." In the musical setting, the chorus are used to represent these mariners in verses where there is some division or inner struggle, where references to the real world often dominate – such as verses two, four and six. For the verses outlining the argument which promotes life on the island (three, five and seven), however, the musical material is reserved for the soprano soloist. As Parry wrote to Sedley Taylor in connection with the work's first performance:

> I tried to make music a comment on the poem and to follow the alternation of the human longing for ease and repose and languorous self-indulgence, and the irrepressible impulse that reminds men that they were not meant to take their ease and do nothing in "Lotosland". The soprano solo is as it were the "inner spirit" referred to in verse 2, and the chorus the human creatures with their protests against their haunting memories and their restless feelings of destiny driving them

---

[65] A sense of urgency within the Lotosland context is suggested at the soprano soloist's cries, "O rest ye, brother mariners" (173), by a fusion of these two approaches in the tempo indication of *Allegro tranquillo*.

whither they would not. The moods are alternated and so are Solo and Chorus. But for the life of me I cannot put it decently.[66]

This association of the delights of Lotosland with the female voice is made even more effective by further subdivisions in the choral writing. The mariners in the poem are obviously male, and the passage which begins "Dear is the memory of our wedded lives, / And dear the last embraces of our wives" (114–115), leads to the logical setting for men's voices only. In the final verse this same texture is used for "We have had enough of action, / ... / careless of mankind" (150–155), which contrasts with the description of the lotos eaters, "For they lie beside their nectar, / ... / girdled with the gleaming world" (156–158), which is sung by the female members of the choir. The sheer sound of the female voice as representative of Lotosland, as opposed to the male voices which equate to responsibility and the real world, is reinforced by the inclusion of the preliminary recitation; not only does the (presumably) male narrator throw the female voice into relief, but the structure represents a move from speech (associated with Ulysses and the real world) to music (the domain of the lotos eaters). This therefore has parallels with the poetic structure; Theodore Redpath, for example, notes that the poem "starts with narrative, but continues over a great span with modulated lyrics gathering in momentum of incantatory power" (119).

The most persuasive element of the musical characterization, however, is Parry's use of a soprano soloist to represent the inner voice of the mariners; the actual sound of the female voice has therefore been used to transform Tennyson's covert suggestion of the siren into an overt physical presence; the separation of soloist and chorus in performance terms also adds to the sense of opposition and debate as the mariners come to their decision. The seductive and intoxicating quality of the soprano's continual coaxing suggests a siren of real power. In one sense this mirrors Parry's awareness of the qualities of the female voice in other choral works. In the ethical cantatas such as *The Soul's Ransom*, and particularly *Voces Clamantium* (via the "Vox consolatoris"), the female voice often has a comforting role, countering the more strident Biblical proclamations of the male soloist. The *Ode on the Nativity*, a setting of William Dunbar, develops this idea (particularly in the section for soprano soloist, "Sinners be glad and penance do"), and in addition associates the voice with an ecstatic quality, particularly at the first vocal entry, "Rorate coeli de super!" In *The Lotos-Eaters*, however, what is striking is Parry's employment of a cumulative battery of aural effects to present the soprano's material, with something of a rhetorical approach. If we take three successive appeals by the female voice, encouraging the mariners to remain on the island, each illustrates a different element (Exs 6.6a–c): firstly, the sense of a siren's call suggested by an introductory long note, which we therefore initially respond to as a pure sound; secondly, the use of repetition in the vocal part to create a soporific

---

[66] Parry to Sedley Taylor, 4 June 1892, Cambridge University Library Add. MS 6259, cited in Dibble, *C. Hubert H. Parry*, 297.

effect; thirdly, a more declamatory approach attempting to convince through force of argument. An awareness of the importance of the soprano's role is also illustrated by concerns voiced by Parry after a rehearsal of the work: "some of it might well be improved, especially the male chorus, & the accompaniment of 'How sweet it were' which gets in the way of the voice."[67]

Example 6.6a: Parry, *The Lotos-Eaters*, opening of stanza 3

Example 6.6b: Parry, *The Lotos-Eaters*, opening of stanza 7

---

[67] Diary, 13 June 1892.

Example 6.6c: Parry, *The Lotos-Eaters*, stanza 7, figure BB

The continual promotion of the delights of Lotosland by the female soloist eventually leads to the final line of the poem, "O rest ye, brother mariners, we will not wander more." Again it is the soprano soloist who commands each phrase – "O rest ye," "brother mariners," and "we will not wander more" – all of which are immediately taken up in turn by the chorus. The latter phrase represents the climactic point of the work, as the soprano sustains the highest note in the entire setting, a top A (which is eventually transferred to the sopranos in the chorus).[68] To reinforce the mariners' decision, however, Parry repeats the words "we will not wander more" (highlighting the flexibility which a musical setting can enjoy), but significantly, this time it is the chorus who lead the soloist – instead of simply responding to a seductive stimulus, they are now taking responsibility themselves (this is not the case in the poem, as the inner voice is not physically separate from the mariners). The music for this textual repetition is the final cadence in the work (the ultimate resolution of the tonal conflict), for which Parry reserves a combination of a 7–6 and a 4–3 suspension, arguably the most beautiful moment in the entire piece (see Ex. 6.7). Not only is the final stanza the one example in the setting where both soloist and choir are represented,[69] but the passage "O rest ye ... we will not wander more" is the only point where soloist and chorus are combined, thus

---

[68] This climactic pitch has only been used once before in the work: by the chorus sopranos at the word "hurled" in the final stanza (156); here, the duration of this pitch is only a minim.

[69] It is significant that the setting of this final stanza occupies roughly a third of the performance time of the entire piece (around 11 minutes from a total of c. 33 minutes).

reinforcing the sense that the poem's inner conflict has been resolved. Parry's push towards an end-focused resolution of the tensions (harmonic, structural, textual) surrounding the mariners' plight therefore has much greater momentum than its poetic counterpart, given the sense of decision-making at the end of the narrative introduction in the latter; although Parry includes the narrative, the decision at the end of the Choric Song is heightened by being made in musical terms, rather than those of recited speech.

Example 6.7: Parry, *The Lotos-Eaters*, ending

What are we to make of Parry's reading of Tennyson's poem? Some might suggest that the very fact that the composer employed such a luscious, seductive sound-world as an evocation of the life of ease reinforces the message that we should return to our lives of responsibility. One could argue that the seductive world would have to be expressed in a powerful fashion to make any threat to the real world a meaningful one. Parry's apparent distrust of such a sound-world have been noted by both Arnold Bax, who suggested that Parry regarded sensuous beauty of orchestral sound as "something not quite nice" (28), and Ralph Vaughan Williams, who felt that Parry "had an almost moral abhorrence of mere luscious sound."[70] However, the word "mere" is significant here, as Parry's reaction seems to have been confined to works where he felt the sound-world was attempting to make up for deficiencies in form or content. This position is illustrated by his comments on Hector Berlioz:

> The means are in excess of the requirements; or rather what should be means becomes requirements, because the effect is made by the actual sound of the instruments, and often not at all by the music which they are the means of expressing.[71]

Although Parry had the opportunity in *The Lotos-Eaters* to develop a didactic tone, particularly in the large-scale choral genre, the sensual nature of the setting is what strikes the listener. For a convincing interpretation of Parry's response to Tennyson's poem, I would therefore suggest a return to Robert Bernard Martin's comments quoted earlier, this time reformulating his summation in musical terms:

> It is no accident that the most [musically effective passages] nearly all come either from the stanzas pressing the claims of the magical isle or from the conclusion, in which the mariners decide to remain there. [Parry] is subtly loading the dice by the sheer mellifluousness with which he presents one side of the case, so that stern devotion comes out a poor second. This may not have been totally intentional, but whether or not it was is irrelevant; what matters is that [Parry's] best method of argument was not rational but sensual.

Although Martin dismisses the question of intent, in Parry's case we may be able to take this further. Parry certainly seems to have been aware that his chosen text was slightly racy; on his copy of Tennyson's poetry, he asterisked "The Vision of Sin," and noted on the title page, "Tithonus; which should ever be classed with the Lotos Eaters and Œnone and some others of Tennyson's diviner inspiration is in the set with Enoch Arden." Although what Parry was responding to exactly in these poems is open to conjecture, several features are surely significant. In his desire for death, Tithonus the immortal indulges in dream and reminiscence, with imagery of indolence:

---

[70] Ralph Vaughan Williams, "A Musical Autobiography," *National Music and Other Essays* (Oxford: Oxford University Press, 1963) 182.
[71] Parry, *The Art of Music*, 5th ed. (London: Kegan Paul, Trench, Trubner & Co., 1894) 303.

> while I lay,
> Mouth, forehead, eyelids, growing dewy-warm
> With kisses balmier than half-opening buds
> Of April, and could hear the lips that kissed
> Whispering I knew not what of wild and sweet,
> Like that strange song I heard Apollo sing,
> While Ilion like a mist rose into towers. ("Tithonus," 57–63)

In "Œnone," Paris, in judging between Herè, Pallas and Aphrodite (representing arguments in favour of power, virtue and beauty respectively) for the prize of the golden apple, eventually "surrenders quietly to the allurements of sense and passion" (Kanda, 61). Apart from the desire for death once again (Œnone's "I am all aweary of my life" [32]) the poem also displays languorous nature imagery:

> The swimming vapour ...
>   Puts forth an arm, and creeps from pine to pine,
> And loiters, slowly drawn.
>   ...
> The purple flower droops: the golden bee
> Is lily-cradled: (3–5, 29–30)

Parallels with the strong sensual imagery of "The Vision of Sin" are even more obvious:

> Dreams over lake and lawn, and isles and capes –
> Suffused them, sitting, lying, languid shapes,
> By heaps of gourds, and skins of wine, and piles of grapes. (11–13)

More specifically, Tennyson's use of musical imagery in these poems may have been particularly attractive to the composer, especially the concept of song as related to the strange, the fantastic and the sensual, as in "The Lotos-Eaters." The reference to the "strange song" of Apollo in "Tithonus" (62) has already been mentioned. In "The Vision of Sin," "Low voluptuous music" (17) provides an undulating sound world, moving to its climax, "Stormed in orbs of song, a growing gale" (25), and Œnone's mournful song represents "a music slowly breathed, / A cloud that gathered shape" (40–41). In relation to Parry's own perceptions of his musical setting, his comments after the first performance of *The Lotos-Eaters* are also revealing:

> The audience seemed to like it well enough. But strangely enough it evidently did not please [J.A.] F[uller] Maitland and [Charles] Graves. I suppose they have made up their minds what sort of Music I ought to write & object to my trying to widen my field.[72]

---

[72] Diary, 13 June 1892.

"Trying to widen my field" represents a statement of intent, and acknowledges that *The Lotos-Eaters* was somehow different from several other compositions. Rather than the dichotomy between Tennyson's poetic intent and result suggested by J.B. Steane above, the conflict here would seem to be between preconceptions surrounding Parry's role as a composer, and a result which he may have intended.

This conflict is illustrated by critical reaction to the work. J.A. Fuller-Maitland, in *English Music in the Nineteenth Century*, dismissively bracketed *The Lotos-Eaters* with the setting of Algernon Charles Swinburne's "Eton" as "a purely secular section of Parry's work," whereas it is the "sacred or semi-sacred works" (*Judith, De Profundis, Ode on St Cecilia's Day* and *L'Allegro ed Il Penseroso*) which "at some point or other raise the nobler emotions of the intelligent hearer to the highest pitch."[73] It is striking that the works of which Fuller-Maitland most approved were all Festival commissions, from Birmingham, Leeds, Gloucester and Norwich respectively. His relegation of *The Lotos-Eaters* to a minor area of Parry's output suggests that for the critic, *The Lotos-Eaters* was disappointing in not providing the necessary moral uplift for the audience; this may also explain why the work was rarely performed, particularly in Parry's lifetime.

There are parallels here with early critical responses to Tennyson's poem. In considering the reaction of contemporary critics, one notices that very few suggested any obvious moral content or "message." On the contrary, R.H. Horne suggested that "we know nothing of him [Tennyson] except that he is a poet," and that we would find it difficult to "pronounce distinctly upon what may be called the mental intention of his poetry."[74] This was echoed in some other criticisms of the 1842 *Poems* which called for a clearer message and a greater element of didacticism.[75] Francis Garden, writing in the *Christian Remembrancer*, wanted more "ordinary duties and sympathies,"[76] and Richard Monckton Milnes felt that Tennyson still had to show that "he comprehends the function of the poet in this day of ours, to teach still more than he delights, and to suggest still more than he teaches."[77] Whilst such reactions were to the *Poems* as a whole, the fact that "The Lotos-Eaters" was not held up as an example of didactic poetry by these writers may be significant. Either the message of the poem was not perceived as one which promoted responsibility, or, if it did, it was not presented strongly enough. Just as Fuller-Maitland may

---

[73] J.A. Fuller-Maitland, *English Music in the XIXth Century* (London: Grant Richards, 1902) 201. From this perspective, it is interesting that the other significant choral composition on which Parry was working in 1892 was the oratorio *Job* – in contrast to "The Lotos-Eaters," this represents the composer in his most Ruskinian vein. Swinburne's "Eton: An Ode" was written to celebrate the 450th anniversary of the school.
[74] Horne, rpt. in Jump, *Tennyson: The Critical Heritage*, 164.
[75] For criticisms of the 1842 set of *Poems*, see Shannon, *Tennyson and the Reviewers*, 60–96.
[76] Francis Garden's unsigned review of the 1842 *Poems* originally appeared in the *Christian Remembrancer* 4 (July 1842): 42–58. Partially rpt. in Jump, 100–102.
[77] Richard Monckton Milnes's critique of the 1842 *Poems* originally appeared in *Westminster Review* 38 (October 1842): 371–390. Partially rpt. in Jump, 138.

have felt a certain sense of betrayal in that Parry had abnegated his role as a moral voice, so these critics felt that Tennyson's poetry was similarly lacking.

Edward Elgar: "There is sweet music" (1907)

As mentioned earlier, Elgar included Parry's *The Lotos-Eaters* in a Worcester Philharmonic Concert of 1902, and was therefore familiar both with the poem and with its musical potential. In terms of expectations surrounding Elgar's setting, one might lean more towards an aesthetic interpretation, rather than a didactic one. Michael Kennedy, for example, has suggested that the composer indulged in musical escapes from reality ("he fled to the historical past of Caractacus, the literary past of Falstaff, the chivalry of Froissart"), that he was "a man of swift and ready emotional response," and that "he turned events of any kind into music without questioning their ethical or political, sociological or humanitarian basis."[78] Unlike several Victorian composers, Elgar attains a certain flexibility by not being associated solely with choral music;[79] he had no significant role as an educator, and his contributions to defining the role of the composer tended to stress national concerns rather than any sense of moral responsibility.[80] In addition, in contrast to Parry's large-scale choral work, Elgar chose to set Tennyson's poem as a part-song – a genre which had no inherent textual restrictions, was small-scale, and, with its relatively lowly status (particularly associated with amateur performance) had no specific didactic associations. Elgar noted in a letter to Ivor Atkins (1869–1953) that his Tennyson setting would "please village choirs,"[81] and the Op. 53 set as a whole which contained this work represented potential test pieces for choirs at the Morecambe Festival. However, the dedicatee of another of the part-songs, W.G. McNaught (1849–1918), felt that the Tennyson setting deserved a higher status than a simple competition piece:

> I have been gazing at "There is sweet music" and am longing to hear it done by a real live choir. It will give some conductors a bad quarter of an hour. I have decided not to use it on a sight test at Morecambe.[82]

---

[78] Michael Kennedy, *Portrait of Elgar*, 3rd ed. (Oxford: Oxford University Press, 1987) 163.
[79] Elgar's choral works themselves display a variety of approaches to both form and content; where subject matter is concerned, they include references to British history in *Caractacus* (1898), religious faith in *The Dream of Gerontius* (1900), and a musical essay on creativity in *The Music Makers* (1912). The oratorios *The Apostles* (1903) and *The Kingdom* (1906) also contain a significant "human" element in the detailed treatment of the character of Judas.
[80] See, for example, Elgar, *A Future for English Music*: "There are many possible futures. But the one I want to see coming into being is something that shall grow out of our own soil, something broad, noble, chivalrous, healthy and above all, an out-of-door sort of spirit" (57).
[81] Elgar to Ivor Atkins, 17 January 1908, *Edward Elgar: Letters of a Lifetime*, ed. Jerrold Northrop Moore (Oxford: Clarendon, 1990) 192.
[82] W.G. McNaught to Elgar, 9 March 1908, *Elgar and his Publishers: Letters of a Creative Life*, ed. Jerrold Northrop Moore, 2 vols (Oxford: Clarendon, 1987) 2: 693. McNaught felt that

Although obviously performable as a self-contained composition, by placing "There is sweet music" at the head of a group of part-songs, the context of the set as a whole has to be considered. The remaining three part-songs are settings of Lord Byron ("Deep in my Soul"), Percy Bysshe Shelley ("O wild west wind"), and Elgar himself ("Owls"). This suggests something of an anthology, and the temptation is to define a common factor between the poems, such as a general sense of mystery or enchantment, or the more specific image of falling leaves which is present in all but the Byron; compare, for example, Shelley's "O wild West Wind! / ... / Make me thy lyre, e'en as the forest is, / What if my leaves are falling like its own!" (1, 57–58),[83] Elgar's "What is that? Nothing; / The leaves must fall, and falling, rustle" (1–2), and Tennyson's "There is sweet music here that softer falls / Than petals from blown roses on the grass" (1–2). The first three songs are dedicated to close friends, the final setting to "my friend Pietro d'Alba" – the pet angora rabbit which belonged to Elgar's daughter Carice. Given the bizarre nature of this dedication, along with the tendency for Elgar scholars to approach the composer primarily from a biographical standpoint, it is inevitable that "Owls" has provoked the most discussion – particularly as the composer subtitled this setting "An Epitaph." However, the Tennyson setting is in many ways the most interesting, particularly where the nature of the subject matter can be seen to influence the compositional structure of the work.

By setting only the first stanza of Tennyson's poem (lines 46–56), unlike Parry's complete reading, Elgar avoids any real sense of debate. There is therefore no separate characterization of the inner spirit to coax the mariners towards a decision to remain on the island, and no reference to the poetic revisions, viewed by some critics as central to the didactic argument. Although one might suggest that a knowledge of the complete poem could be significant for any listener (representing a hidden didactic context, thus mirroring the argument of critics such as F.E.L. Priestley and Jerome Buckley above),[84] it is more likely that the obvious reflection of the subject matter in the initial stanza (the intoxicating "sweet music" [1]) would be the main focus of any interpretation. A musical setting via the genre of the part-song (with no particular didactic expectations) might be predisposed to stress the sensual aspect of the poem anyway, especially given the nature of Tennyson's musical imagery. The setting is also a more realistic depiction of the poetic genre – a Choric Song represented by an unaccompanied song for choir.

---

the metronome marking of crotchet = 44 was "slow for some parts", but realized that "anything like a jaunty rhythm will upset the idea."

[83] Elgar sets the first half of line one of Shelley's poem, "Ode to the West Wind", followed by lines 57–71. See Elgar, *Four Part-Songs, Op. 53* (London: Novello, 1908, rpt. 1892). All subsequent references to the score refer to this edition. The setting of "Deep in my Soul" excerpts lines 347–354 from Byron's *The Corsair: A tale.*

[84] See footnote 25. Similarly, Celeste Langan's essay in this volume, "Scotch Drink & Irish Harps: Mediations of the National Air," notes the significance of another "unseen" presence – in this case music, where lyrics are printed on their own.

164   THE FIGURE OF MUSIC IN 19TH-CENTURY BRITISH POETRY

Example 6.8: Edward Elgar, "There is sweet music" (1907), opening

Compositional strategies employed in the setting itself capture the sense of indolence and intoxication perfectly. The first four lines of the poem, sung by the male voices only, set the tone (see Ex. 6.8). Although the score notes a time signature of four crotchet beats to the bar, as a listening experience the metre and placing of the barlines is ambiguous. The impression is simply one of a delivery of text involving a variety of syllable duration, with occasional lingerings (crotchet or dotted crotchet) interspersed with the quicker-paced quavers. Akin to a heightened form of recitation, the elongated pitches of syllables such as "There," "sweet," "mu-," "soft-," "on," "grass," "night," "still," "walls" and "pass" allow these words to stand out. Even more striking is the elongation of the shorter second syllable in words which in speech would normally be unstressed, such as "petals," "roses," "waters" and "granite." This technique, which adds to the soporific atmosphere, was deliberate, as Elgar's letter to August Jaeger, criticizing Parry's word-setting, illustrates:

> One word as to my treatment of words, not only in this op. but always. I hold that *short* syllables may be sustained occasionally for the sake of effect: just as an actor does. There is one good dear man against whom I wd. not think anything but the greatest admiration & that is Parry. But he almost if not quite annoys me in the way he sets the words which swarm in our English – two syllables, both short, the

first accented e.g. *petal*. Set in an ordinary way a poem sounds like reading a newspaper paragraph. (original emphasis)[85]

Elgar's choice of the word "petal" as an example of Parry's approach suggests that he probably had Parry's setting of *The Lotos-Eaters* in mind.

Example 6.9: Elgar, "There is sweet music," bars 8–11

Having clearly established the key of G major, the male voices come to rest on the tonic at the word "pass." The subsequent entry of the female voices over the men's held bottom G, however, undermines the tonal structure by being in a different key – A flat major (see Ex. 6.9). Elgar was particularly excited by

---

[85] Elgar to August Jaeger, 17 January 1908, *Elgar and his Publishers*, 2: 694.

the juxtaposition of these two key centres, noting, "in two keys at once!"[86] Rather than Parry's technique of covert transformation of tonality, therefore, Elgar relies upon juxtaposition to suggest disorientation. Although the pitches for "There is sweet music here that softer falls / Than petals from blown roses on the grass" (46–47) imitate the music sung by the male voices, the position of the text within the succession of pitches is altered, now lingering upon the syllables "mu-," "falls," "blown" and "grass." Elgar's harmonic and melodic dislocation is therefore an effective evocation of the effects of the lotos fruit, and highlights Tennyson's association of music with altered states of conciousness in the poem.

The sensual nature of the setting is in evidence throughout. For example, there is a subtle range of dynamic markings: at no point does the setting go beyond *mezzo forte*, and the majority of dynamics are marked at *pianissimo* or *pianississimo*; the final chord, marked *pppp*, suggests that sleep has indeed been induced. Expression marks direct the singers to produce smooth and expressive contours, and *ritardandos* and *a tempos* provide a guide to the flow of the music. Elgar was obviously at pains to make sure that performers could capture the atmospheric nature of the work:

> I do not think I have overdone the [expression] marks[:] you see nothing emotional is ever performed in strict time & it takes conductors *years* (literally) to find out a reading: you have only to think of the way people play Brahms (Symphonies or anything) now and compare it with the want of "reading" they obtained even ten years ago. I have only put sort of *emotional* marks for the conductor to do the best he can with. I wish you could have heard the *Morecambe choir under* [R.G.H.] *Howson* sing four or five years ago: you wd then fully appreciate what I have tried to do. (original emphasis)[87]

Some of the most seductive passages in the part-song include the syncopated chromatic writing to represent the word "hangs" (Ex. 6.10), and the use of an expressive appoggiatura or grace note, illustrated by the imitative entries of the male voices at the line "Than tired eyelids upon tired eyes" (51)[88] shown in Ex. 6.11; the latter example also illustrates the way that Elgar occasionally alters time signatures in the work, which obviously affects approaches to phrasing in performance, and adds to the sense of disorientation. The soporific effect produced by the internal textual repetition in this passage is even more marked at the end of the work; here the word "sleep" is repeated, almost in the manner of an incantation, dovetailing the gendered chords (representing the two harmonic worlds) of G and A flat (see Ex. 6.12). The female/male (or vice

---

[86] Elgar to Ivor Atkins, 17 January 1908, *Letters of a Lifetime*, 192.
[87] Elgar to August Jaeger, 26 April 1908, *Elgar and his Publishers*, 2: 693–694.
[88] While Ricks's *The Poems of Tennyson* has "tired," Elgar's part-song has "tir'd."

versa) echoing of text is in evidence throughout the setting, as is the hypnotic restatement of lines and phrases within the male or female choral group.

Example 6.10: Elgar, "There is sweet music," bars 26–28

168 THE FIGURE OF MUSIC IN 19TH-CENTURY BRITISH POETRY

Example 6.11: Elgar, "There is sweet music," bar 17

MUSICAL REACTIONS TO TENNYSON 169

Example 6.12: Elgar, "There is sweet music," ending

170   THE FIGURE OF MUSIC IN 19TH-CENTURY BRITISH POETRY

Example 6.13: Elgar, "There is sweet music," bars 36–41

Example 6.13 continued

Despite the constant repetition, however, the delivery of poetic lines follows the sequence of Tennyson's poem until page twelve of the vocal score, by which time both sets of voices have completed the text. At this point, the female voices hold a long C flat, which is then treated enharmonically as the male voices repeat the opening two lines of the poem, set to the music with which the part-song began. As an obvious recapitulatory device, one might expect a second reading of the entire poem. Sure enough, the female voices enter with a reference to their initial music, but instead of the first two lines, Elgar jumps to the last two lines of the stanza (see Ex. 6.13). This provides a suitable method of bringing the work to a close, but the sudden departure from Tennyson's poetic sequence disorientates the listener (again evoking the effects of the fruit) – a process which is heightened further when the sequence of appoggiaturas shown in Ex. 6.11 is reclaimed by the male voices to sing "And in the stream the long-leaved flowers weep, / and from the craggy ledge the poppy hangs" (55–56). Elgar's use of repetition in general also reflects the importance of small-scale repetition in Tennyson's initial stanza of the Choric Song; in the poem, however, the effect is more one of hypnotic incantation rather than disorientation, with the reiteration of "tired" (51), "Music" (5, 7), or the formulations "And through," "And in," "And from" (54–56).[89] Throughout Elgar's setting, therefore, the listener (and indeed, the performer) is invited to enter the intoxicating world of Lotosland and to experience the sense of beauty, confusion and reverie induced by the fruit. As a mood-picture, and not a measured argument, there is no reference to the dangers of submitting to this temptation, and it is clear that the siren-song has been successful.

Tennyson's depiction of the subject of music in "The Lotos-Eaters" was significant. It illustrates how music's association with altered states, sensuality and the power to enchant – issues which were echoed throughout nineteenth-century culture in general – could be effectively explored within a poetic framework; this was achieved through the reworking of a familiar mythological narrative, with the incorporation of a musical structure (a Choric Song) as a vehicle for the promotion of the life of ease, and for the persuasive powers of music itself. Given the real opportunities for further exploration of these themes within a musical setting (allowing music to represent itself), it is not surprising that composers took up the challenge. Parry's earlier work reformulated Tennyson's poetry by assigning a female gender to the inner voice, thus making Tennyson's covert siren overt, and, in practical terms, by separating this voice off from the choral mariners. Together with the male/female division in the chorus, this highlights the sense of debate within the poem. The cumulative nature of the soprano's seductive coaxing (characterized by the use of third-related keys, vocal rhetoric, and the composer's acknowledgement of the sheer beauty of vocal sound) and the use of small-scale repetition towards the end of the work very much suggests a gradual move towards a final decision.[90] Elgar, on the other hand, responded with a realistic setting (the use of unaccompanied choir) of Tennyson's text; this avoids the sense of debate, and instead highlights the mariners' drugged state through the juxtaposition of keys, rhythmic dislocation, choral division, and partial recapitulations. In reinterpreting the subject of music as music,

---

[89] As in the previous footnote, Ricks's *The Poems of Tennyson* has "tired" and "through," while Elgar uses "tir'd" and "thro.'"

[90] An acknowledgement of the effectiveness of Parry's setting of *The Lotos-Eaters* also has implications for his reception. His setting of a "dangerous" text such as Shelley's *Prometheus Unbound* need not be viewed as something of a solitary aberration; in relation to Parry's association with hedonism, biographical details usually considered as marginal (a love of cars, fine wine, good food, cigars) could be taken more seriously, and an acceptance of Parry's ability to explore pure beauty of sound could also have some impact upon negative attitudes regarding his approach towards orchestration. For a discussion of the latter, see Allis, *Parry's Creative Process*, 110–112.

these two responses to Tennyson's "The Lotos-Eaters" represent an interesting addition to the literary debate over the poem. Parry and Elgar can therefore be identified as two strong readers of Tennyson's text.

Chapter 7

"Monna Innominata" and Christina Rossetti's Audible Unhappiness

Yeo Wei Wei

"It is always her own voice – no echo – a woman's voice, curiously sweet, fantastically sad," wrote Amy Levy of Christina Rossetti.[1] Poetry is evoked as an intimate space where the poet's voice is heard, speaking herself, making the particularity of her womanhood, "no echo" of any other, audible.[2] Unfathomable layers seem to lie beneath the printed surface of the voice. This chapter attends to what Eric Griffiths outlines as "a double nature in printed poetry": in "the absence of clearly indicated sound from the silence of the written word," the text contains "hints at voicing" even as it is laid out in "an achieved pattern on the page."[3] In Christina Rossetti's "Monna Innominata" (1881), a sequence of fourteen sonnets and a prose preface, gender and poetic voice are interrelated concerns. In the work Christina creates the distinct persona of an unnamed courtly lady, but she makes the lady sound just like her, creating a resemblance that strikes any reader familiar with her lyric voice, thus turning Levy's identification of her voice and person (a commonplace in contemporary reviews) on its head.[4] The illusion also creates a mirror-like space as the poet is able to see and hear herself from an outside perception of the persona, and this duality manifests itself in the polyphonic quality of the work. Reflexivity in "Monna Innominata" revolves around the poet's disparate and irreconcilable interests for female selfhood in poetic creation and love. This chapter explores the ways in which reflexivity operates not only through direct utterance in the sonnets, but also through implied (silently voiced) exchanges with other poets, most evident in the framing of each sonnet with

---

[1] Anon., "The Poetry of Christina Rossetti," *Woman's World* 1 (February 1888): 180.
[2] The figure of echo in Christina Rossetti's poetry is discussed by Angela Leighton in *Victorian Women Poets: Writing Against the Heart* (London: Harvester, 1992) 148–151.
[3] Eric Griffiths, *The Printed Voice of Victorian Poetry* (Oxford: Clarendon, 1989) 60. For a definition of voicing, see Chapter 8, n. 15.
[4] When referring to Christina and Dante Gabriel Rossetti, this essay uses given names instead of surnames to avoid confusion between the siblings.

epigraphs of paired quotations from Dante and Petrarch.[5] "Audible unhappiness" denotes the actual sound of Christina's "anxiety of influence."[6]

While tracing the aural dimensions of "Monna Innominata" as a manifestation of Christina's sizing up of herself against other masters, the chapter also explores the trope of music as Christina understood it, particularly in its bearing on her self-assessment as Christian poet. Christina's self-imaging and contesting of the Sapphic model of female song has been discussed by feminist scholars.[7] In a recent critical study, the question of the female poetic voice, particularly in the nineteenth century, is problematized as a "fantasy of origin" so that to approach a poet under the rubric of "voice" is tantamount to caging the poet within the ideology that delimited her poetics during her lifetime.[8] While this is useful to bear in mind, my chapter addresses the question of voice from a different angle, focusing on Christina's reflexive moves around the question itself. This chapter proposes that Christina tests the ideological boundaries of female orality through a daring and powerfully aural engagement with literary history, showing her acknowledgment of her debt to great and esteemed male voices within it even as she seeks to sing over and above them. In his book *Rhythm and Will in Victorian Poetry*, Matthew Campbell examines the prosodic innovations behind the many voices found in the poetry of Tennyson, Browning, Hopkins and Hardy. Although my chapter does not carry out prosodic analysis, it does share Campbell's interest in "the bodily experience of a poetry which is conscious of itself as voiced sound."[9] Campbell investigates the relation between speech and will, "a sense of agency which is posited central to the identity to the self"; in the rhythms of poetic speech he uncovers ambiguities that resonate semantically and aurally. Similarly, a crisis of poetic agency is audible in "Monna Innominata," a self-conscious work of female poetic will and the embodiment of conditions that circumscribe the very coming-to-be of the work itself.

In the preface of "Monna Innominata" Christina outlines her cause, questioning the absence of women poets from the beginning of the lyric tradition: she imagines that if silence had not been imposed upon the "unnamed ladies, 'donne innominate'" of that time, "many a lady" could have shown that she "[shared] her lover's poetic aptitude"; and she highlights the unhappy legacy of the inequality – heroines such as Beatrice and Laura,

---

[5] I will be paying more attention to Christina Rossetti's engagement with Dante in this essay. For a study of Petrarch's influence in her work, see Michele Martinez, "Christina Rossetti's Petrarca," *Essays and Studies* 56 (December 2003).

[6] Harold Bloom, *The Anxiety of Influence* (New York: Oxford University Press, 1973). Dante's influence on Christina Rossetti and the rest of her family has been treated in Alison Milbank, *Dante and the Victorians* (Manchester: Manchester University Press, 1998).

[7] Leighton, 118–163. See also Yopie Prins, *Victorian Sappho* (Princeton: Princeton University Press, 1999).

[8] Alison Chapman, *The Afterlife of Christina Rossetti* (Basingstoke: Macmillan, 2000) 28–45.

[9] Matthew Campbell, *Rhythm and Will in Victorian Poetry* (Cambridge: Cambridge University Press, 1999) 5.

unsympathetic creations of femininity by male poets who "have come down to us resplendent with charms, but ... scant of attractiveness."[10] In "Monna Innominata" she sets out to correct these two injustices: the woman speaker, Christina's unnamed lady as the title tells us, is precisely one of the troubadours' unnamed ladies freed from silence. Speaking for herself, unlike the ladies before her who appear in literary works in the capacity of mute addressee and muse, the Monna Innominata is an unmediated and thus dearer representation of femininity. Christina's aim is not only for such a lady to speak and be heard, but also to establish a vital relation between the voluble nature of her presence and her attractiveness to the reader. This is clear from the last paragraph of the preface:

> Had such a lady spoken for herself, the portrait left us might have appeared more tender, if less dignified, than any drawn even by a devoted friend. Or had the Great Poetess of our own day and nation only been unhappy instead of happy, her circumstances would have invited her to bequeath to us, in lieu of the "Portuguese Sonnets," an inimitable "donna innominata" drawn not from fancy but from feeling, and worthy to occupy a niche beside Beatrice and Laura. (Preface, "Monna Innominata")

"Monna Innominata" represents a determined bid for authenticity and authority in female self-representation through voice. Nor are male poets the only ones subject to this challenge – Christina applies the same terms in the distinction of her poetics from Elizabeth Barrett Browning's in the preface.

Deciphering the somewhat opaque reference to Elizabeth Barrett Browning's "Sonnets from the Portuguese" reveals that the Monna Innominata's projected historicity underpins Christina's sense of the value of her sequence: that through the sequence a historical void is filled as an unnamed lady of the historically mute past is allowed to speak as woman and poet. Christina presents this radically, and furtively, in her ranking of the Monna Innominata over Elizabeth Barrett Browning's Lady in "Sonnets from the Portuguese." The secretive nature of the comparison is suggested by Christina's opaque phrasing; more shall be made of this later. If, as Isobel Armstrong argues, Christina's criticism of Barrett Browning's "Sonnets from the Portuguese" is taken in a strictly biographical sense, this may account for the "happiness" of the "Great Poetess" but not Christina's reproach of their basis in "fancy."[11] It is only in seeing the comparison in the light of Christina's

---

[10] Christina Rossetti, preface, "Monna Innominata," in *The Complete Poems of Christina Rossetti: A Variorum Edition*, ed. R.W. Crump, 3 vols (Baton Rouge: Louisiana State University Press, 1979–1990) 2: 86. All subsequent citations from Christina Rossetti's poems are from this edition and are given in the text with line numbers.

[11] Isobel Armstrong's reading comes from understanding that "in Victorian terminology to be 'happy' was to be married." The reference to Barrett Browning's happiness in the context of criticism of her lady speaker might thus be interpreted as Christina's hint that Barrett Browning "might have been a different and perhaps a greater poet if she had remained single".

issue with Barrett Browning's Lady's historicity that the meaning of the terms – "unhappy" and "happy," "fancy" versus "feeling" – can be deciphered. The latter pair encapsulates the different historicities of their poetic personas, explained in a letter from Christina to her brother Dante Gabriel Rossetti (5 September 1881):

> The Lady [in "Sonnets from the Portuguese"] ... I was not regarding as an "innominata" at all, – because the latter type, according to the traditional figures I had in view, is surrounded by unlike circumstances.[12]

One might infer that the comparison foregrounds, or further emphasizes, the Monna Innominata's contemporaneity with the "donne innominate." In the same letter to Dante Gabriel, Christina writes: "[s]urely not only what I meant to say but what I do say is, not that the Lady of those sonnets is surpassable, but that a 'Donna innominata' by the same hand might well have been unsurpassable" (98). Christina's claim that "Monna Innominata" provides an "inimitable portrait" implies that the Portuguese Lady's sixteenth-century historical identity falls short on the same count in comparison. The implicit assertion is that there is a greater measure of authenticity in her work.

The claim of veracity in the Monna Innominata's historicity is not the only aspect of the work's boldness. Gender inequalities within the lyric genre are severely questioned. The subject of song and of singing, coming from the historical relation of lyric poetry and song, confronts the patriarchal limits of the lyric tradition by questioning some of its discriminatory assumptions and tropes. In Sonnet 2, the trope of the lovers' memorable first meeting from the courtly love tradition is subverted. The Monna Innominata cannot remember the first meeting: "I wish I could remember that first day, / First hour, first moment of your meeting me, / ... / So unrecorded did it slip away" (1–2, 5). In the second quatrain Monna Innominata laments her ignorance of her significance to the male lover-poet: "So blind was I to see and to foresee, / So dull to mark the budding of my tree / That would not blossom yet for many a May" (6–8). The lines imply, however, that the reason for her forgetfulness lies in her exclusion from the outset from any sense of the event's relevance to her as a woman and a poet. A similar vein of criticism is found in Sonnet 4 where the Monna Innominata speaks of how she is loved as "what might or might not be", as something "construed" by her lover (7, 6). The pressing need for self-representation is directly expressed in Sonnet 11, opening with the lines: "Many in aftertimes will say of you / 'He loved her' – while of me what will they say?" (1–2). In Sonnet 1 the Monna Innominata's unhappiness at her

---

See Isobel Armstrong, *Victorian Poetry: Poetry, Poetics and Politics* (London: Routledge, 1996) 345.

[12] Christina Rossetti to D.G. Rossetti, 5 September 1881, *The Family Letters of Christina Georgina Rossetti, with Some Supplementary Letters and Appendices*, ed. William Michael Rossetti (London: Brown, Langham, 1908) 98.

insufficiency and incompleteness of self reveals her thorough mediation by her poet-lover: her "sweetest 'when'" is "when he comes"; the "songs [she] sang" and her life were "sweet because [he] called them sweet" (6, 13, 14).

Even as Christina questions the constraints placed upon women in the lyric tradition, her own writing was being interpreted within a gendered framework. A juxtaposition can be drawn between what contemporary reviews of her writing meant when they wrote of her songlike or musical verse and Christina's confrontation of gender inequalities in the meaning and implications of song from the time lyric poetry began in "Monna Innominata." The song analogy evokes form and effects – the sweetness of tone, the lyricism of texture, the brevity of the composition – in reviews of Victorian women's poetry, these are all qualities designated as fitting for the verse of women.[13] Edmund Gosse opined in line with convention when he wrote that "women, in order to succeed in poetry, must be brief, personal, and concentrated."[14] The analogy bears a different significance for male poets. Earlier on in the century, Percy Bysshe Shelley's and William Hazlitt's writings employ the music analogy to convey a perception of harmony in poetry as creative transcription of harmony in nature.[15] The analogy implies the cosmological significance of poetic works since a poem renders audible, visible, and thus comprehensible, the order of the world.[16] It also carries a conception of the poet as instrument in the sense that he relates what nature impresses upon him like a lyre played upon by a wind through poetry, combining description and imagination (Abrams, 50). The suggestion of such contiguity and correlation between poet and world seems to have been absent in descriptions of women's poetry as songlike. Woman's relation to song in affect continued its sway in Christina's own time; its influence is seen not only in nineteenth-century perceptions of women's poetry, but it also played a part in restricting the kind of music contemporary women composers could make. Women composers were "extraordinarily successful as song writers," according to an astute businessman, William Boosey, who sent texts to many of the women

---

[13] Similar expectations defined the boundaries of women composers in the nineteenth century. See Phyllis Weliver, *Women Musicians in Victorian Fiction, 1860–1900* (Aldershot: Ashgate, 2000): "both female amateurs and professionals could compose, but their pieces should be melodious, graceful music for voice and/or piano. Only men should write powerful, theoretically rigorous music for large-scale, public works like symphonies and operas" (25–26). For a detailed study of the practical financial and ideological constraints on women composers in the nineteenth century, see Sophie Fuller, Chapter 3, "Women Composers During the British Musical Renaissance, 1880–1918," diss., King's College, University of London, 1998, 82–139.

[14] Edmund Gosse, "Christina Rossetti," *Critical Kit-Kats* (1896), in *The Victorian Poet: Poetics and Persona*, ed. Joseph Bristow (New York: Croon Helm, 1987) 138.

[15] M.H. Abrams, *The Mirror and the Lamp: Romantic Theory and the Critical Tradition* (1953; Oxford: Oxford University Press, 1971) 48–52. See also the essays by Susan Bernstein and Kimiyo Ogawa in this volume.

[16] See Edward Lippman, *A History of Western Musical Aesthetics* (Lincoln: University of Nebraska Press, 1992), Chapter 1, for the origin of the association between musical and cosmic harmony in Platonic and Pythagorean ideas.

composers whose works he published to encourage them to write more songs.[17] In music as well as in poetry the meaning of song was ideologically gendered and it bore fruit that fitted the mould. The proliferation of lyrics in women's poetry and the important place of women composers in the culture of the Victorian drawing-room song make this evident. "[M]id-Victorian song ... was a genre that not only embraced stylistic features, from sentimentality to simple tunefulness, that were regarded as 'feminine', but also appeared to have been dominated by women" (Fuller, 104). In poetry the construct of femininity in the separate spheres ideology also leaves a clear imprint: the association of women's verse with the conventional notion of their innate sweetness makes the harmony in their poetry simply an effect of the harmony that "naturally" abides in their female persons. In *Middlemarch*, Will Ladislaw's conversation with Dorothea about poetry reflects this:

> "To be a poet is to have a soul so quick to discern that no shade of quality escapes it, and so quick to feel, that discernment is but a hand playing with finely-ordered variety on the chords of emotion – ...."
>
> "But you leave out the poems," said Dorothea. "I think they are wanted to complete the poet .... I am sure I could never produce a poem."
>
> "You *are* a poem – and that is to be the best part of a poet – what makes up the poet's consciousness in his best moods," said Will, showing such originality as we all share with the morning and the spring-time and other endless renewals.[18]

When an anonymous writer in 1833 said in *Fraser's Magazine* that "there never yet existed a female possessed of personal loveliness who was not only poetical in herself but the cause of poetry in others," the "poetical" nature of women here refers to "the sweet humanities of existence" fully manifest in their persons.[19] According to an anonymously written article in the journal *Living Age*, "a woman's personality dominates and permeates her character to a greater degree than does a man's" and this is why women's "creative mental life is less distinct from the outer practical one than is the case with men," so much so that "it is rare to find the spirit of a woman's work and her conduct in complete antagonism."[20]

Reviewers praised the sweetness of Christina's verse as an attribute of her virtuous femininity. The view of an anonymous critic that "[h]er lovely verse was simply the expression of a lovely personality, exquisitely feminine, sweet and pure, good and worshipful" was widely held.[21] Sonnet 12 of "Monna

---

[17] William Boosey, *Fifty Years of Music* (London: Benn, 1931). Cited in Fuller, 90–91.
[18] George Eliot, *Middlemarch*, Cabinet ed., vol. 1 (1874; Edinburgh: Blackwood, 1878) 341–342.
[19] Anon., "The Female Character," *Fraser's Magazine: For Town and Country* 7 (1833): 601.
[20] Anon., "Some Women Poets," *Living Age* (1 April 1899): 26–34.
[21] Anon., "Miss Rossetti's Poems," *Saturday Review* (February 1896): 196. Cited in Edna Kotin Charles, *Christina Rossetti: Critical Perspectives, 1862–1982* (Selinsgrove: Susquehanna University Press, 1985) 62.

Innominata" was singled out for its display of selfless love. T. Hall Caine wrote: "[t]enderness more true, and resignation more beautiful, ... do not find utterances in English poetry."[22] Hers was a voice from the hearth, noted a reviewer who praised her simplicity in her use of "the homeliest words" and "rhythms in which the art consists in a seeming disregard of art."[23] The association of her diction and home was also made by Arthur Symons who praised her style for "its sincerity, leading to the employment of homely words where homely words are wanted, and always of natural and really expressive words."[24] The critic H.B. Foreman spoke highly of the "reticence in [Christina Rossetti's] songs of the affections," noting that the "very essence of maidenly delicacy" is found in poems like "A Birthday" where "healthy happiness and the ringing melody of a joyful heart" does not break forth in an "unmeasured and uncomely burst ... of excessive openness of expression."[25] His sentiments are echoed by Symons who wrote: "[t]his equable style ... has no italics, no waltz beats, nothing insistent ... absolutely no display" (338). The poet seems to have been complicit in sustaining her acceptable feminine public image. Verses that did not cohere with her image as poet-saint, such as "Cousin Kate," "Sister Maude," and "A Triad," were withdrawn from subsequent imprints of *Goblin Market* after appearing in the first edition of 1862 (Charles, 66–67). In the context of "Monna Innominata," perhaps it was to distance herself from the potentially controversial voice of her persona that the latter's distinctive historicity is emphasized in the preface. Yet by the same stroke the preface heralds the emergence of a kind of female song that is unconventional and without precedent. It gives the reader a foretaste of the work's ambition – ambition that vaults over the estimation of Christina's contemporaries, overturning their gendered interpretations and boundaries. Self-assertiveness in "Monna Innominata" chimes with the tonic key, as it were, of *A Pageant and Other Poems*, the volume in which "Monna Innominata" first appeared: the second poem in the volume is suggestively titled "The Key-Note" and it speaks of the poet's "commitment to continue singing in answer to the silence of winter."[26]

"Music" and "song" in "Monna Innominata" have a wider resonance than feminine sweetness; although this is not directly articulated, its traces can be found in the work's intertextual arrangements. The significance of music in Christina's poetics emerges particularly in her self-comparison with Dante, the poet she admired most. Petrarch's relative inferiority will be explained later. Writing about heaven in *Time Flies* (1885), Christina evokes it as a place of

---

[22] T. Hall Caine, *Academy* (27 August 1881): 152. Cited in ibid., 40.

[23] Anon., *Saturday Review* (January 1895). See ibid., 56.

[24] Arthur Symons, "Miss Rossetti's Poetry," *London Quarterly Review* 68 (July 1887): 339.

[25] Anon., "Criticism on Contemporaries. No. VI. The Rossettis. Part 1. Christina Rossetti," *Tinsley's Magazine* 5 (August 1869): 63–64.

[26] Diane D'Amico, *Christina Rossetti: Faith, Gender, and Time* (Baton Rouge: Louisiana State University Press, 1999) 150. I thank Phyllis Weliver for drawing my attention to the significance of this poem's title. See Christina Rossetti, *A Pageant and Other Poems* (London, Edinburgh, 1881).

music, suggesting heaven's infinite richness and variety through the association with music.[27] She elaborates on this vision of the heavenly afterlife in *The Face of the Deep* (1892): "[h]eaven is revealed to earth as the homeland of music: of music, thus remote from what is gross or carnal; exhibiting like-wise an incalculable range of variety, which rebukes and silences perverse suggestions of monotonous tedium in the final beatitude."[28] This image of heaven suggests the vital influence of Dante's conception of heaven in *Paradiso*. The heavenly spheres are home to God's community of the saved whom Dante the protagonist not only meets and speaks to, but also hears in varied and extraordinary ways. In *Paradiso* 10: 64–81 and 24: 151–154, lights and St Peter respectively sing as they circle around Dante. In *Paradiso* 14: 118–119, the lights of souls in the sphere of Mars form a cross that vibrates "*come giga e arpa, in tempra tesa / di molte core, fa dolce tintinno*."[29]

Music features substantially in Christina's measurement of herself as Christian poet against the standard set by Dante in the *Commedia*. The flipside of this is that music can also be representative of Christina's anxiety of influence in relation to Dante. In one of her essays Christina writes that the *Commedia* is like "organ music," "sustained" and "sonorous" in its timbre, projecting a "majestic swelling and sinking continuity of sound" through its *terza rima*.[30] This brings to mind the distinction of male and female song in Sonnet 4 – the former is "loftier" whilst the latter is compared to "the friendly cooings of [a] dove" (2, 3). The comparison suggests a contrast of eloquence and grandeur to a homelier style. Perhaps the Monna Innominata's self-consciousness here is telling of her poet's as she places herself in the same pantheon as Dante. The association between Dante and music is reinforced in "An Old-World Thicket," another poem from *A Pageant and Other Poems*, where Dante is again allusively evoked through an epigraph ("*Una selva oscura*" – a reference to the dark wood at the start of the *Commedia*) and in the narrative of the poem. The music of Dante's great work is not mentioned anywhere, but the strange aural experience of the poetic persona in the middle of a mysterious wood can be interpreted as embodiment of the poet's anxiety of influence in relation to Dante, albeit within the folds of a fictive narrative. The poetic persona hears a heavenly music in the middle of a mysterious wood and is consequently driven to despair by this physical manifestation of the ideal:

---

[27] Christina Rossetti, *Time Flies: A Reading Diary* (London: SPCK, 1885) 29.

[28] Christina Rossetti, *The Face of the Deep: A Devotional Commentary on the Apocalypse* (London: SPCK, 1892) 352.

[29] "as a viol and harp, stretched and tuned, make a sweet sound of many strings to one who cannot distinguish the melody." For other instances of music in *Paradiso*, see 12: 6; 15: 4; 20: 22–24; 23: 109–110; 25: 131–132. On the subject of Dante and music, see John Stevens, "Dante and Music," *Italian Studies* 23 (1968): 1–18.

[30] Christina Rossetti, "Dante, An English Classic," *The Churchman's Shilling Magazine and Family Treasury* (October 1867): 201, 200.

> Sweetness of beauty moved me to despair,
>   Stung me to anger by its mere content,
>   Made me all lonely on that way I went,
>   Piled care upon my care,
> Brimmed full my cup, and stripped me empty and bare: (46–50)

The thicket is Eden-like and it emanates a perfect music; the persona is physically overwhelmed by these manifestations of perfection, for against them she finds herself well beyond par.

Music features not only in the poem's dramatization of Christina's measurement of self against Dante; it is also a key element in the resolution of the unhappiness that such comparison gives rise to. In this sense music acts as a reminder of heaven and the irrelevance of earthly weights and measures that is found there as well as in all Godly places and hearts. When the persona's crisis has crossed its worst point and before calm is restored, a curious aural phenomenon takes place, surfacing an internal process of self-reasoning:

> Without, within me, music seemed to be;
>   Something not music, yet most musical,
> Silence and sound in heavenly harmony;[31]

Diane D'Amico's exploration of the Christian element in Christina's focus on song has revealed that in the later part of her life Christina became more responsive to Biblical texts that describe heaven as a place of song. The moral significance of music and its opposites, dissonance and silence, is a new characteristic in the later poetic and religious prose writings.[32] The effects in sound, including that of their absence, are literal translations of inner states of being, or of one's unspoken but nonetheless present desires and preoccupations. Dissonance and reticence are effects of worldliness, whereas music conveys purity and transcendence of the earthly (D'Amico, 152). Since silence for Christina is an effect of sinfulness, then here, the conquering of silence through its mixture with sound suggests a process in which sin or an earthly desire is rebuked and quelled.[33] The "heavenly harmony" does not come from heaven but from the self's moral instruction: it is through submission to God that the persona wins her struggle to overcome the ungodly thoughts and feelings that had brought on the crisis in the first place.

The poem's ending and the persona's resolution on the note of submission is significant. Christina's unhappiness at her belatedness to Dante goes against the grain of Christian teaching on how submission and obedience to God are

---

[31] Christina Rossetti, "An Old-World Thicket," *A Pageant and Other Poems* (1881) 141–143.
[32] See D'Amico's excellent study of music references in Christina's religious poetic and prose writings (152–154).
[33] See Christina Rossetti, *The Face of the Deep*: "when earth first saw the light in panoply of beauty the morning stars sang together and all the sons of God shouted for joy: sinless earth, for sinless it then seems to have been whether or not inhabited, called forth instead of silencing an outburst of celestial music" (241).

reflected through performance and acceptance of one's given place or musical part.[34] Christina's understanding of heaven as a place of music provides a framework for her understanding of this:

> Perhaps one reason why music is made so prominent among the revelations vouchsafed us of heaven, is because it imperatively requires living agency for its production ...
>
> The music of heaven, to become music, must have trumpeters and harpers as well as harps and trumpets, must have singers as well as songs. (*Time Flies*, 29, 30)

Yet this belief in the rightfulness of every place in heaven is confronted by Christina's own keen sense of her displacement as woman and poet on the earth that is governed by authority that comes from such a heaven. She is trammeled in her own "living agency" by her sex, an awareness which vexed her self-comparison with Dante whom she rated higher than Petrarch because of her greater admiration for the standard of Christian agency found in his art. Before going into Dante's perfection in this respect for Christina it is necessary to see what Christina understood as Christian agency.

The seed of Christina's Christian unhappiness is buried inside a conviction that human performance will always fall short of God's standard. She writes about the difficulty of meeting the standard, beginning with its ineffability:

> Whilst Unity appears as the sole existence essential to be conceived, our conceiving it as separate from ourself [*sic*] attests at once our likeness and our unlikeness to it. That which we conceive is on our own showing other than ourselves who conceive it: yet to conceive that which has no existence is (I reverently assume) the exclusive attribute of Almighty God, Who out of nothing created all things.[35]

The struggle to meet adequately the demands of the imperative begins with the problem of conception. The limits of human faculties constrain as they necessarily define understanding, not only of the task at hand but also the promise in store. The limits of the mind are predetermined, but Christina's apprehension is of an additional shortcoming which can be helped, a falling-short of will or self-discipline. As she put it in her writing on disinclination:

> DISINCLINATION may never go such lengths as to make us purposely omit a single duty, yet may it colour and dwarf our whole conception of duty .... Conscientious, and more especially scrupulous, persons seem characteristically open to this sin of

---

[34] In studies of poetic influence, under the shadow of Harold Bloom's *The Anxiety of Influence*, "belatedness" is a term that refers to the chronological difference between an earlier and a later poet. It connotes the unhappiness of the later poet.

[35] Christina Rossetti, *Letter and Spirit: Notes on the Commandments* (London: SPCK, n.d.) 27.

> Disinclination, even while they toil persistently along the narrow path; Disinclination makes them (so to say) graze the hedge on one side or other at every step; thorns catch them, stones half trip them up, a perpetual dust attends their footsteps, grace and comeliness of aspect vanish. Though they dare not shut themselves up comfortably indoors with the slothful man (Prov. 22.13), they are haunted by the "lion without", and dwell on the probability of his catching them at every corner. They observe the wind even while they sow, and study the clouds while they reap; thus combining into one unseemly whole the discomforts of obedience and of disobedience. (*Letter and Spirit*, 35)

The movement toward God's love is made on account of it being unlike the kinds of love we know in our realm of things. The endeavor requires application of will to an end beyond our powers of conception and understanding. Its reward in this life is a problem, given its ineffability and infinite measure. Not giving in to disinclination demands whole-hearted obedience, a bending of will to the serving of God. God's love commands absolute and unconditional obedience. To abide by one's love for God consists of efforts toward meeting the standard in spite of limitations and weakness. In Christina's understanding of this, self-surrender is taken to be the solution and the imperative condition: "[a] self-surrendering awe-struck reverence is all that beseems us in contemplating this Mystery of Mysteries, the Trinity in Unity." (*Letters and Spirit*, 12) Self-surrender does not translate simply into a watershed gesture of acceptance, nor does it imply total inner resolution. Its essence is of process – the Christian's subjection of self to a process of relentless and unrelenting self-inquisition, of indefatigably taking oneself to task:

> The Bible records for our encouragement instances of persons who needed to overcome themselves in the first place: that done, their circumstances turned out favourable ... the paramount motive for what we do or leave undone – if, that is, we aim at either acting or forbearing worthily – is love: not fear, or self-interest, or even hatred of sin, or sense of duty, but direct filial love to God. (*Letter and Spirit*, 35)

The prerequisite of commitment to love is an admission of the need for self-abnegation. William Michael Rossetti highlights this aspect in his criticism of Christina's propensity for "self-postponement" and her inclination toward "self-sacrifice": "[s]he was replete with the spirit of self-postponement, which passed into self-sacrifice whenever that quality was in demand."[36] The choice of terms is somewhat misleading. Postponement and sacrifice do not convey

---

[36] *The Poetical Works of Christina Rossetti, with a Memoir and Notes by William Michael Rossetti* (London: Macmillan, 1904) lxvii.

the force of resistance, the tension and strife, within a self convinced that it must first be "overcome" before it can proceed to love.

The Christian duty of self-surrender came into conflict with Christina's poetic vocation. As artist, her every act must needs be a pronouncement and assertion of self. Most of Christina's poems display the conflict of contradictory drives, the self-asserting versus the self-abnegating. Her every endeavor toward poetic achievement and greatness is leaden-footed and to a certain extent, crippled by anxiety of straying. The overcoming of self entails flattening of ego, repression of ambition. Christina's problem with this can be inferred from the strain of resentment in all her songs of renunciation. There is will to resistance in spite of intention to commit self-postponement. Her lyrics are often about death, loss, doubt, failure, but they are the product of an ego unshakably self-possessed and keen on success. Goals may be admittedly impossible, as in the lament of "De Profundis":

> Oh why is heaven built so far,
>   Oh why is earth set so remote?
> I cannot reach the nearest star
>   That hangs afloat. (1–4)

Yet in this poem from *A Pageant and Other Poems*, resignation is tempered characteristically with resolve, self-control exercised in forceful gestures of trying: the poem ends with her settling to "strain [her] heart" and "stretch [her] hands" to "catch at hope" (15, 16). "Pastime," a poem in the same volume, betrays a steely inner edge, stern guardian against the slightest chance of unproductive despair:

> A boat amid the ripples, drifting, rocking,
>   Two idle people, without pause or aim;
>   ...
> Better a wrecked life than a life so aimless,
>   Better a wrecked life than a life so soft; (1–2, 9–10)

The element of struggle is a constant in Christina's writing, an attribute of her life as Christian, woman and poet. It features in her attitude toward Dante because the common ground between them on two of these aspects gave rise to comparison and competition. How Christina placed herself in relation to Dante shows her coping not only with the challenge or liability of being a later poet, but also her sense of their relation as Christian artists, as poets who strive, explore and articulate what it means to live responsibly as Christians.

Criticism on "Monna Innominata" has mostly dealt with the gender implications of Christina's use of quotations from Dante and Petrarch as epigraphs. In such readings the grouping of Dante and Petrarch as a pair of male poets whose interests are opposite to that of Christina is frequently assumed. However, this instance is not mirrored in every part of the sequence.

Most of the epigraphs relate in non-uniform ways to the sonnets they are attached to as a pair. Christina speaks with Dante and Petrarch, but the writings of the poets chosen for their dialogue suggest the disparity between them that their appearance in print belies. The only place that gives an inkling of the unannounced disparity in Christina's attitude towards the two poets is the preface where she ranks them by way of introduction: Dante is "altissimo poeta," superior to Petrarch, "a great tho' an inferior bard". Beyond "Monna Innominata," Christina's lesser regard for Petrarch compared to Dante is evident from the fewer instances of allusion and reference to the former in her oeuvre. In the work, the poets' appearance is misleading; appearing in pairs side by side, the epigraphs conceal their unequal ranks. Close reading shows that a wider circumference of associations is found through the Dante epigraphs, suggesting the limits of Petrarch, limits that are quietly emphasized through the unstated comparison with Dante.

The greatness of Dante over Petrarch signifies that his kind of music is most desirable to Christina. This begs the question: what are the terms that feature crucially in their comparison? How do Dante's *cantos* surpass Petrarch's *canzoniere*? The different ends that are served by their ladies in the works that appear in "Monna Innominata" provide a clue. Like the pairing of the epigraphs, the mention of Laura alongside Beatrice in the preface creates a specious impression of equivalence. The fact that Christina quotes Dante in the *Commedia* rather than *La vita nuova* is significant in this respect: Laura's presence is evoked through the epigraphs from Petrarch's *Rime sparse*; Beatrice's presence does not take center stage in the *Commedia* in the same way that it does in *La vita nuova*, but her appearance in the later poem confirms the vital role she plays in Dante's achievement of poetic greatness.[37] Christina's choice of text reveals her appreciation of Beatrice in this light, her recognition of Beatrice's uniqueness in the courtly lyric tradition. Beatrice is elevated through the higher objective of the *Commedia*; the poem is centered on God rather than Dante's love for Beatrice, and the reunion of Dante and Beatrice demonstrates the way in which the new emphasis makes the *Commedia* a more consummate work of art than *La vita nuova*. Dante's poetic promise at the end of the earlier work about courtly love is affirmed by the *Commedia*, a poem about Godly love. There is no such progression in Petrarch's career.

For Christina, Dante's poetry provides a standard of Christian and poetic achievement that is not found in the fixedly subjective attentions of Petrarch's art. Artistic autonomy is less unresolved in the *Commedia* than in the *Rime sparse*. While Dante asserts his artistic will through witness to God's love, Petrarch's consecration of Laura and the laurel, both richly self-referential

---

[37] *La vita nuova* (vernacular lyric poems with prose narrative and commentary) was compiled in 1292; Dante began writing the *Commedia* around 1307. It is not known when he finished it, but he died in 1321. Petrarch wrote the *Rime sparse* between the early 1330s and the mid 1350s. In 1366, Petrarch began to put together a definitive version of the *Rime sparse*, a task of revision, transcribing and re-arrangement that he continued well into the last year of his life.

images, projects an egocentric trinity. As John Freccero put it, Petrarch's representation of Laura betrays "at the linguistic level the essence of poetic autonomy," creating a "poetic strategy" that "corresponds, in the theological order, to the sin of idolatry":

> Petrarch makes of [the laurel] the emblem of the mirror relationship *Laura-Lauro*, which is to say, the poetic lady created by the poet, who in turn creates him as poet laureate. This circularity forecloses all referentiality and in its self-contained dynamism [poet-Laura-laurel] resembles the inner life of the Trinity as the Church fathers imagined it. One could scarcely suppose a greater autonomy.[38]

The common view is that the penitential tone of the *Rime sparse* carries the freight of Petrarch's oscillation between a tendency to idolatry and Christian knowledge.[39] Yet it can be argued, as Freccero has done, that the refrain of this struggle carries also the tune of poetic self-assertion:

> By accusing his persona of an idolatrous passion Petrarch [confirms his strategy of autoreflexivity, thus] affirming his own autonomy as a poetic creator. To psychologize about "spiritual torment" in the [*Rime sparse*] is to live the illusion that Petrarch was perhaps the first to create. (40)

As a comparison of the epigraphs attached to Sonnet 14 in "Monna Innominata" shows, Dante's and Petrarch's distinct centralities in poetic self-affirmation are significantly regarded by Christina. The fusion of poetic agenda and Christian agency is achieved to markedly different degrees in Dante and Petrarch, manifest in the poets' different approaches to love. In Dante, love dwells in the hearts of the community who recognize that the greatest measure of love is found in God, whereas love in Petrarch is limited. The protagonist in the *Commedia* and the poetic persona in the *Rime sparse* represent their poets' distinct emphases through the kinds of journeys they make in the course of the works. Dante's *personaggio* travels to return to the straight way that he lost in the dark wood and the journey through the other world leads him eventually to God, ending the poem with an actual vision of love. Petrarch's persona does not travel beyond the realm of his eye and mind; his understanding of love is based on the self's desire to possess the other. Petrarch's loving gaze at Laura does not extend beyond himself. The epigraphs to Sonnet 14 reflect the distinction through their contrast:

---

[38] John Freccero, "The Fig Tree and the Laurel: Petrarch's Poetics," *Diacritics* 5 (1975): 40, 37.
[39] For the alternative view, see Giuseppe Mazzotta, "The Canzoniere and the Language of the Self," *Studies in Philology* 75 (1978): 271–296.

> "*E la Sua Volontade è nostra pace.*" – DANTE.[40]
> "*Sol con questi pensier, con altre chiome.*" – PETRARCH.[41]

The Dante epigraph is taken from Piccarda's speech in *Paradiso* 3. She is encountered in the moon, the first sphere of Paradise where souls whose only fault lies in inconsistent faith appear to Dante and his guide. The Petrarch epigraph is a quotation from the sestina "*Giovene donna sotto un verde lauro.*" The commemoration of a historic moment, Petrarch's first meeting with Laura, may be the stated aim of the sestina, but it registers more closely a process of introspection: the poetic persona is more intent on viewing the event through its transformations in his head than on recording it factually. Laura's portrait is thus formed as an inseparable part of the persona's self-image. Not whole in herself, her image consists of an assemblage of beautiful body parts; if once a historical person, her historicity has been appropriated to serve Petrarch's poetic self-interest. In the sestina the poetic persona's self-centeredness is a constant. The phrase "*Sol con questi pensier*" paints an image of solitary introspection whereas the picture of a community of kindred souls is conjured by the use of the plural "*nostra*" in the Dante epigraph. In *Paradiso* 3 the line conveys the souls' happy allegiance to God through obedience to His Will. God's community is filled with love and light, embodied by the warmth and the luminosity of the souls in the canto (*Paradiso*, 3: 69, 3: 109–111, 3: 118). The beauty of their souls translates into a physical beauty that makes them unrecognizable (58–60). The contrast between the beauty that is praised here and in Petrarch's poem is striking: for Dante, truth is "*bella,*" bearing "*il dolce aspetto,*" giving radiance to the souls who have it; for Petrarch, beauty, embodied by Laura, is found in an inaccessible and strange femininity – cold, pale, like snow long without sun ("*più bianca et più fredda che neve / non percossa dal sol molti et molt'anni*"). The relation between the persona and Laura consists solely of the former's gazing at the latter such that Laura exists only as a reflection in his eyes. Unlike the souls in *Paradiso* 3, Laura's beauty does not reflect the greatness and love of God, only the mastery of her poet-lover. The phrase "*altre chiome*" reflects the persona's advanced years but at the same time it evokes his triumph over time. Through his craft Laura's "*chiome*" have turned into gold for posterity; the laurel's golden crown stands for poetic greatness. The worldly triumph of self in Petrarch's lyric contrasts with the dismissal of earthly measures in Dante, voiced by Piccarda:

> *Chiaro mi fu allor come ogne dove*
> *in cielo è paradiso, etsi la grazia*
> *del sommo ben d'un modo non vi piove.* (*Paradiso*, 3: 88–90)[42]

---

[40] In his good pleasure we have each his peace.
[41] Alone with these my thoughts, with altered hair.
[42] Now plain it grew to me, how everywhere / In heaven is Paradise, though the Chiefest Weal / His grace not equally distributes there.

Against such resonances in the epigraphs, the Monna Innominata's retreat into silence in Sonnet 14 is curious. It is at this point, near the end of the sequence, that a distance between poet and persona becomes most apparent. Reflexivity takes on a severely self-critical edge. Significantly, Christina's self-checking is audible in her subtle censuring of the Monna Innominata through Dante. At times the space between sonnets and epigraphs seems to swell with Christina's unhappiness with the persona. These are instances where sympathy with Dante on grounds of Christian understanding can be said to override Christina's other concerns that are nonetheless voiced through the Monna Innominata. The Dante epigraphs in Sonnets 1, 2, 7, 8, 11, 12, 13, and 14 come from cantos with vocal music that is sung in worship. Psalms and hymns sung by souls in *Paradiso* point to the fusion of music and poetic agency in Christian ministry. In contrast, the Monna Innominata's song is worldly and self-centered. The rift between the Monna Innominata's approach to song and that implied by Christina's quotations from Dante consists of the conflict of earthly and Godly interests within the poet herself. This is embodied by the dissonance of the sonnets, heard only through comparison with the heavenly music allusively evoked through the epigraphs. Two other instances of juxtaposition suggest the poet's mixed feelings towards the Monna Innominata. The epigraphs to Sonnets 4 and 10 come from *Paradiso* 1 where Dante hears the music of the heavens. He marks "[*l*]*a novità del suono*" (the newness of the sound) (*Paradiso*, 1: 82) in "*l'armonia*" (the harmony), a song of desire and love for God generated by the motions of the Primum Mobile, that is, motions of the desire in every one of its parts that yearns for the Empyrean. The sound of a harmony beyond comparison in the epigraph to Sonnet 4 strikes a subtle contrast to the subject of the sonnet: the comparisons that rule secular love relations. This suggests reproach of the Monna Innominata in the space between the Dante epigraph and Sonnet 4. In the case of Sonnet 10, however, a refrain of empathy with the Monna Innominata's longing for the perfection of afterlife is discernible. For both Sonnets 4 and 10 the Dante epigraphs come from contexts where comparisons of earthly nature are evoked. Their new setting in the epigraphs lend a resonance to their words that is not found formerly in *Paradiso* 1: evoking the wordless and incomparable music of the heavenly spheres, the epigraphs imply the inconsequentiality of human comparisons in the face of the divine.

In Dante, Christina finds a model of Christian poetics worthy of emulation. Her reflection on the two variants of his name reveals as much: "*Dante* (giving) befits one who has enriched the after ages; *Durante* (enduring) suits no less that much-enduring man."[43] Yet, as "An Old-World Thicket" suggests, her sense of the perfect standard in Dante gives rise to anxiety. The aural also features in relation to Christina's unhappiness from the incompatibility of her secular and Christian hopes in "Monna Innominata," not simply in the

---

[43] Christina Rossetti, "Dante, The Poet Illustrated Out of the Poem," *The Century Magazine* 27 (February 1884): 567.

narrative but as part of its form. Christina's sympathy with Dante in preference over Petrarch is embodied in the interactive space of sonnet and epigraph. This aspect of the poets' exchange is not declared in the preface; indeed, it seems to be a secret that the work's gender polemic cannot admit. There is a hint of Christina's different regard for Dante and Petrarch in the texts that she chose to represent them: the *Commedia* is clearly a work of greater magnitude and breadth than the *Rime sparse*. The voices of the poets that distinguishes them for her is implied in that choice and they resonate through the allusive aural dimensions of the epigraphs, snatches of lyrics from Dante's and Petrarch's song. The vocalizing of other poets through implied exchanges with the Monna Innominata and her echoes of predecessors invokes poetic tradition through embodiment. Christina was very taken with this method, going so far as to marvel at its originality in a highly uncharacteristic fashion: "I rather wonder that no one (so far as I know) ever hit on my semi-historical argument before for such a treatment, – it seems to me so full of poetic suggestiveness."[44] "Poetic suggestiveness" gives apt description of the sequence's aspect of hidden and declared relations with other poets. As the reference to Elizabeth Barrett Browning suggests, the Monna Innominata's parity with Beatrice and Laura and her superiority over the Portuguese Lady seems to be based on a system of poetic value, but its workings are not self-evident and the way in which the evaluation is simply stated without further qualification in the preface suggests that unquestioning acceptance of its validity is required of the reader. Christina's obscurity and silence succeed in eliding the issue of poetic standing that she raises confidently in the preface at a precise point: that is, where she might have explained exactly why her Monna Innominata is superior to the Portuguese Lady. The greater age of the Monna Innominata is Christina's justification for her advantage over Barrett Browning's portrait, but behind this lies an inaccessible logic. Her use of terms as binaries without any accompanying key as to how they are meant to function and her tone of strident purposefulness in the preface suggest that the inaccessibility is due more to intentional secrecy than oversight.

The Monna Innominata's historicity is accorded its curious significance, featuring crucially in Christina's comparison with Barrett Browning as well as in that with the male poets of tradition because it is the cornerstone of Christina's claim to a particular rank in poetic history and tradition. Such determined comparison with other poets, whether contemporary Victorian or historically remote, suggests Christina's self-consciousness about her own historicity as poet. Christina's secret anxiety can be uncovered by decoding the enigmatic language used in her reference to Barrett Browning. The pairing of "unhappiness" with "feeling" and "happiness" with "fancy" is curious, but the mystery may be solved, I think, if one refers to Shakespeare's Sonnet 32.

---

[44] Christina Rossetti to D.G. Rossetti, 5 September 1881, *Family Letters of Christina Rossetti*, 98.

> If thou survive my well-contented day
> When that churl Death my bones with dust shall cover,
> And shalt by fortune once more re-survey
> These poor rude lines of thy deceasèd lover,
> Compare them with the bett'ring of the time,
> And, though they be outstripp'd by every pen,
> Reserve them for my love, not for their rhyme,
> Exceeded by the height of happier men.
> O, then vouchsafe me but this loving thought:
> "Had my friend's Muse grown with this growing age,
> A dearer birth than this his love had brought
> To march in ranks of better equipage;
> > But since he died and poets better prove,
> > Theirs for their style I'll read, his for his love."[45]

Casting his mind to the future, the poet sees the surpassing of his present work by later poets whose advantage rests simply in their belatedness: these poets are "happier men" for they attain greatness through their birth at a maturer stage of history, expressed through the figures of "height" and "growing age." The later poets are "happier" by dint of their better talent or their living in more opportune times for writing.[46] They possess better "style," showing "better equipage" in tandem with "the bettering of the time." Happiness accompanies belatedness.[47] Against such impossible competition, the poet claims the strength of sincerity. His lines are "poor," "rude," and "outstripped by every pen," but they are inscriptions of feeling, of "love," rather than instrumentations of "rhyme" and "style," features of fancy. I use Christina's terms here to point to the unaccredited source of her comparative frame. The association of "unhappiness" and "feeling" in the preface of "Monna Innominata" echoes Shakespeare's pairing of the poetic persona's churlishness with the emphasis on feeling in his poetry. The unsurpassable value of feeling is claimed in both instances, reinforcing the sense that Christina is echoing Shakespeare.

Shakespeare's audible presence in "Monna Innominata" is not limited to the preface; the sonnets in the sequence provide a larger and more suggestive space for echoes. For instance, the conceit and its expression by the couplet in Shakespeare's Sonnet 109 ("For nothing this wide universe I call, / Save thou, my rose; in it thou art my all") resonate again in lines from Sonnet 1 of "Monna Innominata" ("For one man is my world of all the men / This wide

---

[45] All citations from Shakespeare are from *The Complete Works of Shakespeare*, ed. David Bevington, 3rd ed. (London: Scott, 1980).

[46] *William Shakespeare: The Sonnets and A Lover's Complaint*, ed. John Kerrigan (London: Penguin, 1995) 215.

[47] Making the same association in one of her two essays on Dante, Christina wrote: "we ... in nineteenth century [sic] England are happier ... than our forefathers." See *Dante, An English Classic*, 200.

world holds; O love, my world is you" [7–8]). The first sonnet also echoes Shakespeare's Sonnet 39 in the speaker's ambiguity about the period of her lover's absence, wishing he were with her but also reluctant to lose the creative space the absence grants her. "Come back to me, who wait and watch for you: – / Or come not yet, for it is over then" (1–2), are the lines in the Monna Innominata's speech that call to mind the self-divisive indecision voiced in Shakespeare's Sonnet 39: "O absence, what a torment wouldst thou prove, / Were it not thy sour leisure gave sweet leave / To entertain the time with thoughts of love, / ... / thou teachest how to make one twain, / By praising him here who doth hence remain!" (9–11, 13–14). "In our two loves there is but one respect" (5), writes Shakespeare in Sonnet 36; in Sonnet 4 of "Monna Innominata" there is a similar line: "For one is both and both are one in love" (11). The resemblance to Shakespeare's sonnets can be explained by the common use of iambic feet. However, as Christina's appropriation of Spenserian meter suggests, imitation of an earlier poet makes the poet an unannounced aural presence in her writing.[48] Interestingly enough, at one time Christina did express interest in studying the influence of Italian literature on Spenser.[49]

Given that Shakespeare is manifestly echoed in "Monna Innominata," it is curious that his name is absent from the work, and all the more so given the mindfulness of tradition found in the preface. Further, it seems that acknowledgement is begrudged the English sonnet tradition as a whole. Instead, a challenge is posed to the continental lyric tradition from the Middle Ages to the Renaissance, to poets who wrote in non-English languages. The absence of English sonneteers does not preclude Christina's engagement with the sonnet in English literary history; it merely reinforces the sense that she was self-conscious about her place as poet. As a poet who wrote predominantly in English, why did she nominally exclude the English sonnet tradition from her project? Even the historicity of the Monna Innominata is incongruous to the language she speaks: she is Christina's "donna innominata" speaking up on behalf of the silent ladies of her time, answering back in English to poets who composed their courtly lyrics in Provençal and medieval Italian. Christina treats the subject of Dante's and Petrarch's different language in the same manner as Shakespeare's influence in her work – by not speaking of it, but subtly introducing it into "Monna Innominata" through the sound of words on the page, witnessed in the insertion of untranslated quotations from the two Italian poets as epigraphs into the sequence.[50] Just as Shakespeare's influence

---

[48] See Yopie Prins, "Victorian Meters," *The Cambridge Companion to Victorian Poetry*, ed. Joseph Bristow (Cambridge: Cambridge University Press, 2000) 109–110. Prins discusses the secrecy and revelation through sound in Christina's imitation of Spenser's meter in "February Eclogue" in her own poem, "Winter: My Secret."

[49] See Mackenzie Bell, *Christina Rossetti: A Biographical and Critical Study* (London: Hurst and Blackett, 1989) 33.

[50] No translations were provided for the epigraphs until William Michael Rossetti's edition of Christina's *Poetical Works* in 1904.

is discernible in the sonnets, the different sounds of Italian and English are evoked in the space between epigraphs and sonnets. That the difference in language is as furtive and unannounced as Shakespeare's presence suggests reluctance to deal with the place of "Monna Innominata" in the English literary canon. This offers a sharp contrast to the image of the poet that is painted by Christina's confident speech in the preface, but it is one that is not entirely unexpected when viewed in the light of the extreme hopes and fears that dramatized Christina's every engagement with the question of her place in poetic tradition.

One of two sonnet sequences in *A Pageant and Other Poems*, "Monna Innominata" mirrors the transitional poetics of the volume as a whole. As D'Amico has shown, *A Pageant and Other Poems* marks the beginning of a new phase in Christina's writing: the beginning of a shift of influence from the book of Ecclesiastes to the First Epistle of St John; from the theme of vanity of vanities to that of God's love (149). The volume is different from the ones that preceded it in that Christina dispenses with the separate section of devotional verse. It seems that the volume represents Christina's conscious effort at intertwining her roles as lyrical and religious poet. The offering of religious and non-religious poems as a whole suggests this, as well as the organization of the volume. It opens with a dedicatory sonnet to the poet's mother, a quietly intimate piece about a daughter's love. The poem at the close of the volume, "Love Is Strong As Death," reveals a starkly contrasting poetic voice: in two short stanzas Christina lends her voice to two scenarios at death, the non-believer and the believer, and for both she is strident, conveying the depth of despair of the first and the height of affirmed love that is found by the second. Interpersonal love and love for God are themes that weave through and by one another in *A Pageant and Other Poems*; and the voice that is used for these causes may differ in tone and timbre as shown in the comparison of the opening and closing poems. The volume's varied textures suggest the diversity that exists in the poet's lyrical and Christian modes. "Monna Innominata" reflects the diversity found across the volume; more importantly, it reveals the tensions that are caused by divisive interests. "Vanity of vanities" is a repetitive theme across Christina's writings. The counsel of the Teacher in Ecclesiastes is taken very much to heart, as these instances show, but the frequentness of the refrain comes perhaps from an acute sense of how much she needed that reminder to herself. The struggle between Christina's desire to achieve fame and honor as poet and her Christian knowledge that such earthly goals yield ephemeral gains is played out in "An Old-World Thicket." In "Monna Innominata" the struggle is no less present, but it is borne far more secretively. The aural complexity of "Monna Innominata" acts as a portrait of the artist in sound, revealing her torn self, divided in its aspects as woman, poet and devout believer.

Chapter 8

The "silent song" of D.G. Rossetti's *The House of Life*

Phyllis Weliver

> Now it is part of the ideality of the highest sort of dramatic poetry, that it presents us with a kind of profoundly significant and animated instants [*sic*], a mere gesture, a look, a smile, perhaps – some brief and wholly concrete moment – into which, however, all the motives, all the interests and effects of a long history, have condensed themselves, and which seem to absorb past and future in an intense consciousness of the present....
> It is to the law or condition of music, as I said, that all art like this is really aspiring; and ... the perfect moments of music itself, the making or hearing of music, song or its accompaniment, are themselves prominent as subjects.[1]

Walter Pater's essay on Giorgione describes how the painter is drawn to "the perfect moments of music" (165), a subject that Dante Gabriel Rossetti also explores in his sonnet sequence, *The House of Life* (1881),[2] where the sonnet is defined in the first line as a "moment's monument."[3] Indeed, Rossetti and Pater

---

[1] Walter Pater, "The School of Giorgione" (1877), *Walter Pater: Three Major Texts*, ed. William E. Buckler (New York: New York University Press, 1986) 165. I am grateful to Yopie Prins, Bennett Zon, Jennifer Nesbitt and Sally Bormann for discussions about this essay and feedback on drafts.

[2] The sonnet sequence comprises 102 poems written during the course of Rossetti's poetic career (1847–1881). While some of the sonnets were written for the final version of *The House of Life* (published along with two historical narratives in *Ballads and Sonnets* [1881]), a shorter version of *The House of Life* had already appeared in Rossetti's *Poems* (1870). Before the 1881 publication, Rossetti labored at the ordering of the sonnets. However, despite his efforts, the sequence does lack cohesion, a fact that has drawn critical comment from the first. See David G. Riede, *Dante Gabriel Rossetti Revisited* (New York: Twayne, 1992) 120; John Hollander, *The Work of Poetry* (New York: Columbia University Press, 1997) 193.

[3] Dante Gabriel Rossetti, introductory sonnet, *The House of Life*, *Dante Gabriel Rossetti Collected Writings*, ed. Jan Marsh (London: Dent, 1999) 275. All subsequent citations from *The House of Life* are from this edition and are given in the text with line numbers. The poem on Giorgione is written about the painting in the Louvre, *Le concert champêtre*. Pater mentions Rossetti's painting style as similar to Giorgione's, but he does not analyze Rossetti's poems in

respond quite similarly to the painter, as can be seen in Rossetti's "A Venetian Pastoral, by Giorgione." The sonnet recounts the moment when, in the words of the preface, "two cavaliers and an undraped woman are seated in the grass, with musical instruments."[4] The poem continues:

> Whither stray
> Her eyes now, from whose mouth the slim pipes creep
> And leave it pouting, while the shadowed grass
> Is cool against her naked side? Let be: –
> Say nothing now unto her lest she weep,
> Nor name this ever. Be it as it was, –
> Life touching lips with Immortality. (8–14)

As John Dixon Hunt rightly comments, the sonnet attempts to capture the instantaneity of the painting, which represents music-making: "Giorgione, by the very nature of his art, has forever left the recorder poised at the girl's mouth."[5] While the topic of the painting represents a moment, it is made as permanent ("Life touching lips with Immortality") as the "moment's monument" of *The House of Life*. Music is a recurring theme in Rossetti's poetry and in its emphasis on the moment it anticipates the primacy of music in aesthetic writing, as much as do Pater's essays.[6]

Pater is obviously the more usual figure to associate with the aesthetes, but his indebtedness to the Pre-Raphaelites was noted from the first by critics.[7] However, scholars have virtually ignored the musical images in Rossetti's poetry, a fact that seems especially strange given the emphasis placed on music by Pater and by aesthetic writing. In Rossetti's poems, music recurs, but it is more than a "theme." It is concretely present in structural and figurative elements in Rossetti's poetry, and this "music," in the obliteration of the distinction between matter and form, mimics the speaker's aspired unity of soul and body, of himself and his lover, and finally of his own personality. In this, Rossetti's sonnets anticipate Pater's famous ideal: "*All art constantly aspires toward the condition of music.* For while in all other kinds of art it is possible to

---

his essay. Another essay by Pater, "Dante Gabriel Rossetti" (1883) *The Bibelot* 5.10 (1899): 321–338, addresses poetic style.

[4] "A Venetian Pastoral, by Giorgione." There are two versions of this poem, from 1850 and 1870. I am using the latter text. It is interesting that several of Rossetti's *Sonnets for Pictures* include music. See "An Allegorical Dance of Women, by Andrea Mantegna" and "A Marriage of St Katharine [by Hans Memmeling]."

[5] John Dixon Hunt, "A Moment's Monument: Reflections on Pre-Raphaelite Vision in Poetry and Painting," *Pre-Raphaelitism: A Collection of Critical Essays*, ed. James Sambrook (Chicago: University of Chicago Press, 1974) 244.

[6] One aesthetic writer, Oscar Wilde, even comments on the same set of images, texts, and ideas: Giorgione's *Le concert champêtre*, Rossetti's "A Venetian Pastoral, by Giorgione," the "moment's monument" of *The House of Life*, music and time. See Oscar Wilde, *The Critic as Artist* (1891), rpt in *Oscar Wilde: The Major Works*, ed. Isobel Murray (Oxford: Oxford University Press, 1989) 259, 283, 288.

[7] See John Morley, "Mr. Pater's Essays," *The Fortnightly Review* 13 (1873): 469–477.

distinguish the matter from the form, and the understanding can always make this distinction, yet it is the constant effort of art to obliterate it." (Pater, "Giorgione," 156; original emphasis) Indeed, Pater admired that Rossetti had "a structure and music of verse, a vocabulary, an accent, unmistakably novel, yet felt to be no mere tricks of manner adopted with a view to forcing attention."[8] This "structure and music of verse" is found, in part, through the arrangement of *The House of Life*. While the sonnets communicate the subjects of love and loss, of increasing fragmentation of self, and notions about art, any sense of narrative in the sonnet sequence is dependent on the overall form. There is no storyline except as occurs from the ordering of the sonnets: those about unity in love give way to those about loss, which are then layered with sonnets about fragmented personality. In this, *The House of Life* "*aspires toward the condition of music*" since sequencing is essential to determining meaning in formal music analysis: it is the sequential order in which themes are presented, return and transform that the attentive listener is supposed to be able to reproduce in his mind, as well as the relations and developments that occur between themes, as based on this order.[9]

As Christina Bashford and Catherine Dale have discussed, this type of analysis was being actively taught to many audiences for the first time in Victorian Britain through the use of program notes, a practice that originated in Britain and seems to be a specifically British phenomenon during the nineteenth century. Using prose passages and musical examples, these analytical notes pointed out what was important to listen for during the concert; the focus was on compositional form, such as identifying themes and their transformations, and the audience was meant to concentrate on these structural elements.[10] This emphasis on the musical work was quite different from eighteenth-century norms of concert going, which included conversing during the music and listening attentively to star performers more than focusing on the composition.[11] The importance to *The House of Life* is that Rossetti was interested specifically in sequence. Not only does *The House of Life* rely on sequencing to cohere, to establish meaning, and to develop the meaning of certain phrases and ideas that repeat and gain meaning as they mutate, but teaching nineteenth-century

---

[8] Walter Pater, "Dante Gabriel Rossetti," 322.
[9] For a comparison of musical structure to narrative in literature, see Robert Adlington, Chapter 4, "Temporality in Post-tonal Music," diss., University of Sussex, 1997.
[10] Christina Bashford, "Not Just 'G.': Towards a History of the Programme Note," *George Grove, Music and Victorian Culture*, ed. Michael Musgrave (Basingstoke: Palgrave, 2003) 115–142, 301–318. See also Catherine Dale, *Music Analysis in Britain in the Nineteenth and Early Twentieth Centuries* (Aldershot: Ashgate, 2003).
[11] See Christina Bashford, "Learning to Listen: audiences for chamber music in early-Victorian London," *Journal of Victorian Culture* 4 (1999): 25–51; Jennifer L. Hall-Witt, "Representing the Audience in the Age of Reform: Critics and the Elite at the Italian Opera in London," *Music and British Culture, 1785–1914: Essays in honour of Cyril Ehrlich*, eds Christina Bashford and Leanne Langley (Oxford: Oxford University Press, 2000) 121–144. In the middle decades of the nineteenth century, program notes accompanied some London concerts such as the Philharmonic Society and the Crystal Palace Saturday Concerts, gradually occurring more often in the 1870s and becoming the norm by the 1880s (Bashford, "G").

audiences to listen to structural units in music mirrored the Victorian emphasis on prosody (the study of meter) – on reading in terms of what Yopie Prins calls "predictable intervals."[12]

Figure 8.1: Rossetti's illustration for the introductory sonnet of *The House of Life*

---

[12] As Prins demonstrates, meter was increasingly "measured in predictable intervals" in Victorian poetry: "[t]he Victorians increasingly conceptualized meter as a formal grid or pattern of spacing, created by the alternation of quantifiable units .... Thus, when Patmore writes in his 'Essay on English Metrical Law' that 'the sequence of vocal utterance shall be divided into equal or proportionate spaces,' the very process of measuring such 'proportionate spaces' turns 'vocal utterance' into a temporal or spatial 'sequence.'" Rather than simply trying to mimic everyday language and speech rhythms, temporal sequence was an important part of compositional style and technique in Victorian poetry, just as it was in formal musical analysis. See Yopie Prins, "Victorian Meters," *The Cambridge Companion to Victorian Poetry*, ed. Joseph Bristow (Cambridge: Cambridge University Press, 1999) 90. Citations from Coventry Patmore are from his *Essay on English Metrical Law: A Critical Edition with a Commentary*, ed. Mary Roth (Washington, D.C.: Catholic University of America Press, 1961) 15.

Rossetti's interest in sequence is noteworthy because, as Jennifer Ann Wagner documents in *A Moment's Monument*, groups of sonnets were usually referred to as a sonnet *series* in the nineteenth century (220). While a series leans toward the notion of ordering, a sequence refers to change and development within a collective. This emphatically returns the focus of "the sonnet" to being one item in a larger whole, which was how the sonnet was commonly conceived before Shakespeare's *Sonnets* began to make each individual sonnet more independent, resulting in subsequent poets writing individual sonnets, outside of a sequence or series.[13] Rossetti appears to have introduced the term "sequence" into more common usage with the title to his 1881 *The House of Life: A Sonnet-Sequence* and this, it seems to me, must relate to Rossetti's notion of *The House of Life* as a single poem, with sonnets serving as stanzas (Italian for "rooms").[14]

In Rossetti's sonnets "music," then, is not heard literally, but understood figuratively. Indeed, our first glimpse of the sonnet sequence is through a picture that represents the sonnet as music (see Fig. 8.1). Rossetti interpreted his design that illustrates the introductory sonnet as "the Soul is instituting the 'memorial to one dead deathless hour,' a ceremony easily effected by placing a winged hour-glass in a rose-bush, at the same time that she touches the fourteen-stringed harp of the Sonnet, hanging round her neck."[15] The sonnet is not just *like* a musical instrument, it *is* the harp, with each line constituting one string of the instrument. Moreover, because the personified Soul plays the sonnet instead of singing or saying it, the picture emphasizes non-text-based music as an important component of "voicing" the soul.[16] In this, it is important that while Rossetti envisioned *The House of Life* as putting in action "a complete *dramatis personae* of the soul," music is not one of the fragmented, "personified emotions"[17] of the soul. Rather, it is communication itself.

---

[13] S.K. Heninger, Jr, "Sequences, Systems, Models: Sidney and the Secularization of Sonnets," *Poems in Their Place: The Intertextuality and Order of Poetic Collections*, ed. Neil Fraistat (Chapel Hill: University of North Carolina Press, 1986) 87.
[14] Jennifer Ann Wagner, *A Moment's Monument: Revisionary Poetics and the Nineteenth-Century English Sonnet* (Madison: Associated University Presses, 1996) 220; Riede, 120; Hollander, *Work*, 193; Jan Marsh, "Introduction," *Dante Gabriel Rossetti Collected Writings*, ed. Jan Marsh (London: Dent, 1999) xxvi.
[15] D.G. Rossetti to his mother, 27 April 1880, *The Letters of Dante Gabriel Rossetti*, eds O. Doughty and J.R. Wahl (Oxford: Clarendon, 1965–1967) 4: 1760. Cited in Wagner, 217.
[16] The idea of "voice" is clearly defined by Prins, who traces how meter can imply voice by referencing Wordsworth's 1802 Preface to *Lyrical Ballads*. Wordsworth discusses how a regular meter communicates an "intertexture" or intermediate voice that is not spoken but is felt and is essential because it provides a regulating force for the passionate, irregular states of mind that are the subjects of his poems. See Prins, 91–92; William Wordsworth, "Preface," *Lyrical Ballads, with Pastoral and other Poems*, 3rd ed. (London: Longman, 1802) i, xlvi–xlvii. For further discussion of Wordsworth and meter, see Eric Griffiths, *The Printed Voice of Victorian Poetry* (Oxford: Clarendon, 1989) 72–74.
[17] D.G. Rossetti to T.G. Hake, 21 April 1870, *The Letters of Dante Gabriel Rossetti*, eds O. Doughty and J.R. Wahl (Oxford: Clarendon, 1965–1967) 992. Cited in Marsh, "Introduction," xxiii.

The sonnet is figured as an instrument – a means of making music – and this process is represented in the sequence as the hope that words will be transformed into music through metrical performance. In this, Rossetti's sonnet plays with the reflexivity of language, or what Herbert F. Tucker calls "poetic spacetime." In his absorbing essay, "Of Monuments and Moments: Spacetime in Nineteenth-Century Poetry," Tucker outlines the nineteenth-century predilection to read space as time (e.g., geology interprets an object in space in terms of its history) and, conversely, time as space (e.g., train timetables, where "temporal succession might be laid out visibly as a spatial field translating minutes into miles").[18] Poetry of the period delighted in a similar interpretation of space and time, where the space of a poem takes minutes or hours to read, and its temporal organization (meter, stanzaic structure) is laid out visually on the page and bound within a material object (a book or journal). Of course, all printed poems combine the temporal and spatial, but Tucker's point is that the conscious use of and reference to form is rampant in Romantic and Victorian verse, despite an avowed dedication to spontaneity, at least in Romanticism. When time or space is then discussed within poetic texts, especially when they "describe an artifact, a built structure" while being "conspicuously built structures in their own right, being either sonnets or else stanzaic poems" (278), there is a reflexive function. Language points to and contemplates its topic and also itself; Tucker's idea is that the spacetime effect "occurs insofar as the structure to which the passage refers images the structure of the passage itself" (278–279).

While Tucker is most interested in poems as representing solid artifacts – as ekphrastic – it seems obvious that poetic language can also be reflexive when what it references is not a spatial structure (a picture, a room, a boat, a skull), but a temporal structure (sequence), and that it is figured and interpreted quite solidly on the page.[19] Of course, material artifacts are also figured in *The House of Life* (the "house" of the title, the "monument" of the opening line, the "harp" of the illustration), but so is the more fleeting: the "moment" and music-making. Pause and process, or a temporal understanding of "structure," is linked to music. When the effect of language is also called "music," a reflexivity occurs. The sonnet sequence interprets and constructs the figure of music (sometimes figuring music as a physical object or body) while also being constructed by ideas about what music is (sequence and meter are temporal, but they appear on the page and so literally construct the space of the poem).

---

[18] Herbert F. Tucker, "Of Monuments and Moments: Spacetime in Nineteenth-Century Poetry," *Modern Language Quarterly* 58 (September 1997): 271. Tucker discusses the introductory sonnet to *The House of Life* in his essay, but he does not consider music as a part of spacetime poetics.
[19] Of course, although frequently perceived as temporal, music can also be discussed as spatial (e.g., atmospheric vibrations, the production of music by body or instrument, or "music" as in sheet music).

While it is not unusual in Victorian poetry to call poets "singers" or poems "songs," it is essential to note that music in *The House of Life* is specifically linked to meter in the poems, which introduces an intermediate voice that is quantifiably there in the sonnets: a presence that can be felt and analyzed through formal units or structures. *The House of Life* acknowledges this as the speaker's aim, one that he feels to be a task of almost impossible proportion, but which he nonetheless attempts. For instance, the octet of "Heart's Hope" (Sonnet 5) depicts the speaker's desire to transform words through rhythmic units into song:

> By what word's power, the key of paths untrod,
> Shall I the difficult deeps of Love explore,
> Till parted waves of Song yield up the shore
> Even as that sea which Israel crossed dryshod?
> For lo! in some poor rhythmic period,
> Lady, I fain would tell how evermore
> Thy soul I know not from thy body, nor
> Thee from myself, neither our love from God. (1–8)

What is hoped for is not merely the ability to write a good poem (the interpretation often put forth),[20] but this task specifically depends on discovering a "word's power" and, even more, on a "rhythmic period," or a unit of speech in Latin rhetorical declaration. This, ideally, becomes "Song" which is given power over nature as it parts the Red Sea, just as Orpheus's music commanded stones and beasts. In keeping with this supreme achievement, bringing elements of language together is not only equated metaphorically to song, but it will be used to communicate the unity of soul and body, and earthly love with divine love. More than just stating this purpose, however, this sonnet plays with form, making sound and meter stand out by contradicting the usual 10-beat, iambic pentameter line of the sonnet. Although the poem on the page looks like a traditional Petrarchan sonnet, there are actually 11 beats in lines 1, 2, and 4 of the octet. Even line 5 has 11 beats since the exclamation point serves as a pause, adding a beat. Moreover, by including dactyls at the ends of some lines, the meter is concretely brought to the attention of the reader as a "voice" that is even more important than syntax. For instance, the triplets in lines 5 and 6, "period" and "evermore," encourage the reader to continue the same rhythm when she comes to "body, nor" in the next line, despite the fact that the comma and enjambment work against this sound. In this case, the power of the words occurs through meter that is not hinted at, but can be physically marked as well as concretely heard. This formal structure privileges sound as well as sense, creating a voice beyond the

---

[20] Riede, 138–139; Richard L. Stein, *The Ritual of Interpretation: The Fine Arts as Literature in Ruskin, Rossetti, and Pater* (Cambridge, MA: Harvard University Press, 1975) 193.

subject of the poem that is dependent on form, just as the speaker finds that "Thy soul I know not from thy body."[21]

It is important to be specific here: I do not mean that we find a poetic "music" in the sense meant by scholars who use musical metaphors to explain the sound of poetry.[22] Indeed, in this sense Rossetti is not regarded as a "musical" poet. William Rossetti, after all, reported that his brother had no musical gift, nor the "craving to be constantly hearing music," a fact that was such common knowledge that A.J. Hipkins also commented in the 1883 *Musical Review* that Rossetti had "no decided musical ear" apart from the "cadence and inflection" of poetry, concentrating instead on the "harmony of line and proportion that many painters have noticed in musical instruments, inherent in their essential configuration."[23] Certainly, Rossetti was fascinated by music, as is clear from his own musical instrument collection and how often he depicted musical instruments in his paintings, experimenting not just with line but also with color. While the painted instruments are invested with more meaning than Hipkins gives them, as demonstrated by Suzanne Fagence Cooper's research into gender and music in the paintings whereby "musical motifs [were used] to produce a deliberately sensual and physical effect,"[24] it does seem that

---

[21] The accents in Rossetti's poems sometimes work so much against natural speech rhythm as to have sparked critical comment (approving and disapproving) ever since the poems were first published. For instance, William Michael Rossetti criticizes "Willowwood," considering it "a grave defect in versification that the word 'willowwood' should have been treated as if it constituted a dactylic rhyme, chiming (only too imperfectly) with 'widowhood' and 'pillow could'". What is important is not whether the effect of this seems mannered, but rather that part of the art of writing Victorian verse was to introduce what Pater terms "the control of style". See William Michael Rossetti, "Notes," *The Works of Dante Gabriel Rossetti*, ed. William Michael Rossetti (London: Ellis, 1911) 654; Pater, "Dante Gabriel Rossetti," 322. A dactyl is a unit of three syllables of which the first is stressed and the last two are unstressed.

[22] For explication of what John Hollander calls the "music of poetry," see the introduction to this volume of essays.

[23] A.J. Hipkins, "The Musical Instruments in Rossetti's Pictures," *The Musical Review* 2.1 (13 January 1883): 27; William Michael Rossetti, *Some Reminiscences of William Michael Rossetti* (London: Brown, 1906) 191. See also Dianne Sachko MacLeod, "Rossetti's Two Ligeias: Their Relationship to Visual Art, Music, and Poetry," *Victorian Poetry* 20.3-4 (1982): 90; A.J. Hipkins, "The Musical Instruments in Rossetti's Pictures," *The Musical Review* 5.1 (3 February 1883): 75-76.

[24] This citation is from the work done by Suzanne Fagence Cooper for our collaborative paper, "A 'rapturous undersong': music in D.G. Rossetti's pictures and *House of Life* poems," The Rossettis: Cosmopolitans in Victorian London Conference (St John's College, Cambridge, 7/01). Fagence Cooper demonstrates that this physicality of musical images occurs in Rossetti's paintings beginning around 1860 and is in sharp contrast to contemporaries, "especially Burne-Junes and Whistler, for whom music was an ethereal art." Fagence Cooper demonstrates that after the 1850s, music is more than an object or prop for Rossetti; it becomes a subject and a recurring motif that appears in "his studies of beautiful, fleshly women throughout the 1860s and 1870s." What is fascinating about Fagence Cooper's work is that frequently in the paintings of women and musical instruments, a narrative is missing: there is no link made between the subject and a literary or historical figure, as there are in so many of Rossetti's other paintings. While Fagence Cooper concludes that this makes music itself a subject, it seems to me that a slightly different, if complementary, conclusion can be drawn.

imaginatively reproducing the sound of particular instruments or music itself was not what creatively interested Rossetti.

Rather, Rossetti's poems feature recognized instruments that have associative meaning, but then deny them that meaning in order to decontextualize them, and so the poem.[25] What is emphasized, then, are "The problems of reading, interpreting, making sense," as Antony H. Harrison notes, so "that we become finally more interested in surfaces, in techniques and their employment, than the subject matter being presented."[26] The mental quest for deeper meaning beyond the surface of the text is not barren since it turns up what might be called the "participatory effort" at making meaning and the formal techniques for achieving this.

The poems rely on this hermeneutical attempt in order to demonstrate the futility of historical contextualizing and so shift the reader into a response based on analyzing or perceiving the purely formal. Indeed, the process is furthered because while the idea of discussing music as representational was certainly explored in the nineteenth century,[27] music has frequently been perceived to have a special place in the creative arts precisely because it is supposed to elude representation.[28] As I explain below, *The House of Life* plays with this idea since, by referencing historic instruments, it suggests that these instruments might be historicizing, but then denies them that function. By this process, music in *The House of Life* helps to create what J. Hillis Miller calls the linguistic moment: "This is the moment when signs are cut off from any extralinguistic grounding

---

The lack of narrative in the paintings parallels the lack of narrative in *The House of Life*, further supporting the idea that Rossetti was experimenting with ways in which the other arts could become, in their non-referentiality, like music. He emphasizes, in short, a sensual experience of "art for art's sake."

[25] For the idea that Rossetti's images sometimes do not have the religious meaning that we expect, and that meaning exists on the surface, see Jerome J. McGann, "Rossetti's Significant Details," *Victorian Poetry* 7 (1969): 41–54. For the notion that this creates what Rossetti calls "mystery" since the "surface effect of the image rests on a sense of inaccessible depth" see John Barclay, "Consuming Artifacts: Dante Gabriel Rossetti's Aesthetic Economy," *Victorian Poetry* 35 (1997): 18.

[26] Antony H. Harrison, *Victorian Poets and Romantic Poems: Intertextuality and Ideology* (Charlottesville: University Press of Virginia, 1990) 93.

[27] For instance, in Herbert Spencer's (1820–1903) writings about the evolution of human expression, music was perceived to induce precise physiological reactions, emotions and associations in all human beings, notions that became hugely influential for subsequent nineteenth-century texts on music aesthetics. Herbert Spencer, "The Origin and Function of Music," (1857) *Essays: Scientific, Political, and Speculative* (London: Longman, 1858) 359–384.

[28] The perception of music as nonrepresentational is exalted by the aesthetes, where structure and content ideally slide together, as seen by Pater's comments (*"All art constantly aspires toward the condition of music"*) and by the idea of *l'art pour l'art*. The latter notion reached Britain in the 1860s through Théophile Gautier's and Charles Baudelaire's writings and was developed by the aesthetic poet Algernon Swinburne (1837–1909). Swinburne lodged with D.G. and William Michael Rossetti in the Cheyne Walk house and was infamously attacked alongside Rossetti in Robert Buchanan's "The Fleshly School of Poetry: Mr D.G. Rossetti." See Jan Marsh, "Introduction," xx; Gautier, *Mlle. de Maupin* (1835); Baudelaire, *Les Fleurs du Mal* (1857); Leonée Ormond, *George Du Maurier* (London: Routledge, 1969) 243–248.

and become fascinating in themselves, in their self-sustaining and self-annihilating interplay."[29] Music can go one step further than language since, as Pater also noticed, musical compositions are commonly perceived to exist in terms of formal structure, or the relations between pitches and rhythms (a fact which does not necessarily preclude semiotic interpretation). However, *The House of Life*, by using certain *instruments* that *might* be used as signs, uses methods similar to deconstructing words, where the sign must first be referenced before it can be deconstructed. This relies on the "interplay" of signs as both representational and not representational, as absent and present. Indeed, the "sign by definition is the presence of an absence" writes Miller (345), and this notion of something both present and missing might also be used to describe music itself.

The concept of an ephemeral voice as materializing from the page, of presence and absence, is crucial to understanding *The House of Life* where communication comes not only from the speaker, but also from the soul, Love and the writing of the beloved. While this would seem to suggest an unembodied voice, it actually roots ideas of spirit and voice as tangibly present in the writing – an idea crucial to the sonnets' frequent topic of the unity of physical and spiritual love. For instance, silent music is a recurring trope in the sonnet sequence, as in the opening stanza of "The Love-Letter" (Sonnet 11) where the speaker notes how his beloved pours her heart onto the printed page:

> Warmed by her hand and shadowed by her hair
>   As close she leaned and poured her heart through thee,
>   Whereof the articulate throbs accompany
> The smooth black stream that makes thy whiteness fair, –
> Sweet fluttering sheet, even of her breath aware, –
>   Oh let thy silent song disclose to me
>   That soul wherewith her lips and eyes agree
> Like married music in Love's answering air. (1–8)

While the words of the letter are obviously visual as the ink flows onto the page, "silent song" suggests that aural elements also exist in writing and in reading silently to oneself. The words are further compared to a song that discloses the lover's soul: in lines 4–8, the intangible spirit is made tangible through a music that the speaker finds situated on the page. Taken one step further, this concept refers not only to the love letter written by the beloved, but also to the sonnet entitled "The Love-Letter" and to the sonnet sequence in general. In *The House of Life*, the voices of the soul and Love are not only the words that we read as sonnets, but they are also communicated by their physical presence, either through personification or through making the body itself "Like ... music." In the sonnet above, while the "Sweet fluttering sheet" is most obviously the printed page, it might also refer to the beloved's hair,

---

[29] J. Hillis Miller, "The Mirror's Secret: Dante Gabriel Rossetti's Double Work of Art," *Victorian Poetry* 29 (1991): 344.

fluttering with her breath. In this, the hand, hair, lips, eyes and breast ("heart") become a living sheet, with the heart's "articulate throbs" becoming the "silent song." This music is not a sung or played musical composition, but rather a communication that emerges from the physical body as page; it is the "Love-Letter" in this poem.

Since "silent music" is a recurring trope in *The House of Life* and the musical instruments in the sequence cannot really be heard, they should be read as tropes. Indeed, while Rossetti is known for ekphrastic poems (poems that address a real work of visual art), when it comes to music, real compositions are not referenced in his poems nor are Victorian instruments. This fact is important for considering not just what is represented, but also for issues of interpretation. If an actual piece of music had been referenced, the Victorian reader would either already know it or would be able to find it and hear or play it. It would be what I call a "musical artifact": a piece of music or a musical instrument that exists outside the text, just as Rossetti described actual paintings and Keats wrote about the real Elgin Marbles.[30] Victorians themselves saw music as, in part, consisting of objects that could be displayed and interpreted historically and geographically. They exhibited instruments, scores and libretti as artifacts in the musical exhibitions at the Crystal Palace at Hyde Park (1851) and Sydenham (1854–1936). While some of the musical objects displayed were from the Victorian period, historical instruments were also exhibited at the Crystal Palace and the South Kensington Museum. The Hyde Park Crystal Palace displayed for the most part instruments that demonstrated technological innovation, but there were still hautboys exhibited by Johann Christoff Selboe of Copenhagen and Frederic Triebert of Paris. The South Kensington Museum (later The Victoria and Albert Museum) displayed lutes from European and Eastern countries, including two Italian lutes dating from *c*. 1580 and the early seventeenth century, and a seventeenth-century Italian hautboy.[31] Musical performances were even sometimes called "exhibitions" at the Crystal Palace, opening up the idea that actual performances referenced in literature might be considered "artifacts" by literary critics and musicologists.[32]

If Victorian or subsequent readers knew or searched out the musical piece or even an exotic instrument referenced in a poem, then they actively participated in making and understanding the poem's meaning. Because they knew precisely

---

[30] For a discussion of referencing real works of visual art in the poems of Ruskin, D.G. Rossetti and Pater, see Stein, 7–10.

[31] See Michael Musgrave, *The Musical Life of the Crystal Palace* (Cambridge: Cambridge University Press, 1995) 161–166; Peter and Ann Mactaggart, eds, *Musical Instruments in the 1851 Exhibition* (Welwyn, UK: Mac & Me, 1986) 70, 71; Carl Engel, *Descriptive Catalogue of the Musical Instruments in the South Kensington Museum*, 2nd ed. (London: Eyre, 1874) 226, 241, 322.

[32] The items displayed also included letters, manuscripts and other personal belongings of composers, portraits and busts of composers, and objects used by performers (e.g., props from operas). An argument could be made for including some of these items as "musical artifacts," but it seems to me that they are not made as important as the instruments and musical compositions in Victorian fiction and poetry.

what the artifact was, they collapsed the distance between themselves and the poet or the speaker. The reader could hear the specific musical piece in her inner ear when she read about it and this makes the world described by the poem seem at least partially concrete, while also making the poem itself three-dimensional because in hearing the composition internally, the music is played not on the page itself but rather in the imaginative leap that the reader makes to reproduce the music.[33]

Rossetti's sonnets do indeed reference medieval and Romantic instruments, but as I mentioned above, they are used as tropes; they are "musical artifacts" that are manipulated. For instance, at times music is specifically figured as Love strumming the lute, an important point because the active personification of Love recalls medieval Italian poetry as much as the lute references medieval music.[34] While the lute is a frequent presence in nineteenth-century poetry, its specific historic associations are usually lost.[35] Rossetti, however, seems to suggest some historical referentiality by combining the lute with other elements found in medieval Italian poetry. For example, the lute as an appropriate, historically accurate instrument for Love, occurs in "Love's Lovers" (Sonnet 8):

> Some ladies love the jewels in Love's zone
>   And gold-tipped darts he hath for painless play
>   In idle scornful hours he flings away;
> And some that listen to his lute's soft tone
> Do love to vaunt the silver praise their own;
>   Some prize his blindfold sight; and there be they
>   Who kissed his wings which brought him yesterday
> And thank his wings to-day that he is flown.
>
> My lady only loves the heart of Love:
>   Therefore Love's heart, my lady, hath for thee
>   His bower of unimagined flower and tree:
> There kneels he now, and all-anhungered of
> Thine eyes grey-lit in shadowing hair above,
>   Seals with thy mouth his immortality.

The lute is one of several accoutrements by which Love is identified, to the point where some ladies value the surface details of love more than real love, or "the heart." The identification of Love with the lute also occurs through sound: the

---

[33] Celeste Langan posits the term "hallucination" for a similar concept. See Celeste Langan, "Understanding Media in 1805: Audiovisual Hallucination in *The Lay of the Last Minstrel*," *Studies in Romanticism* 40.1 (2001): 49–70.

[34] The sonnet sequence includes both the lute (Sonnets 8 and 49) and the hautboy (Sonnet 9), instruments that were commonly used in medieval Europe, not in Victorian Britain.

[35] See John Hollander's synopsis of the conflation of Apollonian, Biblical, Celtic, classical, and contemporary references in the image of the lute to the point that "when an English Romantic poet writes of a 'lute', he will mean almost anything but that by-then-obsolete instrument." *Images of Voice: Music and Sound in Romantic Poetry* (Cambridge: Heffer, 1970) 12.

alliterative l's serve to link together love, Love, ladies and lute. The effect is to reference medievalism, but not necessarily to plunge the reader into a medieval setting.[36] Rather, the lute is simply part of the iconography of Love in *The House of Life*.[37] However, this iconography seems to take a second seat in "Love's Lovers" to sound itself, as "love" and "Love" are repeated to the point where they are reduced to mere words; the meaning conveyed is almost lost if not simply confused by repetition and by the same word being used for the emotion "love" and the personification "Love." While the limited lexicon emphasizes sound over meaning, however, these repeated words do not make the poem "just like a song," but rather demonstrate how Rossetti denatures language for a similar effect to how music itself is often perceived to be beyond signification.

Similarly, in a reference to the Aeolian harp, "Monochord" (Sonnet 79) warps Romantic associations with the instrument in order to depict the isolation and despair of the speaker.[38] This contrasts with the use of the instrument to express unity between poet and life, as exemplified in Percy Bysshe Shelley's *Alastor* (1816):

> and deep noon-day thought,
> Has shone within me, that serenely now
> And moveless, as a long-forgotten lyre
> Suspended in the solitary dome
> Of some mysterious and deserted fane,
> I wait thy breath, Great Parent, that my strain
> May modulate with murmurs of the air,
> And motions of the forests and the sea,
> And voice of living beings, and woven hymns
> Of night and day, and the deep heart of man.[39]

In this, the poet Alastor envisions himself as a lyre, playing with divine inspiration, or "breath," which makes his lyrics vibrate with wind and water.[40]

---

[36] In his discussion of the display of artifacts in museums, Stephen Bann explains that when individual objects add up to envelop the viewer in a sense of having stepped into a particular period and place, the artifacts function as synecdoches – taken together the parts create a larger sense of the whole. See Stephan Bann, *The Clothing of Clio: A study of the representation of history in nineteenth-century Britain and France* (Cambridge: Cambridge University Press, 1984) 83–86.

[37] In D.G. Rossetti's pictures, the personified Love is also identified with music, although not with the lute. In "The Rose Garden" Love plays a psaltery and in "Michael Scott's Wooing" Love touches a polystringed monochord (Hipkins, 27, 75).

[38] See Susan Bernstein's and Kimiyo Ogawa's essays in this volume for further discussions about the Aeolian Harp and its uses in Romantic poetry.

[39] Percy Bysshe Shelley, *Alastor, The Complete Poetical Works of Percy Bysshe Shelley*, ed. Neville Rogers (Oxford: Clarendon, 1975) 2: 40–49.

[40] Comparisons between sound waves, light waves and water waves frequently occurred in nineteenth-century Britain, and were sometimes used to discuss the bond between people, as in the mesmeric relationship. I discuss this in *Women Musicians in Victorian Fiction, 1860–1900: Representations of music, science and gender in the leisured home* (Aldershot: Ashgate, 2000). While there is not space to explore it here, it is worth noting that a similar connection between

Motion is positive and unifying, a point worth remembering in comparing *Alastor* with *The House of Life*, where the speaker frequently expresses alarm at motion, as in "Monochord." Rossetti's sonnet was originally published in 1870 with the title "Written During Music" and then republished in *The House of Life* with a new title and first line. While both versions reference Romantic tropes, the original text, "Is it the moved air or the moving sound", more obviously demonstrates the actual presence of music, while the revised text highlights the elements of sky and sea that often surround the Aeolian harp in Romantic poetry:

> Is it this sky's vast vault or ocean's sound
>   That is Life's self and draws my life from me,
>   And by instinct ineffable decree
> Holds my breath quailing on the bitter bound?
> Nay, is it Life or Death, thus thunder-crown'd,
>   That 'mid the tide of all emergency
>   Now notes my separate wave, and to what sea
> Its difficult eddies labour in the ground? (1–8)

While the speaker identifies himself with the instrument as Alastor did – as if he is the harp – the instrument has obviously been transformed from the multi-stringed wind harp to the single-stringed monochord. Reworking common Romantic associations with the Aeolian harp, Life (the moving air, the domed sky, or the ocean's sounds) "draws my life from me," or "breath." This directly contrasts with Shelley's poem where the breath of an "other" inspires creation. Unlike this Romantic configuration of poet in communion with divinity and the natural world, however, Rossetti's sonnet expresses deep isolation, where his "separate wave" labours to the sea rather than modulating or vibrating with it.

The single string of the monochord also expresses this solitary state; he is not the multi-stringed harp, and although he is played upon by the wind, this "other" portends Death. This relates to the greater theme in *The House of Life* about the loss of the beloved – an "other" figure who brought emotional desolation instead of the antiphony promised in "Youth's Antiphony" (Sonnet 13), where "Love breathed in sighs and silences / Through two blent souls one rapturous undersong" (13–14). This "rapturous undersong" is love singing one song in two people. Both speak, but they are dependent on each other to make the sonnet and even to finish the lines: "'I love you, sweet: how can you ever learn / How much I love you?' 'You I love even so, / And so I learn it.'" (1–3). The lovers echo each other, and these words, this "antiphony," is figured as lovers' speech. In contrast, the single string of the poet in "Monochord" is played upon by "Life or Death" as he questions what is this "That draws round me at last this wind-warm space, / And in regenerate rapture turns my face / Upon the devious coverts of dismay?" (12–14) The "rapturous undersong" has become "regenerate rapture," and the "wind-warm space" drawing round him and drawing life from him replaces the two voices of the lovers. Although it brings some regeneration, this rapture

---

self and the external world is expressed in the citation through the idea of sound waves.

ultimately looks upon dismay. Far from becoming one with nature, Rossetti's speaker is sucked dry. The metaphor of the harp as poetic mind is darkly present, since the speaker, played upon by Life, has his breath, notes and communication expire on the air as they sound. In referencing Romantic tropes, it is important that we find another meaning than expected. Instead of communion and transcendence, we find the speaker isolated in terms of his relation to the natural world, his psyche, and the condition of his poetic mind: his "quailing" breath is in marked contrast to the inspirational breath and modulations imagined by Alastor.

Thus, using musical instruments as he does, Rossetti references particular historical contexts, but they do not add up to one historical setting. References to the Aeolian harp bring deeper meaning to the poem, but they do not serve to plunge us into a recreated Romantic past, just as the medieval instruments do not steep us in medievalism. *The House of Life* emphasizes different associations than expected and creates an opacity of text. This occurs not just in terms of historical period, but also in the type of music played: real compositions are not only absent, but the Aeolian harp, by its very nature, plays random music which cannot be exactly reproduced in the reader's imagination. It cannot really be heard, as a "musical artifact" could be.

Besides instruments, the mythical Orpheus is a musical figure that is variously invoked in the sonnets and is expressly identified with the speaker's roles as poet and lover. The Sonnet is not only a harp, but the poet/lover is figured as Orpheus, and the effect of his communication is imagined to be like Orphic song. Perhaps unsurprisingly, Rossetti reconfigures and subverts the traditional trope of Orphean power; normally the image conflates the eloquence of poetry and music with a view of expressing "a man's power to shape the physical world," as Richard Leppert puts it.[41] At the beginning of the sonnet sequence, Orpheus is associated as usual with the power of music and with physical, even erotic, presence. Importantly, the poet's figuration as Orpheus includes a "song" that functions like my earlier discussion of sequence and musical composition. At the end of the first stanza of "The Kiss" (Sonnet 6), for example, the speaker refers to Orpheus's song as a "lay":

> For lo! even now my lady's lips did play
> With these my lips such consonant interlude

---

[41] Orpheus and music as representing "male power over nature", where "art and power are one and the same" is discussed in terms of visual representation in Richard Leppert's *The Sight of Sound: Music, Representation and the History of the Body* (Berkeley: University of California Press, 1993) 131, 133. See also John Hollander, *The Untuning of the Sky: Ideas of Music in English Poetry, 1500–1700* (1961; New York: Norton, 1970) 163–176, 347–348; Sue E. Coffman, *Music of Finer Tone: Musical Imagery of the Major Romantic Poets* (Salzburg: Institut für Anglistik und Amerikanistik, Universität Salzburg, 1979) 128, 301. For some of the references to Orpheus in Romantic poetry, see Samuel Taylor Coleridge, "To William Wordsworth," 45–47; William Wordsworth, *The Prelude*, 1: 227–233; Wordsworth "To the Clouds," 60–65; Percy Bysshe Shelley, *Prometheus Unbound*, IV, i, 415–417; Shelley, "Orpheus."

> As laurelled Orpheus longed for when he wooed
> The half-drawn hungering face with that last lay. (5–8)

In the next poem, "Nuptial Sleep" (Sonnet 6a), "lay" reappears, this time in lines 8 and 14:

> At length their long kiss severed, with sweet smart:
>   And as the last slow sudden drops are shed
>   From sparkling eaves when all the storm has fled,
> So singly flagged the pulses of each heart.
> Their bosoms sundered, with the opening start
>   Of married flowers to either side outspread
>   From the knit stem; yet still their mouths, burnt red,
> Fawned on each other where they lay apart.
>
> Sleep sank them lower than the tide of dreams,
>   And their dreams watched them sink, and slid away.
> Slowly their souls swam up again, through gleams
>   Of watered light and dull drowned waifs of day;
> Till from some wonder of new woods and streams
>   He woke, and wondered more: for there she lay.

Positioning "lay" at the ends of stanzas emphasizes its importance, making the poems move to the word, and repeating the word highlights the associative meanings between the sonnets. Not only is "lay" a song in Sonnet 6, but it refers to lying down in Sonnet 6a. This is made clear through the development of the word "kiss," which refers not only to kissing but also to consummation in "Nuptial Sleep." While "lips" in Sonnet 6 become associated with "mouths," "married flowers" and "knit stem" – thereby demonstrating the metonymic process of association and variation – repeating key words is also metonymic in *The House of Life*: a single word, in developing more meanings as it is used in different contexts, spins out the associations and multiple referents contained within any one signifier. Meanings layer on top of each other, arching over the boundaries between individual sonnets, and linking them into a sequence. In this, the order is important for tracing developments of meaning. It is important that the musical "lay" comes before the sexual "lay," showing not only the connection between music and desire in Rossetti's sonnet sequence, but also that music is envisioned as at least coming before union, if not being a tool for achieving it.

However, this sense of music's erotic potential and potency is balanced with its flipside: the ultimate failure of Orpheus to revive Eurydice. In imagining this dual role, the speaker reflects the sense of emptiness and presence that I have been discussing: music is deeply embedded in the speaker's psyche for its ability to exist as reassuringly, physically present and worryingly absent, causing a sense of both power and impotence. As I have explored, the simultaneously material and ephemeral quality of sound functions on the level of the words on the page (in metrical structure), but it also figures in terms of the hoped-for power of music itself to unite body and soul. In "The Kiss," the speaker compares the presence of his beloved and their physical intimacy to the absence of and longing for that very body:

> For lo! even now my lady's lips did play
> > With these my lips such consonant interlude
> > As laurelled Orpheus longed for when he wooed
> The half-drawn hungering face with that last lay. (4–8)

Using the myth of Orpheus, the speaker envisions not having his wife, and this loss is figured as Orpheus's desire not simply to resurrect Eurydice but to kiss. It is through music that this physicality will be reinstated to Eurydice (the physicality of her body) and also to Orpheus (the physicality of sexuality), associating music's power with solid bodily presence, sensuality and desire. Significantly, this quatrain is positioned just before one of the most sensual stanzas in the sonnet sequence. However, it is at the very moment before possession that the idea of loss occurs, perhaps carrying forth ideas found in the preceding sonnet, "Heart's Hope," where the speaker doubts his poetic ability to capture the essence of their love in verse. In effect, it is not only his ability to retain his lover and their sexuality that the speaker doubts, but also his ability to express himself, as the mythical Orpheus also failed in his task to regain Eurydice, despite his powerful music.

Indeed, in the first of the four "Willowwood" sonnets (Sonnet 49),[42] the speaker perceives himself as having Orpheus's experience:

> I sat with Love upon a woodside well,
> > Leaning across the water, I and he;
> > Nor ever did he speak nor looked at me,
> But touched his lute wherein was audible
> The certain secret thing he had to tell:
> > Only our mirrored eyes met silently
> > In the low wave; and that sound came to be
> The passionate voice I knew; and my tears fell.
>
> And at their fall, his eyes beneath grew hers;
> And with his foot and with his wing-feathers
> > He swept the spring that watered my heart's drouth.
> Then the dark ripples spread to waving hair,
> And as I stooped, her own lips rising there
> > Bubbled with brimming kisses at my mouth.

The sonnet functions on several levels: the beloved is imagined to replace personified Love, she is a reflection of the speaker himself, and the myths of Narcissus and Orpheus are referenced. The Orpheus myth is alluded to as

---

[42] The four "Willowwood" Sonnets were written in 1868 and published in the *Fortnightly Review* (March 1869) and in Rossetti's *Poems* (1870), before being included as Sonnets 49–52 of *The House of Life*. See Marsh, "Notes," *Dante Gabriel Rossetti Collected Writings*, 497.

music becomes the sound of the lover's voice and it is this that transforms the image into her eyes, hair and lips, as Orpheus would have resurrected Eurydice's body through his music-making. Moving toward the kisses at the end of the poem also references the way that "The Kiss" imagined Orpheus longing for Eurydice's kiss. In Sonnet 49, music only imaginatively resurrects the lover's form and her kisses, and it is important that this imagined sensation brings tears. The sonnet focuses on the present moment as an emotional, sensory moment. Instead of meditating on what loss means and trying to understand it, as occurs in poems like Wordsworth's "Surprised by Joy," Rossetti's sonnet focuses on conjuring up the lost beloved; it engages with emotions surrounding the desire for unity and painfully depicts the reality of physical separation and loss. Music's link with sensation is a traditional association, but what is significant here is that while music calls up the experience of physical presence and sensation, it is only in the imagination that it seems real.[43]

What becomes interesting is how music and its representational or non-representational qualities play into the striving after unity and meaning, as expressed by the sonnets. As I discussed above, the speaker associates music with the power of uniting lovers, and so with desire. However, the fact is that the speaker loses the beloved, expresses an increasingly fragmented psyche, and is unable to root himself and his poems in a single historic moment, while still suggesting the search for context. This process is concretely demonstrated in the "Willowwood" sonnets. Sonnet 49 emphasizes how the speaker is imagining and feeling, and this imagination includes the appropriate medieval accoutrement for Love's communications. Imagination and sensation are the focus of the poem as we step into the speaker's mind and heart rather than accessing a recreated historical moment. The "musical artifact" assists this process as it is an actual historic object, but it then works not to create a real spatial and temporal present, but rather an imagined moment with the lost beloved. The result is to send the speaker spiraling not only into his imagined connection with the beloved, but also into the nightmarish fragmentation of memory and psyche that the following "Willowwood" sonnets describe.

Rossetti's sonnet sequence, then, partakes of the Victorian urge to collect, catalogue and display artifacts, but finally frustrates the search for ultimate meaning in this direction; it steps beyond socially situating these objects, suggesting instead an orientation toward musical instruments and the playing of music that fits the aesthetic principle of *l'art pour l'art*. And while this "*condition of music*" as presence and absence can be seen structurally and figuratively in *The House of Life*, the idea of presence and absence also says something about the literal "condition of music" in nineteenth-century Britain, as perceived by the music profession. Is Britain *das Land ohne Music* or is it not? Music professionals responded with an emphatic "not," and then

---

[43] For a further discussion of the links between music, sensation and nineteenth-century theories of imagination, see Emma Sutton's and Michael Allis's essays in this volume, and my *Women Musicians in Victorian Fiction*.

proceeded to qualify and worry at the statement. In 1889, music critic Francis Hueffer (1843–1889) was already reflecting music's exponential increase in nineteenth-century England in his book, *Half a Century of Music in England, 1837–1887*, but also defending the state of English composition. If England really was the land without music, then would there have been so much attention paid to music's place in culture and to issues regarding how to promote "good" music, how to encourage British composition, and how to make music a lasting presence in the nation?[44] The problem could be rephrased in terms of Pater's "moments of music" or Rossetti's "moment's monument": how to monumentalize the moment of music? How to take fleeting time and immortalize it in space ("monument")? And how to take British musical "progress" – a keyword of the period – and not only encourage it, but display and exhibit it, whether in performance, in museums, or on the page (in journals, musical tracts, poetry and prose, and musical score notation). Indeed, the monumental Royal Albert Hall built near Exhibition Road to memorialize Queen Victoria's music-loving consort seems to encapsulate all of the components I have mentioned (exhibit, display, moment, monument, music).[45] In these cases, the temporal, transient, transcendent art form of music is constructed as material object, and its spatial display celebrates and further propels the idea that Britain is indeed musical. Rossetti's poetry, therefore, participates in constructing the Victorian idea of music as double: as presence and absence, spatial and temporal, moment and monument.

---

[44] See Francis Hueffer, *Half a Century of Music in England, 1837–1887* (London: Chapman, 1889) 25, 27; Anon., "Classical Music and British Musical Taste," *Macmillan's Magazine* 1 (1860): 384–385; Anon., "The Education of Audiences," *The Musical Times* 3 (1 December 1848): 79; Henry Leslie, "Music in England," *Macmillan's Magazine* 26 (1872): 245–253; Anon., "Contemporary Music and Musical Literature," *Westminster and Foreign Quarterly Review* ns 31 (1867): 384–400; William Pole, "The London Musical Season," *Macmillan's Magazine* 4 (1861): 448–455; Joseph Bennett, "The Condition of Opera in England," *Macmillan's Magazine* 20 (1869): 260–265.

[45] The proximity of the Royal Albert Hall (1867–1871) to sites of exhibition such as The Victoria and Albert Museum (begun in the 1850s), Imperial Institute (1887–1893), and the museums of Natural History (1837–1881), Science (1907), and Geological (1933–1935) only emphasize its own function of display, as does its location on land bought by the proceeds of the Great Exhibition. The Albert Hall's monumental and memorializing functions are further emphasized by its neighbor sitting across the street in Hyde Park, the Albert Memorial (1876), with its statue of the Prince.

Chapter 9

"The Music Spoke for Us": Music and Sexuality in *fin-de-siècle* Poetry

Emma Sutton

> Those who have never known a lover's sin
>   Let them not read my ditty, it will be
> To their dull ears so musicless and thin
>   That they will have no joy of it, but ye
> To whose wan cheeks now creeps the lingering smile,
> Ye who have learned who Eros is, – O listen yet a-while.[1]

In 1881, Oscar Wilde published his first and only collection of poetry, in which "Charmides," from which the stanza above is taken, was included. With its references to unnamed sins and physical debilitation, its classicism and celebration of erotic love, the poem exemplifies many of the characteristics with which *fin-de-siècle* British poetry is frequently associated. Its musical allusions, too, are representative of the widespread attention to and celebration of music in much late-nineteenth-century poetry and aesthetic theory. Wilde's cautionary interjection employs musical sensibility as a means of differentiating those "who have learned who Eros is" from those who have not; his subject is, he suggests, intelligible only to those whose "ears" can appreciate the "music" of his work. This is, as we shall see, one of many associations in his work of music with erotic love: both "Charmides" and the volume as a whole are suffused with references to music. Wilde's equation of musical sensibility with a state of erotic experience is an evocative starting point for this essay, which examines representations of music and sexuality in British poetry of the *fin de siècle*.[2] From Wilde's homoerotic images of classical lyric musicians, to Arthur Symons's accounts of heterosexual infatuation, to the "Sapphic song" of collaborative female poets "Michael

---

[1] Oscar Wilde, "Charmides," *Poems* (London: Bogue, 1881) 115–120.
[2] In the essay below, I use the term literally, to denote the 1880s and 1890s, rather than a particular *Zeitgeist*.

Field," musical allusions were employed, I will argue, as a means of delineating, exploring and imagining sexual experience and identity.

During the *fin de siècle*, there was considerable, disparate attention to the relations between music and sexuality. Whether explicit or allusive, discourses about music and about sexuality were, I would suggest, mutually constitutive. That the *fin de siècle* was the period in which modern conceptions of sexuality and sexual identity were established is widely accepted.[3] During the 1880s and the 1890s, the concepts of sexual types – "the homosexual," "the lesbian" and so on – emerged, a phenomenon which arguably privileged sexual preference and activity as definitions of individuals' personal and social identity. German, British and French sexologists speculated about the relations between sexual tastes and traits of personality or "temperament," and sexuality became not only a means by which scientists could classify individuals, but a formative influence on individuals' conceptions of their own personality or self. A number of sexologists, including Magnus Hirschfeld (1868–1935), Marc-André Raffalovich (1864–1934) and Havelock Ellis (1859–1939) turned their attention to the relations between sexuality and musical sensibility, examining in particular the purported affinities between musicality and homosexuality;[4] in certain discourses, references to musical tastes, aptitude and sensibility were utilized and perceived as indications of sexual inclination or practice.[5] Concurrently, musical form, effect and sensibility became influential elements in the mental and physical sciences, employed as means of investigating and elucidating the structure and function of various mental and physical processes. As Phyllis Weliver has recently demonstrated, music was particularly important in the work of a number of British, French and American associationist psychologists, whose analyses of the form and effects of music documented the interdependence of mind and body, and the corporeal elements of even such apparently cerebral facilities as memory.[6] Their hypotheses suggested that there were affinities between the structure and consumption of music and formative elements of individual identity, including memory and emotion. They also emphasized and lent scientific credence to the ancient association of music with the sensual and the corporeal. Music was thus

---

[3] See, for example, Elaine Showalter, *Sexual Anarchy: Gender and Culture at the Fin de siècle* (London: Virago, 1992); Jeffrey Weeks, *Coming Out: Homosexual Politics in Britain, from the Nineteenth Century to the Present* (London: Quartet, 1977) 3–4.

[4] See Magnus Hirschfeld, *A Categoric Personal Analysis for the Reader* (1899), trans. or adapted by Xavier Mayne, (c. 1908), cited in Neil Bartlett, *Who was that Man? A Present for Mr Oscar Wilde* (Harmondsworth: Penguin, 1993); Marc-André Raffalovich, *Uranisme et Unisexualité: Etude sur différentes manifestations de l'instinct sexuel* (Lyon: A. Storck and Paris: Masson, 1896) 185–189; and Havelock Ellis, *Studies in the Psychology of Sex: Volume 1: Sexual Inversion* (London: University Press, 1897) 17.

[5] See Wayne Koestenbaum, *The Queen's Throat: Opera, Homosexuality and the Mystery of Desire* (London: Penguin, 1994) 190; Philip Brett, "Musicality, Essentialism, and the Closet," *Queering the Pitch: The New Gay and Lesbian Musicology*, eds Philip Brett, Elizabeth Wood and Gary C. Thomas (New York: Routledge, 1994) 9–26.

[6] Phyllis Weliver, *Women Musicians in Victorian Fiction, 1860–1900: Representations of Music, Science and Gender in the Leisured Home* (Aldershot: Ashgate, 2000) 58–97.

associated not only with "atypical" sexual desire and identity, but also with eroticism and sensuality in general. These perceptions were augmented by the extensive debates about the purportedly unprecedented sensuality of some recent music (notably that of Richard Wagner), the subjects and effects of which were frequently identified as "excessively" erotic. The association of music and sexuality had, then, particularly topical and contentious overtones in this period.

A number of musicologists have recently proposed that music is constitutive of sexual and, more broadly, personal identity; this insight was anticipated, I propose, in the representations of music in late nineteenth-century poetry.[7] Musical analogies became a medium for representing personal, private, even solipsistic aspects of individual experience, and also for articulating what we might call more "public" sexual identities. Given the reciprocally-influential discourses about music and sexuality at this date, I will consider how *fin-de-siècle* poetry was informed by and modulated these debates. This essay considers what these texts might tell us about late-Victorian perceptions of music and of sexuality, and about the role of poetry as a medium for these subjects. The essay touches, too, on the relations between this poetry and the extensive corpus of British and other verse in which music was used as an analogy for the sensual or erotic. The prevalence of musical allusions in *fin-de-siècle* poetry might equally be explained with reference to Paterian or Symbolist aesthetic theory; or to the prominence of music in bourgeois domestic life and leisured "culture"; or to the prominence of musical references in poetry (such as that of Charles Baudelaire or Paul Verlaine) by which a number of *fin-de-siècle* poets were particularly influenced. Here, I wish to draw attention to an additional explanation of these musical allusions, and to emphasize their relation to contemporary discourses about sexuality. In so doing, we might recover some of the contemporary overtones of this poetry which would otherwise (to borrow Wilde's term) remain "musicless" and mute.

My starting point is a number of examples in which sensuality and sexual desire are represented in musical terms, a characteristic which is particularly explicit in Arthur Symons's "During Music" (1892):

> The music had the heat of blood,
> A passion that no words can reach;
> We sat together, and understood
> Our own heart's speech.
>
> We had no need of word or sign,
> The music spoke for us, and said

---

[7] See, for example, Susan McClary, *Feminine Endings: Music, Gender, and Sexuality* (Minneapolis: University of Minnesota Press, 1991) 26.

> All that her eyes could read in mine
> Or mine in hers had read.[8]

Symons's text evokes the sensuality both of the performance conditions and of the effect of this music, vividly delineating the intimacy and the reticence of this occasion of public musical consumption, and the expectation of mutual desire. While the musical text is unidentified, it is more than likely that Symons had Wagner's music in mind here, and probably *Tristan und Isolde* in particular; he had certainly attended performances of the music drama by this date and, in common with many of his contemporaries, was fascinated by the sensuality of Wagner's work.[9] His concern, however, is not a specific performance, but rather music's ability to represent – and stimulate – erotic desire. The music to which the characters are listening exposes and heightens the narrator's own desire, and that of his companion, increasing the characters' understanding of themselves and of each other. The performance is both revelatory, and simply reiterative of what is already half-perceived by both characters; the music's representational and affective capacities are repeatedly characterized as superior to those of speech. He suggests, that is, that music has not only the capacity both to stimulate desire and to illuminate sensual and psychological states, but that it has a greater epistemological authority and scope. Symons is better known, perhaps, for his evocations of dancers and music hall performers than of musicians, but many of his vignettes of theatrical life include references to musical performances. In his poetry, music is almost invariably associated with erotic desire. *London Nights* (1895), for example, includes (as its title suggests) many references to the *demi-monde*, and the collection is itself structured as a musical composition with the groups of poems divided by "intermezzos." The volume includes "To Muriel: At the Opera," a text delineating the narrator's desire for his companion; her decollete dress and white bosom again emphasize the tensions between decorum and erotic display inherent in certain forms of musical performance.[10] Symons's work suggests that the equation of music and the erotic was a product both of the performance conditions of certain genres such as opera and music hall, and of the affective properties of music. These musical allusions, occurring as they do in texts which repeatedly explore the exotic, the artificial and the sensual, augmented the association of music with illicit heterosexual desire. Placed within his explorations of contemporary urban life, they recurrently associate music with worldly eroticism.

Symons, then, repeatedly employed musical allusions in his delineations of a complex, self-consciously "modern" psychological condition. The influence

---

[8] Arthur Symons, "During Music," *Selected Writings*, ed. Roger Holdsworth (1974; Manchester: Carcanet, 1989).

[9] For a discussion of Symons's Wagnerism, see Stoddard Martin, *Wagner to "The Waste Land": A Study of the Relationship of Wagner to English Literature* (London: Macmillan, 1982).

[10] Arthur Symons, *London Nights* (London: Smithers, 1895) 50.

of music on perceptions and representations of contemporary sensibility and sexual experience is evident too in the work of a number of his contemporaries, in which heterosexual and homosexual desire was represented in musical allusions shaped by the language and theories of contemporary science. Katharine Bradley[11] and Edith Cooper lived and wrote together in what we would now understand as a "lesbian" relationship; *Underneath the Bough* (1893), published under their pseudonym Michael Field, includes "My heart is a violin," in which the narrator explores the relations between erotic desire and musical effect through an allusion to birdsong:

> Again my heart-string bears
>   The merciless vibration,
> As that trill comes unawares
>   To incite, and tease with cessation
>   When just awaking
>   The music into fire:
>   O heart, a viol quaking
>   With vain desire![12]

The poem delineates the corporeality and sensuality of the narrator's response to the birdsong, and also suggests an implicit, unspecified erotic relationship; it might be read as a dramatization of a moment in the relationship between the two female poets. The allusions to "fire," "teasing," "heart" and "desire," and the anthropomorphic image of the poet as a viol, imply an erotic subject – that the narrator is pained not only by the qualities of the bird's song, but also by the recollection or anticipation of an absent lover. The personification of music, and its representation as an autonomous, active entity, further imply that the poem's subject is not only one of birdsong and musical consumption, but also that of an intimate relationship between individuals. The strikingly corporealized image of the poet as a viol or violin draws both on Romantic images of the poet or of poetic sensibility as a harp or lute,[13] and on the vocabulary and metaphors of contemporary science. The image is, I would suggest, inflected by contemporary neurology; its representation of the visceral and instinctual aspects of desire recalls images of the nervous system and nerves as a stringed instrument current in scientific discourse. Their use of a musical image in which to represent the corporeal aspects of desire may have

---

[11] I have followed Bradley's preferred spelling of her name. See Michael Field, *Music and Silence: The Gamut of Michael Field*, chosen, annotated but not edited by Ivor C. Treby (n.p.: Blackland, 2000) 16–17.

[12] Michael Field, *Underneath the Bough*, in Sight and Song *1892 with* Underneath the Bough *1893*, intro. by R.K.R. Thornton and Ian Small (Oxford: Woodstock, 1993) 9–16.

[13] Further discussion of this image may be found in Kimiyo Ogawa's essay in this volume, "'Suspended' Sense in *Alastor*: Shelley's Musical Trope and Eighteenth-Century Medical Discourse" and, likewise, in Susan Bernstein's "On Music Framed: The Eolian Harp in Romantic Writing," and Phyllis Weliver's "The 'silent song' of D.G. Rossetti's *The House of Life*."

been suggested, then, by the experiments of neurologists and psychologists in which these domains were represented as interdependent. Similarly, in "Charmides," Wilde describes his protagonist at the lovers' tryst: "his nerves thrilled like throbbing violins / In exquisite pulsation" (129–130). Symons, too, in "The Armenian Dancer," published in 1906 though probably written around the turn of the century, portrayed sexual desire in similar images, beginning:

> O secret and sharp sting
> That ends and makes delight,
> Come, my limbs call thee, smite
> To music every string
> Of my limbs quivering.[14]

The narrator's instruction to the dancer to "smite / To music" his limbs or "strings" suggests both that her movements are accompanied by music, and that his desire for her is the stimulus to poetic creativity. Contrasting the intimacy and privacy of the "secret" "sting" of desire with the abrupt, dramatic production of music, Symons's image is one of violent, immediate and unmediated inspiration prompted by erotic desire. Here, the relation between sexual inspiration and the public poetic voice is itself a subject of the poem. Symons explicitly identifies sexuality or erotic experience as a legitimate subject of poetry – indeed as the source of poetry or music.

Symons published "Music and Memory" in *Silhouettes* (1892), which included a section entitled (alluding to Frédéric Chopin and James McNeill Whistler) "Nocturnes." His text (like Wilde's "The Burden of Itys," in which music is described as "the Art / Which is most nigh to tears and memory" [303–304]),[15] suggests that music and erotic desire were associated partly because of contemporary scientific exploration of the affinities between the structure of mental processes and music. "Music and Memory" obliquely alludes to contemporary investigations into musical structure and memory by psychologists such as Freud's tutor Jean-Martin Charcot (1825–1893) – these scientific explorations of music and memory are evoked by the physiological vocabulary of the "brain." Symons's text describes the (implicitly male) narrator's recollections of a woman, presumably a lover, in these terms:

> Music, soft throbbing music in the night,
> Her memory swims
> Into the brain, a carol of delight;
> The cup of music overbrims
> With wine of memory, in the night.[16]

---

[14] Arthur Symons, "The Armenian Dancer," *Selected Writings*, 1–5.
[15] The title alludes to the narrator's reiterated "burden" or ostinato.
[16] Arthur Symons, "Music and Memory," *Silhouettes*, 2nd ed. (London: Smithers, 1896) 6–10.

The poem's reiterative structure evokes the cyclical, cumulative structure of memory, emphasizing, perhaps, the aural properties rather than the "argument" of the language. As the poem develops, the equation of music and memory becomes more absolute, until her returning memory is described simply as "Music in music." His evocation of a state of languorous desire is simultaneously an exploration of memory: the text's eschewal of logical argument or conventional narrative development recreates the reiterative structure of memory and of music themselves. The poem explores the structure rather than, for example, the rhythmic or harmonic qualities of this music. In this respect, it suggests the influence of contemporary experimentation with musical form (such as that of Wagner's *unendliche Melodie* or of post-Romantic French composers).[17] Though Symons does not specify to what music the narrator is listening, his text evokes late-nineteenth-century rather than, for instance, Classical or contrapuntal structures; the formal innovations of a number of late-nineteenth-century composers suggest why it was that analogies between music and memory were made by scientists and artists at this date.

Music was, then, frequently used to allude to the sensual or erotic, and musical images were also used more specifically (as "Charmides" suggested) to contrast states of innocence and erotic experience. In "Céleste," published in *London Nights*, Symons's allusions to "an unknown tongue of love" (8) delineate the adolescent girl's position on the cusp of erotic experience, between childhood and adulthood. She is described as a "child," to whom "Love's music" is at present inaudible or unintelligible.[18] In "The Harlot's House" Wilde also employed musical images as a measure of sexual and moral integrity. In this text, a couple walking in the street observe on the blinds the shadows of figures in a brothel, from which "We heard the loud musicians play / The 'Treues Liebes Herz' of Strauss." The reference to Strauss points to the incongruity of these declarations of love, and also emphasizes, like Symons's work, the sensuality suffusing much public music-making. The patrons and dancers are represented as grotesque marionettes, their seductions taking the form of a stylized dance accompanied by "horn and violin"; when the narrator's "pure" female companion enters, the brothel's music founders and "the tune went false".[19]

In Wilde's work, music is often associated with sexual experience, particularly that perceived as a Fall, as in "Helas!", the lament which stood as the preface to his collection of poems, demonstrates:

---

[17] Symons's poem suggests a form of music in which thematic development is the predominant syntax and in which, as in the work of these composers for example, Classical distinctions between "statement" and "development" were effaced.
[18] Arthur Symons, "Céleste: The prelude," *London Nights*, 1, 4.
[19] Oscar Wilde, "The Harlot's House," *Complete Works of Oscar Wilde* (Glasgow: HarperCollins, 1994) 5–6, 11, 31.

> To drift with every passion till my soul
> Is a stringed lute on which all winds can play,
> Is it for this that I have given away
> Mine ancient wisdom, and austere control?
> Methinks my life is a twice-written scroll
> Scrawled over on some boyish holiday
> With idle songs for pipe and virelay,
> Which do but mar the secret of the whole.
> Surely there was a time I might have trod
> The sunlit heights, and from life's dissonance
> Struck one clear chord to reach the ears of God:
> Is that time dead? lo! with a little rod
> I did but touch the honey of romance –
> And must I lose a soul's inheritance?[20]

In this text, the poet is represented both as musician and instrument – the youthful confident young musician sure of his moral integrity and ability to strike a "clear chord" contrasted with the pained experience of the powerless lute. The sonnet employs the passivity and receptivity of the lute as an unwelcome image of lost musical, implicitly poetic, authority and control: sexual experience – the "honey of romance" – has resulted in the loss of creative and moral autonomy. The text, as the title emphasizes, is an exclamation of regret and anguish, with the questions registering the narrator's disbelieving dismay; his Fall is resoundingly attributed to illicit, sinful, erotic experience. The poem evokes "the medieval" through its allusions to the lute and "virelay," augmenting the sense of a moralized, implicitly Christian prohibition on erotic experience. Yet the images of the palimpsest, the "ancient" wisdom and the scroll alternately suggest a classical context, and the sonnet could be read as a reflection on a "Fall" from the Platonic relationship of older sage with young disciple. Here, music represents both personal integrity or poetic gift (the clear chord), and erotic experience (the "idle songs" which deface the scroll); the contrasting musical images of "songs" and the "clear chord" differentiate with finality the states of erotic innocence and experience. With its allusions to the loss of spiritual and, less specifically, personal integrity, the poem identifies sexual experience as a profoundly formative or transforming aspect of individual experience.

The significance of the analogy between music and erotic experience in Wilde's work and imaginative *topos* is confirmed in "ΓΛΥΚΥΠΙΚΡΟΣ ΕΡΩΣ" ("Bittersweet Love"). Published as the final section of the 1881 edition of the *Poems*, erotic experience and musical or poetic creativity are again represented as mutually exclusive. The narrator laments his condition of "common clay," that he has not "From the wildness of my wasted passion ...

---

[20] There is, perhaps, an echo of this poem in Wilde's description of Aubrey Beardsley's provocative, androgynous illustrations for *Salome* (with its repeated musical allusions) as "naughty scribbles a precocious boy makes in the margins of his copy book". Oscar Wilde, cited in Matthew Sturgis, *Aubrey Beardsley: A Biography* (London: HarperCollins, 1998) 158.

struck / a better, clearer song", and regrets that his lips have not been "smitten into music by the kisses / that but made them bleed".[21] Similarly, the narrator in "Silentium Amoris" ("The Silence of Love") declares: "thy Beauty make[s] my lips to fail, / And all my sweetest singing out of tune" (5–6). In contrast to "Helas!", the narrator makes clear that it is desire, rather than experience, which has muted him, but the poem similarly represents the poet as a lutanist and singer: "surely unto Thee mine eyes did show / Why I am silent, and my lute unstrung" (13–14). The submerged pun on the "unstrung" poetic voice, and the "undone" state of sexual experience, emphasizes the paralyzing effects of sensual desire and experience. Again in "Heart's Yearnings," an early poem written while at Magdalen College, Oxford, erotic love divides a state of eloquence or musicality from that of muteness or dissonance:

> Surely to me the world is all too drear,
>   To shape my sorrow to a tuneful strain,
> It is enough for wearied ears to hear
>   The Passion-Music of a fevered brain,
>   Or low complainings of a heart's pain.[22]

If Wilde repeatedly used musical images to differentiate between different stages of erotic experience and to portray sexuality as a threat to poetic autonomy, his protestations, were, of course, refuted by the texts themselves, in which thwarted creativity becomes the subject of successful literary compositions. Why, then, did he repeatedly adopt musical images to delineate threats to authorial and personal autonomy? Here, the "Passion-Music of a fevered brain" may begin to suggest an explanation. Wilde's allusion to contemporary *Weltschmerz*, and to anatomical or neurological discourses, suggests that music offered a novel ontological framework in which to delineate the tragic and mysterious elements of a distinctive *"fin-de-siècle"* psychological condition.

The familiarity, even banality, of the association of the musical and the erotic by the 1890s is suggested in "The Three Musicians," one of the poems published in *The Savoy* by the artist and writer Aubrey Beardsley, who was, with Symons, editor of the journal. The poem, which narrates the pastoral stroll of three musicians, two of whom are observed by a tourist consummating their desire, highlights with knowing audacity the association of sexual experience and music. It blithely alludes to pornographic musical images,[23] describes the musicians reflecting on and singing snatches of Wagner's, Gluck's and "Franz Himmel's" music, and draws on the association of professional musicians with the bohemian. Its fey octosyllabic lines suggest, perhaps, the form of the

---

[21] Oscar Wilde, "ΓΛΥΚΥΠΙΚΡΟS ΕΡΩΣ," *Poems*, 2, 5–6, 9–10.
[22] Oscar Wilde, "Heart's Yearnings," *Complete Works of Oscar Wilde*, 1–5.
[23] See Linda Gertner Zatlin, *Aubrey Beardsley and Victorian Sexual Politics* (Oxford: Clarendon, 1990) 151–154.

"roundelay" to which the figures allude; certainly, in its glib references to erotic exploits it recalls an insouciant dancing song:

> The three musicians stroll along
>   And pluck the ears of ripened corn,
> Break into odds and ends of song,
>   And mock the woods with Siegfried's horn,
> And fill the air with Gluck, and fill the tweeded tourist's soul with scorn.[24]

In Beardsley's text, music is both prop and synonym for seduction. The majesty and dignity of the grand opera to which they allude – particularly the subject of tragic love with which Gluck is famously associated through *Orfeo* – is undercut by their erotic exploits, and through the irreverence and indifference with which they juxtapose operatic subjects and styles. "The Three Musicians," and the context in which it was published – a journal that was widely perceived as the mouthpiece of the decadent aesthetic movement after Wilde's imprisonment for homosexual offences, and which was suffused with musical allusions and coded references to homosexuality – might also remind us of the topical political overtones of these musical allusions.

Here, unexpected affinities between Wilde's and Beardsley's poetry – the musical allusions of which appear, at first glance, antithetical in their tone and details – become apparent. Both writers drew on and augmented the association of music and sexuality – particularly homosexuality. Though Beardsley's poem narrates a heterosexual seduction, the youth and effeminacy of the "slim, gracious boy" (11) are emphasized. Beardsley's camp equation of musical aptitude or sensibility with the effeminate or (homo)erotic – a characteristic evident in his black and white drawings and prose as well as in his small poetic *oeuvre*[25] – is indebted, I would suggest, to the prominence of music in the poetry of a number of his immediate predecessors and contemporaries, including Wilde. Wilde's images of classical musicians, many of which included homoerotic allusions to youthful beauty, frequently accompanied melancholic laments for unspecified states of emotional loss or tragic experience. If these texts were published before Wilde himself apparently developed any homosexual relationships, and certainly before he was known as a provocatively effeminate public figure, they nonetheless bore out homosexual interpretation. For example, his allusions, in "The Burden of Itys," to music's ability to "make sorrow beautiful" (242) and to the "untented wounds" (245) and "dead voiceless silence" (244) permit interpretation as allusions to homosexual subjects. In "The Garden of Eros," the nineteenth century is repeatedly characterized as one of cultural and specifically poetic

---

[24] Aubrey Beardsley, "The Three Musicians," *Poems*, ed. Matthew Sturgis ([Edinburgh]: Tragara Press for the Eighteen Nineties Society, 1998) 21–25.
[25] See Emma Sutton, *Aubrey Beardsley and British Wagnerism in the 1890s* (Oxford: Oxford University Press, 2002).

decline — a "starved age" "so sceptical and so dogmatical";[26] it is contrasted with a loosely-defined state of "classical" pre-eminence, such that Wilde's subject may be read both as a lament for a loss of aesthetic grace, and also as nostalgia for an age of homoeroticism. Music is personified as Adonis — the god famed more for his beauty than his musicianship:

> Yet tarry! for the boy who loved thee best,
>   Whose very name should be a memory
> To make thee linger, sleeps in silent rest
>   Beneath the Roman walls, and melody
> Still mourns her sweetest lyre, none can play
> The lute of Adonais, with his lips Song passed away. (121–126)

By the 1890s, when Beardsley was writing, allusions to music, and to nameless suffering in silence (like Lord Alfred Douglas's "Love that dare not speak its name"[27]), invited readings as allusions to taboo sexual subjects.

Given that music had become, by this date, a prominent element in British and other homosexual discourse, and that musical allusions were self-referentially employed by figures including Walter Pater and Wilde to allude to homoerotic and homosexual subjects, the prevalence of musical allusions in the poetry of the British decadence movement should be reconsidered in these terms. The musical references in the work of Wilde, Beardsley, John Gray and others who were perceived as representatives of British decadent art might be seen as contributions to the implicit homoeroticism of much decadent writing, intended as discrete allusions to homosexuality and perceived in these terms by informed contemporary readers. Such an interpretation is supported, for example, by John Gray's "Parsifal," first published in *The Dial* in 1892, and included in *Silverpoints* (1893), a volume which was, famously, a seminal text of British decadent art. Gray's sonnet, an "imitation" of Verlaine's treatment of the Wagnerian theme,[28] emphasizes the innocence of Wagner's "virgin boy" (2) in "robe of gold" (12), and his resistance to the female sexuality represented by the flower-maidens and the "Woman Beautiful" (5). His frailty, passivity and chastity are contrasted to the fleshly sensuality of the women with their "round proffered arms" (2) and "mobile breasts" (4); the phallic "holy Javelin" (9) rather than Wagner's protagonist is the locus of dynamic energy in the poem. Gray's sonnet (the Princeton manuscript of which was dedicated to Wilde)[29] makes no explicit reference to Wagner's music drama, which was itself shortly to become explicitly identified as a "homoerotic" work,[30] but the operatic source is evoked in the celebrated final line "And oh! the chime of children's voices in the dome" (14).

---

[26] Oscar Wilde, "The Garden of Eros," *Poems*, 113, 114.
[27] Douglas uses this phrase in his poem, "Two Loves" (1894).
[28] See Paul Verlaine, "Parsifal," in *Oeuvres Poétiques Complètes*, ed. Jacques Borel (Paris: Gallimard, 1962).
[29] Ian Fletcher, ed., *The Poems of John Gray* (Greensboro, NC: ELT Press, 1988) 299.
[30] See, for example, Oscar Pannizza, "Bayreuth and Homosexuality," trans. Isobel Vetter,

In Michael Field's work, musical allusions similarly provide a framework in which to explore and delineate homoerotic desire and homosexual identity. Their sequence of poems based on fragments of Sappho's work, *Long Ago*, was published in 1889; unsurprisingly, their work, like Wilde's, draws heavily on images of classical lyric musicians. While we should remember that Sappho was not unequivocally identified as "a lesbian" at this date, and while a number of the poems refer to her heterosexual desire for Phaon, Bradley and Cooper were clearly stimulated by Sappho's role as a musician and exponent of same-sex desire. The sensuality of their poetry may have been legitimated in part by the emergent figure of "the lesbian" as an individual defined by their erotic inclinations and practice (their friendship and correspondence with Havelock Ellis may well have increased their familiarity with the theories of contemporary sexology);[31] their poems also, of course, contributed to an emerging self-conscious corpus of "lesbian" writing. In poem XVII of *Long Ago*, Sappho the singer and lyre-player leads a choir of young women in moonlit dances and song, lamenting her isolation from the community of young virgins:

> And Sappho touched the lyre alone,
> Until she made the bright strings moan.
> She called to Artemis aloud –
> ...
> ["]For maidenhood still do I long,
> The freedom and the joyance strong
> Of that most blessèd, secret state
> That makes the tenderest maiden great["].[32]

Music again differentiates between different states of erotic experience: Sappho's role as singer and musician is implicitly attributed to her greater maturity and erotic experience. It is also, of course, her means of reflecting on these experiences, and of articulating her desire for participation in the eroticized community of female dancers. Sappho's role as a musician and public figure is one to which we shall return; here, I wish to emphasize the sensuality with which the instrument itself, and the act of playing, are described. These characteristics are especially prominent in the exuberant unpublished poem "A Lyre: to her god," written in 1903, which begins:

> It is not I, but thou, o god, art growing old;
> Thou art grown strange, neglectful of thy lyre,
> Well-tuned it is, & ripe to thy desire,
> And thou to other tunes thy flock dost fold:
> By the passion of thy moods I am controlled[33]

Wagner 9 (April 1988): 71–75.
[31] Chris White, "The Tiresian Poet: Michael Field," *Victorian Women Poets: A Critical Reader*, ed. Angela Leighton (Oxford: Blackwell, 1996) 149.
[32] Michael Field, *Long Ago* (London: Bell, 1889) 19–21, 25–28.

With playful conceit the sonnet explores the relationship of musician and instrument; it might equally be read, of course, as a dramatization of an episode in the creative and personal relationship of the aunt and niece. The lyre's reproaches combine mock-heroic despair with plaintive regret; the abandoned lyre's situation is described as one of "muteness" and of "enrapt & mouldering fire" (7), emphasizing the betrayal of erotic love as well as of collaborative performance. Again, the vocabulary of secrecy and silence suggests a homoerotic subject. But the lyre's monologue ultimately modulates into triumphant self-assertion: "But thou dost touch me not; touch me & I shall sing / All of myself: though wilt be caught listening." (13–14) The couplet jubilantly inverts the lyre's subsidiary role in collaborative performance, emphasizing the affective and seductive power of music. The female lyre's boisterous challenge to the musician suggests that the poem is, in part, an exploration of their collaborative literary and personal relationship. It invites interpretation as an expression of an egalitarian partnership rather than a hierarchical relationship of creator (musician) and medium (instrument); the unconventional musical images are used to delineate an "alternate" form of romantic and collaborative relationship. As in Wilde's, John Gray's and Beardsley's work, music is a means of articulating unconventional forms of eroticism and sexuality – and in its inventive variations on the mechanics of musical performance, the poem re-imagines and explores the poets' and women's relationships.

In "Nella Trista Valle" ("In the valley of sorrows"), Michael Field evoked the seductive potential of music and of musical performance. The text was one of four sonnets published in the *Hobby Horse* in 1891 and written after a performance of Gluck's *Orfeo*.[34] The sonnets, dedicated to Julia Ravogli who sang the role of Orfeo (scored, in the 1762 version, for an alto castrato), explore the musical and dramatic properties of the performance – in particular, elements of the erotic and of gender ambiguity. The sonnet alludes to the sensuality of dramatic, especially, operatic performance – to the spectacle, cross-dressing and erotic subjects with which the genre was commonly associated. Orpheus is termed:

> Wanderer of the lute,
> With thy young lover's voice so fresh in woe
> For passion of three thousand years ago (1–3)

The character's youth – and androgyny – are emphasized: the male lover, performed by a woman disguised as a man, sings in what was, by the nineteenth century (in contrast perhaps to the great era of the castrati), a vocal register unequivocally perceived as "feminine." Moreover, the singer's desire is, of course, directed towards another female performer. The poem delineates

---

[33] Michael Field, "A Lyre: to her god," *Music and Silence*, 1–5.
[34] Michael Field, *A Shorter Shīrazād: 101 Poems of Michael Field*, chosen, annotated but not edited by Ivor C. Treby (n.p.: De Blackland, 1999) 41.

the eroticism of both the dramatic performance, and of the poets' response to the visual and aural ambiguities of the character's gender. The poets'/audience's language is overtly that of romantic flirtation:

> Nay, I think, we love thee most
> Bearing thy limpid music through the host
> Of chaos, till the roar begins to wane; (9–11)

Possibly because the sonnet is explicitly identified as a response to a real performance, the narrative voice is plural, speaking perhaps on behalf of the entire audience, but also for Cooper and Bradley: the sensual account of the singer's voice and appearance, then, takes on authorial overtones. The banal act of reflective evaluation of the "favorite" moments of a performance becomes the occasion of a subversive evocation of unconventional desire, and a means of exposing the mutability and ambiguity of gender in Baroque opera.

If this text documents the erotic terms in which performers and fellow listeners were perceived by members of the audience, Poem XXXIV in *Long Ago* offers an intriguing counterpart to these images. It begins:

> "Sing to us, Sappho!" cried the crowd,
>   And to my lyre I sprang;
> Apollo seized me, and aloud
>   Tumultuous I sang. (1–4)

In contrast to a number of Michael Field's poems (such as "A Lyre: to her god") which were not intended for publication, here musical analogies are used to delineate a sense of public, social sexual identity. Narrated from the perspective of the lyricist Sappho, the poem describes her initial unexpectedly hostile reception from the audience, imaged as "men who jeer" (6). The hostile listeners are imagined as masculine, but once Sappho begins to recall more benevolent relationships between the two, the audience is portrayed in feminized terms:

> There is a gift the crowd can bring,
>   A rapture, a content;
> Pierian roses scarcely fling
>   So ravishing a scent (9–12)

In this instance, the relationship of performer and audience is portrayed from the perspective of the musician – and in terms of a despotic seduction of the audience. Sappho's calculating domination of the audience is imagined as an erotic relationship between the two parties, a seduction which is the product of her own eroticized musical inspiration: "I paused: the whistling air was stilled; / Then through my chords the godhead thrilled" (XXXIV, 21–22). The entire process of inspiration and public performance is thus portrayed in highly eroticized and sensual terms, incorporating both homoerotic and heterosexual images. The text suggests that they conceived the public role of the poet, their relationship with audiences or readers, in terms of an erotic relationship; indeed, in this instance, as a sexual conquest and re-gendering of the initially masculine operatic audience. Such examples, and their numerous references to their poetry as "song," might be seen as attempts to delineate an emergent public homosexual identity.

The familiar analogy of poetry and song appears in a number of the texts which I have been considering, often used to draw attention to the lyricism of such poetry as well as to its performative, public qualities – its interaction with readers or audiences. This sense of the public, almost institutionalized role of poetry is particularly conspicuous in Field's work, in which they frequently draw on the figure of the classical lyric musician as an antecedent of their own role as poets. That this analogy had clear personal overtones is evident, representatively, in their celebrated declaration of poetic and personal devotion in *Underneath the Bough*:

> My Love and I took hands and swore,
>   Against the world, to be
> Poets and lovers evermore,
> To laugh and dream on Lethe's shore,
> To sing to Charon in his boat,
> Heartening the timid souls afloat[35]

Though the poem explicitly identifies their sexual and poetic identity as unconventional and anti-social in the sense of beleaguered, their poetic role is nonetheless conceived as one of public ministry. Their "song" is addressed to those in liminal or marginal states of existence, but is all the more necessary and benevolent for that. Similar personalized images of their work as a form of "song" are frequent: in *Underneath the Bough* alone, the texts are organized into "Books of Songs," and "An Invitation," for example, begins "Come and sing, my room is south".[36] If such an analogy was a commonplace of nineteenth-century poetry, it had also – as Margaret Reynolds has suggested – specific topical reference by the *fin de siècle*. Describing Michael Field's relation to the Sapphic fragments as a "duet, a collaboration, a singing in unison which gave new freedoms and new permissions," Reynolds emphasizes the shift in perceptions of Sappho and of music at this date. Alluding to the various nineteenth-century operatic versions of Sappho's story by Rossini and Gounod, for example, she suggests that the cultural and sexual integrity represented by *bel canto* opera offered a liberating image for female poets. The association of *bel canto* with "natural" song, like the sexologists' identification of homosexuality as "natural" or inherent, offered a legitimating model both for their personal and creative lives.[37] Thus the prevalence of images of song in

---

[35] Michael Field, Song 18, Book 3, *Underneath the Bough*, 4–9.
[36] Michael Field, "An Invitation," *Underneath the Bough*, 1.
[37] Margaret Reynolds, "'I lived for art, I lived for love': The Woman Poet Sings Sappho's Last

their work might suggest not only their sense of their public vocation as poets, but a confidence in their sexual identity.[38]

The images of song and "natural" music or sexuality which inform Michael Field's work, also shape that of John Davidson and Wilde. Davidson's poetry associates music with a form of sensual sublime, and is, in some cases, probably informed by, though it does not explicitly refer to, specific musical texts – such as Wagner's *Tannhäuser*. "A Ballad of Tannhäuser" (1896) makes repeated references to the song with which the Venusberg, the domain of erotic love, is associated; Tannhäuser's seduction is attributed as much to the effects of this "dulcet melody" as to the beauty of Venus. After Tannhäuser's apparently fruitless journey to Rome in search of absolution, he returns to the Venusberg:

> The air, a world-enfolding flood
>   Of liquid music poured along;
> And the wild cry within his blood
>   Became at last a golden song.[39]

This form of song, rather than expressing a poet's role as public spokesman, has become an image of panthean, cosmic energy. In "Panthea," Wilde similarly employed an image of cosmic music to celebrate erotic love which anticipated that of Davidson in "A Ballad of Tannhäuser":

> We shall be notes in that great Symphony
>   Whose cadence circles through the rhythmic spheres,
> And all the live World's throbbing heart shall be
>   One with our heart; the stealthy creeping years
> Have lost their terrors now, we shall not die,
> The Universe itself shall be our Immortality.[40]

The image combines disparate musical allusions – to symphonic music and the celestial music of natural religion – to draw on the generic association of music with the sensual and instinctual. Here, music denotes the sublime and infinite, the image of symphonic music indicating the seamless fusion of seemingly endless parts. If we have traveled a considerable distance from the neo-Platonic celestial harmony to which Wilde alluded in "Helas!", these images are nonetheless united by their attention to the analogies between music and sexuality. In Davidson's text, as in "Panthea," sexuality is represented as a dynamic cosmological force, ubiquitous and without limit. Rather than

---

Song," in Leighton, 287, 302.

[38] For further discussion of the analogy of poetry and song, and of "Sapphic song" in nineteenth-century poetry, see Yopie Prins, *Victorian Sappho* (Princeton: Princeton University Press, 1999).

[39] John Davidson, "A Ballad of Tannhäuser," *The Poems of John Davidson*, ed. Andrew Turnbull, 2 vols (Edinburgh: Scottish Academic Press, 1973) 157–160.

[40] Oscar Wilde, "Panthea," *Complete Works of Oscar Wilde*, 175–180.

identifying sexual experience as a cause or indication of the isolation of the modern individual, these texts identify sexuality as an expression of cosmic unity and order. Reworking the image of celestial harmony into a jubilant celebration of sexual experience, they affirm the ecstatic properties of musical and erotic experience.

These musical allusions, then, are united by an attention to the affinities between musical form, performance and effect, and the psychological and physiological complexities of erotic experience. If some common strands are immediately apparent – the anthropomorphic representation of relations between musician and text or musician and instrument; the sensuality of musical performance and effect; the perception of music as a formative, even revelatory, influence on personal identity – we may well be struck too by the protean mutability and diversity of these images. They suggest the ambiguities and richness of music within contemporary musical life and in discourses about music, its status as both one of the most decorous forms of bourgeois culture, and its subversive, even heterodox, elements. Drawing on and augmenting the equivocal position of music with late-Victorian cultural discourse, these texts suggest its centrality to understandings and delineations of the newly-theorized domain of sexual identity – and, more broadly, to self-knowledge and representation. And, equally importantly, to the delineation of "*fin-de-siècle*" experience itself.

Chapter 10

Sappho Recomposed: A Song Cycle by Granville and Helen Bantock

Yopie Prins

Musical (De)Cadence

"To be a disembodied voice, and yet the voice of a human soul; that is the ideal of Decadence," Arthur Symons declared in his 1893 manifesto on "The Decadent Movement in Literature."[1] The disembodiment of voice was a musical ideal transported from French Symbolist poetics, which read poems as evocation of infinite resonance, detached from the body of a speaker "and yet" embodied in sound. Music was idealized by poets such as Paul Verlaine, whose credo *de la musique avant tout chose* was translated by Symons from French to English:

> Music first and foremost of all!
> Choose your measure of odd not even,
> Let it melt in the air of heaven,
> Pose not, poise not, but rise and fall.[2]

According to the first stanza of "Art Poétique," the perfect measure of poetry is music, when the spoken language dissolves into musical cadence. The poem aspires to "the air of heaven" where breath of the body transformed into pure spirit, and material form is spiritualized. Rather than assuming an original speaking voice, we are asked to read the poem as music that resounds without beginning and without end: not posited ("pose not, poise not") at one fixed point, but forever rising and falling, in elusive measures "odd not even." The cadence of the decadent voice is a fall (*de* + *cadere*) into disembodied echo, and thus, at the very moment of its emergence, voice is already fading.

---

[1] Arthur Symons, "The Decadent Movement in Literature," *Harper's New Monthly Magazine* 87 (November 1893): 862.
[2] Translation by Arthur Symons of lines 1–4 of "Art Poétique" by Paul Verlaine, quoted in John Munro, *The Decadent Poetry of the Eighteen-Nineties* (Beirut: American University of Beirut, 1970) 52.

This idea(l) of music echoed throughout the Decadent Movement at the end of the nineteenth century, when a new literary sensibility emerged along with a new musical culture in England. In his chapter on "The Condition of English Song in 1900," Stephen Banfield notes that literary decadence coincided with "a radical transformation in the aesthetic status of English song," as English composers turned to poetry for inspiration and became known especially for setting poems to music.[3] They sought to define their own national tradition by drawing on the poetic culture of late Victorian England, turning the English art song into a musical genre distinct from the popular ballad, the German *Lied*, the French *mélodie*, the Italian aria, and songs from other traditions. Periodicals such as *The Vocalist* (founded in 1902) were dedicated to the promotion of English art songs as these circulated with increasing popularity in print and performance, in private salons and public concert halls.[4] But how could English composers recreate the disembodied voice of decadent poetics in song? The challenge for them was to turn a musical metaphor into actual music, as a musical performance rather than a metaphorical form. What the audience was invited to "hear" in such a performance was a voice poised at the vanishing point, always receding.

My essay will trace the rise and fall of a decadent voice in a late Victorian song cycle, entitled *Sappho: Prelude and Nine Fragments* (1900–1906), with music composed by Granville Bantock and libretto composed by his wife, Helen Bantock. In this cycle, the complex relation between music and lyric is figured through Sappho, the very personification of lyric as the genre came to be read at the end of the nineteenth century. I have argued in *Victorian Sappho*, what we now call "Sappho" is in many ways an artifact of Victorian poetics: the hypothesis of a female persona singing at the origins of a Western lyric tradition, whose long-lost song echoes through the centuries.[5] According to this ideology of lyric reading, our assumption of a speaker produces a desire for the "original" voice of Sappho, as a longing that can never be fulfilled. The following pages are a postscript (or musical postlude) to this argument, as I

---

[3] Stephen Banfield, *Sensibility and English Song: Critical Studies of the Early 20th Century* (Cambridge: Cambridge University Press, 1985) 2–4. I also thank Lewis Foreman for sharing with me his expertise on Bantock.

[4] On musical culture in England at the turn of the century, see Meirion Hughes and Robert Stradling, *The English Musical Renaissance, 1840-1940: Constructing a National Music*, 2nd ed. (Manchester: Manchester University Press, 2001). On the cultivation of music in Victorian England, see Maurice Willson Disher, *Victorian Song: From Dive to Drawing Room* (London: Phoenix House, 1955); Nicholas Temperley, ed., *The Lost Chord: Essays on Victorian Music* (Bloomington: Indiana University Press, 1989).

[5] For an historical account and a theoretical critique of the idea of Sappho that emerges in Victorian poetics, see Yopie Prins, *Victorian Sappho* (Princeton: Princeton University Press, 1999). On Sappho's association with the sister arts (poetry, art, music) in nineteenth-century England, see Margaret Reynolds, *The Sappho History* (Basingstoke: Palgrave MacMillan, 2003). In her reading of Christina Rossetti in the present volume, Yeo Wei Wei also invokes a (Sapphic) model of female lyricism that reflects Victorian ideas about women's relation to song.

transpose the problem of reading voice in lyric into a question about hearing voice in music. How does the song cycle composed by the Bantocks prolong our longing for the voice of Sappho?

The revival of Sapphic song is predicated on its loss, and thus revolves around the paradox of a voice beyond hearing. As the title of *Sappho: Prelude and Nine Fragments* already suggests, the musical personification of Sappho by the Bantocks assumes her fragmentation. The Sapphic persona of their song cycle is not a unitary person with a unified voice, but a medium for "sounding through" (*per + sona*). I analyze various invocations and revocations of Sapphic voice, to show how Sappho is an equivocal figure for the performance of voice, both in lyric and in music. These songs equivocate: between vocal and instrumental performance, between harmonic resolution and dissolution, between words and music, between different kinds of desire. By attending to such equivocations, I suggest that the phonic effect of Sapphic song – its "Sapphonic" appeal, to echo a phrase introduced by Elizabeth Wood in *Queering the Pitch* – is a form of resonance that disembodies voice "and yet" gives body to echo. If we listen with an ear attuned to such resonance, we can understand the song cycle as a simultaneously lyrical and musical attempt by the Bantocks to embody the ideal of Decadent poetics: a musical (de)cadence where the voice of Sappho is forever fading into the distance.

In addition to reading the figure of music in nineteenth-century poetry, I therefore propose a way of reading the figure of poetry in music as well. This is a reciprocal relation, but also one of mutual interruption. In his chapter on "Song" in *Music and Poetry*, Lawrence Kramer emphasizes an "agonic" relation between poetry and music that pulls the voice in different directions, between two attempts to be heard. Instead of understanding song expressively (as if the music "expresses" the poem, and vice versa), he argues that song is a "dissociation of speech: a loosening of phonetic and syntactic articulation and a dissolving of language into its physical origin." Song is always a "transmemberment" of speech according to Kramer, who points to moments when it exceeds the spoken language through "overvocalizing," by which he means "the purposeful effacement of text by voice."[6] In a later essay, "Beyond Words and Music: An Essay on Songfulness," Kramer draws a similar distinction between song as "enunciation" and the song as "vocalization," in order to argue that "enunciated song must continually posit the possibility of its interruption by or transformation into vocalized song." He describes "occasions on which song became deeply moving, not as an expressive fusion of text and music, but as a manifestation of the singing voice, just the voice, regardless of what it sang." The relation between words and music is less agonistic here, now understood not as purposeful effacement of text but simply going "beyond" it: "[t]he text on these occasions doesn't matter, is even better if unknown; song here works not by what it signifies, but by the material

---

[6] Lawrence Kramer, *Music and Poetry: The Nineteenth Century and After* (Berkeley: University of California Press, 1984) 130, 132.

presence of its signifiers."[7] In rising toward "songfulness," the singing voice falls away from meaning into pure sound and resonance.

Such "occasions" are another way of falling into decadence, like the moment evoked by Symons when music appears "first and foremost of all" and, listening to the language dissolving into its physical origins, we "let it melt ... rise and fall." But if this is the vanishing point toward which the song cycle by the Bantocks aspires, it is important to note that their spiritualization of Sapphic song happens through the materialization of a "voice" that presents itself not only in the interruption of words by music, but also in the interruption of music by words. While the decadent ideal seems to locate music beyond language (*musique avant tout chose*) nevertheless these mediums are internal to one another, each using the material presence of its own signifiers to produce an idealization of the other. In *Sappho: Prelude and Nine Fragments*, the musical remembering of Sappho is a transmemberment, but not a transcendence, of that dismembered poetic corpus.

The Bantocks and Wharton's *Sappho*

Granville Bantock stands out from his generation as the most literary of the composers associated with the English Musical Renaissance. He began his compositional career as one of the "English Wagnerians," and proved unusually prolific in composing vocal music.[8] He studied from 1888–1893 in London at the Royal Academy of Music, and founded *The New Quarterly Musical Review*, a journal published in London from 1893–1896 that announced grand ambitions for the future of English music. In the first issue, a "Prefatory Sonnet" compared this ambitious venture to the adventures of Jason and the Argonauts, as a "Golden Quest" for which "we seize the oars, and with full voice and strong / Launch forth into the unknown deep with song."[9] Although the journal ran aground after several years, by 1900 Bantock had successfully launched himself forth "with full voice" and "with song" as a composer, known especially for his musical settings of poetry in song cycles, choral symphonies and orchestral tone poems. Many of Bantock's compositions were inspired by nineteenth-century poets such as Percy Bysshe Shelley, Samuel Taylor Coleridge, Robert Browning, Algernon Swinburne,

---

[7] Lawrence Kramer, *Musical Meaning: Toward a Critical History* (Berkeley: University of California Press, 2002) 52–53.

[8] For a brief narrative of Bantock's career, see Peter J. Pirie, "Bantock" in *The New Grove Dictionary of Music and Musicians*, ed. Stanley Sadie (London: Macmillan, 1980) 2: 123–125. See also Peter J. Pirie, "Bantock and his Generation," *The Musical Times* 109 (August 1968): 715–717; Trevor Bray, *Bantock: Music in the Midlands before the First World War* (London: Triad, 1973).

[9] Lines 12–14 from "Prefatory Sonnet," *The New Quarterly Musical Review* 1.1 (May 1893) 1. The sonnet was composed by H. Orsmond Anderton, who met Bantock as a student at the Royal Academy of Music and helped him edit the journal.

George Meredith and Oscar Wilde, and also by English translations of exotic poems such as *The Rubayait of Omar Kayam*, *Ghazals of Hafiz*, *Songs from the Chinese* and *The Garland of Meleager*. In addition, he collaborated with Helen Bantock on various songs and several large-scale choral works.[10]

The artistic and literary talents of his wife, born Helena Franceska Von Schweitzer, were an inspiration to Bantock early in his career. Educated in Germany and France, she wrote poetry and attended art school in London, where she became engaged to Granville Bantock. During their engagement she composed words for the 36 songs included in *Songs of the East*, and when they were married in 1896 he composed their wedding march; soon thereafter he also composed the *Helena Variations*, an orchestral work dedicated to Helen F. Bantock with "[t]houghts and reflections on some of your moods written during a wearisome absence," and spelling out in musical notes the initials H.F.B. (in a recurring motive of B sharp, F, and B flat). Under her newly Anglicized name, she published *The Love Philtre and Other Poems* in 1897, followed by *A Woman's Love* in 1911. In addition to working on the libretti for Bantock's songs, she designed covers for several of his early musical scores, and by all accounts was "of inestimable help to him in countless ways, besides showing her own powers as a poetess."[11]

In 1904 the Bantocks moved to Birmingham, where Granville was appointed Principal of the School of Music, and in 1908 he took over Edward Elgar's chair as Peyton Professor of Music at Birmingham University. In a family memoir, their daughter Hermione Myrrha Bantock (born during the period when the Bantocks were occupied with ancient Greece) recalls in particular the passion for poetry shared by her parents:

> This pleasure in reciting poetry aloud just for the joy of it was common to all the Bantocks, and a pastime in which my father often joined. It was from him, of course, that the idea originally developed, for we had grown up to the sound of quotations from the Greek and Persian poets interspersed with sayings from the Bible, the Chinese philosophers, and Shakespeare. My mother also read poetry very beautifully; it was her great love.[12]

About her mother, Myrrha Bantock writes that she "differed from the typical Edwardian lady" in "her serious outlook and her intellectuality" (15), and that she continued reading and writing well into her eighties, "in her own romantic world of poetry, literature, music and art" (181). As for her father, "it is impossible not to be impressed with the wide range of his reading: he must have gone through a tremendous number of books" (57). To prove how his

---

[10] A list of songs by Bantock is included in Banfield, *Sensibility and English Song*, 2: 407–415.
[11] H.O. Anderton, *Granville Bantock* (London: Lane, 1915) 33.
[12] Myrrha Bantock, *Granville Bantock: A Personal Portrait* (London: Dent, 1972) 140. Subsequently, page numbers from her memoir will be cited in the main text.

"knowledge of and feeling for literature were quite exceptional" (85), she devotes a chapter to "Our World of Books." Many of his colleagues also admired his literariness, as we learn in *Our Favourite Musicians*: "[t]he range and quality of Bantock's literary interests are to be traced in the course of his compositions. A list of the poets and poems that have induced him to write music, chronologically, would be sign and token of a wealth of appreciative reading far transcending that of any other musician known to the world. His house is filled with books."[13]

Among the books that filled the house of the Bantocks was a late Victorian edition of the Sapphic fragments, entitled *Sappho: Memoir, Text, Selected Renderings and a Literal Translation* by Henry Thornton Wharton.[14] What the Bantocks found in Wharton's *Sappho* was more than a mere compilation of Greek texts. As an amateur philologist, Wharton drew on the authority of nineteenth-century Classical scholarship to create a popular edition that would appeal to a wide range of readers. In addition to juxtaposing the textual fragments of Sappho in Greek with his own "literal" translations in prose and with literary imitations by various English poets, Wharton sought to reconstruct Sappho herself as the image of the perfect Poetess. His book included an elaborate frontispiece depicting "Sappho" in profile (see Fig. 10.1). More Victorian than Greek, this portrait of lyric perfection was engraved by J. Cother Webb and based on a painting by Lawrence Alma-Tadema, whose signatures are reproduced below the image as if they are its co-authors, along with Wharton, of Sappho. Above the image, Sappho's name is spelled out in Greek letters, directly across from the title page, where her name appears again, transliterated in English. Thus Sappho seems to gaze from the frontispiece toward her name on the title page, as if she is looking forward to – perhaps even, longing for – her own translation. She is the personification of dead letters revived in a living language, a feminine form to be animated by means of prosopopoeia, first giving face to the name of Sappho and then a voice as well.[15]

Not only is Wharton's book prefaced (literally) by the face in the frontispiece, but to bring this figure to life Wharton included a long preface, entitled "Life of Sappho." Here, based on scanty evidence, he imagines how Sappho lived and sang her songs. "Her poems or μέλη were undoubtedly written for recitation with the aid of music," Wharton writes, not unlike "what is called in modern days the *Song* or *Ballad*" (44; original emphasis), and he

---

[13] Sydney Grew, *Our Favourite Musicians, from Stanford to Holbrooke* (London: Fouls, 1924) 144.

[14] The first edition of Wharton's *Sappho* (London: Lane, 1885) was followed by a second edition in 1887, a third edition in 1895, and a posthumous fourth edition in 1898 that included a memoir of Wharton (who came to be known as "Sappho Wharton"). I quote from the 1895 edition, the one most likely used by the Bantocks for their song cycle.

[15] On the prosopopoeia of Wharton's edition, simultaneously giving a face to the name of Sappho and defacing it, see my discussion of "Wharton's Rend(er)ings," in *Victorian Sappho*, 52–73.

imagines that "she sang softly and plaintively, and at a higher pitch than any of her predecessors" (45). According to Wharton, Sappho's claim to fame as a lyric poet came first and foremost through her music, and for the benefit of his musical readers he speculates in some detail on the composition of Sappho's melodies. Following ancient scholiasts and contemporary Classical scholars, he suggests that Sappho might have invented the ancient Mixolydian mode, and he even re-prints a scale in musical notation, "the scale of our G major without the F# or leading note .... called in the early Christian Church 'the angelic mode'" (45–46). He also describes the instruments that provided musical accompaniment for Sapphic song, "a kind of harp" and other "kinds of many-stringed Lesbian lyres which cannot now be identified" (46). Although it is difficult to identify these sounds with any historical accuracy, Wharton leads his readers toward an imaginative reconstruction of Sappho's music.

To further instruct his readers Wharton makes a metrical notation of the Sapphic stanza, "the metre commonly called after her name ... because of her frequent use of it. Its strophe is made up thus" (47):

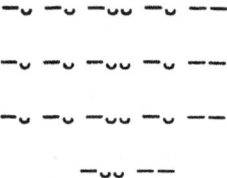

With this representation of Sappho's distinctive meter (an alternation of syllables that are scanned long and short in Greek, with the last syllable of each line either long or short), Wharton invites the reader to "hear" the rhythms of her song, turning a graphic notation into an audible form. To emphasize this audibility he quotes several lines from Swinburne written in Sapphic stanzas, because "nothing repeats its rhythm to my ear so well." This fantasy of sound is transferred from his own "ear" to that of the reader, as Wharton writes at the end of his essay: "[w]ith such lines as these ringing in the reader's ears, he can almost hear Sappho herself singing 'Songs that move the heart of the shaken heaven, / Songs that break the heart of the earth with pity, / Hearing, to hear them'" (47). Wharton asks us to "hear Sappho herself singing" in Swinburne's Sapphic stanza, as if his meter could recreate the original sound of her songs and thus bring Sappho back to life through his essay, "Life of Sappho." But the critical word in Wharton's claim that we "can almost hear Sappho herself" is *almost*, for in Swinburne's poem it is not Sappho's singing but the reiteration of our own hearing ("hearing, to hear them") that creates Sapphic song: what we hear is a resounding echo, "ringing in the reader's ears" as an effect of reading.

Designed to help readers translate Greek letters into a lyrical image of Sappho, Wharton's book inspired the Bantocks to re-imagine the lyrics of Sappho in song. Out of the scattered Sapphic corpus, a dismembered body of many parts, Wharton created a seemingly unified, composite portrait that allows Sappho to be remembered as the ideal Poetess and the very embodiment of lyric as a genre: a muse "singing" through the centuries, even though her song is lost. Along with the frontispiece and the preface, the iconography of Wharton's front cover serves as a reminder of this musical effect. The 1895 edition features a decorative blue cover embossed in gold with a lyre at the center, and in each corner we see the Greek letter *psi* (Ψ). It is the first letter in Sappho's name and its shape is reminiscent of Sappho's lyre, graphically representing the link between lyric and music. Helen Bantock used this edition to transpose Wharton's translations into a poetic sequence that Granville Bantock then composed into songs for contralto and orchestra. The final page following the final song in the cycle echoes the front cover of Wharton's edition, by depicting a lyre as the poetic frame for their musical composition. The Sappho "composed" by Wharton as a musical figure (or muse) for lyric was thus "recomposed" by the Bantocks as lyrical figure for music.

They recomposed Sappho over a span of several years, starting around 1900 when Helen Bantock selected the words from various Sapphic fragments and combined them into nine songs that Bantock set to music, one by one. It was a collaboration based on mutual exchange of ideas, as Bantock wrote to his wife in 1904, "I have been copying out the Sappho Song with its unfinished ending as you suggested, and commenced work on another of them .... which will have to be more lyrical."[16] More than an hour long, the song cycle was completed in 1905 and a piano-vocal score published in 1906, with an elaborate illustration on the front.[17] (see Fig. 10.2) Like the frontispiece of Wharton's *Sappho*, the name is presented in Greek letters and transliterated into English letters that promise a translation of Sappho into living song. But unlike Wharton's edition, the focal point of the image designed by the Bantocks is not a portrait of the poetess but a tripod burning incense: a crucible, perhaps, where music and text are combined to produce the essence of Sappho, her body transformed into the spirit, or "perfume," of inspired Sapphic song. So the Bantocks invite us to hear Sappho in a spiritualized, musical form.

---

[16] Quoted by Lewis Foreman in his program note for "Sir Granville Bantock: Sappho and Sapphic Poem" (Hyperion CD, 1997) 7.
[17] Piano-vocal score, *Sappho, Nine Fragments for Contralto*, words selected by Helen F. Bantock, set to music by Granville Bantock, Deutsche Übersetzung von Joh. Bernhoff (Leipzig: Breitkopf and Hartel, 1906). All subsequent references to the score, including musical examples, refer to this edition. The complete orchestral score is published by Breitkopf & Härtel. I am grateful to the Northwestern University Music Library for lending the piano-vocal score, and to University of Michigan Photo Services for reproducing the front cover.

Figure 10.1: Frontispiece and title page, Henry Thornton Wharton's *Sappho: Memoir, Text, Selected Renderings, and a Literal Translation*

Figure 10.2: Cover illustration, piano-vocal score, *Sappho: Nine Fragments for Contralto*

The Lesbian School of Music

The lost songs of Sappho provoked much speculation not only among the philologists and poets included in Wharton's edition, but among historians of music as well. With the emergence of historical musicology and ethnomusicology in Victorian England, there were numerous attempts to reconstruct ancient Greek music, although the actual pitches, timbres, rhythms, melodies and harmonies remained (and to this day remain) open to debate. Since no one really knew what the music of the Greeks sounded like, reading Greek musical notation was a matter of hypothesis at best. Nevertheless it was a topic that preoccupied musicologists, many of whom were trained in Classics at the end of the nineteenth century. Granville Bantock was aware of their debates, in longer musicological treatises of the period and in his own journal: *The New Quarterly Musical Review* published several scholarly articles about musical notation for instruments and voices in ancient Greece, charting in detail the transposition of notes and scales into letters of the Greek alphabet.[18] And contemporaneous with Wharton's first edition of Sappho, John Frederick Rowbotham (1859–1925) published *A History of Music* in three volumes (1885–1886), the second of which was dedicated to "The Music of the Elder Civilizations and the Music of the Greeks." Along with other books circulating at the time, Rowbotham contributed to the esoteric, exotic and erotic appeal of ancient Greek music for Bantock's compositions.

In his study of nineteenth-century British musicology, Bennett Zon situates Rowbotham among general histories of music that imposed an aesthetic template on an evolutionary model.[19] Rowbotham narrates the history of music as a chronological progression through different instruments: the drum stage, the pipe stage, and the lyre stage, evolving from primitive music to higher forms of musical expression. The lyre stage is associated with more advanced forms of civilization, such as the lyric age of Greece, where Rowbotham locates the transformation from "sensuous" into "spiritual" music: the accompaniment of voice by the lyre, he believes, allowed for the subjection of sensuous sound to the words of the singer. Throughout his historical study, Rowbotham tries to distinguish between the "musical" and "poetical" elements in music through a series of oppositions: one originates in sound, the other in words; one is sensuous, the other intellectual; one is instrumental, the other vocal. But these distinctions do not hold, as Bennett Zon points out: "[i]nterestingly, in Rowbotham's book the sequence of chapters on drum, pipe, and lyre is in itself arrested after the pipe stage, or before the lyric stage, by a chapter on the voice" (200). This interruption in Rowbotham's argument

---

[18] Three painstakingly detailed articles appeared in *The New Quarterly Musical Review*: C. Abdy Williams, "The Musical Notation of Ancient Greece" in No. 6 (August 1894): 53–59, continued by Williams in No. 9 (May 1895): 1–16, and followed by a response from Cecil Tor, "Modern Notions of Ancient Music" in No. 10 (August 1895): 82–87.

[19] For discussion of John Frederick Rowbotham, see Bennett Zon, *Music and Metaphor in Nineteenth-Century British Musicology* (Aldershot: Ashgate, 2000) 193–201.

suggests a confusion or equivocation about whether to align "voice" with the musical or poetical elements in music, and it seems that Sapphic song is especially equivocal in disrupting the distinction between instrumental and vocal performance.

Rowbotham dwells at length on the lyric poets of Lesbos, where "there was Melody in the air," beginning with Terpander who "joined words to the prelude which the Lyre had used to play alone."[20] Rowbotham describes the musical developments that culminated in "the high state of perfection which Greek singing had reached under the influence of the Lesbian School of Musicians" (127). Of course the greatest of these musicians was Sappho, whose Lesbian song is understood to be lesbian song, as Rowbotham is free to imagine: "she panted for that love which seems so strange, where women love each other" and "invented strange ways of gratifying their passions" (90). He associates Sappho's erotic style with an inventive musical style: "[a]nd she was full of fire and passion, and is the acknowledged mistress of the Systaltic or 'Thrilling' Style of Music, of which very likely she was the inventress, and so it is out of compliment to her introducing a new style into Music that Plato has called her the Tenth Muse" (91–92). Simultaneously a woman and a muse, Sappho marks a critical turning point in Rowbotham's speculative history, because she embodies both sensuous and spiritual music. Her song is a convergence of musical and poetical elements, combining rhythmic and melodic innovations to create highly eroticized poetry that appeals to the passions as well as the intellect.

The so-called "Thrilling Style" of Sappho is defined by Rowbotham first as an effect of meter, breaking up the flowing hexameters of Homer through patterns of phrasing that contrast with the rhythm of the epic line. The Sapphic meter is "a woman's Hexameter," according to Rowbotham, who compares a line of the Sapphic stanza to dactylic hexameter in order to illustrate how Sappho falls one foot short of Homer.[21]

> Perhaps she is not tall enough and cannot reach so high; for look, when we come to compare it with the real Hexameter, lo! it is one foot too short.
>
> Hexameter: —ᴗᴗ —ᴗᴗ —ᴗᴗ —ᴗᴗ —ᴗᴗ ——
>
> Sapphic: —ᴗ —ᴗ —ᴗᴗ —ᴗ —ᴗ

Only in the fourth line of the Sapphic stanza, does Sappho finish "her Hexameter as all Hexameters of course ought to be finished," with a dactyl and

---

[20] John Frederick Rowbotham, *A History of Music* (London: Trubner, 1885–1886) 2: 45.

[21] A line in dactylic hexameter is divided into six metrical feet, composed primarily of dactyls (a long syllable followed by two short syllables) and ending with a spondee (two long syllables). In his comparison of Homeric and Sapphic meter, Rowbotham illustrates how a line of six dactyls might be aligned with a line in the Sapphic stanza (2: 97).

a spondee (known as an "Adonic" line) echoing the last two feet of the Homeric line. This is an example of "the feminine heroic," according to Rowbotham: rather than striking up the lyre as a prelude to recitation of epic battles that went on and on, Sappho used the lyre as harmonious accompaniment to her love songs that had greater variation in phrasing and contrast of accents. She was able to "reduce these conflicting elements into order ... by the perfection of her phrasing," and it was this "clear phrasing ... which characterized Sappho and all the Lesbian School" (96–97).

Along with its rhythmic innovation, Rowbotham emphasizes the melodic cadence of Sapphic song. "Now what the Lesbian School of Music did for the development of the Art, briefly was this: They introduced the Systaltic Style, and .... they also developed the Musical Period to its perfection" (101). While in Homeric recitation the voice dropped down in the spondee at the end of every line, the Sapphic stanza sustained the voice over four lines before the Adonic conclusion, "so that the concluding cadence of the voice was put off for a comparatively long time, and the ear was trifled with and its expectation kept alive for that marked ascent or descent of the voice" (102). While Rowbotham tries to isolate the precise notes in the cadence of Sapphic song, he is ultimately more interested in making it sound familiar to nineteenth-century ears: "[w]hat would be the effect of this extension of the Musical Period and the protraction of the Cadence on the Voice?" he asks, and answers, "[i]t is plain the Voice would gain greatly in sustaining power ... so that the tone of the Voice would become greatly beautified and enriched .... And it was natural that a woman should come to the fore as the exponent of the new ideas, which had expressed themselves in the form of song ... much in common with our *Lied* form" (111–112). Indeed, he makes the prolongation of the cadence in Sapphic song sound like late Romantic music, where a desire for harmonic resolution is intensified by being (infinitely) prolonged. Rowbotham hints at the erotic undertones (or overtones) of this musical effect: "[i]f Sappho's loves were not always excited by the voice .... it was at any rate her glory 'to sing lovely strains, that should please the ear of her soft-skinned companions'" (112). The voice straining to sustain itself over a longer musical period made Lesbian song into lesbian song, those "lovely strains" that excited the women of Lesbos, at least sometimes if not always.

The Bantocks played on an ambiguous identification of and with the "Lesbian music" of Sappho, some of whose love songs were addressed to women while others celebrated marriage. On the one hand, the song cycle created by husband and wife seemed like the offspring of heterosexual desire, as their daughter claimed: "[t]he combined work of my parents produced a song cycle of unique and particular beauty, showing that the two collaborators had a rare sympathy towards the poetess and an understanding of Greek thought" (144). On the other hand, their sympathetic understanding of "Greek thought" also turned Sappho into a figure for other forms of desire. Myrrha Bantock claims that her mother had special "feminine insight" into Sappho's love songs:

> Using nine fragments of *Sappho* with wonderful feminine insight, she succeeded in linking them together with a few additional lines of her own. The result was the nine songs which G.B. composed for contralto voice and orchestra. These songs are quite the most beautiful he wrote for the female voice. The Colonel found the fifth, "The Moon Has Set," particularly lovely as a piece of mournful atmospheric writing and a complete contrast to the effective refrain in the "Bridal Song." (100)

In contrast to the bridal song (Song VIII), the fifth song evokes a solitary Sappho "ever maiden," while other songs in the cycle present Sappho pining for other objects of desire: a nameless girl (song I), a girl named Atthis (song II), "the sweet-voiced nightingale" (song III), "soft Aphrodite" (song IV), a girl with "lovely laughter" (song VI), "delicate Adonis" (song VII), and "rosy-armed, pure Graces, sweet-voiced maidens" (song IX). Sapphic *eros* seems to circulate through the song cycle in different forms, and with different objects of desire, depending on the listener.[22]

Perhaps this is why, as Myrrha Bantock implies, one of the listeners most attuned to the autoerotic and homoerotic elements in the cycle is "the Colonel," Bantock's loyal amanuensis H. Orsmond Anderton.[23] He wrote his own memoir of Bantock, in which he rhapsodizes about "intense eroticism ... carried to an enormously higher power of beauty, range, and exaltation in the *Sappho Songs*" (73), and he describes at length how "the peculiar beauty of this phoenix among poetesses seems to have entered into the composer's heart" (84). He praises the "fervid glow" produced by "daring harmonies and varied rhythms" in the songs, and their "passionate abandonment" (84–85). Anderton also admires the passion of the orchestral prelude that sets the tone for the entire cycle:

> The *Prelude* is opened by the harp, languidly in 5/4, with spread chords that look like two chords combined, but which are really, of course, high powers of single chords. These are answered first by 'cellos alone, and afterwards by clarinets and strings. The *Prelude* is full of passion, and fitly ushers in the songs that follow. (84)

The aesthetic effects of Bantock's music are highly eroticized in this account. The *Prelude* seems to begin with a musical structure of call and response:

---

[22] On the "reciprocally-influential discourses about music and sexuality" and the circulation of heterosexual and homosexual desire through music in the late nineteenth century, see the essay by Emma Sutton in this volume.

[23] During their student years at the Royal Academy of Music, Anderton traveled with Bantock to Bayreuth to hear Wagner's *Tristan*, and later he lived with the family as Bantock's amanuensis. Myrrha Bantock writes affectionately of the Colonel that "he never showed the slightest interest in anything female while he was with us, beyond his genuine affection and courtly admiration for my mother. The Greek athlete was his ideal and he much admired the statue of the Discobolos on the top of his desk, which nowadays might have marked him as having homosexual tendencies!" (7)

evoking Sappho at her lyre, the harp plays three arpeggios to awaken the orchestra, which responds each time with more instruments in a mounting melody. Then high violin trills interrupt this languid suspension and the *Prelude* begins in full force, as an initiation into the sensuous melodies of Sapphic song.

To recreate the trilling, thrilling style of Sappho, Bantock may have learned much from the Lesbian School of Music, but he learned even more from the European school of music of the late nineteenth century. Rather than attempting an "authentic" reconstruction of Sappho's original melodies, his song cycle exemplifies a post-Wagnerian musical idiom. Bantock's *Prelude* is a tone poem, a voiceless song in which the instruments of the orchestra (especially the English horn) play the part of Sappho's voice accompanied by the lyre. The opening chords of the *Prelude* create an ambiguous tonality, as we see in the piano-vocal score (see Ex. 10.1).

Example 10.1: Granville and Helen Bantock, *Prelude*, bars 1–4

The opening arpeggios, superimposing an A flat major seventh chord over a D flat major seventh chord in the lower register, are a sequence of alternating major and minor thirds. These resonating chords introduce a range of harmonic possibilities without a clear resolution, in anticipation of the shifting moods and rhythms of Sappho's song throughout the cycle. The musical motives introduced in the *Prelude* are sung with words later on in the cycle, but here they exist independently of words, as if musical inspiration precedes the lyrical impulse.

In fact much of this music seems inspired by Wagner's *Tristan und Isolde* (1861), often described by critics as a drama of desire, or as John Reed suggests, "*Yearning* is perhaps a preferable term, and the German *Sehnsucht* (which implies hankering, longing, or pining as well) is better yet." (original emphasis)[24] With its wandering chromaticism, continual modulations, half-diminished seventh chords, and infinitely prolonged cadences, Wagner's *Tristan* creates a sense of longing that marks the emergence of a decadent style in music. The Wagnerian echoes in Bantock's *Prelude* serve as signifiers of a free-floating desire that will never be fulfilled.[25] To intensify the

---

[24] John R. Reed, *Decadent Style* (Athens, OH: Ohio University Press, 1985) 200–201.
[25] This point was confirmed in conversation with Byron Adams, who has analyzed in detail the musical permutations of Wagner's *Tristan* in Bantock's *Prelude*. On British responses to

(auto)eroticism of this desire, Bantock also echoes the sensuous sonorities of Debussy's *Prélude à L'après-midi d'un Faune* (1892),[26] and if we listen carefully we can hear the lush orchestration of Tchaikovksy in the lower strings, the fire of Richard Strauss in melodramatic outbursts from the brass, the pathos of Rachmaninov, and some hints of Elgar.

All this musical echoing might lead us to conclude that the music of Granville Bantock is derivative, and indeed Bantock was criticized for lack of originality, as his daughter regrets to admit: "[s]ome critics have remarked that Bantock's work contains unconscious reminiscences of Strauss and other composers" (163). Despite the large-scale ambition of his compositions, there may be something lacking, a void in the center of his most dramatic musical moments. Yet in a cycle of songs that revolves around the absence of Sappho's voice, the refraction of musical ideas in a spectrum of echoes is effective – indeed affective – because it produces affect through the manipulation of various echo effects. What his music lacks in elaborate counterpoint or rigorous structure, it makes up in rich melodies and subtle orchestration, described by his daughter as "the Bantock quality":

> His harmonic idiom, warm and richly romantic, is matched by a masterly and expansive orchestration. He delighted in the mellow tones of cello and double bass. These he employed with great skill, obtaining a fullness of emotional sound which he often and suddenly contrasted with hauntingly beautiful, even nostalgic, passages for upper strings and wood-wind [*sic*]. The Bantock quality was unmistakable. He used brass instruments with especially telling effect, and dramatic values were enhanced by the manner in which he repeated what, in their day, were strident discords. There are few British composers of his time whose music could portray the same range of human passions, ecstasies, sorrows and spiritual longings. (88)

The Sappho songs exemplify – indeed, they amplify – Bantock's particular strength as a composer, whose idiom is so full of resonance it creates an "especially telling effect."

Sir Thomas Beecham, the much-revered conductor of British music and another friend of the Bantock family, also praised the composer for "having the quick penetration of the true lyrical writer for reaching the heart of a poem and re-creating it in fitting and telling turns of melody."[27] Beecham conducted the *Prelude* and considered the Sappho songs among Bantock's greatest

---

Wagner, see Emma Sutton, *Aubrey Beardsley and British Wagnerism in the 1890s* (Oxford: Oxford University Press, 2002).

[26] The idea of Sappho also inspired Debussy, who composed songs and music for harp in response to Sapphic imitations by Pierre Louys. Bantock may have been familiar with Debussy's *Chansons de Bilitis* (1897–1898) when he started composing his Sappho songs.

[27] Sir Thomas Beecham, *A Mingled Chime: An Autobiography* (New York: Putnam, 1943) 111.

achievements. But what do its turns of melody tell us? The song cycle does not narrate a story as such, nor does it reconstruct Sappho as its narrator: there is no development of a character, no dramatic action, no narrative progression. The Sapphic fragments juxtaposed in Wharton's edition are re-composed by the Bantocks into a series of crises, climaxes and shifts of mood that evoke the perpetual movement of desire. In this respect the musical structure of the cycle recalls Rowbotham on the prolonged musical period of Lesbian song: the concluding cadence of the voice is put off so that the ear's expectation may be "kept alive for that marked ascent or descent of the voice." Each of the Bantock Sappho songs performs its own variation on that "protracted cadence," variously ascending or descending in a virtuoso vocal performance.

Hymn to Aphrodite

Starting in 1906, the Bantock songs were performed on various occasions, sometimes separately and sometimes together, sometimes with piano and sometimes with orchestra.[28] The first song in the cycle, "Hymn to Aphrodite," was premiered by a Canadian contralto with piano accompaniment on 25 May 1906 at the Aeolian Hall in London: a resonant space for the performance of Sapphic song, because of its name as well as its acoustics.[29] This song (the longest in the cycle) is a prolonged invocation to the goddess of love, and it performs a gradual amplification of voice through a series of complex echo effects, both textually and musically. Although provoked by words, these evocative effects are difficult to put into words. To suggest how Sapphic song resonates between instrumental and vocal performance, I will present a few musical examples, but with the understanding that what we try to read, or hear, in these songs can only be an echo, of an echo, of an echo ... ad infinitum.

The "Hymn" is based on the only text of Sappho to survive intact: it is the first poem in Wharton's edition, given first in Greek and then in various English versions. One notable feature of Wharton's "literal" rendering is that he retains the female pronouns in Greek, to show that Sappho is praying to Aphrodite for the love of a girl. Helen Bantock's libretto follows Wharton in retaining the effect of the pronouns in the original text, but she also strove to retain more of its metrical effects: when we compare her poetic version to his prose translation, we see she has strategically altered the syntax and sequence

---

[28] A recent recording of the song cycle featuring Susan Bickley (mezzo-soprano) and the Royal Philharmonic Orchestra (Vernon Handley, conductor) is available on the compact disk, *Sir Granville Bantock: Sappho and Sapphic Poem* (Hyperion Records, CDA66899, 1997). In his program notes for the CD, Lewis Foreman surveys the performance history of the Sappho songs, from 1906 to 1996, fifty years after the death of Bantock (7–9).

[29] Newly renovated in 1903, the Aeolian Hall was advertised in 1904 as "a concert-hall and show-room for the instruments of the Aeolian Company," with walls "paneled to the height of eight feet six inches in fumed mahogany" to produce "good acoustical qualities." Quoted by Percy Scholes, *The Mirror of Music 1844–1944* (London: Novello, 1947) 1: 212–213.

of Wharton's words for better rhythm. Where Wharton translates the first stanza into a rather monotonous sentence ("Immortal Aphrodite of the broidered throne, daughter of Zeus, weaver of wiles, I pray thee break not my spirit with anguish and distress, O Queen"), Helen Bantock translates the invocation to Aphrodite into something like a Sapphic stanza:

> Daughter of Zeus, immortal Aphrodite,
> Queen of the broidered throne, distress'd I pray thee,
> Weaver of wiles, break not my heart with anguish,
> O Goddess, hear me!

In phrases like "Immortal Aphrodite," and "break not my heart with anguish" we can hear the second half of a line in Sapphic meter (−⌣⌣ −⌣ −−). And in "distress'd I pray thee" and "O Goddess hear me," we hear the final Adonic coda at the end of the Sapphic stanza (−⌣⌣ −−) . Although these patterns of quantity (long and short syllables in Greek) and accentuation (stressed and unstressed syllables in English) may not align perfectly in Classical and Victorian prosody, nevertheless Helen Bantock allows each to echo the other in her version of the Sapphic stanza.

Example 10.2: Bantock, "Hymn to Aphrodite," Song I, bars 1–12

The music composed by Granville Bantock also partially recapitulates Sapphic meter in his own rhythm. We hear the metrical pattern (again, the second half of a line in the Sapphic stanza: –⌣⌣ –⌣ – – twice before the words begin (see Ex. 10.2). Although the time signature is 4/4, the rhythm of the first four measures creates a syncopated counterpoint, until we arrive firmly on the downbeat in measure 5. Meanwhile the bass line descends in an Aeolian scale (from D to C to B flat to A to G to F to E to D), evoking Sappho's poems (written in the Aeolic dialect) and the modal melodies of Sapphic song. With these special metrical and melodic effects, the introduction creates a musical frame for the song as an "archaic" form revived in the present. The "Hymn to Aphrodite" is thus presented (made present) to the listener as a musical artifact from the past, not an authentic recreation of the original Sappho but a self-consciously self-archaizing performance.[30]

After the opening fanfare, performed by woodwinds in the orchestral version, the song proceeds from measure 5 in a more familiar stately hymn that is reminiscent of English church music. The formal invocation to Aphrodite alternates between F major and D minor chords, but the minor key begins to take over in the transition to distress and anguish. The line "distress'd I pray thee" is musically stressed with the suspension of dissonant half steps: in measure 12 we hear F and E natural on the first beat resolving to D on the second beat; and we hear E and D natural on the third beat resolving to C sharp on the fourth beat. When the song is performed with orchestra, these suspensions are doubled by the French horns, paradoxically amplifying and displacing the vocal performance of the singer as she descends into the lower registers of the voice. Indeed, her voice is barely audible when she sings the final words of the first stanza: "O Goddess, hear me." It is difficult to hear this plea, unless we listen carefully to the way it resounds, repeated twice by voice and then carried over by solo oboe and English horn. The song is sustained by this interplay between the voice and the instruments of the orchestra. When the voice drops out in the interlude between the first and second stanzas, the instruments carry on the musical momentum.

The strings in the orchestra introduce a dramatic tonal and temporal shift at the beginning of the second stanza, which marks the return of the voice with a vision of the goddess Aphrodite. Wharton's translation of this divine epiphany is a long breathless sentence in prose: "[b]ut come hither, if ever before thou didst hear my voice afar, and listen, and leaving thy father's golden house camest with chariot yoked, and fair fleet sparrows drew thee, flapping fast their wings around the dark earth, from heaven through mid sky." But the Bantocks

---

[30] Bennett Zon has suggested to me that we might even think of the composer as archaeologist, with Bantock (an ardent collector of exotic artifacts) presenting his Sappho songs as an archaeological discovery, and thus transporting the listener into a museum of musical artifacts. This would fit with the ethnographic account of Lesbian song in Rowbotham's *History of Music* as well. I am grateful to Bennett Zon for illuminating conversations about a self-consciously historicizing turn in British music and musicology at the end of the nineteenth century.

allow this passage to breathe, breaking it up into shorter cadences and emphasizing the music of the Sapphic stanza:

> Now hither come, as once before thou camest,
> Hearing my voice afar, and lean to listen;
> Camest with golden chariot, leaving swiftly
> Thy father's dwelling.

Helen Bantock begins her translation with "now," unlike Wharton. Carefully balancing the verb between present imperative and past tense – between "now hither come" and "before thou camest" – she emphasizes more than Wharton the present moment of performance, here and now. In his musical setting, Granville Bantock amplifies this effect by repeating the phrase "now hither come," rearranging the rhythms of the Sapphic stanza into the flow of a gradual musical crescendo that leads gradually toward a resurgence of voice. After the fading of the voice at the end of the first stanza, we are asked to hear the voice revealed anew in the following stanzas; indeed the call to Aphrodite, to recall her "hearing my voice afar" in the past, also serves as an appeal to the responsive listener, who might "lean to listen" to this song in the present.

The third stanza makes a subtle shift from the past to the present, where through a series of musical effects Aphrodite can be heard "descending" once again:

> Beautiful, fleet thy sparrows drew thee hither,
> Round the dark earth from heaven's height descending,
> Whirled they with wings through deeps of middle aether,
> Fluttering came they.

In the orchestration for this passage, there is rapid movement in the orchestra with descending and ascending lines to suggest the descent of the chariot, and a fluttering sound in the flutes to suggest the flutter of wings in the air, or "middle aether" in Helen Bantock's translation. The vocal line also becomes more ethereal as it flies freely up and down the register, and we hear breathy variations on the word "hear," like "hither," "heaven," "height," as well as the alliteration on "whirling wings" that make the voice sound airy, until the orchestration finally leaves it behind, suspended in mid-air. These might seem like mimetic effects, in which the orchestration is "expressing" or "representing" the words, but mimesis also seems to go in the other direction, with the words echoing and perhaps even representing the music. The phrase "mid-aether" hovers in the middle range of the voice, and the final phrase "fluttering" is repeated several times, making the voice sound like one of the flutes that introduced this stanza.

What follows is a musical epiphany, not only of the goddess but also of the voice that is invoking her. At this pivotal moment in the song, when we seem to hear the voice of "Sappho" ventriloquizing the voice of "Aphrodite," the music composed by Granville Bantock emphasizes the mediation of these voices by the instruments of the orchestra. Between the third and fourth stanzas is a carefully placed harp arpeggio (recalling Sappho's lyre, from the *Prelude*) that sets the scene for this transformation of mortal into immortal voice:

> Then thou, blest one, with lips immortal smiling,
> Didst ask – "Why weepest thou? What is befallen?
> Whom wouldst thy heart and beauty draw to love thee?
> Who wrongs thee Sappho?"

The transition between voices (graphically marked by the dash after "ask –" in Helen Bantock's translation) is made audible in distinct brass chords and a dramatic pause in the music. Then, to emphasize the quotation marks around Aphrodite's questions, the musical setting introduces a new triplet rhythm that is sustained throughout the address to Sappho. Here the structure of address is reversed (no longer Sappho to the goddess but now the goddess to Sappho), culminating in the moment of naming Sappho at the end of the stanza: "Who wrongs thee Sappho?" This question is repeated in Bantock's musical setting, amplified by brass chords that resound on each syllable of the name of Sappho. The O in Sappho is made to resonate, as if Aphrodite is echoing back the vocative O that we heard in Sappho's earlier invocation, "O goddess" in stanza 1. As each voice seems to be invoking the other, they are called into being as echoes of one another.

The voicing of the name – re-composing Sappho not only in letters but in an omega of sound – is a provocative reconfiguration of lyric apostrophe (the rhetorical figure of address that allows something absent to be made present through invocation). Jonathan Culler has argued that "the lyric is characteristically the triumph of the apostrophe," insofar as apostrophe seems to make present not only the object that is invoked, but also the invoking subject.[31] According to Culler, "[t]he poet makes himself a poetic presence through an image of voice, and nothing figures voice better than the pure O of undifferentiated voicing" (142). But the display or "triumph" of apostrophe in lyric is also its defeat. Foregrounding the trope is embarrassing according to Culler, for when it is exposed *as* a trope, apostrophe creates a self-reflexive awareness that "the potential addressee of every apostrophe [is] the apostrophic 'O' itself" and "every apostrophe an invocation of invocation" (144). This would defeat the point of a lyric reading when it is predicated on the assumption of a speaking subject or an original voice.

What Culler calls the "embarrassment" of lyric apostrophe is precisely what Bantock's song successfully performs, perhaps even to excess and without embarrassment: we are invited to listen to the infinite resonance of an invocation of invocation. "Hymn to Aphrodite" is addressed to its own variable voicing, making the addressee of the apostrophe the apostrophic O itself. If

---

[31] Jonathan Culler, "Apostrophe," *The Pursuit of Signs: Semiotics, Literature, Deconstruction* (Ithaca: Cornell University Press, 1981) 149.

voice is figured in lyric as "the pure O of undifferentiated voicing," in song we hear the differentiation of the O. The distinction between lyric apostrophe and apostrophe in song is not that one produces a "fictional" voice while the other is produced by a "real" voice, but that the figure of voice is performed according to the particular forms and conventions of each medium. When Susan Bickley sings the "Hymn to Aphrodite," for example, we hear a different timbre during the words of Aphrodite, a shift in the sonorous texture of the voice that prolongs the O without belonging to any persona in particular: it does not belong to "Aphrodite" who calls upon Sappho, nor to "Sappho" who recalls Aphrodite, nor to the translator who translates the Greek, nor to the poet who transposes the translation, nor to the composer who composes the song, nor even to the singer who sings the song. Rather, the song uses apostrophe to create a figure of and for its own vocal performance: the echoing of the O in the name of Sappho.

Moving beyond this self-reflexive moment, the fifth stanza makes a transition from the words of "Aphrodite" back to the words of "Sappho" (the former explicitly in quotation marks, the latter implicitly):

> "She who spurns gifts shall give: who flies shall follow;
> If she loves not, unwilling soon shall love thee."
> Ah come, from care release, fulfil my yearning;
> Help, I beseech thee.

The music builds up in a crescendo to a climactic moment, "soon shall love thee," a phrase that is repeated with a decrescendo along with the disappearance of the goddess, fading into the distance. This promise of erotic fulfillment is followed by a tremolo in the strings, a harp glissando and then a dramatic pause. The Aphrodite section ends as it began, lyrically framed by the sound of a harp, to evoke a divine voice that is conjured from and then returned to a resonant silence.

From this point onward, the song gradually moves from a barely audible sigh in "Ah" to the reiteration of "Help," and finally back to the vocative "O goddess hear me," as it was heard in the beginning of the song. But when Bantock's "Hymn to Aphrodite" circles back in this ring composition characteristic of ancient Greek hymns, it does so with elaborate orchestration to create a more sonorous ending. As the voice seems to call out with greater force and power, the orchestra responds by amplifying the prayer to Aphrodite so that it may be heard again, in ornamented form. The final stanza is a recapitulation of the first, except this time we hear the plea to "hear me" in a triumphant major chord. The "Hymn to Aphrodite" thus seems to project a voice for Sappho after all, finally filling the lyric vocative – its empty "O" – with sound.

Rather than concluding with this apparent triumph of invocation, however, the song ends with its echo. During the climactic F major chord (beginning in measure 3, Ex. 10.3) we hear ascending scales in the orchestra to suggest the rising of the voice; but then the voice drops down an octave and we hear a half-

252   THE FIGURE OF MUSIC IN 19TH-CENTURY BRITISH POETRY

diminished chord during which a descending bass line fades into its final resolution.

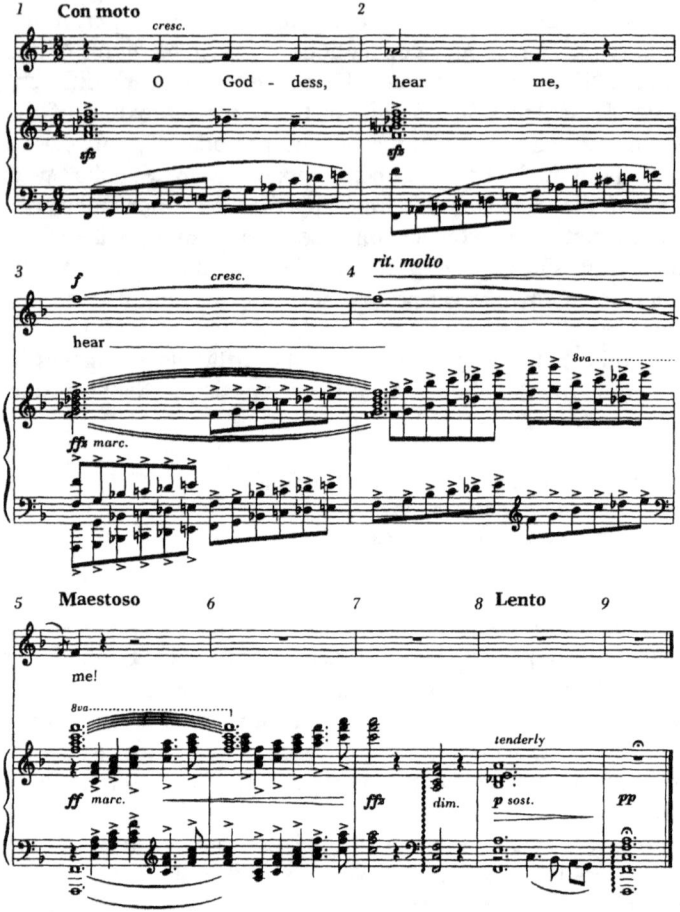

Example 10.3: Bantock, "Hymn to Aphrodite," Song I, bars 113–121

In the last two bars marked "Lento," the lower strings of the orchestra perform the fading of Sapphic voice, as a spectral image of the music we have just heard. What we hear in other words (or: other than words) is its resonance, a silence that will resound but only if we learn another way of listening.

Sapphonic Voice

We might call the phonic effect of this Sapphic voice, "Sapphonic." Elizabeth Wood explores the erotic undertones and overtones of "a Sapphonic voice," which may be heard as "a particular voice that thrills and excites" but can also be understood, more generally, as a transgression of vocal categories: it "crosses boundaries among different voice types and their representations to challenge polarities of both gender and sexuality as these are socially – and vocally – constructed."[32] In Wood's account, "Sapphonic voice is a destabilizing agent of fantasy and desire" (32), and she gives a variety of examples from songs and operas that create "Sapphonic space for the female singer-lover to voice lesbian desire" (45). While the song cycle by the Bantocks may not "voice" an exclusively or even specifically lesbian desire in our current understanding, its destabilization of voice mobilizes a movement of desire that we can listen to "Sapphonically." The song cycle requires unusual versatility from the contralto, who must sing across the *passagio* of the voice, excessively crossing the break between the lower and upper registers identified as "masculine" and "feminine," in order to perform the rise and fall of Sapphic song. Traversing the polarities of voice and gender and sexuality, *Sappho: Prelude and Nine Fragments* creates a new acoustic and erotic space for what has been called (from Rowbotham to Wood) the "Thrilling Style" of Sappho.

The ten-minute *Prelude* to the cycle sets the scene for this prolongation of desire, as I have already suggested, with its wandering harmonies and echoing orchestration. Long before the singer begins to sing, Bantock's instrumentation already evokes, and indeed provokes, a desire of and for Sapphic song. This interplay between voice and instruments creates the Sapphonic appeal of Bantock's Sappho songs. "He thrust aside the influence of the German masters and made daring experiments in orchestration," according to Myrrha Bantock; "[n]ot only did he lead the way in this respect, but he also evolved new techniques with voices, and in his choral works used them almost as if they were instruments; in this way he achieved fantastically effective results" (99). She further quotes one of Bantock's contemporaries at the School of Music in Birmingham to confirm this view: "Bantock achieved international repute in the early opulent days of this century when orchestral and vocal resources were virtually unlimited. No other composer of his generation has been able to surpass his skill in writing for voices or instruments" (103). Of all the songs he composed (more than 400), Bantock's Sappho songs come closest to justifying this extravagant claim. It is Bantock's skill in writing "for voices or instruments," or rather, in writing for voices *as* instruments, that makes these songs so provocative.

Composed for a voice that moves across vocal boundaries, the song cycle demonstrates the sensuous sonority of Sapphic song even while dramatizing its inaudibility. As we hear the texture of the voice intertwining with the timbres of the orchestra, the melody is no longer carried by the voice but realized in a space between the vocal and instrumental lines, as something unvocalized. Again and again, what we hear is the disappearance of the voice. As we have noticed in "Hymn to Aphrodite," the invocation "O goddess hear me" falls to a

---

[32] Elizabeth Wood, "Sapphonics," *Queering the Pitch: The New Gay and Lesbian Musicology*, eds Philip Brett, Elizabeth Wood and Gary C. Thomas (New York: Routledge, 1994) 28.

pitch so low it is barely heard over the orchestra at the end of the first stanza. Although the invocation is amplified in the higher range of the voice at the end of the song, nevertheless the song subsides into echo in its final measures.

The next song in the cycle descends even lower, thematically and melodically, to the house of Hades. The "fluttering" effects we heard in Song I ("Hymn to Aphrodite," describing the arrival of Aphrodite) become the "flitting" of a shadowy voice among the shadowy dead in Song II ("I loved thee once, Atthis," describing the departure of Atthis) (see Ex. 10.4).

Example 10.4: "I loved thee once, Atthis," Song II, bars 64–68

The vocal line is reduced to a monotone, finally reiterating just a single note on C, while a bass line descends chromatically to produce a spectral effect. There is a series of diminished chords dropping down in triplet rhythms, and to emphasize the suspended animation of the voice at this low point in the song, the passage is marked "poco lento with hollow voice." There is a similar moment in the seventh song of the cycle, also marked "with changed and hollow voice." These moments suggest a hollowing out of voice, so that it can be heard as pure echo of something not there. What we hear, in other words, is not the presence of the Sapphic song but its absence.

The longing for a voice impossible to hear is theorized by Slavoj Žižek, in his suggestive essay on the songs of Robert Schumann.[33] Žižek argues that

---

[33] In "Robert Schumann: The Romantic Anti-Humanist," Slavoj Žižek focuses on an "inaudible inner voice" in Schumann's songs, extending a musical analysis by Charles Rosen through the psychoanalytic framework of Jacques Lacan, in order to argue that "this 'absolutely inaudible' sound provides an exemplary case of the Lacanian *object petit a*." He concludes that "the very

these songs give form to the silence of a (barred) subject, no longer a person but a formal structure of absence that produces infinite longing. "Sappho" is the proper name for this formal structure in the Bantock songs: the paradox of a voice that cannot be heard, and is not the expression of any subject. Instead of listening for a melody that "voices" the inner life of a subject, we hear a failing melody; its unrealizable sonority is, according to Žižek's logic, "elevated into the *structural principle* of the unheard voice" (199; original emphasis). Another way to understand this paradox is Carolyn Abbate's analysis of Debussy, who (like Bantock) discovered images of unimaginable sound in Symbolist aesthetics. In her chapter on "Debussy's Phantom Sounds," Abbate shows how the attempt to realize "heard and unheard sound" in his early song settings leads to the musical realization in *Pelléas et Mélisande* of inaudible sound; when the voice of Mélisande "becomes quite audibly an object that recedes to far distances, away from human discourses, at one with the instruments," it paradoxically "approaches, as much as any voice that exists as sung reality could approach, the unrealizable sound of a song that can never exist."[34]

So also the Sappho songs recomposed by the Bantocks give form to the unrealizable sound of a song that can never exist, by performing the continual rise and fall of Sapphic voice. These cadences are heard in a fluctuating pattern within each individual song and throughout the cycle as a whole, where we see a range of markings for the vocal performance: "beseechingly" and "con moto, with anguish" in Song I; "regretfully," "bitterly," "feebly," "with yearning," "murmuring," "tenderly," and "in a hushed voice" in Song II; "peacefully" and "dreamily" in Song III, "sonore" and "cantabile" and "appassionato con molto espressione" in Song IV; then "dreamily" and "plaintively" "with yearning" in Song V; and again "con molto passione" in Song VI; "sadly" and "tristamente" in song VII; "con dolzessa" and "tenderly" in song VIII; "lightheartedly" and "(as if far distant)" in song IX. These markings for vocal expression are not expressive of a subject, but serve to indicate the continual equivocation of Sapphic song as it is suspended between different forms of articulation.

In the last song of the cycle, the marking for the voice "(as if far distant)" in parentheses is especially evocative. While Song IX begins as another invocation ("Muse of the golden throne, O raise that strain"), mid-way through the singing is interrupted by an orchestral silence, a pause that marks the distance between the present song and the singing of the past. Then we hear the drawing of breath for final inspiration – or is it expiration? – of Sapphic song, and the singer performs the final words of Song IX (see Ex. 10.5). As the singer repeats the phrase, "Hither now, Muses" (in measure 1 and again in measures 3, 4, and 7) it almost sounds as if she is singing, "Hither now,

---

formal structure of Schumann's music expresses the paradox of modern subjectivity: the bar ... on account of which 'infinite longing' is constitutive of subjectivity." Slavoj Žižek, *The Plague of Fantasies* (London: Verso, 1997) 199, 205.

[34] Carolyn Abbate, *In Search of Opera* (Princeton: Princeton University Press, 2001) 162, 179.

music," an apostrophe to music. But instead of making the music present, the song makes it increasingly absent as the orchestration becomes increasingly transparent, raising the strain higher and higher, until the voice fades away on the word "come." From measure 8 onward, we see the voice disappearing into the distance, pointing toward a Sapphic song that is impossible to hear except as resonance. The vocal line dissolves into the vowel "o" and then the hum of "m" (in measures 8–9 and 15–17), and in measure 16 the instrumental line is marked "*ppp possible*": *pianississimo*, as soft as possible. While the voice is vanishing in this long diminuendo, its echo is prolonged by the orchestration, as the strings continue playing, ever softer and ever higher, for another fourteen measures. Finally their ethereal sound, like the music in the poem by Symons, seems to "melt in the air of heaven." Thus Sapphic voice recedes into the distance, disarticulated yet infinitely desirable.

Example 10.5: "Muse of the golden throne," Song IX, bars 41–57

Example 10.5 continued

I have argued that the simultaneous rise and fall of Sapphic song in the cycle composed by the Bantocks embodies the cadence, or decadence, of a disembodied voice that can only be heard as an echo, forever diminishing. In doing so, I have transposed the question of "voicing" lyric into a musical question: although literary studies and musicology define "voice" differently, these two disciplines can benefit from reciprocal interrogation and interruption of a term we often take for granted.[35] Sappho has been the central figure in my

---

[35] For a general discussion of voice within literary studies, see Donald Wesling and Tadeusz Slawek, *Literary Voice: The Calling of Jonah* (Albany: State University of New York Press, 1995). On the problem of voice in lyric reading more specifically, see Jonathan Culler, "Changes in the Study of the Lyric," and Paul de Man, "Lyrical Voice in Contemporary Theory,' in *Lyric Poetry: Beyond New Criticism* (Ithaca: Cornell University Press, 1985). For a juxtaposition of musicological and literary approaches to voice, see the special issue of *New Literary History* 32.3 (Summer 2001). For other ideas about voice in musicology, see Edward T. Cone, *The Composer's Voice* (Berkeley: University of California Press, 1974); Carolyn Abbate, *Unsung Voices: Opera and Musical Narrative in the Nineteenth Century* (Princeton: Princeton University Press, 1991); Lydia Goehr, *The Quest for Voice: On Music, Politics, and*

argument because the Sapphic fragments are a memorial to lyric as a genre no longer (if ever) heard. For the Bantocks, this silence was a provocation to re-imagine the relation between music and poetry. By turning the unheard voice of Sappho into an ideal vanishing point toward which his own music aspires, Granville Bantock "opened vistas of music hitherto unseen." This phrase came as high praise in a memorial tribute to the composer:

> He greatly developed existing techniques, particularly in respect of vocal and instrumental sonorities. In both of these directions he broke fresh ground .... Few composers have piled up greater masses of vocal or orchestral sound; few have used voices or instruments with a surer sense of their character .... Words, for him, opened up vistas of music hitherto unseen, but it must not be supposed that this happened to the detriment of the words; Bantock had too good a literary sense for that.[36]

Bantock's contemporaries admired the Sappho songs in particular because of the innovative interchange between vocal and instrumental sonorities, between lyrical and musical elements. Along with the "good literary sense" of Granville Bantock's music, Helen Bantock's lyrical translations of Sappho also made good musical sense. In their collaboration, each depended on the other to open up a space for resonance between different forms of composition, recomposing the figure of Sappho to find the interface between music and language. Sappho is the personification of that interface, simultaneously provoking and interrupting the idealization of poetry by music and the idealization of music by poetry. What we come to hear in *Sappho: Prelude and Nine Fragments* is not a persona with a voice, but a resounding desire to idealize what is always an equivocation.[37]

---

the *Limits of Philosophy* (Oxford: Oxford University Press, 1998); and Chapter 3 on "Voices" in Alastair Williams, *Constructing Musicology* (Aldershot: Ashgate, 2001).

[36] In her "Appendix: In Memoriam," Myrrha Bantock quotes various tributes to her father after his death, including these words from Mr Kennedy Scott (186).

[37] This paper was presented with music on various occasions: at the William Clark Memorial Library; the Royal College of Music; the American Musicological Society; Vanderbilt University; the University of Bristol; the "Victorian Soundings" conference at University of California, Santa Cruz; and the Rackham Interdisciplinary Seminar on music and lyric at the University of Michigan. I am grateful to these audiences who allowed my argument to resonate between reading and hearing the notes, and I wish to thank Phyllis Weliver for encouraging the completion of this essay as postscript.

Index

Abbate, Carolyn 255
Abrams, M.H. 74–75
Ackroyd, Peter 86–87, 102
Act of Union (1707) 36
Adorno, Theodor 32–33, 39, 48, 87
Aeolian harp 11, 13, 19
  and Coleridge 81–84
  construction 75
  definition 60–61
  and D.G. Rossetti 206
  dualism 76–77
  and Fourier analysis 71, 73
  as metaphor 52–53, 74–75
  origins 53, 75
  in Romantic writing 70–84, 207
  and Shelley 20, 52, 53, 59, 64–65, 206
"air," meaning 20
  see also national airs
Allis, Michael 6, 15, 22, 23, 24, 132–173
Alma-Tadema, Lawrence 235
Anderson, Benedict 15, 20
  on nationalism 28–29
Anderson, Erland 61
Anderton, H. Orsmond 243
Anger, Suzy 119
Armstrong, Isobel 16
  Victorian Poetry 10, 141, 176
art, and morality 125
Ashton, Rosemary 118
Atkins, Ivor 162
Auerbach, Nina 137

Bahti, Timothy 48
Banfield, Stephen 231
Bantock, Granville
  career 233
  compositions, inspired by poetry 233–234
  Helena Variations 234
Bantock, Granville & Helen
  Sappho: Prelude and Nine Fragments 24, 237–258
    "Hymn to Aphrodite" 246–252
    "I loved thee once, Atthis" 254
    "Muse of the golden throne" 255–256
    musical extracts 244, 247, 252, 254, 256–257
    musical influences 244–245
    "Sapphonic voice" 252–258
  Sappho, Nine Fragments for Contralto 237
    cover illustration 239
Bantock, Helen
  A Woman's Love 234
  The Love Philtre 234
Bantock, Myrrha 234, 242–243, 245, 253
Barrell, John 102–103
Barthes, Roland 33, 38
Bashford, Christina 196
Bax, Arnold 141, 159
Beardsley, Aubrey 23
  "The Three Musicians" 13, 221–222
Beattie, James 31
Beecham, Thomas, Sir, on Granville Bantock 245–246
Beecher, Henry Ward 130
Beer, Gillian 117
  Darwin's Plots 17
Beer, John 100, 101, 104–105
Beethoven, Ludwig van 28
Berlioz, Hector 159
Bernstein, Susan 15, 17, 20, 21, 70–84
Bishop, Henry 45, 46
Blake, William 4

antinomianism 105–106
poetry
  music in 93–95, 98–106
  musical settings 86
  vision in 105–106
works
  "Chimney Sweeper" 91–92, 97, 98
  The Four Zoas 96
  "Holy Thursday" 90, 97–98
  Jerusalem 104
  "Laughing Song" 94–95
  The Marriage of Heaven and Hell 90
  Milton 96, 100
  "On Another's Sorrow" 90
  Songs of Experience 95
  Songs of Innocence and Experience 21, 88, 90, 91, 96
    "The Echoing Green" 89, 90
    "The Garden of Love" 98
    "The Little Girl Lost" 89
    "The Little Vagabond" 96–97
    "The Song of Los" 99
    "Thel" 99–100
Blind, Mathilde 116
Bloch, Ernst 87
Bloom, Harold 15
Bodenheimer, Rosemarie 118
Bonaparte, Felicia 131
Boosey, William 178
Bradley, Katharine 217, 226
see also Field, Michael
Brewer, John 39, 41
Bridges, Robert 12
Brookfield, William 139
Browning, Elizabeth Barrett 190
  "Sonnets from the Portuguese" 176
Browning, Robert
  Essay on Percy Bysshe Shelley 69
  musical images, use 13
Buckler, William E. 135
Burney, Charles 53–54
Burns, Robert 4, 20, 26
  Excise Officer 37, 41–42
  Lallans dialect, use 29
  and "localization" 40–41
  on paper 42–43
  works
    "The Author's Earnest Cry and Prayer" 38
    "John Barleycorn" 38
    Notes on Scottish Song 39–40
    Poems, Chiefly in the Scots Dialect 31, 41
    "Robin Adair" 36
    "Scotch Drink" 37, 38
    Scots Musical Museum, contributions 32, 39, 41
    "To a Mouse" 34

Caine, T. Hall 180
Campbell, Matthew, *Rhythm and Will in Victorian Poetry* 175
capitalism 20
Carlyle, Thomas, on music 124
Channing, William Ellery 124
character, and music 129–130
Charcot, Jean-Martin 218
Chartism 10
Cheyne, George 67
  English Malady 60
Chomsky, Noam 20
chord
  as a nerve 56
  in Shelley 54–55, 67
climate, and language 44
Coleridge, Samuel Taylor, "The Eolian Harp" 81–84
Collins, Wilkie, *The Woman in White* 137
Cooper, Edith 217
see also Field, Michael
Cooper, Suzanne Fagence 201
Cowper, William 105
Croker, John 133, 134
Cronin, Richard, *Colour and Experience...* 53
Crook, Nora 57
crowd theory 4
Culler, Jonathan 250
Cunningham, Allan 85
Current Musicology 8

Dahlhaus, Carl 26, 49
Daiches, David 38–39
Dale, Catherine 196
d'Alembert, Jean le Rond 76

INDEX

D'Amico, Diane 182, 193
Dannreuther, Edward 123, 142
Dante
  influence on Christina Rossetti 181–183, 187–188, 189–190
  La vita nuova 186
  Paradiso 181, 189
Darwin, Erasmus, *Zoonomia* 55
Davidson, John 23, 228
  "A Ballad of Tannhäuser" 228
Davis, Leith, on Thomas Moore 43, 45
Davy, Humphry 12
De Man, Paul 6, 74
Debussy, Claude
  Pelléas et Mélisande 255
  Prélude à L'après-midi d'un Faune, influence on Granville Bantock 245
Decadent Movement 230–231
Deen, Leonard W. 101–102, 103
Delius, Frederick 141
Derrida, Jacques 72, 73, 75
Dibble, Jeremy 143
Dietz, Vivien 37
Drummond, William, Sir 58
Du Maurier, George, *Trilby* 3, 136–137, 138

Elgar, Edward 22, 132
  "There is sweet music" 162–173
    dynamic markings 166–167
    musical examples 164, 165, 167, 168, 169, 170, 171
Eliot, George 21
  and music 119–122
  poems, music in 108–112
  works
    "A College Breakfast-Party" 120
    "Arion" 110–111
    Armgart 13, 110
    Daniel Deronda 117, 120–121
    "Erinna" 109
    "Ex Oriente Lux" 113, 120, 126
    "How Lisa Loved the King" 111–112
    Middlemarch 179
    Scenes of Clerical Life 117
    "Stradivarius" 111, 118
    "The Legend of Jubal" 22, 107, 112–131
    The Mill on the Floss 137
Ellis, Havelock 214, 224
Emmet, Robert 44
emotion, and music 128–129
Excise Office 41

Fairchild, B.H. 104
Ferber, Michael 102
Feuerbach, Ludwig, *The Essence of Christianity* 119
Field, Michael 4, 23, 217, 228
  "A Lyre: to her god" 224–225, 226
  Long Ago 224, 226
  "My heart is a violin" 217–218
  "Nella Trista Valle" 225–226
  Underneath the Bough 217, 227
Fitch, Donald 86
folksong tradition 26
Foreman, H.B. 180
Fourier analysis 17, 20, 21, 79
  and the Aeolian harp 71, 73
Fourier, Jean-Baptiste-Joseph 71
Fraser's Magazine 179
Freccero, John 187
Freud, Sigmund, *The Interpretation of Dreams* 2
Froude, James A., *The Nemesis of Faith* 128–129
Frye, Northrop 88

Gellner, Ernest 39
Gibson, Evan K. 64
Ginsberg, Allen, influence of Blake 86
Giorgione 194, 195
Gluck, Christoph, *Orfeo* 222, 225
Godwin, William 58
Gosse, Edmund 178
Grabo, Carl 66
Gray, Beryl 119
Gray, John 23
  "Parsifal" 223
  Silverpoints 223
Grew, Sydney, *Our Favourite Musicians* 235
Griffiths, Eric 12, 136, 174
Guiton, Derek 57

Haines, Simon 62

Haldane, Elizabeth S. 116
Hardy, Barbara 109
harmony 75–76
Harrison, Antony H. 19, 202
   Victorian Poets and the Politics...
   10–11
Hartley, David 59, 65, 68
   Observations on Man 58
Haweis, H.R., Rev, *Music and Morals*
   123, 126
Hazlitt, William 30, 47, 178
Heaney, Seamus 40
   The Makings of a Music 12
Helps, Arthur 124, 130
Herder, Johann Gottfried von 31
Hermitage, George 106
Herschel, William 17
Hill, Peter 42
Hipkins, A.J. 201
Hirschfeld, Magnus 214
Hoffmann, E.T.A. 76–77, 78
Hoffmann, J.J., *Lexicon Universale* 75
Hollander, John 12, 13
Holmes, Richard 58, 59
Homer, *Odyssey* 133
homosexuality, and musicality 214, 222–223
Hopkins, Gerard Manley, use of counterpoint 12
Horne, R.H. 135, 161
Hughes, John 15, 21, 85–106
Hume, David 58
Hunt, John Dixon 195
Hunt, Leigh 55
   "A Thought on Music" 14
   "Paginini" 13–14
   "The Lover of Music..." 13
Hutton, R.H. 116

interdisciplinarity, 19th century studies
   14–19
intertextuality 9, 19

Jaeger, August 165
James, Henry 109, 116
Janowitz, Anne, *Lyric and Labour* 10
Johnson, Barbara 78
Johnson, James, *Scots Musical
   Museum* 27

Johnson, Mary Lynn 86
Jones, W., *Physiological Disquisitions*
   75

Kennedy, Michael 162
Kingsley, Charles, on music 127–128
Kircher, Athanasius, *Musurgia
   Universalis* 75
Kivy, Peter 31
Kramer, Lawrence 6, 9, 24
   Music and Poetry 7–8, 232

Lacoue-Labarthe, Philippe (co-author),
   The Literary Absolute 47
Lallans dialect 29
Lamb, Charles 128
Langan, Celeste 15, 19–20, 25–49
language
   and climate 44
   and nationalism 29
Larrissy, Edward 91, 92, 97
Lawrence, William, *Lectures on
   Physiology...* 56
Leighton, Angela 118
Lesbos, lyric poets 241–246
Levi, Peter 139
Lévi-Strauss, Claude 6
Levy, Amy 174
   A Minor Poet and Other Verse 1
   "June-Tide Echo" 1, 3, 4
   "Sinfonia Eroica" 1–2, 3
Lewes, George Henry 108
   The Foundations of a Creed 17
Lippman, Edward A. 93
Living Age 179
Lloyd, David 40
Locke, John 74
Lucas, John 105

McGann, Jerome, *The Poetics of
   Sensibility* 52
Macmillan's Magazine 22, 122, 124, 125
McNaught, W.G. 162
Martin, Robert Bernard 139–140, 159
Marx, Karl 35–36
Mee, Jon 105
mesmerism, and music 136–137
metaphor

Aeolian harp as 52–53, 74–75
and philosophical discourse 72
Miller, J. Hillis 202, 203
Milnes, Richard Monckton 161
The Monthly Magazine 50, 56
Moore, Thomas 20, 26
  drinking songs 45–46
  on music 44–45
  public performances 43–44
  works
    "Erin! The Tear and Smile in Thine Eyes" 47
    Irish Melodies 27, 32, 43, 44, 45, 46–47
    "Melologue upon National Music" 44
    "Oh! Breathe Not His Name" 44
    A Select Collection of National Airs 27, 45
    Selection of Popular National Airs 32
    "'Tis the Last Rose of Summer" 34
morality, and art 125
Muggletonians 106
Murphy, Peter, *Poetry as an Occupation...* 41
music
  and character 129–130
  Charles Kingsley on 127–128
  in D.G. Rossetti's poems 195
  and the divine 87–88
  ecstasy 77–78
  effect on the senses 54
  and emotion 128–129
  George Eliot
    attitude to 119–122
    poems 108–112
  and mesmerism 136–137
  metaphoric use 12
  and morals 126–127
  as object 18–19, 212
  as objects 204
  in poetry 4–5, 9, 11–12, 14, 51
  and prosody 12, 197
  and science 20, 21, 50, 52
  and sexuality 23, 213–229
  Thomas Carlyle on 124
  Thomas Moore on 44–45
  in Victorian society 122–130, 211–212
  and women composers 178–179
Musical Review 201
musicality, and homosexuality 214, 222–223
musicology, postmodern 8–9, 15

Nancy, Jean-Luc (co-author), *The Literary Absolute* 47
nation, and national airs 30, 45, 48
national airs
  definition 27–28
  materiality 33–43
  and nation 30, 45, 48
  and poetry 26
nationalism
  Benedict Anderson on 28–29
  and language 29
  and print culture 28–29
nerve, chord as 56
The New Grove Dictionary 26
The New Quarterly Musical Review 233, 240
Nietzsche, Friedrich 87
  The Genealogy of Morals 96
Novello, Vincent 55, 64

Ogawa, Kimiyo 15, 20, 21, 50–69, 73
Oliphant, Margaret 117
O'Neill, Michael 91, 102
Orpheus 23, 208–211

Paley, Morton D. 104
Palgrave, Francis, *The Golden Treasury* 123
paper
  Robert Burns on 42–43
  symbolism 41, 42–43
Parry, Hubert 22, 132, 137
  cantatas 144, 155
  The Lotos-Eaters 141–162 (Tennyson)
    critical reaction 160–161
    musical extracts 146–148, 154, 156–157, 158
    soprano soloist 155–156, 157
    tonal structure 148–149, 153–154
Pater, Walter 23, 123, 194, 195–196,

264 INDEX

223
Peacock, Thomas 57
Petrarch, influence on Christina Rossetti 175, 180, 183, 185, 186–188
place names, and evocations 40
poetry
  ideology 18
  and the national airs 26
  and politics 10–11
  and punctuation 12, 13
  sexuality in 215–229
poets, Chartist 10
politics, and poetry 10–11
Powers, S.B. 59
Priestly, Joseph
  air, experiments 33–35
  Experiments and Observations... 33, 35, 49
  "factitious airs" 34, 47
Prins, Yopie 6, 15, 19, 24, 192, 197, 230–258
  Victorian Sappho 231
print culture, and nationalism 20, 28–29
prosody, and music 12, 197
Pulos, C.E. 58
Punter, David 91, 97

Raffalovich, André 214
Rameau, Jean-Philippe 76
Ramsay, Allan 26
Reed, John R. 244
Rees, Abraham, *Cyclopaedia* 55–56, 60
Reiman, D.H. 59
Reynolds, Margaret 118, 227
Reynolds, Matthew, *The Realms of Verse* 10
Richards, I.A. 7
Richter, Hans 2
Romantic writing, Aeolian harp in 70–84, 207
Rossetti, Christina, on disinclination 183–184
  "A Birthday" 180
  A Pageant and Other Poems 180, 181, 193
  "An Old-World Thicket" 181, 189, 193

  "De Profundis" 185
  Goblin Market 180
  "Monna Innominata" 22, 174–193
    Dante's influence 181–183, 187–188, 189–190
    music in 180–181
    Petrarch's influence 175, 180, 183, 185, 186–188
    reflexivity 174–175, 189
    Shakespeare's influence 191–193
  "Pastime" 185
  The Face of the Deep 181
  Time Flies 180
Rossetti, D.G. 177
  music, interest in 201–202
  poetry, music in 195
  works
    "A Venetian Pastoral" 195
    The House of Life 23, 194–212
      Aeolian harp 206
      introductory sonnet, illustration 197
      meter 200
      music in 196, 198, 200, 202–204, 206–11
      musical instruments in 205–206
      Orpheus myth 208–211
      reflexivity 199
      sonnet sequencing 196–197, 198–199, 211
Rossetti, William 184, 201
Rousseau, Jean-Jacques, *Reveries...* 62, 65
Rowbotham, John F., *A History of Music* 240–241
Ruskin, John 143

Sappho 19, 24, 224
  poetry
    meter 236, 241–242
    style 241–242, 253
  as Victorian construct 231
Schelling, F.W.J. 87
Schiller, Friedrich 29
Schopenhauer, Arthur 87
Schumann, Robert 254
science, and music 20, 21, 50, 52

Secor, Cynthia 117
Seeley, J.R., *Natural Religion* 125
sexologists 214
sexuality
  and music 23, 213–229
  in poetry 215–229
Shakespeare, William
  influence on Christina Rossetti 191–193
  Sonnet 32 190–191
Shelley, Mary 61
Shelley, Percy Bysshe 178
  and the Aeolian harp 20, 52, 53, 59, 64–65, 206
  chord, use 54–55, 67
  musical knowledge 57
  on the soul 61–62
  theory of necessity 56, 57
  works
    Alastor 20, 50, 53, 57, 58, 59, 61–69, 73, 74, 80–81, 206, 207
    Defence of Poetry 51, 53, 54, 62, 69
    Hymn to Intellectual Beauty 58, 59
    "Mont Blanc" 51, 58, 66
    "Mutability" 58, 59, 63
    "Ode to the West Wind" 78–80
    "On Life" 58–59
    "On Love" 52, 58, 59, 64
    Prometheus Unbound 51
    Queen Mab 55, 61, 62, 64
    "The Retrospect" 64
    "To Constantia" 64, 67
Simcox, G.A. 116, 125
Sinclair, John, Sir
  History of Public Revenue 41
  Statistical Account of Scotland 39, 41
siren imagery 137–138
Smiles, Samuel
  Character 125, 129
  Self-Help 125
  Thrift 125
Solie, Ruth A. 15, 21–22, 107–131
soul
  location in body 60
  Shelley on 61–62
Spedding, James 133

Spencer, Herbert 108
Stanford, Charles Villiers 142
Stanley, A.P. 124
Steane, J.B. 161
Stephen, Leslie 117
Stevenson, John, Sir 32
"suspend," definition 67
Sutton, Emma 2–3, 13, 15, 23, 213–229
Symons, Arthur 4, 23, 180, 213
  "Céleste" 219
  "During Music" 215–216
  London Nights 216, 219
  "Music and Memory" 218–219
  "The Armenian Dancer" 218
  "The Decadent Movement in Literature" 230
  "To Muriel" 216
"sympathy," medical definition 63–64
synaesthesia 78
syncopation, definition 72–73

Tennyson, Alfred
  In Memoriam 119–120
  "Œnone" 160
  "The Lotos-Eaters" 22, 132
    criticism 134
    Elgar's musical setting 162–173
    interpretation 138–141
    music in 134–141, 172–173
    Parry's musical setting 141–162
    source 133
  "The Sea Fairies" 137
  "The Vision of Sin" 160
  "Tithonus" 160
Tennyson, Charles 139
Thompson, E.P. 106
Thompson, James, "The Castle of Indolence" 75
Thomson, George 28
Tomlinson, Gary 8
Trotter, Thomas, *A View of the Nervous Temperament* 55
Trumpener, Katie, *Bardic Nationalism* 46
Tucker, Herbert F. 199
Twining, Thomas, *Two Dissertations...* 54

Utilitarianism 11

Vaughan Williams, Ralph 159
Vauxhall Gardens 57
Verlaine, Paul, "Art Poétique" 230
vibration, theory of 58, 59
Victorian society, music in 122–130, 211–212
Vlock-Keyes, Deborah 12
The Vocalist 231

Wagner, Jennifer A., *A Moment's Monument* 198
Wagner, Richard 2
  Parsifal
    influence on Parry's *Lotos-Eaters* 153
    musical extract 150–152
  Tannhäuser 228
  Tristan und Isolde
    influence on Bantock 244
    influence on Symons 216
Wallace, Alfred Russell 128
Wallen, Jeffrey 73
Wash Act (1784, 1786) 37–38
Watts, Isaac 105
"web," as metaphor 16–17
Webb, Daniel, *Observations...* 54
Weliver, Phyllis 74, 137–138, 194–212, 214
  Women Musicians in Victorian Fiction, 1860–1900 74

Wesley, Charles 105
Wharton, Henry Thornton, *Sappho...* 235–236
  frontispiece & title page 238
whisky making 38–39
Whytt, Robert 60, 63–64
Wilde, Oscar 23
  "Bittersweet Love" 220–221
  "Charmides" 213, 218
  "Heart's Yearnings" 221
  "Helas!" 219–220, 228
  "Panthea" 228
  "The Burden of Itys" 222
  "The Garden of Eros" 222–223
  "The Harlot's House" 219
  "Silentium Amoris" 221
Williams, Alastair 6, 8
Winn, James A., *Unsuspected Eloquence* 7
women composers, and music 178–179
Wood, Elizabeth 252–253
  Queering the Pitch 232
Wood, Henry, Mrs, *East Lynne* 138
Wordsworth, William 12

Yeats, W.B. 12
Yeo Wei Wei 15, 22, 174–193

Žižek, Slavoj 254–255
Zon, Bennett, *Music and Metaphor* 71–72, 240

For Product Safety Concerns and Information please contact our EU representative GPSR@taylorandfrancis.com
Taylor & Francis Verlag GmbH, Kaufingerstraße 24, 80331 München, Germany